D1276378

Dance of
LANGUAGE

Susan O'Connor

authorHOUSE®

AuthorHouse™
1663 Liberty Drive, Suite 200
Bloomington, IN 47403
www.authorhouse.com
Phone: 1-800-839-8640

©2008 Susan O'Connor. All rights reserved.

No part of this book may be reproduced, stored in a retrieval system, or transmitted by any means without the written permission of the author.

First published by AuthorHouse 12/19/2008

ISBN: 978-1-4343-1452-9 (sc)

Library of Congress Control Number: 2008902715

Printed in the United States of America
Bloomington, Indiana

This book is printed on acid-free paper.

To Patrick, my dance partner,
and to Kate and Rachel,
who know how to dance

Acknowledgments

This book has been in the making for thirty-six years, at least. It's difficult to put a time frame on the experiences of learning and loving language. In whatever time it took to write it, however, a number of people contributed ideas and examples included in the book, if not inspiration and support. Without my students there would not be a book, and I thank them for years of trial and error, for their responses to what worked and what didn't in each lesson. I am also grateful for the use of some of their pieces of writing, which I have acknowledged in those sections. From the administrators of the T.H. Rogers School in the Houston Independent School District, I received valuable support, allowing me to use revised versions of the book for eight consecutive years. Finally, I want to thank my family and friends—my husband Patrick, whose love of language taught me many valuable lessons and whose knowledge of word processing often saved me time and effort, my daughters who encouraged me to continue writing, and my friends who were patient with and understanding of my absence in their lives. As always, I will be eternally grateful to my mother who first introduced me to that wonderful journey called reading.

Contents

Acknowledgments. 3

Chapter 1
Dancing...A Metaphor II

Chapter 2
Writing: Building a Base 15

    The Writing Journal 20

Chapter 3
Writing Short Fiction 22

    Writing Workshop: Part 1 24
    Activity 1: What makes a piece of writing original? 25
    What is Plagiarism?. 26
    Activity 2: What makes a good plot? 26
    Activity 3: What is your own unique style of writing? 29
    Activity 4: What makes good fiction writing? 31
    Activity 5: Where do writers get ideas for plots? 32
    Activity 6: How important is characterization? 33
    Writing Workshop: Part 2 34
    Step 1: Practice with perspective and story elements 34
    Step 2: Practice with characterization 35
    Step 3: Clarify kinds of conflict: Physical and intellectual plots 36
    Step 4: Create plot outlines. 36
    Step 5: Create tension in plots 37
    Step 6: Observe how tension is created in film. 41
    Step 7: Combine character and conflict 45
    Step 8: Let your characters speak: Write dialogue 46
    Step 9: Add a third character. 49
    Step 10: Consider ways to begin your story 49
    Step 11: Create a strong plot 50
    Step 12: Focus on diction. 51
    Step 13: Meet in writing response groups 51

Chapter 4

WRITING SCRIPTS 53

How to Turn a Great Short Story into a Script. 54
From Story to Script: Tips for Writing and Producing a Play 55
Three Times Three: An Exercise in Scriptwriting 56

Chapter 5

WRITING ESSAYS. 63

Writing a Critical Essay about Literature 63
A Model for Essay Writing 63
To Be or Not to Be… Finding Substitutes for *Be* Verbs 66
Basic Writing Guide .66
Writing Personal Essays and Memoirs 67
Refining Your Writing: A Checklist 72

Chapter 6

RHETORIC AND DIALECTIC: 75

Two Arts in the Dance of Discourse 75

Chapter 7

THE STUDY OF LITERATURE 81

Literary Terms 87

Chapter 8

THE AMERICAN RENAISSANCE: ROOTS AND LEAVES. 91

Drawing Conclusions from a Chronology. 92
Hawthorne's Contemporaries in the American Renaissance 100
From Emerson and Thoreau…Back to Plato 111
Plato's Theory of Ideas 113
Your Philosophy: A Gift 115

Chapter 9

ANALYZING LITERATURE 116

Mastering the Steps of the Dance 116
Hawthorne's Use of Archetypes 117
Sacrifice and the Life/Death/Life Archetype 118
The Hero's Journey: Forsyth's *Whispering Wind*. 119

Chapter 10

AN EXAMINATION OF FIVE STORIES BY HAWTHORNE. 122

Story #1: "The Maypole of Merry Mount". 123
"The Maypole of Merry Mount," A One-Act Play. 124
Hawthorne: A Life of Isolation, Rejection, Mystery, and Joy 128
The Maypole, Past and Present. 130
Tree Symbolism. 131
"The Maypole of Merry Mount" Reading Assistance 134
Archetypes in Hawthorne's "The Maypole of Merry Mount" 135
Literary Tools from Freud and Jung 138
The Peascods, a Maypole Dance 140
"The Maypole of Merry Mount": Putting Thoughts on Paper 141
The Fantasticks: A Study in Archetypes 143
Story #2: "Dr. Heidegger's Experiment" 147
Story #3: "Rappaccini's Daughter" 149
Story #4: "The Minister's Black Veil" 153
Story #5: "Young Goodman Brown" 157
Allegory in Hawthorne's "Young Goodman Brown" 159
Thesis Sentences for Writing about Hawthorne's Short Stories 162
Symbolic Illusions 162

Chapter 11

THE SCARLET LETTER 164

Keeping a Journal 164
Conflict in *The Scarlet Letter*. 166
Antithesis in *The Scarlet Letter*. 166
Moral Exemplars in Hawthorne's Writing 167
Metaphors in *The Scarlet Letter* 168
Symbolism in *The Scarlet Letter* 170
Sample Journal Responses 173
Chapter Synopses for *The Scarlet Letter* 175
The Scarlet Letter Essay: Writing, Editing, and Revising 179
Suggested Essay Topics 180
Looking at Student Models 181
The Art of Quilt Making in America 186
Making a Paper Quilt Using Symbols 187

Chapter 12

MODERN AMERICAN LITERATURE 188

The Harlem Renaissance and Beyond 189
Lindy Hop: A Dance for Harmony and Healing 193

Harper Lee's *To Kill a Mockingbird:* Text and Film 194

To Kill a Mockingbird, A Study Guide 196

Maslow's Hierarchy of Needs. 198

Lawrence Kohlberg's Stages of Moral Development 199

Chapter 13

HERITAGE OF HUMANITY: ESPRIT DE CORPS, OR BETRAYAL? 200

Study Guide Terms 201

Heritage of Humanity Questions 202

Readings 203

Paulo Coelho's *The Alchemist*: A Wisdom Tradition 213

Study Guide Questions 214

Learning About Ourselves and Others 216

Friendship and Bestiality in John Knowles's *A Separate Peace* 217

Mandalas and Labyrinths 221

Celebrating Cultural Diversity: Touchstones 224

The Tasting Party 225

Chapter 14

THE ENGLISH RENAISSANCE: THE DANCE OF SHAKESPEARE 227

Watching, Reading, and Discussing *Twelfth Night* 231

Who Is Shakespeare? 232

Shakespeare's Poems and Sonnets 234

Shakespeare's Plays 235

A Chronology: Shakespeare in The Elizabethan and Jacobean Periods . . .236

Shakespeare and Elizabethan Life 239

Celebrating Twelfth Night 240

Recipes for a Twelfth Night Celebration 241

Re-enacting St. George and the Dragon 244

"Saint George and the Dragon" 245

Hoboken Brawl: An Elizabethan Circle Dance 250

Verse Speaking: Shakespeare's Stage Directions 251

Twelfth Night: Preparing the Text for Acting. 257

"Circle Dance": A Modern View of Shakespeare. 258

Chapter 15

A CLASSICAL APPROACH TO WORD STUDY 294

Latin and Greek Roots: Improving Vocabulary 295

Latin in Our Everyday Speech 315

Chapter 16

FIVE-MINUTE GRAMMAR 324

    Grammar Terms. 326
    Parts of a Sentence 329
    Kinds of Sentences 330
    Phrases 330
    Clauses 331
    Usage 331
    Practice Sentences 331
    A Guide for Punctuation and Grammar Usage 341

Chapter 17

TRADITIONS THAT ENRICH OUR LANGUAGE 352

    An Introduction to YOU: A Two-Page Spread 352
    Valentines in Literature. 353
    The Quest Letter 353
    A Reading List 355

WORKS CITED 370

How can we know the dancer from the dance?
W. B. Yeats
"Among School Children," 1928

CHAPTER I

Dancing...A Metaphor

The announcement of a school dance is generally enough to pique the interest of students to start planning to be there. There's a nervous twitter when the day arrives. I enjoy being there, too. Just watching on the sidelines of that dance can be illuminating—the joy, the energy, the reckless abandon!

Maybe you remember dancing when you were a child. Perhaps you celebrated the arrival of spring by weaving colorful ribbons and dancing around a Maypole. The steps weren't difficult, but sometimes the dancers forgot who they were—under or over?—and the result was usually laughter and slightly bulging ribbons unevenly woven around the pole. In pieces of literature rich with imagery and symbolism, the concept of dancing is often dominant because its elements have so strong a resemblance to the elements that make up our lives—the diverse steps in choreography, the partners, the moods, the missteps, the reasons for the dance.

Dancing in a circle, for example, encourages a kind of magic that seems to strengthen and protect whatever it encloses. As a significant part of world mythology, the meaning of dancing in any shape or form has grown in complexity while other symbols—hands, feet, the heavens, and thread, for example—connect with it and enhance its powerful image. The dance, as both symbol and metaphor, provides an ancient instrument by which we can understand and know ourselves. It is little wonder then that dancing has become an expression of emotions—the dance of love, of anger, of joy and thanksgiving; the dance of entreaty; the rain dance, the fertility dance; and the dance of imitation, the dance of creation, the dance of the planets, and the dance of angels around the throne of God.

Dancing has thus come to be a manifestation of human growth and maturation that, as Jung reminds us, leads to individuation, or becoming the people we were meant to be.

In this handbook, you will see the steps that we will follow as we move through the dance of language. Though not always graceful in the beginning, you will become more adept and feel more at ease as you increase your knowledge, step by step, of how the language works and how it can work for you.

The contents of this book, just like the contents of our language, are impossible to organize in sequential order. Unlike some kinds of dances that require strict choreography, our language demands that we know and use many skills concurrently. The order of the literature study here is, however, sequential because the skills and knowledge for critical analysis in this book build on each other and prepare students for reading and writing and thinking about the pieces that follow.

Because writing contests, which usually begin early in the fall semester, give students opportunities to be rewarded for their creativity and effort, I have placed the section on fiction writing at the beginning of the book. Right from the start, students should see themselves as authors as well as critics.

Serious students of dance must understand not only the inner workings of the body and the bones and muscles that allow the body to move but also the importance of maintaining balance and conditioning. How similar to the student of language who must also comprehend the different ways in which words, phrases, and sentences are selected and combined to form the framework that allows our language to move gracefully and to *move us*—to inform, to persuade, to entertain, to touch our hearts and minds. This handbook, therefore, includes tools for maintaining strength in studying many aspects of language.

If you're in a classroom, your teacher may choose to do only selected activities from this book. Because the ideas included here support a core curriculum in the humanities, most of the units and even individual activities can be isolated easily from the body and used to enhance other areas of study. Classic ideas tend to support each other and form cohesive patterns. Some of the people you will read about include Aristotle, Plato, Emerson and Thoreau, Freud and Jung, and the Roman and Greek poets, philosophers, and statesmen—those who have left us with the marvelous gifts of the foundation of our thinking and of our language.

No handbook on language would be complete without a literary reading list as well as a list of sources for enriched study. In order to proceed in our pursuit of higher levels and more sophisticated dances, we must aim ever so high in choosing to read. I tend to lean toward the proverbial "just read everything you can get your hands on" philosophy, and so these lists are only a place to begin. Browse and add your own titles. According to the Bowker Annual Library and Book Trade Almanac 2006, book title output for all categories numbered 149,859 (516). Try to imagine, if you can, what that means in terms of available choices for reading material. Now, there has to be something printed that interests you! Remember, good readers make good writers.

Finally, what would a handbook called *Dance of Language* be without actual dance steps? The literature in this course begins with the American Renaissance and ends with the English Renaissance. Included in both studies are the steps for two popular English circle dances of the seventeenth century. These dances offer students a sensory, kinesthetic approach to complement and encourage their learning, as well as immerse them in the culture of a people for whom dancing was literally an essential part of life. We will also take a peek into the dance movements that lifted up a people through depression and war and into their own heritage and culture, and continue to do just that today. George and Ira Gershwin wrote many Tin Pan Alley tunes in the 1920s and '30s to convince people who were down and out that dancing was the cure.

In "The Dance of Life," 1923, essayist Havelock Ellis concludes that dancing is the most beautiful of the arts because it not only reflects life; it is life. Dancers, as well as those who simply have a keen understanding of Ellis's statement, have expressed their feelings about dancing and used its perfect metaphoric quality to communicate their ideas. I have seasoned this handbook with my own favorites, sprinkled here and there. Once you read them, you will begin to see them again in places you may have never noticed before.

Art, perhaps the earliest of storytellers, has a unique dance that lends its steps to my own path in life. In October of 1872, French Impressionist painter Edgar Degas (1834-1917) traveled from France to New York and boarded a train for a long journey to New Orleans, Louisiana. His subjects for the next year would focus on his family and life in this cultural city. Degas's mother, Celestine Musson, was the daughter of Germain Musson and Marie Celeste Rillieux—my matriarchal family name. Marie Celeste and Marie Antoinette Rillieux were sisters, both born in New Orleans to a prominent old French family. Their parents, Vincent Rillieux and Marie Tronquette, the respected matriarch of New Orleans, were also my maternal grandmother's great-great grandparents. Georgine Susan White Hill, my grandmother, who was also born in New Orleans, and Degas's mother were cousins. Georgine's mother, Jeanne Felicie Mercier (granddaughter of Marie Antoinette Rillieux) married Denis Prieur White and at the age of twenty-seven moved in the same New Orleans society as her cousin Edgar Degas during the short time he lived and painted in New Orleans.

A copy of Degas's *Blue Dancers* hangs in my family room as a reminder, not only of the metaphor of dance, that archetypal rhythm of the universe and the theme of this book, but also of the great need for the stories that connect our lives.

More than ever, my own classroom structures must include ritual, another kind of dance that depends on language to keep it fueled and connected to meaning and purpose. The opening ritual might include a routine of coming into the room and warming up with grammar and writing or looking at the day's agenda and getting prepared for the class. This daily task not only teaches students what to expect; it also shows them what organization looks like and how it can be rehearsed and eventually achieved.

Ordinary days need to be recognized, too, in a way that is as meaningful as the more celebrated events in life. Although it's fun to try new ways of approaching learning, I much prefer the heightened sense of awareness provided by doing activities that have stood the test of time in generating creativity in students. Each year students engage in the particular activities that students before them have done: writing for the Scholastic Art & Writing Awards competition, learning the Maypole dance for the story we reenact each fall, constructing *The Scarlet Letter* journal and symbol quilt, sampling the delicious food at the Heritage and Culture Book Tasting Party, performing scenes from *Twelfth Night* and celebrating winter holidays of the English Renaissance, and finally, writing the quest letter that will be mailed their senior year of high school. This sampling of rituals in my classroom develops pride and continuity and closeness between all the members of the class. My desire is to help students share in a fuller experience through rites that help us connect and live well. I want students who come into my class not only to know what to expect but also to look forward to the program of events planned for them. Teenagers today have so much pressure and uncertainty growing up. Research shows that predictable outcomes and meaningful rituals produce healthier people. What we do now, the choices we make today about how well we live, will have an effect on what happens to us tomorrow.

True ease in writing comes from art, not chance,
As those move easiest who have learned to dance.
Alexander Pope
An Essay on Criticism, 1711

CHAPTER 2

Writing: Building a Base

What could be more joyous than dancing to music that stirs your very soul? Is there not a song that makes all of us want to move something—hands, fingers, feet, arms, hips, head, the vibration traveling up and down our bodies from our ears to our feet? The music of ABBA does it for me. One summer my husband Patrick and I found ourselves engulfed in the wave of a London theatre filled with music and dancing at the end of the smash West End hit *Mama Mia*. It was almost a spiritual experience as the audience stood up and began dancing in the aisle. Even my friends and family would have been a bit surprised to see us clapping and swaying along with the rest of the merry makers. To this day the memory of it still energizes me.

As a metaphor of life, moving to the rhythm of the universe, dancing lends its depth of meaning to the language we use in every way and for every purpose. Before you limit this image to the beautiful language of Shakespeare or some loftier language of other classic poets and philosophers, remember the extraordinary power of simple words, the ones that express appreciation or love or understanding between ordinary human beings. Recall the words of a friend offering comfort or a funny story that lifted your spirits and made your side ache from laughter. Yes, the apology, the explanation, the consent, the awaited diagnosis, the plan—even when we don't remember the words, how easily we can recall the way the meaning behind the words changed our lives. Words create that flicker of understanding that captures a moment of enlightenment, of fully understanding.

When Annie Dillard wrote about the existence of beauty and grace in nature, ever present even though we might be unaware, she presented us with this challenge: "The least we can do is try to be there" when it happens (*Pilgrim at Tinker Creek*, 7-8). So it is with language, waiting for us to receive the words ready to be used for our every need, and all we have to do is be there. Because we live in a world of dynamic, fluid language that conforms to the shape of each human vessel into which it is poured, we can have its enormous potential for communicating just by acknowledging that it is already ours.

Writers of fiction tell us that the wants and needs of characters drive the plot of a story. Perhaps we are those diverse characters with our own unique wants and needs expressed through language. The ability to use words to get what we want and need starts from the earliest years of our existence. Toddlers understand quickly how using words, limited though they may be, gets their wants and needs met. Examples, of course, abound in literature; they are the *raison d'etre* of fiction. In Hawthorne's *The Scarlet Letter,* Hester Prynne endures the town's reproachful, taunting remarks rather than leave the place of her crime and punishment, with one desire in her heart—to be near her daughter's father, whose name is shrouded in secrecy. Abandoned, Hester uses her needle and thread to support herself and her child, and her response to their inquiry—will you name the father?—drives the plot of the story.

While Hester may be American literature's greatest heroine, no character is more admired and emulated than Atticus Finch in Harper Lee's *To Kill a Mockingbird.* Given the difficult task of defending a black man wrongly accused of raping a white woman in Alabama in 1932, Atticus's love of justice and his need to be a model of ethical behavior for his two children Jem and Scout compel him to accept the case. His defense is impeccable, even though he knows he has little chance of succeeding in this small Southern town with clearly drawn lines of race, class, and gender. His words of passion and courage seem familiar as they linger in a place deep within us: "It's when you know you're licked before you begin but you begin anyway and you see it through no matter what" (112).

Wants and needs drive the plots of drama as well as fiction. In Lorraine Hansberry's inspiring play *A Raisin in the Sun,* Walter Lee struggles to become the man he wants to be, challenged at every turn by poverty and racial prejudice that have pushed him away from the opportunities to rise up in a white man's world. In the end, his need for respect and dignity triggers an unexpected decision that alters the outcome of the life of his family.

Frederick Forsyth's words give us a character who wants what the rest of us want, to live life in peace and love. Hired by the government as a scout to help General Custer's men move the Indians back on the reservation in Montana, Ben Craig rescues a young Cheyenne woman from the army's murderous hands. He falls in love with her, even though she is promised to another man, and spends the rest of his life searching for her. His need to have Whispering Wind as his wife propels him into a journey beyond the grave.

My earliest remembrance of words takes on the image of my mother in a rocking chair with a story book in her hands and a little girl sitting on her lap. An Indian boy lost in the snow is discovered by a Pilgrim girl, who subsequently brings whites and Indians together for a thanksgiving feast. It was a story she read over and over, and even today I see reading as comfort, not a bad beginning to life. The scene shifts to summer and I am older. The library is cool and quiet, and I am living in the Pink Motel, until I move on to Cannery Row. Move to the other side of the library and I am fifteen, discovering plays. I read every edition of *Best Plays*, and I am suddenly on the stage. I never really understood Van Druten's *I Am a Camera* until much later, but I loved the title. I, too, saw myself as a camera, amassing snapshots as experiences and *words* swirled past my eyes. I was building a base of experience and knowledge for whatever future lay ahead. What I wanted to do was *tell* those stories, the real ones and the made up ones. In *The Secret Life of Bees*, Sue Monk Kidd's character August Boatwright says, "Stories have to be told or they die, and when they die, we can't remember who we are or why we're here" (107). When I learned to put words together to tell the stories I had gathered, I became a writer.

And I have been a writer for as long as I can remember. Writing has been an old friend I could always rely on. I even fell in love with my husband Patrick because he wrote beautiful letters from across the Atlantic. As a child I spent a lot of time in the sweltering back seat of my father's Chevrolet, with long extended trips to the Gulf coast of Mississippi every summer to visit my grandmother. From a pre-adolescent's perspective on life, I composed a number of essays in my windblown head as the hours crept alongside the ocean front highway. Although letters are the earliest account of putting words on paper, I do remember creating a little story when I was thirteen. It was the first piece of fiction anyone had ever asked me to write, and it was a joy, probably the happiest remembrance of that year. Looking back, I recall it was more a vignette of a little girl playing beside a brook and accidentally dropping her shoes in, but I was enchanted with this simple fantasy, so happy that someone asked me to write about it and express the only life that felt real in those difficult times. I don't remember writing again until ninth grade when I joined the speech and debate team. Mr. Taylor taught me how to write a speech for an oratory contest, and three years later my senior English teacher Miss Whitten taught me how to write essays and a research paper. I adored these teachers. We wrote an essay every Friday on a topic of our choice. On Monday morning I got it back with a grade and one sentence at the top stating what she liked about it. In those days, writing was not really part of anyone's required curriculum—there was an occasional contest, but certainly no serious assessment or accountability in writing. I suppose there existed some sort of belief that knowledge of writing was innate. You either had it or you didn't. I never viewed writing as tedious or forced, however. I welcomed opportunities. Nevertheless, when I arrived on the steps of college English, I struggled with uncertainty and lack of confidence at times as I tried to produce a worthy paper for each professor whose expectations seemed miles apart. I must have eventually written something of worth, but not without hard work. Like all the other experiences, this, too, made me a better writer.

Over the years I read everything I could and then taught myself how to improve my writing, keeping both personal and professional journals. Watching my two daughters also keep journals, I have seen the significant effects of continuous writing on their lives. Both began writing in a blank book when they learned how to hold a pencil and form letters. What I suspected then and strongly believe now is that people who write also see themselves as readers and scholars and individuals who feel they have a voice that makes a difference in people's lives. As my own writing journey becomes circular through a life of letters, essays, articles, journals, stories, poetry, plays, and books, I continue to write and to teach what I have learned over time.

Publishing student work has been a good and even essential response to writing, but it didn't compel me enough to do it until years later when I began compiling my students' original poems, stories, essays, and plays and could see the positive effect on them. The *Houston Chronicle* published articles about famous young Houstonians written in collaboration by my students and a sister school. Later the *Chronicle's* "Texas Magazine" sponsored a short fiction contest for writers aged six to eighteen, which awarded a cash prize and the honor of having the stories published and illustrated in their Sunday magazine. Today the Scholastic

Art & Writing Awards, the oldest and most prestigious foundation that recognizes young artists and writers in America, pays tribute to its winners from the stage of Carnegie Hall in New York City each summer. Recognition is a curiously addicting phenomenon. It's a good and necessary thing for your family, friends, and teachers to tell you your writing is good, but it is potentially life changing for a well-established national foundation to tell you you're the best young writer in America.

I sometimes reflect on exactly what actions make a difference in the outcome of writing success for students, fiction or otherwise. Providing opportunities to write and publish while focusing on the importance of writing obviously comes first, but good stories don't get written without the application of concrete methods and lots of practice. Failure to succeed in writing is like the proverbial student who never learns to swim because he never gets in the water. Workshop style writing with enough work on drafts in stages, helpful response, and a frequent return to the editing process has always worked best for my students as well as for myself as a writer.

Nonfiction writing has a different aim, and so it requires a slightly different process. Although prewriting, writing, editing, and proofreading are still the necessary steps, years of observation indicate trouble in two areas—prewriting and editing.

Prewriting is limited to the strength of the writer's background. I believe that everyone has something to say, a story to tell, but is that enough? A rich and varied store of experiential as well as core knowledge enables the writer to work with a broader range of ideas for discourse. The student who is culturally literate is often a more effective writer. Prewriting, therefore, is not just a graphic organizer but also a resource to which the writer can turn for content and support.

The problems of editing are similar to those of prewriting. Although it helps to have a natural rhythm and ear for words, students usually haven't had enough guided practice with varying their sentence structure and combining ideas. Although Kellogg Hunt's research indicates that sophistication in syntax is developmental (1965), student writing can become more sophisticated with instruction and practice.

I recently worked with several students who were having difficulty writing an essay on *The Scarlet Letter*. I stood at my old-fashioned chalkboard and took them through the process of writing an introduction using the ideas of one particular student who volunteered his thesis sentence. After using this method with one student, I asked the others to plan at least three supporting ideas for their theses and write a draft elaborating on the first one, including textual support. The next day, I began with one student at a time to model the kind of thinking and questioning I would do for my own writing, while helping the students to connect or reconnect with their own styles of editing in the process. The students, receptive to this help, were willing to think about changes and additions to their writing. We repeated this process throughout the writing of the essay with favorable results. Whether writing or swimming, those areas you want to improve require focus and attention.

As a student of the English language arts, you will watch your skills progress in stages if you apply the tools in this book to your writing. You may have already been successful with several different forms. A review of your writing tells you that you are able to think logically and communicate ideas in an organized way. In fact these skills have worked wonders for you.

Perhaps your large experiential background, rich with resources and networking, explains your ability to generate ideas and information and grasp new ideas quickly, or perhaps you were one of the fortunate ones born with the gifts of articulation and eloquence. You experienced success with language at every stage. Not everyone, however, has been so fortunate with his or her progress in writing. Certainly one valid reason could be poor instruction, but I have also witnessed another problem: fear of failure. Too often students who engage in writing—from journal entries and essays to short fiction, plays, and poetry—arm themselves with a bottle of correction fluid on their desks, so fearful are they of making mistakes, even on rough, often handwritten drafts, or they sit at a blank screen and stare at it. What this actually does is make students feel immobilized and incapable of producing even one sentence, much less an entire composition.

While this image may seem exaggerated, when I ask students like you to tell me what they think and feel about a particular topic, all too often their initial response is a blank. Suddenly they have no thoughts, at least not easily retrievable ones, or they can't decide what they think. Or maybe they don't recognize their thoughts as being valid when they have them. Whatever the reason for this sudden dearth of words, the fact remains that fear stifles creativity and prevents the free flow of thoughts that should be a writer's *modus operandi* for success.

How does one learn to fear writing? What makes you afraid at times to express your own original, creative ideas? Whatever the cause, you can take action as a writer to combat this block. Can you allow yourself to write without evaluating your work in the beginning, to open your mind, let thoughts flow freely, and refrain from making judgments about what you write? If you can, you have taken the first step to writing improvement.

Photographers often say you have to take a hundred pictures to get one good one. This advice seems to apply to writing as well. Words produce more ideas, which produce more words. A blank page produces more blank pages. How will you know you have achieved your goal without having lots of words to plow through? Invest in words and practice, and your return will be elaboration and precision, forerunners to eloquence. With encouragement, opportunities, and guidance, in addition to instruction—from a teacher, a mentor, or yourself—you *can* improve the quality of your writing.

Students sometimes come to a screeching halt when they find little or no connection between their experiences and ideas and the teacher's assigned writing topic. Thus the planned accumulation of knowledge and experience can encourage thinking and build a reserve so that students feel more prepared for written discourse. Simply put, this book can enrich your knowledge base. Although it can't give you enough actual experiences to make up for everything that's missing from your life, it does offer you some fragments of the foundations of thought. Inside these covers you will find a place to begin:

Aristotle's literary ideas and means of rhetoric

Freud's id, ego, and superego

Jung's archetypes, motifs, and beliefs about human behavior

Plato's ideas about reality, specifically the allegory of the cave and the ring of Gyges

Emerson's philosophy of self-reliance

Maslow's hierarchy of needs

Kohlberg's levels of moral development

Common psychological and philosophical ideas: moral ambiguity, tolerance for ambiguity, man's bestiality, the concept of "the other," *esprit de corps*, and betrayal

Latin and Greek roots, expressions, and sayings

The historical and philosophical background for a number of literary pieces by well-known authors including Hawthorne, Emerson, Thoreau, Claude McKay, Langston Hughes, Harper Lee, John Knowles, Maya Angelou, Frank O'Connor, Frederick Forsyth, Annie Dillard, Lorraine Hansberry, Mary Oliver, Paulo Coelho, and the enigmatic William Shakespeare.

Throughout this handbook you will examine pieces of literature closely and develop deeper interpretations of their components. Symbols, themes, figurative language, philosophy, and psychology will help you to unravel the mysteries of literature while building your knowledge base for writing. Once you understand these ideas and learn how to apply them to literature, you can make these tools your own for adding the depth you need for growth in writing. You will also find many opportunities to write with various modes, purposes, and audiences in mind. Sometimes you will see student models that show you examples of what is possible. Whether you are crafting a personal essay, a poem, a short story, a letter, a play, or an analytical essay on a piece of literature, you will find the writing easier and the final product more rewarding when you garner all possible resources about you for the job. The time invested to make sure you have an adequate supply when you need just the right experience, image, or word is time well spent.

The Writing Journal
● ● ● ● ●
Getting Started

Your writing journal can be your greatest resource. From the start, give it an attractive cover, write in it consistently, and take care of it. This book is not a notebook to be tossed carelessly and hurriedly into a locker, under a bed, in a closet, or under a pile of papers and then discarded in a moment of cleaning frenzy. Once you see the quantity and the quality of your thoughts and ideas stored in this journal, you will want to keep it, treasure it, and refer to it as long as possible.

Start with a good sturdy composition book. Have a little fun with it before you get serious. Decorate it with your favorite designs and sayings—perhaps a Latin phrase or quotation that represents your philosophy of life—and then cover it with laminating or contact paper that is somewhat waterproof, or keep it in a large plastic zipper bag.

The first of many entries will be your writing history, followed by the responses suggested in the section on writing short fiction. After that you will see journal prompts scattered throughout the book in almost every chapter and section. Why should you continue journal entries long after you have written and submitted your short story to the Scholastic Art &

Writing Awards competition, or any other writing contest? Simple answer: writing records thinking, and practice does make perfect, or at least much improved. Over time you will become more adept at thinking quickly. Remember the adage, how do I know what I think until I see what I say? Besides, writers who continue to submit their stories, essays, poems, plays, and even novels to Scholastic have a greatly increased chance of achieving those coveted Silver and Gold Portfolio Awards, and that means cash awards to take to college. In the end, the contest isn't the reason to write. It's only a valuable benefit of the journey toward increasing your skill with the language you will use to communicate for the rest of your life.

If you're one of those students who habitually say, "I can't write," you need to do three things: first, stop thinking and saying those words. Your brain is going to start believing you and you really will have writer's block. Second, become a reader—good readers make good writers. And finally, let yourself write without needing to be perfect the first time. In fact, give yourself permission to make lots of mistakes and write garbage. Just know there is a flower growing in that compost heap. Keep writing until you uncover it. The more you learn about writing and the more you practice, the sooner you will see the qualities of an articulate writer that you admire in other people.

You will have opportunities to respond to numerous journal prompts throughout this handbook. Some will relate directly to the information in the chapter, and some prompts will ask you to consider similar ideas. Your journal then will be a record of your thoughts and ideas for use in longer pieces of writing. Although most of the journal entries will not be drafts of more structured pieces, the connections you will make between your ideas and the literature, philosophy, history, and psychology that you will read can help you to create more complex pieces of writing.

One particular novel will contribute ten short essays to the journal contents. The guided study of Hawthorne's *The Scarlet Letter* incorporates five specific tools for studying literature that will be useful for an intensive study of other great works in literature.

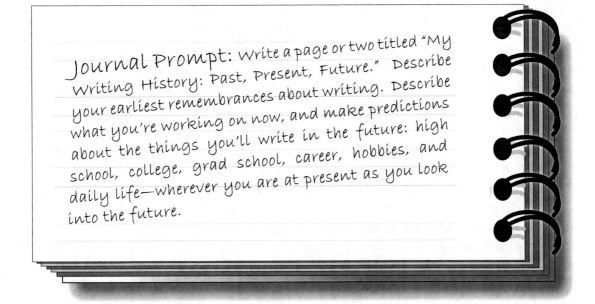

Journal Prompt: Write a page or two titled "My Writing History: Past, Present, Future." Describe your earliest remembrances about writing. Describe what you're working on now, and make predictions about the things you'll write in the future: high school, college, grad school, career, hobbies, and daily life—wherever you are at present as you look into the future.

Did ye not hear it?—No! 'twas but the wind,
Or the cat rattling o'er the stony street.
On with the dance! Let joy be unconfined:
No sleep till morn, when Youth and Pleasure meet
To chase the glowing hours with flying feet.

George Noel Gordon, Lord Byron
Childe Harold's Pilgrimage, canto III st. 22
1812-18

CHAPTER 3

Writing Short Fiction

Writing a story seems simple on the surface. We read stories; we watch stories; we live stories. Put characters together in a plot that has a beginning, middle, and an end, and it's almost like magic. Actually, it's a little more complicated than that, but once you understand the makeup of each part of writing a story, and once you realize that writing takes dedicated persistence and perseverance, arriving at a plan for the basic plot structure is not the insurmountable task that it seems.

You know from studying literature that the beginning of a story introduces the initial action of a situation. Characters with wants and needs appear, and the reader starts to see little by little what motivates the actions of each one.

The ancient Greek philosopher Aristotle called the next part of the story the rising action, the pace increasing as the characters pursue their goals. If the characters succeed too easily, the reader will begin to get bored. The main character, or protagonist, must face challenges, stumbling blocks, and problems in order to increase the tension of the conflict. The antagonist, the character who tries to prevent the protagonist from reaching his goals, contributes to the tension. The details are important here. How does the protagonist react to these problems in the conflict? Do they alter the main character permanently? How does the main character find the strength to overcome the difficulties in a creative way, or does she simply give up? The reader expects the writer to provide answers to the most crucial questions. Believability is at stake.

The end begins with the climax, the most intense part of the story, and continues through the falling action and the denouement, the unraveling of the plot that leads to the final outcome. If everything has fallen into place as you planned and anticipated, the reader will be satisfied with the kind of plausibility that evolves naturally through details.

The decisions you make about plot will result from the characters you want to write about, their goals, and their motives. Once you have an idea for your story, you must decide on the force behind your characters' actions. Will it be a physical adventure-suspense challenge, or an inner conflict of human nature and relationships between people? Or will it be a combination of the two?

One way to start developing your short story is to make some basic decisions about the protagonist. Make notes in your journal. Is it a boy or a girl? How old? Does the character live in a small town or a big city? What does he want and need? What problems does she encounter? What are his relationships with family and friends? Once you begin to flesh out the character you are inventing, you will watch the character take the story where she wants it to go. You have invented a character from the inside out with wants and needs and problems that will affect what happens. Once the story takes you where it wants to go, you have no choice but to follow the plot.

The best stories come from your own teenage experience—what you are and know and whom you know—and other people's experiences that you are familiar with. Powerful characterization, however, needs to come from inside yourself. You are inventing characters who represent your imagination and your thoughts, beliefs, and experiences.

What motivates your character? What does he need to reach his goal? What does she want in order to satisfy a longing? What are his internal conflicts? What are her external conflicts? Give your characters a realistic life and inner structure so they will be believable. People are complex, and so must your characters be. How are your characters' personal traits in conflict with their wants and needs?

Avoid stock or stereotyped characters. Create a realistic, unique person with realistic wants and needs. If you could describe yourself in a word to capture the essence of you, what would it be? Your character has the same potential. How could you describe in a word your character overall? Why did you choose that word? What does it imply?

An equally important task in the development of characters is a consideration of the various circumstances and settings in which you place them. An active imagination is essential but not sufficient. To make your story seem acceptable to the reader as believable, you must know what you're talking about, and nothing takes the place of experience. If you don't have the experience you think you will need for your story, make an attempt to get it. It is easier said than done, right? Do the research. Frederick Forsyth, a best selling novelist for many years, was called a "one-time journalist turned thriller writer" by the *Sun-Herald* on September 19, 2004 ("Master"). The article explains how Forsyth prepared to write his most current book at the time, *Avenger*. "He researched for six months, visited Serbia to scout the location of the horrific murder that starts the book, then talked to teenage hackers, aeroplane and security experts to weave the story of crime and retribution together." The reporter asked Forsyth how he wrote his book. His reply was, "Ten pages a day times 50 days is a book. You just have to say to yourself, 'I am not getting up from this table until I have done ten pages.' I start at the beginning and finish at the end. I don't go back and revise. I leave that to the editor. It needs a fresh, shrewd pair of eyes to pick up passages that could be better, inconsistencies, continuity, and so on."

Keep these ideas in mind throughout the process of developing your story:
1. Know what your characters want and need.

2. Create tension.

3. Make sure things happen for a reason.

4. Do the research necessary to create believable characters and settings.

By now you are getting the message that character and plot are inseparable. The actions of the characters determine the plot, and yet have you noticed how variations of the same plot keep surfacing? You might be wondering if even one more version remains of the traditional girl-meets-boy plot, and yet writers continue their never ending pursuit of creating yet one more variation on the theme. Plots are not new; how we treat them can be. Several people have distilled story structures down to a select number as a foundation for all stories written. Ronald Tobias, in his book *Twenty Master Plots*, categorizes twenty traditional plots, such as quest, pursuit, rescue, escape, transformation, love, and sacrifice, to name several. If you stopped to list all the stories you know, you could easily begin to sort their plots as well as subplots into common categories.

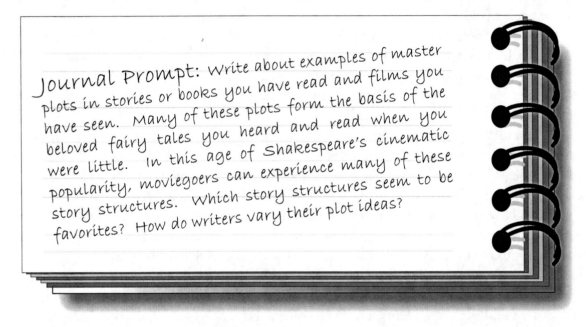

Journal Prompt: Write about examples of master plots in stories or books you have read and films you have seen. Many of these plots form the basis of the beloved fairy tales you heard and read when you were little. In this age of Shakespeare's cinematic popularity, moviegoers can experience many of these story structures. Which story structures seem to be favorites? How do writers vary their plot ideas?

WRITING WORKSHOP: PART 1
• • • • •

Six activities in the first part of this workshop approach to constructing a short story can help you generate ideas and hone your writing skills. Along the way you will discover the answers to these questions that will engender good writing:

1. **What makes a piece of writing original?**
2. **What makes a good plot?**
3. **What is your own unique style of writing?**
4. **What makes good fiction writing?**
5. **Where do writers get ideas for plots?**
6. **How important is characterization?**

Activity 1: What Makes a Piece of Writing Original?

● ● ● ● ●

1. Read the description given for plagiarism. Ask questions if you don't understand or if something needs clarification. If writers use common story structures over and over, what is it that makes a writer's work original? Think about how the details of setting, character traits, motives, unexpected changes (*reversals*), and paradigm shifts (*recognition*) make a story the writer's own.

2. Choose a partner. Then together choose one of the ten basic story elements below. Fill in the gaps in the plot with specific details that could make it a unique story. When you finish, be prepared to share your plot ideas with the class or with a partner.

   Basic plot structures:

   a. The hero goes on a journey, faces obstacles on his/her way (perhaps with another person), and at the end accomplishes a goal that changes his/her life.

   b. Boy meets girl; boy chases girl; boy gets girl.

   c. Character *A* is harassed by character *B*. *A* seeks to gain more power or confidence. *B* is overcome by *A*.

   d. *A* doesn't want to get involved. Action against *A* draws him/her into the situation. *A* decides to take a stand.

   e. *A* and *B* are friends. *A*'s life is threatened, or worse. *B* seeks revenge.

   f. *A* and *B* are not friends. *A* is killed. *B* feels remorse and regret.

   g. *A* has a problem making friends. *B* convinces *A* to do something by befriending *A*. *A* suffers a loss.

   h. *A* is captured. *A* meets *B*. *B* helps *A* escape.

   i. *A* and *B* fall in love. Their love is forbidden. They run away/make plans to run away together.

   j. *A* is the underdog, always losing. *A* finds good fortune. *A* triumphs.

WHAT IS PLAGIARISM?
· · · · ·

With the ever-growing strength of the focus on writing, student writers are feeling the stress of producing original work, from class-assigned essays to short fiction contests. Lack of confidence in one's ability to produce an acceptable piece of writing may be at the heart of this problem, but time also plays a role. How many students procrastinate and find themselves panicking at the last minute with too little time left to complete or even to start the composition? Unfortunately, the availability of compositions and short fiction published on the Internet has attracted the most desperate of procrastinators. Beware! Few students who commit plagiarism actually escape unscathed, and the consequences are far more devastating than the low grade one might receive for a poorly written paper or even the zero for not doing the assignment at all. No one takes dishonesty lightly, especially the officials of a prestigious national writing competition.

The story you have written is not original if...

1. you copied the exact words from another story or copied the words with a few changes.

2. you borrowed the plot from another story, published or not, but used your own words, your own descriptions. (This does not apply to a general plot structure or archetypal pattern.)

3. you heard the story from someone else but didn't read it yourself, and you are not sure of the source. If you're not sure of the source, you're not sure that it *isn't* published somewhere. The risk is too great.

Stories that may follow a master plot, archetypal motif, or common generic story structure, yet are products of your own design in characterization, setting, exposition, resolution, and all other details that make the story uniquely your own—these can be considered original stories.

ACTIVITY 2: WHAT MAKES A GOOD PLOT?
· · · · ·

Aristotle left us a strong foundation for literature. In particular, he defined several terms that we will be using in this workshop, especially in writing tragic plots.

- A *complete plot* consists of two things: 1. One event flows into the next as a natural consequence. 2. The first event does not need explaining, and the last event brings closure to the plot (13-14).

- The *magnitude of the plot* depends on the presence of a change from bad fortune to good fortune or vice versa, and this change must be the result of a sequence of connected events (14). "The change from good fortune to bad corresponds to the failure in action that evokes fear and pity" (Heath xxv).

- *Emotional impact* also contributes to the quality of the plot. Events occur because of their *connection* to the other events. *Astonishment* occurs when things happen contrary to expectation, but "they appear to have happened as if for a purpose" (17).

- *Recognition* occurs with a paradigm shift. The character experiences a change from ignorance to knowledge (18).

- A *reversal* involves a change in the expected outcome of an action (18). See *emotional impact*.

- *Hamartia* is a Greek word that means error. Mistakes that are made in ignorance or through misjudgment, according to Aristotle, make the best plots (21). He also uses this term to include moral errors but not wickedness. Aristotle believed that a character who harmed unwittingly was to be pitied as much as the victim (Heath xxxii).

- Aristotle believed that harm done to someone closely connected to the perpetrator was also a source of fear and pity (23). *Philos* is the Greek word that Aristotle used to describe the person closely connected to the one inflicting harm (Heath xxxiii).

Journal Prompt: The English philosopher Edmund Burke believed that people are motivated by the beautiful and the sublime, but he spoke in agreement with Aristotle in saying those things which strike awe and fear in us are more powerful than the serenely beautiful ones. Write about a scene that struck you with fear or awe.

Do the following exercises:

1. What is a paradigm shift and how can it enhance or change a basic plot structure to make it more interesting?

Paradigm shift: A character exists, conducts his life in a particular frame of mind, and has a certain way of seeing things. Something happens to cause the character to see a person, event, or circumstance in a totally different way. The character shifts the way he sees that person (object, event) because of this new information. He now sees things in a new light.

When working with a plot, constructing a character who experiences what Aristotle called *recognition*—a change from ignorance to knowledge—can have a significant impact on the outcome of the story. The new information received causes the character to do an about-face. That is, when the character sees a person or situation in a new light, his response to it changes, sometimes dramatically. The effect can essentially turn the plot around. The great advantage to this plot structure, of course, is the absence of predictability.

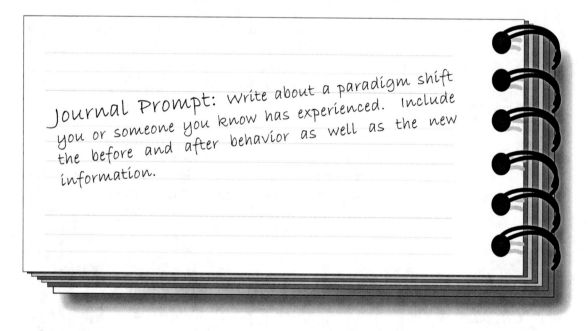

Journal Prompt: Write about a paradigm shift you or someone you know has experienced. Include the before and after behavior as well as the new information.

Choose a partner and one of the following plot structures below. Fill in the details of the plot, noting that the paradigm shift is in parentheses. You must provide the specific information. For example, in number one, what is it that **A** discovers that could make him see **B** in a new light? Construct a situation from the information given.

a. *A* does not take *B* seriously (until *A* discovers something about *B*).

b. *A* is jealous of *B* (until *A* learns more about *B*).

c. *A* does not return *B*'s love. *B* grieves (until *B* learns the truth about *A*).

d. *A* becomes impaired and loses hope (until *B* does something surprising).

e. *A* puts total faith in *B* (until *A* learns the truth about *B*).

f. *A* has solved a mystery (and then finds some surprising, conflicting new information).

g. *A* grieves over a personal loss (and then discovers crucial information about the loss).

h. *A* appears to be evil and tries to prevail over *B* (until *A* learns new information)

i. *A* thinks *B* is inferior and persecutes him for it (until *A* and *B* learn new information).

j. *A* is wealthy, apparently successful, but ruthless. *A* loses his wealth (and learns some surprising truths about himself).

2. Read Ambrose Bierce's short story "The Coup de Grace." Evaluate his story using Aristotle's description of good tragic plots. How does Bierce achieve closure? What or who in the story evokes pity? Does a paradigm shift (astonishment, reversal) occur? What mistake in judgment does the captain make? Is it a mistake? Is he to be pitied, as the sergeant is? Does he not think help will come before the swine attack? Does the situation seem more tragic because the two men are close friends? Does the reader pity the captain even more because his friend's brother, the major, hates him? Write your evaluation.

ACTIVITY 3: WHAT IS YOUR OWN UNIQUE STYLE OF WRITING?
● ● ● ● ●

It has been said that if a story doesn't hook the reader in the first one hundred words, it's not a very good story. Although this may often be the case, I'll let you be the judge. Read the opening paragraphs (about a hundred words each) of as many short stories and novels as you can. As you read, think about the answers to these questions:

a. What kind of story do you think this is, based on the opening?

b. What is the tone (the author's attitude) of the story? What mood has the writer created?

c. What can you tell about the writer's style?

d. Does the opening grab your attention? Why or why not?

Sue Monk Kidd is a masterful storyteller with an extraordinary gift for writing description. The following excerpt is the opening paragraph of chapter 1 of her novel *The Secret Life of Bees*.

> At night I would lie in bed and watch the show, how bees squeezed through the cracks of my bedroom wall and flew circles around the room, making that propeller sound, a high-pitched zzzzzz that hummed along my skin. I watched their wings shining like bits of chrome in the dark and felt the longing build in my chest. The way those bees flew, not even looking for a flower, just flying for the feel of the wind, split my heart down its seam (1).

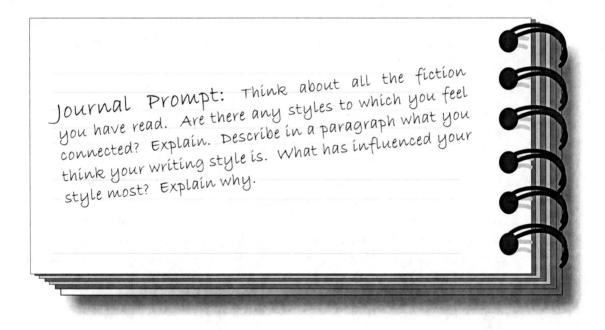

Journal Prompt: Think about all the fiction you have read. Are there any styles to which you feel connected? Explain. Describe in a paragraph what you think your writing style is. What has influenced your style most? Explain why.

ACTIVITY 4: WHAT MAKES GOOD FICTION WRITING?
● ● ● ● ●

A few authors speak out. See if any of these ideas can be helpful to your specific needs.

- Aristotle thought the best plots involve a virtuous person who moves from good fortune to bad fortune, or misfortune is imminent but does not occur. He said that effective plots contain a connected **beginning, middle, and end**, and also **recognition** (a paradigm shift) and **reversal** (a change in the expected outcome).

- Writer Josip Novakovich says, "Gradually fictionalize yourself—create a persona in the first person, who will have your voice and your style of thinking but who will have different biographical facts" (12).

- Creative writing instructors Robert Meredith and John Fitzgerald teach would-be fiction writers that these questions must be answered in order to develop a story:

  Who are the characters involved in the situation?
  Where does the situation take place?
  What is the main event during the situation?
  When does this event happen?
  Why does this event happen?

- Book editor Kathleen Krull counts the following traits as the most important for a story to possess:

  Is the story well written?
  Does it have an opening sentence that grabs?
  Does it target a subject people will want to read about?
  Are the ideas fresh and original?

- Karen Hubert, who teaches genre writing, asserts that good writing has all the right qualities and answers the right questions but most importantly it makes the reader *feel.*

- Stephen King said that every writer needs to read Strunk and White's *Elements of Style,* pointing in particular to omitting needless words.

- Author Joan Lowery Nixon offered several tips for successful fiction writing:
  1. Use sensory perception to bring the writing to life.
  2. Use good strong verbs.
  3. Always start with a good opening sentence.

4. Start with action at the beginning to grab the reader.

5. Make sure every character belongs in the story.

6. Pare your dialogue. Don't waste words. Get rid of extra stuff unless it is important that the characters are hedging.

7. Be careful about slang. It grows old, out of date quickly.

8. Be careful about dialect. It's difficult to write, hard to pull off well.

ACTIVITY 5: WHERE DO WRITERS GET IDEAS FOR PLOTS?
● ● ● ● ●

1. Dig up your own roots by looking at images from your past. It is no secret that bits and pieces of an author's life often surface in his work—the people and the places and events from his own experiences. Writers often muse at the seeming coincidence of self-discovery in the process of writing. Donald Murray, who has for many years taught us so much about writing, does not believe it is by chance that our lives are revealed through our words. He writes, "When we discover what we have said, we discover who we are" (7).

This discovery works for readers, too. Have you ever felt really connected to a character or a place or an event in a book or story? Louise Rosenblatt explains this recognition in this way: "The reader seeks to participate in another's vision—to reap knowledge of the world, to fathom the resources of the human spirit, to gain insights that will make his own life more comprehensible" (7).

Writers entice people of all ages and walks of life into literature by capturing and offering up to readers common human experiences. Psychologist Carl Jung theorized that people across both time and culture recognize these patterns because humans are born knowing these familiar motifs. A well-known **archetype** (*Basic Writings* 301), a word Jung coined to express these universal motifs, is the hero who goes on a quest, a journey in search of something that ultimately changes his life forever. We are living in an age that often questions the existence of modern-day heroes, and yet we can easily recognize the journeys in our lives and their outcomes that often redefine who we are. Author Dan Kirby looks at the average person and simplifies this concept of archetypes by placing portraits from our past, and even our present, into nine categories. Examine his nine images of childhood and see how you can apply them to the building of character and plot in your story.

Nine Images from Childhood

Journal Prompt: Write a **snapshot**. Tell about a "picture" in your past that is frozen in your mind—a person, place, thing, or event that you can still see clearly.

Journal Prompt: Write about **possessions**. Describe one or more objects that were special to you as a child or even today.

Journal Prompt: Write about **boundaries.** Describe where you could and could not go or play when you were little, or write about the more sophisticated boundaries of your life today.

Remember, boundaries can also be rules and restrictions. They can be physical, mental, or emotional.

Journal Prompt: Design a **home schematic**, i.e., a chart listing from top to bottom the following: city, neighborhood, house, special place. Describe each from your childhood. Then choose one to write a short descriptive or narrative piece.

Journal Prompt: Write a **kid portrait**. Describe what you were like when you were a kid. Give as clear a picture as possible, including physical appearance, personality, and interaction with other adults and kids.

Journal Prompt: Construct a circle of **friends** diagram. Draw three circles and write a different age from childhood in each. Extend lines from each circle, and at the end of each line write the name of a good friend. Then choose one person and write about any part of your friendship.

Journal Prompt: Write about **losses and gains**. Make two columns labeled *losses* and *gains*. Fill them in with appropriate people, events, or things. After examining your lists, choose one loss or gain or combination to write a short piece.

Journal Prompt: Face your **fears**. Write about a fear you had as a child that left an impression, or perhaps a fear that you still have.

Journal Prompt: Write about yourself **from someone else's perspective**. Describe how you know or feel you were perceived when you were a child, or how you think you are perceived now.

2. Begin your own collection of ideas from real-life stories in newspapers and magazines. Cut out at least ten articles and glue them in your writing journal. Highlight ideas in the articles that might be useful for your story now or for future stories.

ACTIVITY 6: HOW IMPORTANT IS CHARACTERIZATION?
• • • • •

Aristotle wrote that plot was more important than characters. Many writers today would disagree. Whatever your opinion is, the fact remains that a story must have characters who act and react and move the plot along. In "Writing Workshop: Part 2," we will work on developing different kinds of characters in steps 2, 3, 5, and 6. Remember that we learn about characters in several different ways:

> What the character does
> What the character says
> What other characters say about the character
> How other characters respond to and behave toward the character
> How the author describes the character

Joan Lowery Nixon, author of over one hundred books—many of which are for teens—was asked recently if she based any of her stories on real people. Her answer was no, not directly. A word of caution: a writer may create a character from characteristics of many people she knows, but she never uses the name and personality or circumstances of one person.

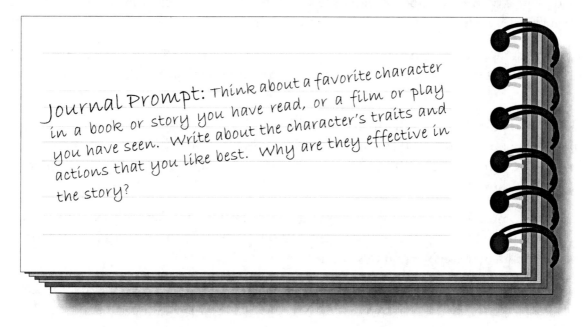

Journal Prompt: Think about a favorite character in a book or story you have read, or a film or play you have seen. Write about the character's traits and actions that you like best. Why are they effective in the story?

WRITING WORKSHOP: PART 2
• • • • •

As we move through the second part of the fiction writing workshop, you will begin to see characters and plot develop. Although you might consider your participation in these activities as mere practice, the ideas you develop can actually be potential short story material. Be sure to include these steps in your writing journal.

STEP 1: PRACTICE WITH PERSPECTIVE AND STORY ELEMENTS
• • • • •

Writers have a saying. The more you write, the more you know what it is you want to say. Now that you have completed Writing Workshop: Part 1, you have begun to collect ideas that can move you closer to uncovering a story. How does the writer move from personal narrative to fiction? How does she put distance between the specific events of her own life and the people she knows in order to turn those events and people into fiction? Step 1 asks you to reshape one of the ideas from the images of childhood. Choose an incident from your life and apply two of the following tasks to that event. Write a page in your journal. You should be able to see fiction taking shape.

1. Change the perspective to third person.

2. Change the age of the protagonist.

3. Change the gender of the protagonist.

4. Change the setting.

5. Change the outcome of the incident.

6. Add or remove a character.

STEP 2: PRACTICE WITH CHARACTERIZATION
• • • • •

Continue your search for character traits by looking at a larger group of people. Choose three examples below and try to draw specifically from your own experiences in addition to what you have learned from reading. Try not to describe one particular person you know when you complete the exercise that follows. Write a sentence or two about each of the three people you are describing in your journal. Remember to *show* what the character does.

Describe someone who

1. is funny

2. is weird or strange

3. is lovable

4. is tricky, deceptive, manipulative

5. loves animals

6. is always negative

7. is conceited

8. is mysterious

9. is popular or not popular

10. does or does not follow rules

Apply several of the character types listed to one of the following plots. Think about how each personality would react differently to the situation. Write a page or two showing the interaction. It is only a sliver of a story and needs no introduction or resolution. Choose one or more of the characters in step 2 and place them in one of the following plots. Show how each character affects the plot.

1. Several characters are trapped together under potentially dangerous circumstances.

2. A character is accused of either a crime or unacceptable behavior.

3. A character falls in love.

4. A character feels betrayed by a close friend.

5. Several characters must work together as a team to accomplish a goal.

Step 3: Clarify kinds of conflict: Physical and intellectual plots
• • • • •

Are you beginning to see the connection between character and plot? Keep these character traits from step 2 in mind as you complete step 3.

In the exercise below, characters *A* and *B* face challenging situations. Let several of these characters interact and write a page or two about what happens. Again, how do specific character traits affect the plot?

1. *A* is physically overpowered by *B.*

2. *A* is not accepted socially.

3. *A* does not take *B* seriously.

4. *A*'s dangerous way of living threatens life.

5. *A* faces uncertainty and grief as he grows up.

6. *A*, who usually escapes anything, is caught.

7. *A* is taken advantage of because of his generosity.

8. *A* is harassed by a seemingly more powerful person.

9. *A* goes through a significant change that she doesn't want.

10. *A* always gets in trouble but wants to change.

Step 4: Create plot outlines
• • • • •

Read each plot description below and choose one to develop. Answer the questions that follow, and then write a page or two integrating this information with the plot. The end product should be a brief plot summary.

Plot descriptions:
1. Character *A* goes on a journey. Character *B* joins *A* along the way. Together they overcome difficulties in order to reach their goal. Both are changed by the experience.

2. Character *A* sets off in a challenging pursuit of a person or thing that will bring him/her a reward of some kind.

3. Character *A* undertakes a journey in order to rescue someone from danger.

4. Character *A*, perhaps along with others, plots to escape from some kind of restraint, captivity, or danger.

5. Character *A* and character *B* are at odds, battling for power or control.

6. Character *A* is considered weak or incapable of succeeding but, through a series of events, actually does succeed in the end.

7. Character *A* experiences an event that enables him/her to see life differently, so much so that character *A* is a changed person. Often the change is a significant or dramatic one.

8. Character *A* sacrifices something precious, perhaps even his/her own life, for the good of someone else. This story sometimes involves a rite of passage, a formal or informal ritual—perhaps the sacrifice itself that a person participates in, indicating that he/she has reached a new level of maturity.

Questions:
1. What are the characters' names?
2. What is the setting?
3. What are the difficulties/dangers they encounter?
4. What are their goals? What rewards/prizes await the characters?
5. Do the characters change? How? Why?
6. What are the major events that help to change the characters?
7. What personality traits of the characters affect the plot?
8. How does the conflict turn out?
9. Are there any other details that are important to the plot? Explain.

STEP 5: CREATE TENSION IN PLOTS
• • • • •

Tension fuels plot. It is the emotional, mental, and physical energy that drives a situation and moves the story along. Tension is the key ingredient that turns a plot summary into a compelling story. So how does a writer create this tension? Look at the plot structures listed below. After each one is a focusing question or two that should lead you to consider the possible causes of tension in each plot. Think about, and discuss with another person if you can, the many different ways you could develop these ideas to create greater tension in the plot of your story. You should discover the sensory images that communicate tension and make the reader empathize, even feel the same discomfort and fear that the character is feeling. The writer can achieve two methods of feeling tension: the reader himself feels it or the reader observes the character feeling it after the reader does, providing dramatic irony.

1. **Plot 1**
    a. Will she survive and reach the goal? How will her life change?
    b. Causes of tension:
        1.) obstacles
        2.) attack, loss, injury
        3.) expectation of gain

2. **Plot 2**
    a. If he survives, what will he gain?
    b. Causes of tension:
        1.) risks
        2.) challenges
        3.) fear

3. **Plot 3**
    a. Will he get the person he is chasing?
    b. Causes of tension:
        1.) facing obstacles in the search
        2.) being led astray
        3.) keeping up, losing the trail

4. **Plot 4**
    a. Will she get revenge?
    b. Causes of tension:
        1.) anger/bitterness that motivates
        2.) dangers, risks, obstacles in the pursuit
        3.) fear of physical or psychological harm
        4.) victimization

5. **Plot 5**
    a. Who is going to win the argument, conflict?
    b. Causes of tension:
        1.) struggle, fight, battle

2.) uncertainty

3.) the breaking point, teetering between winning and losing

6. **Plot 6**

   a. Does he/she rise to the top?

   b. Causes of tension:

       1.) uncertainty

       2.) hope, desire for better fortune

       3.) fear of the more powerful

7. **Plot 7**

   a. Does he/she succumb, give in?

   b. Causes of tension:

       1.) potential evil; danger threatens nearby

       2.) uncertainty

       3.) fear of consequences

       4.) weakness of victim, strength of the powerful

8. **Plot 8**

   a. What transforms his/her life? How is he/she changed?

   b. Causes of tension:

       1.) the event that causes the change

       2.) uncertainty, unknown

       3.) consequences from change, loss, unexpected or unwanted gain

9. **Plot 9**

   a. What causes him/her to grow up, mature?

   b. Causes of tension:

       1.) event or breaking point that starts the maturation process

       2.) loss of innocence

       3.) obstacles—other people or even self tries to prevent maturation

10. **Plot 10**

   a. Are the two lovers successful in getting through all five stages of love? (See chapter 8 for Jung's archetypes and Hawthorne's symbolism: the attraction and meeting, the chase and hiding, the problems, the healing, the bliss.)

   b. Causes of tension:

1.) the chase

2.) the hiding, uncertainty

3.) obstacles, problems, fears, losses

11. **Plot 11**

    a. Who or what is sacrificing or being sacrificed? Why?

    b. Causes of tension:

        1.) fear of pain, death, or loss

        2.) desire for death

        3.) inability to accept the idea of loss after the fact

        4.) pain of death or loss

12. **Plot 12**

    a. What happens when human beings go too far?

    b. Causes of tension:

        1.) building fear of consequences as something accumulates.

        2.) consequences of greed

        3.) pain of loss

        4.) being in a state of denial

Journal Prompt: Choose one of the causes of tension in the plot structures, and write about a tense incident in your own life or the life of someone you know.

STEP 6: OBSERVE HOW TENSION IS CREATED IN FILM

• • • • •

We observe and empathize with the tension in a story whether it is directed at the characters, or, as in dramatic irony, it is caused by characters who experience it after the reader or viewer does. What specifically causes the tension? How does a writer make us feel it? What are the specific techniques a writer uses to communicate dialogue and images of tension?

Watch the following video clips and identify the conflict. Listen and observe the film for details that might contribute to the tension in the clip. Avoid the film's sound effects and music that you could not apply to writing. Then use those details to construct a sentence in your journal that shows tension. This sentence can describe the scene in the film or it can describe one from your imagination. The object is to *show* tension, not just tell about it.

Clip 1: *Mad About Mambo*

> Boy meets girl.
>
> Boy chases girl.
>
> Girl rejects boy.
>
> Girl discovers she needs boy's help.
>
> Boy helps, and girl pays attention.

Clip 2: *School Ties*

Middle-class senior football player is recruited to play for an exclusive New England prep school in the 1950s. Jealousy causes a classmate to accuse him of cheating on an exam, grounds for expulsion from the school. Additional clip: Boys discriminate against and harass a Jewish classmate.

Clip 3: *The Milagro Beanfield War*

A Chicano handyman from Milagro Valley accidentally causes water from a large resort development site to irrigate his small, dry bean field. He suddenly realizes the injustice imposed on him and he incites his neighbors in a war against the developers who want to turn their modest community into a golf and resort area.

Clip 4: *I Know Why the Caged Bird Sings*

A black family in the 1930s hides one of their members to avoid a lynching.

Clip 5: *Ever After*

Girl meets boy and rejects him. She discovers startling new information about him and tries to win him over.

Clip 6: *Finding Forrester*

An instructor at a prep school in New York City becomes engaged in a conflict with a student when that student comes to the rescue of one of the pedant's victims.

Clip 7: *The Emperor's Club*

A history teacher at an old, well-respected prep school holds a competition on classical history each year. He must find a way to cope with the consequences of the kind of rivalry that this contest has produced.

Clip 8: *The Fantasticks*

Luisa hands over her mother's necklace, her most prized possession, to El Gallo as proof that she will return to him and accompany him on a great adventure. She returns, only to become heartbroken, for he has left her, taking the necklace with him.

Clip 9: *Adventures in Babysitting*

A teenage girl on a babysitting job gets a call from her best friend who needs rescuing. She puts the kids in the car and sets off on a journey into the big city to find her friend. She finds much more than her friend.

Clip 10: *Princess Bride*

A young man engages in a battle of wits in order to win the prize: the life of the woman he loves.

Clip 11: *Far and Away*

A young Irish woman is trying to escape the stifling confines of her Victorian family's life. She solicits the help of a poor farm boy whose bitterness makes him reject her.

Clip 12: *Labyrinth*

A teenage girl must stay at home and baby sit her younger brother against her will. Her wish for him to be taken away by the goblins, which she speaks aloud, is granted, when she suddenly finds him missing from his crib.

Clip 13: *Serendipity*

A man and woman meet accidentally—twice. They feel fate has a hand in their meeting, but the woman wants to put fate to the test, to the disappointment and frustration of both.

Clip 14: *The Journey of Natty Gann*

A boy looking for work and a girl searching for her father during the depression of the 1930s travel across country together. When the boy finds work, the girl must decide whether to go with him or continue looking for her father.

Clip 15: *Nicholas Nickleby*

In nineteenth-century England, the Nickleby family loses their father and is betrayed by their uncle. The eldest son, Nicholas, must embark on a journey to save the family against great odds.

Clip 16: *The Importance of Being Earnest*

Two eligible and beautiful women insist that the husband of their dreams must be called Earnest. In a mix-up of identities, Gwendolen and Cecily become instant rivals.

Clip 17: *Regarding Henry*

A high-powered New York attorney, whose greatest weakness is his belief in his own invincibility, is assaulted as he walks into the middle of a convenience store robbery. He survives but must relearn everything, even his own past, which he no longer wants.

Clip 18: *Open Range*

The setting is the late nineteenth-century West when driving cattle in the open range meant survival and a way of life. Four innocent men are hunted down by a ruthless, evil rancher whose greed for land and power must be stopped.

Clip 19: *Zulu*

Outnumbered forty to one, a small garrison of English soldiers in 1879 hold out eighteen hours as four thousand Zulu tribesmen in South Africa launch a fierce and bloody battle.

Clip 20: *Runaway Jury*

Can a jury be influenced by an outsider? A ruthless jury consultant will do anything to win this case. Will the attorneys succumb to the temptation of "buying" jurors who are for sale?

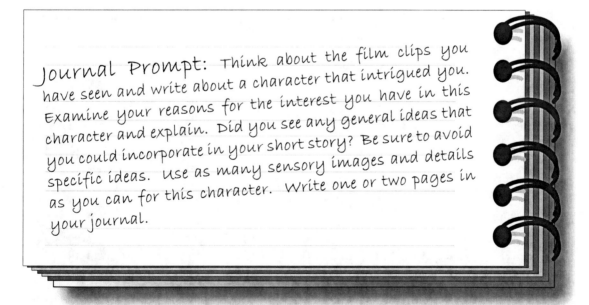

Journal Prompt: Think about the film clips you have seen and write about a character that intrigued you. Examine your reasons for the interest you have in this character and explain. Did you see any general ideas that you could incorporate in your short story? Be sure to avoid specific ideas. Use as many sensory images and details as you can for this character. Write one or two pages in your journal.

Watch *Children on Their Birthdays,* a film based on the story of the same title by Truman Capote. Pay close attention to the characters' wants and needs, which provide the tension in the story. Examine the multiple conflicts:

- Billy Bob's mother, Mrs. Murphy, and her relationship with Speedy

- Billy Bob and his attempt to make and save money to go to the World Series

- Billy Bob and his best friend, Preacher, both falling for the same girl and competing for her attention

- Preacher's desire to hurt other people for his own pleasure or power

- Billy Bob's desire to grow up

- Lily Jane's desire to get to Hollywood

- Lily Jane's desire to make moral restitution with everyone

- Janice and Cora Mae wanting attention from the two boys

- Speedy's desire to marry Mrs. Murphy

- Mrs. Murphy's desire to move on with her life after her husband's death

- Lionel's plan to cheat everyone out of their money

Which scenes would make good short stories in themselves, isolated from the larger story? Do the following activity in a large group discussion:

1. Choose one of the characters from the film. Describe how his or her wants and needs drive the action.

2. Which specific actions create tension? For example, when Billy Bob picks up the rifle, there is a sense of impending doom, and for a moment the scene is a gripping one.

3. Which actions of the characters create a paradigm shift? How does this story element contribute to the tension in the story?

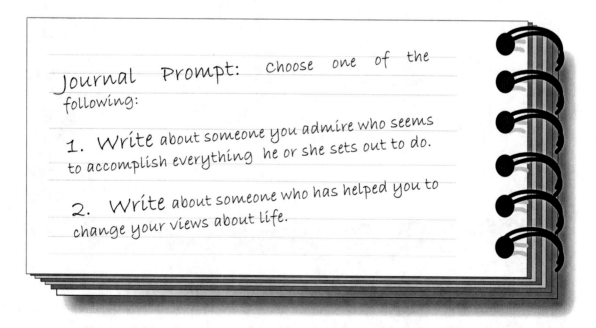

Journal Prompt: Choose one of the following:

1. Write about someone you admire who seems to accomplish everything he or she sets out to do.

2. Write about someone who has helped you to change your views about life.

An important aspect of visual literacy, a cinematic presentation of story elements provides writers with an array of models for sculpting their own characters' wants and needs and tension. Films can also show writers the success they can have when they write about what they know. Often what they know is their own culture.

Shadow Magic is a film set in Peking, China, in 1902. Young photographer Liu discovers a struggling British filmmaker trying to sell the idea of silent moving pictures to an unreceptive, skeptical, and even fearful Chinese audience at the turn of the century. Liu, fascinated with western technology, offers to help him in return for a job. Raymond, the filmmaker, gladly accepts his help and business picks up. But betrayal, love, and a changing world lead to many conflicts as Liu attempts to follow his dreams.

Watch the film and discuss how the writer develops the story through the journeys of both Liu and Raymond. What causes tension in the story?

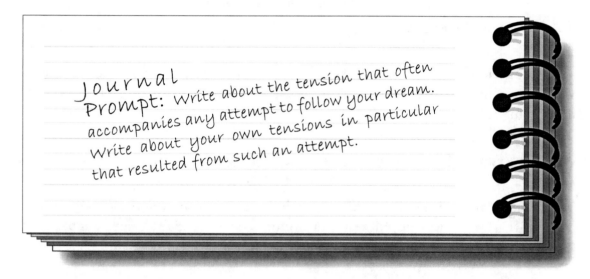

Journal Prompt: Write about the tension that often accompanies any attempt to follow your dream. Write about your own tensions in particular that resulted from such an attempt.

STEP 7: COMBINE CHARACTER AND CONFLICT
• • • • •

Use the information you have been stockpiling to complete these exercises. At this point, you may have begun to write your story. If so, complete these exercises using the characters and plot that are now taking shape in your story.

1. Choose three people you know or that you can create from previous exercises, and construct one character from them. Combine physical traits as well as personality traits. Think of specific details, such as an intriguing voice or an annoying habit, and make this part of your new character's personality. Place the character in a scene, perhaps one that you have already devised or one from another step, and see what happens. Write at least a page.

2. In step 2 you wrote about three people with specific traits. Now choose two of those characters and complete as many of the following details as you can about each one:
      Name, gender, age

Height, weight, eye color, hair color

Parents

Pets

Education, talents, skills

Favorites

Goals and obstacles

3. Place the two characters you detailed in one of the following conflicts. Write a sentence or two summarizing your plot.

    a. *A* wants something that *B* has.

    b. *A* is jealous of *B* and plays a mean trick on *B*.

    c. *A* rescues *B*

4. Complete a home schematic chart for each of your two characters. Tell as much as you can about the character from his environment. Place each character in a city, neighborhood, house, or his or her own special place.

STEP 8: LET YOUR CHARACTERS SPEAK: WRITE DIALOGUE
● ● ● ● ●

Writing dialogue is not just a matter of mimicking real conversations between people. If you do that, your dialogue will result in wordiness and overkill. As an example, try to remember your last casual phone conversation with a friend. Was it something like this?

Maggie: Hey, what's up?

Christine: Not much. What about you?

Maggie: I'm so bored.

Christine: Yeah. Me, too. And it's so hot outside.

Maggie: Yeah. I'm gonna get something to drink. Hold on.

    (She puts the phone down and Christine waits.) Okay.

    I'm back. What'd you say?

Christine: Nothing.

Not exactly titillating dialogue, is it? The exercises in this step will encourage a process of getting words on paper, allowing the dialogue to say what you want it to say, and then paring words to perfection. In the editing process you can get rid of the excess and move the dialogue along so that it doesn't drag.

1. Pretend your two characters know each other well. Write two **A/B** scripts with five to eight dialogue exchanges each.

    a. In the first script, engage them in a scene in which the characters' motives determine their actions. The reader may not know yet what the motives are, but the writer does. One or more characters want or need something urgently.

    b. Now, in the second script, pretend your two characters have just met each other. Think of where they might be and why they might be speaking to each other.

    Use the following format for your A/B script:
    What do you suppose motivates the words and feelings between the two characters in this **A/B** script? What are their wants and needs?

    A: Jim told me about last night.

    B: I don't follow you.

    A: The folder. He said you got the key.

    B: Listen, I don't know what you're talking about. Why do you think Jim would know anything? I suggest you get your story straight. Now, if you'll excuse me....

    A: They found Brigg.

    B: (*She stops and turns around slowly.*) I see. Close the door.

    (And so forth. The two characters continue exchanging dialogue.)

2. Sometimes when people speak, they give more information to the listener than what their words are saying on the surface. The body language of the character can help to reveal what the speaker is really thinking, but loaded words, emotional language, and the speaker's follow-up comments and questions are the strongest indicators of what writers call **subtext**, the underlying meaning or thoughts that enhance the depth of the character as well as the relationship between characters.

    Choose one of the following conversations and write an **A/B** script with eight to ten dialogue exchanges between character **A** and character **B**. Keep this guide in mind:
    He/she says_____. What he/she may be implying is_____.
    Think about why the character is leaving out important information. The **A/B** script should show the characters' subtext. Remember that the details of the conversation, in addition to the characters' actions that create an underlying message, add greater depth to the characters and the plot.

    - A parent giving advice to a son or daughter

    - A student in a job interview

    - A boy talking to a girl he has a crush on

- Two friends planning a guest list for a party
- A girl breaking up with her boyfriend (or a boy...girlfriend)
- A student explaining to a parent why he/she failed the test
- One friend trying to convince another to do something
- A teacher or coach giving advice to a student
- A student explaining a reason for being late, not having an assignment, etc.
- A parent trying to get information from his/her son or daughter
- Two friends arguing and blaming each other
- The new kid at school trying to make friends
- A girl or boy explaining to a stranger why he/she is running away
- One friend consoling another
- A teenager visiting relatives he/she hasn't seen in years

Journal Prompt: Write about a situation, perhaps one of those suggested in step 8, in which you or someone you know engaged in a conversation in which one of the speakers wanted to withhold information or felt compelled to omit parts of the truth, or whose words held a deeper or additional meaning. Describe the speaker's wants, needs, body language, and the actual language that helped to cover up the whole truth.

You can now also draw from your own experience with subtext to create dialogue for characters. Write another **A/B** script with subtext, using your same two characters from the previous assignments or two new ones. Once you have written it, go back and pare it. Get rid of any unnecessary words so that you have the essence of meaning. Remember, you do not want to replicate real conversation with its long pauses and wordiness that create a sluggish pace.

STEP 9: ADD A THIRD CHARACTER
• • • • •

Choose one of the conflicts you have described. Look at your list of characters and find one who might add interest, additional conflict, or reconciliation to the plot. Examine the same questions about this character. How do the three interact? How does the addition of a third character change your plot or help to advance it?

STEP 10: CONSIDER WAYS TO BEGIN YOUR STORY
• • • • •

You are now ready to use the notes you have made from these writing exercises to construct your short story. If you feel you are still not ready, look back at the different methods of gathering information about character and conflict and try again. When you start to flesh out the story, aim for a thousand-word draft and build to approximately three thousand words.

If you want to enter a contest, the Scholastic Art & Writing Awards is by far the best with a time-honored record of recognizing student writing. According to the Scholastic guidelines, which can be obtained from their website, the competition requires that a short story be at least 1,300 to 3000 words and a short short story be 600 to 1,300 words. Whether entering or not, consider the number of ways you can begin your story. Examples are listed below.

1. Circular pattern: The end looks a lot like the beginning, with the main character in the same place where he began, or at least in a similar situation. For example, S. E. Hinton's *The Outsiders* begins with the character Ponyboy stepping out into the sunshine, and it ends with the same words.

2. Flashback: The story begins at the end, in the present, while the narrator returns to the past to recap what happened. For example, *The Outsiders*, as the reader discovers at the end, turns out to be a retelling of a story that a sixteen-year-old boy writes for his English class.

3. An incident that sparks a story but is not really part of the basic plot: It could also be a person, place, thing, or event that causes a character to reminisce. For example, the sugary treats in the shapes of animals in the Mexican market in Katherine Anne Porter's "The Grave" cause the main character to remember a loss of innocence in her childhood. The incident becomes the focus of the story.

4. The narrator mentions a person, thing, place, or event in the beginning that will explain the story as it slowly unravels: For example, Scout Finch implies at the beginning of Harper Lee's *To Kill a Mockingbird* that the entire story has its roots in the breaking of her brother Jem's arm and, of course, the reasons behind it.

5. A character begins to tell a story which becomes the plot: For example, in the 1390s, poet Geoffrey Chaucer used the frame of a pilgrimage to the shrine of Thomas á Becket in Canterbury Cathedral. The thirty travelers, or pilgrims, each participate in a storytelling contest as they gather at the Tabard Inn in Southwark.

Throughout the workshop you have been collecting ideas for your story.

Remember, the best stories come from what you know and like:

Stories from your own heritage and culture

Stories with teenage issues, conflicts, angst

Family stories

Friendship stories

Teen adventure stories

Stories with conflicts complicated by additional conflicts

STEP 11: CREATE A STRONG PLOT
● ● ● ● ●

Evidence that people everywhere enjoy stories clearly shows up in booming box office sales and packed book stores—the large chains, the small independent shops, as well as the numerous discount stores. Cafes attached to these shops with aromatic pots of delicious brews may have some influence, I suppose. Nevertheless, this proof can put to rest the myth that only English teachers love reading stories. When I begin teaching my classes each fall, it is always with the notion of turning readers of stories into writers of stories. My favorite activity of the year revolves around fiction writing and is also the one that is often the turning point for the student who is developing a plot. In an English program that could suffer from the goal of being adequate enough to prepare students to pass a state exam, I sometimes shudder at the amount of time this activity imposes on an already bulging curriculum. The number of national Scholastic winners from my classes in the short fiction category silences that fear. This next activity is a must. Each student stands before a group of peers and outlines the plot of the story she is writing. When she is finished, she poses questions for her audience: Do I need more tension and where? Does everything make sense; is the plot believable? What would make this a better story? The listeners are always ready to respond. The writer jots down their suggestions and decides later whether she will use them or not. I caution the writer not to get caught up in defending what she has written. Although listening to and discussing each student's short story plot consumes precious time, it could easily be the most helpful part of the fiction writing process. Besides, people enjoy listening to a good story.

STEP 12: FOCUS ON DICTION
● ● ● ● ●
Create a word bank for your story.

After you make some decisions about your characters and plot, make a list of strong words for your story. Choose at least five nouns, verbs, adjectives and adverbs. Find twenty new, more precise words or synonyms that could replace these words. Use a thesaurus throughout the process of writing your story, but remember when you finish, you don't need to use all of your new words. Choose the best ones for the job. **Less** is often **more.** Season carefully.

Show, don't tell.

Take a sentence or passage from your short story that would benefit from more description. Use your word bank to make the passage more eloquent, or use other tools, such as symbolism, thematic support, metaphor, or antithesis. ***This one revision alone can mean the difference between a good story and a great story.***

Edit by reading aloud.

Read parts of your story aloud to a listener who is willing and able to give you constructive criticism. Work out problems with plot. Make sure the tension created helps to drive the plot. Look for fresh beginnings, endings, and twists. Do this early in the writing process to smooth out the wrinkles in your plot before you get too far into the development of the story. Reading aloud affords different benefits from reading silently. Decoding words aloud prevents reading the manuscript as the writer would *like* it to be read rather than reading it as it really is on paper.

STEP 13: MEET IN WRITING RESPONSE GROUPS
● ● ● ● ●

Now that you have a draft of your story, you can receive valuable information from other writers through a process of reading it aloud and hearing their comments and questions. It is important for the group to remain supportive, to be good listeners (taking notes about what they hear), and to ask questions that could help the writer develop the story. Try to meet at least three times in your response group. Use the following guide for responding to each other's stories:

Response Group Meeting 1:

1. Record anything you hear that sounds good to you.

2. Note anything that is not clear to you.

3. Listen for information that is either present or absent and seems essential to characterization and plot.

4. Listen for anything that seems to predict or foreshadow. Ask where the writer is taking this idea.

5. Listen and ask questions about the causes of tension in the story.

Response Group Meeting 2:

1. Continue to focus on where the plot is going. Look at the beginning, middle, and end. Does the opening grab the reader's interest? Does it set the conflict in motion? Does the middle continue to develop the conflict and keep it fueled with tension? Does the end tie up loose ends?

2. Does the setting play an important role? What effect does the setting seem to have on the story?

3. Are the characters interesting? What traits, words, situations, and background information are provided? How well are these elements woven into the story? Are they subtle, or abrupt and glaring?

4. Are the ideas fresh and original? Tell the writer which ones are and which are not, but do it in the spirit of helpful criticism.

Response Group Meeting 3:

By this time the writers in your group have added your suggestions to plenty of their own revisions in developing their short stories. It's time to look at word choice and dialogue.

1. Word choice

Avoid too much or too little. Every writer is looking for balance in his or her voice and style, and the only way to achieve this balance is to revise, revise, revise, and give your writing lots of thought. The words the writer chooses have to be consistent with every element in the story: genre, setting, characterization, tension, plot development, dialect, local color, dialogue—everything that makes your story unique.

2. Dialogue

Go back and look at step 8, writing dialogue so your characters can speak. The basic questions you will have as you listen to each other's stories are, first, if the dialogue is appropriate for the characters, and second, if the writer achieved balance—not too wordy but not so sparse that the characters appear weak or insignificant.

LUISA: Couldn't we just sit this one out?
EL GALLO: Ridiculous! When there's music to be danced to.
Tom Jones and Harvey Schmidt
The Fantasticks

CHAPTER 4

Writing Scripts

Writing a play can be a fascinating and quick way to see your work published quickly with unique benefits. A dramatic script enables many people to share your writing in a communal way, as they express their response to your work emotionally and sometimes even verbally. Their faces reveal their feelings as soon as the actors speak the words. From the actors' perspective, *the roar of the greasepaint, the smell of the crowd* summarize the attraction to the theatrical world, but if that is so, the script is the tool that catapults them into that arena.

In a well-written play, the characters speak to each other in a way that allows the audience to feel as if they are eavesdropping on a conversation in the lives of a group of people they really don't know and yet ironically know intimately. Even when the play is not performed on a stage with a proscenium arch open only on one side to the audience, the *fourth wall* still exists. It is that imaginary wall that separates the actors from the audience, wherever the audience is seated. It is through this quite large keyhole that we get a glimpse into their fictional lives. No narration exists in a play, with the exception of a narrator who plays a character that steps through the wall and communicates directly with the audience, offering information that will continue to tell the story. The script must contain words and actions in stage directions that will clearly move the plot forward without confusion. The conversation should be so clear that the audience can see and understand the development of character and plot throughout the play in the backdrop of the situation.

The characters should be believable but not necessarily realistic. Any genre, including fantasy, can be performed as a play. The writer achieves this end by giving the character enough lines in a scene that allow him to divulge information through actions, dialogue, and response. The writer must achieve a balance, letting the character speak enough words that will communicate information and emotion but not so much that the dialogue becomes heavy. For most playwrights, this requires reworking the script and editing it until the sound is right. Imagination and experience are the two great sources for creating characters. In the chapter on writing fiction, you practiced creating characters from real people in your experience. This technique holds true for scriptwriting as well. Bits and pieces of people you know become the parts of a great collage that ends up in the story or on the stage as characters with specific wants and needs. You will remember, too, that it is their wants and needs that drive the plot and create the tension that makes a good story. And don't forget about subtext. For a number of reasons, a more significant meaning could lie beneath the words actually spoken by the characters.

In this chapter, you will learn how to turn a published story into a play. Just remember that the story belongs to another writer. You will also learn how to write a play from your own imagination. The example in this book, in the chapter on Shakespeare, is a modern teenage version of the romantic comedy *Twelfth Night*. Although I loosely followed a favorite Shakespeare convention, the girl disguised as a boy, the story structure is the archetypal girl-meets-boy with my own variations in the conflict.

How to Turn a Great Short Story into a Script
● ● ● ● ●

You have already seen how I took the Hawthorne story, "The Maypole of Merry Mount," and a canto from a long narrative poem, Spenser's *The Faerie Queene*, and turned them into a form that is meant to be seen and not read, a play. Now it's your turn. I've listed some suggestions below for stories written by well-known short fiction and novel writers. Although many playwrights work alone, you might want to work with a partner or several other students to write, direct, and produce your own play based on your chosen piece of literature.

I've listed a few stories that you will find easy and enjoyable to turn into dramatic scripts.
Scenes from *How the Garcia Girls Lost Their Accents* by Julia Alvarez

Scenes from *I Know Why the Caged Bird Sings* by Maya Angelou

"The Devil and Daniel Webster" by Stephen Vincent Benet

"A Tooth for Paul Revere" by Stephen Vincent Benet (*Twenty Grand* collection)

Stories from *The Illustrated Man* or *The Martian Chronicles* by Ray Bradbury

"Fumble" by Katharine Brush (*Twenty Grand*)

Stories about teens from two collections edited by Donald Gallo: *Connections* and *Sixteen*

Scenes from *China Boy* by Gus Lee

"A Very Old Man with Enormous Wings" from *Leaf Storm* by Gabriel Garcia Marquez

"Flight" by John Steinbeck

"The Secret Life of Walter Mitty" by James Thurber

Any lively, humorous story with witty British dialogue from the early 1920s from the collection titled *The Most of P.G. Wodehouse*

"The Man Who Was Almost a Man" by Richard Wright

From Story to Script:
Tips for Writing and Producing a Play

● ● ● ● ●

Knowing where to begin can eliminate the anxiety of getting started. The following tips are listed in a somewhat sequential way, but as writing goes, you must discover what works best for you.

1. After reading the story or excerpt of the novel you chose, plot the events of the story on a line. Select the events you want to include in your script.

2. Make a list of characters in those events.

3. Find the dialogue already written by the author for those characters. Include some or most of it in your script.

4. Look at the narration that you need to turn into dialogue in order to move the plot along toward a conclusion. Will the characters say these lines, or do you need a narrator?

5. Make sure you include stage directions in parentheses.

6. Since this is a play and the audience will not have the benefit of reading narration that fills in necessary information in a short story or novel, you will need to communicate the story through dialogue and acting. Carefully plan out these elements: the words spoken by the characters, the interaction between the actors on stage, and the stage directions that guide their movement.

7. At first don't think too much about the length. When you get ready to do a final draft, write scenes that are not so short that the scene change feels longer than the scene itself.

8. Write scenes that are do-able. Consider props, set, and actions that are within possibility and plausibility. Remember, in play production you can *suggest* a scene. You needn't try to recreate the scene with realism. Keep it as simple as your resources dictate.

9. Choose music to accompany the theme of the play. The audience can hear this music as they wait for the play to begin and also as the play ends.

10. Arrange special, appropriate, but simple lighting for each scene if theatrical lighting is available.

11. Enhance your scenes with sound effects if possible. You have literally hundreds of sounds available on CD now.

13. Choose appropriate costumes and props that help the actors get into character and the audience see the plot evolve.

14. Memorize lines, rehearse, and produce your play for an audience.

THREE TIMES THREE: AN EXERCISE IN SCRIPTWRITING
● ● ● ● ●

One of the most enjoyable exercises my students engage in is a writing and acting exercise that I call "Three Times Three." I ask my students to pair up and plan a conflict between two teenagers and then examine the different ways this conflict could be interpreted and then presented to an audience. For example, students could

- Change the outcome or resolution of the conflict.

- Vary the mood or tone from scene to scene.

- Change the setting, time, and place.

- Have character *A* switch personality traits or attitude with character *B*.

- Increase or reduce the energy level in each scene.

- Vary the level of sophistication of language, or perhaps create a different regional or foreign accent for each scene.

Writers who participate have an opportunity to try out endless possibilities of human interaction, and actors can stretch their own repertoire by creating a variety of roles for the same conflict. After students write and revise their scenes, the result is usually astonishingly brilliant. Although several students might end up with two partners instead of one, they all write short, polished scripts consisting of three scenes, each three minutes long, hence the name "Three Times Three." There's a good reason for doing three scenes. It's traditionally the number of perfect balance, of course, and a mystical, magical number whose components fill our daily lives with their mystery: mother-father-child, beginning-middle-end, the three little pigs, earth-air-water, the three-legged stool—the list goes on. Whatever the reason, *three* creates a satisfying balance in communicating the plays' messages. The production details remain simple: actors performing with minimal props and furniture against a black theatrical curtain with standard full stage lighting, and opening and closing theme music.

Jessica and Leah created the following script in one of my classes, employing two teenage girls, apparently once close friends, in a conflict involving a mutual friend and love interest. Notice the shift in the middle scene toward a circular structure with the final scene. As you might imagine, their audience of fourteen-year-olds loved it.

He's Mine!

Scene 1: *Leah is sitting at a table in the center left of the stage. She is reading a magazine, listening to music, and chewing gum. Jessica storms in.*

Jessica: Since when do you like Jason? (*Leah doesn't respond and starts bobbing her head to the music.*) Ugh. (*Jessica walks over to Leah and pulls out her right ear plug.*) I said, since when do you like Jason!

Leah: I don't know what you're talking about. (*Leah looks away from Jessica.*)

Jessica: Yes, you do! (*Leah looks back at Jessica, who pulls a note out of her back pocket and hands it to Leah.*)

Leah: (*She looks at the note and is shocked by what she sees.*) Oh, my gosh! Where did you get this?

Jessica: I saw you and Katy passing notes in math class today and leaving me out. At the end of class I found it crumpled in the trash can.

Leah: Fine, maybe I do like him.

Jessica: Ugh, I can't believe this! How could you do this to me?

Leah: Do what! It's not like you were going out.

Jessica: But you know I've liked him since fifth grade. We're so close to going out, he already asked me to the dance and everything.

Leah: See? He likes you, not me. But that doesn't mean that I can't like him.

Jessica: (*She sighs.*) As hard as it is for me to admit, you are much prettier and more popular than me. If you do as little as look at Jason, he will totally forget about me.

Leah: Well, it's not my fault if I'm totally irresistible. Some girls have it and others —(*She looks at Jessica.*) don't.

Jessica: Ugh! You have to stop liking him. That's breaking the girl code.

Leah: What girl code?

Jessica: (*She pulls out The Book of Girl Codes.*) Code #54, Section A. (*She shows the book to Leah.*)

Leah: (*She reads the book.*) "A girl cannot like the same boy as her best friend if her best friend has liked him since fifth grade and they are going to the dance together." (*She looks up from the book.*) Did you write this in yourself? (*She rolls her eyes and slams the book down on the table.*) I can't just stop liking him.

Jessica: Why not! You know how much he means to me.

Leah: Suck it up. He doesn't matter that much to you.

Jessica: Yes, he does. (*She stares off into the distance, smiling.*) I love the way his light brown eyes glitter in the sunlight, how his floppy brown hair bounces when he runs, the way his smile always brightens up my day.

Leah: (*She also stares off into the distance, smiling.*) Me, too.

Jessica: (*She glares at Leah.*) Ugh! You disgust me!

Leah: (*She looks back at Jessica.*) Well, it's not so pretty looking from my view, either.

Jessica: (*She gives Leah ugly look.*) This is so stupid. I don't even know why we became friends in the first place.

Leah: Me neither. (*She grabs the magazine and walks up to Jessica.*) Here, take your dumb magazine you let me borrow. (*She throws the magazine at Jessica.*)

Jessica: (*She catches the magazine.*) Fine, I will. (*Both girls begin to storm off-stage in opposite directions.*)

Leah: Fine!

Jessica: Fine!

Leah: Fine!

Curtain

Scene 2: *Leah is sitting at a table in the center left of the stage. She is reading a magazine, listening to music, and chewing gum. Jessica storms in.*

Jessica: Since when do you like Jason? (*Leah doesn't respond and starts bobbing her head to the music.*) Ugh. (*Jessica walks over to Leah and pulls out her right ear plug.*) I said, since when do you like Jason!

Leah: I don't know what you're talking about. (*Leah looks away from Jessica.*)

Jessica: Yes, you do! (*Leah looks back at Jessica, who pulls a note out of her back pocket and hands it to Leah.*)

Leah: (*She looks at the note and is shocked by what she sees.*) Oh, my gosh! Where did you get this?

Jessica: I saw you and Katy passing notes in math class today and leaving me out. At the end of class I found it crumpled in the trash can.

Leah: Fine, maybe I do like him.

Jessica: Ugh, I can't believe this! How could you do this to me?

Leah: Do what! It's not like you were going out.

Jessica: But you know I've liked him since fifth grade. We're so close to going out, he already asked me to the dance and everything.

Leah: See? He likes you, not me. But that doesn't mean that I can't like him.

Jessica: (*She sighs.*) As hard as it is for me to admit, you are much prettier and more popular than me. If you do as little as look at Jason, he will totally forget about me.

Leah: Well, it's not my fault if I'm totally irresistible. Some girls have it and others —(*She looks at Jessica.*) don't.

Jessica: Ugh! You have to stop liking him. That's breaking the girl code.

Leah: What girl code?

Jessica: (*She pulls out The Book of Girl Codes.*) Code #54, Section A. (*She shows the book to Leah.*)

Leah: (*She reads the book.*) "A girl cannot like the same boy as her best friend if her best friend has liked him since fifth grade and they are going to the dance together." (*She looks up from the book.*) Did you write this in yourself? (*She rolls her eyes and slams the book down on the table.*) I can't just stop liking him.

Jessica: Why not! You know how much he means to me.

Leah: Suck it up. He doesn't matter that much to you.

Jessica: Yes, he does. (*She stares off into the distance, smiling.*) I love the way his light brown eyes glitter in the sunlight, how his floppy brown hair bounces when he runs, the way his smile always brightens up my day.

Leah: (*She looks at Jessica with a pitiful face.*) Oh, my gosh, you are obsessed with him.

Jessica: Yes, I am. I really like him a lot.

Leah: Well, don't worry. I won't do anything to try to take Jason away from you. After all, we're best friends.

Jessica: (*She smiles.*) Thank you so much.

Leah: (*She picks up the magazine and an iPod off the table*) You know, I think they opened up that new movie theater at the mall. You wanna go?

Jessica: Sure. I've been dying to see *Mean Girls*!

Leah: Oh, me too! (*Both girls walk off together stage right.*)

Scene 3: *Leah and Jessica are sitting at a table in the center left of stage. They are looking through a magazine together.*

Leah: Oh, my gosh, he is so cute! (*She points to a page of the magazine.*)

Jessica: He sure is. Oh, and so is he! (*She points to a different page.*)

Leah: Yeah, too bad there aren't any cute guys like this at our school.

Jessica: Well, actually, there is one.

Leah: Oh, yeah, that's right.

Jessica and Leah: Jason Michaels! (*They turn their heads toward each other.*) Oh, my gosh! You like Jason, too?

Jessica: (*She stands up and steps away from the table.*) What do you mean by "You like Jason, too?" You know that I've liked him since fifth grade.

Leah: I didn't know you still liked him.

Jessica: Yes, you did! I told you that I am thinking of asking him to the dance.

Leah: What! You're thinking of asking Jason? I was going to ask him.

Jessica: I know you remember me telling you that because you started telling me about how you wanted to go to the dance with Brad.

Leah: Eww, Brad? Jason is more my type.

Jessica: Your type? Since when do you have a type? I thought you would just go with anyone who was desperate enough to go with you.

Leah: (*She glares at Jessica.*) Whatever. I know Jason is going to say yes to me. I'm much   prettier and more popular than you.

Jessica: Have you looked in the mirror lately? I'd be surprised if my pet bull dog would want to be seen in public with you. Besides, I wouldn't be so sure that Jason is going to say yes to you.

Leah: What are you talking about? Did you see the way he was looking at me today all through math class? I can get him in a heartbeat.

Jessica: No way. He was totally staring at me. Plus, he was flirting with me at lunch.

Leah: (*She scoffs.*) He was doing that to make me jealous, duh.

Jessica: Whatever. You're just jealous because last year Wesley dumped you for me.

Leah: Oh, my gosh! That's totally not the way it happened. I dumped him.

Jessica: Well, that's not what he told me.

Leah: Why would you believe him? I don't even know why you went out with him in the first place. That's breaking the girl code.

Jessica: What girl code?

Leah: (*She pulls out* The Book of Girl Codes.) Code 37, Section C. (*She shows the book to Jessica.*)

Jessica: (She *reads from the book.*) "A girl cannot go out with her best friend's ex-boyfriend if her best friend claims to have dumped him but he claims that he dumped her." Did you write this in yourself? (She *rolls her eyes and slams the book down on the table.*) I don't see what the big deal is anyway. If you broke up with him, that means you don't like him anymore. Besides, I only went out with him for a couple of months. You're just upset because you know that Jason likes me more than he likes you.

Leah: That's not true! Katy told me that Ryan told her that Jordan told him that Jason likes me.

Jessica: Oh, I'm sure. (*Jason walks by.*) Look, here comes Jason. Why don't we just find out which of us he will choose.

Leah: (*She runs up to Jason.*) Hey, Jason. You wanna go to the dance with me?

Jessica: (*She runs up next to Leah.*) No, you want to go with me, right?

Leah: No, he's going with me. Look at him. He's ignoring you.

Jessica: No, he's not. He's going with me.

Leah: How can you say that? He just said himself that he wants to go with me.

Jessica: No, he didn't. You haven't let him speak a word since you came up to him. Let's just ask him. Jason, pick one of us to go to the dance with.

Jason: Well, I—

Jessica: See. He wants to go with me!

Leah: He doesn't want to go with you. Are you kidding me? You'd be lucky if anybody wanted to go with you. You're never going to get Jason. He's all mine. You can just stop trying.

Jessica: (*She speaks simultaneously.*) Yes, he does. You're the one he doesn't want. No one wants you and it's not hard to see why. Now I can tell why Wesley dumped you. You're just a preppy, self-centered girl who thinks every guy wants her. Well, you need to realize that there are other girls who are better. (*As Leah and Jessica are arguing, Jason carefully slips away and exits stage right.*)

Leah: (*The arguing trails off.*) Wait…what?…Jason! Look you made him leave!

Jessica: What? I made him leave? You're the one who was acting all crazy.

Leah: Good job. Now he hates both of us. This is so stupid. I don't even see why we became friends in the first place.

Jessica: Me, neither. Consider this friendship over.

Leah: Fine, I will.

Jessica: Fine!

Leah: Fine!

Jessica: Fine!

Curtain

I am a watcher. The job of a journalist is to watch, observe, study and sit on the sidelines. They should be on the parapet above the ballroom watching the dance go on and report on it, not go down there and do a jig. I am a reporter sitting watching the great fandango.

Frederick Forsyth, *The Sunday Herald*
September 19, 2004

CHAPTER 5

Writing Essays

WRITING A CRITICAL ESSAY ABOUT LITERATURE
• • • • •

Wouldn't it be great if everyone could just start writing and end up with a well-organized, fluent essay that articulately sheds an interesting new light on a literary work? Think it's not possible? Not necessarily, but it does take practice and preparation. The trouble is that students of English are in different places in their mastery of the language. I have found that it helps first to have a specific scheme for organizing and presenting ideas. The trick to using this plan is to know when to stop leaning on it and when to venture out to experience more sophisticated dimensions of writing. There comes a time when, in order to achieve growth in one's ability to write using more complex structures and ideas, the writer must let go of the formulaic writing that once was considered helpful scaffolding. If you are the writer who needs to gain more confidence or who has too little experience explaining your ideas in writing, you may need some help. If you're ready to take a step toward ending up with that well-organized, fluent essay I mentioned earlier, then this formula is for you.

Sometimes students find themselves stuck, unable to write at all because they don't know how to present an idea and then support, elaborate, and extend it to larger truths. The following structure is a place to begin. Each segment—introduction, body, and conclusion—below offers suggestions about how to get your ideas on paper in paragraph form. If you don't need the strict prescriptive form given, just follow the guidelines in a way that helps you best.

A MODEL FOR ESSAY WRITING
• • • • •
Introduction

One example of an effective introduction contains about five sentences organized in deductive order, from general to specific. Before you write even one sentence in the introduction, however, you must construct a thesis sentence. See sentence 5.

Sentence 1: Write a broad statement, a generalization, about your topic or the idea on which you want to focus. You can usually narrow the topic of your thesis to one or two words and then write a general statement about it. When writing to analyze literature, you need to show how a concrete idea reveals an abstract one. For example, Hawthorne's diction and imagery in his description of Roger Chillingworth (concrete) reveals the theme of balance (abstract).

Sentence 2: Write a sentence that flows from the first in order to elaborate on that idea. In this way the writing becomes less general because you have added information to it. The reader learns more about your topic.

Sentence 3: Write a sentence that flows from the second. This sentence adds another dimension to the original thought. It is an observation, another way of perceiving the idea first introduced. It moves the reader closer, however, to the idea in the thesis.

Sentence 4: Write a sentence that introduces this idea: writers sometimes, or perhaps *often*, address this theme in their work.

Sentence 5: This sentence is your thesis, the idea that finally evolves from the generalization and all the sentences that follow it.

Body Paragraphs

Write three or more body paragraphs, each containing at least one group of related sentences that are organized by making a point, giving an example, which is often a quotation, and offering commentary on it. The following suggestion includes two such groups for each paragraph.

Sentence 1: State the first of several, usually three to five, sub-points about your thesis. Each body paragraph will focus on a different sub-point.

Sentence 2: Give an example or quotation that supports the sub-point. Remember to use a parenthetical reference when offering quoted material.

Sentence 3: Write a sentence of commentary about sentence 2. *Commentary* includes a relevant comment or explanation of the example or quotation you used in sentence 2. This sentence serves to clarify what you mean and where you are headed in terms of supporting the thesis.

Sentence 4: Write another idea about your sub-point.

Sentence 5: Give an example or quotation that supports sentence 4.

Sentence 6: Write a sentence of commentary about sentence 5.

Conclusion

An effective conclusion contains five to seven sentences using inductive order, specific to general.

Sentence 1: Restate the thesis. In other words, write a sentence that says almost the same thing as your thesis statement. This sentence is not as formal as the thesis you wrote in your introduction.

Sentences 2, 3, and 4: Summarize and make observations about the ideas you have asserted in your essay.

Sentences 5, 6, and 7: Offer implications and draw conclusions. You have now drawn some conclusions about the ideas themselves. What do these ideas mean in terms of the bigger picture? Do these ideas bring to mind a cause/effect relationship, or any other kind of relationship? What underlying meanings exist behind these ideas? You might end with an appropriate quotation that encourages new ideas and further contemplation on the subject.

Introduction

Begin with a generalization. Build to the specific thesis by making each sentence, which connects to the previous one, more and more specific. The thesis, the last sentence in the introduction, states the main idea of the essay.

Body

Write at least three paragraphs, each clearly supporting the thesis. The structure that includes elaboration in order of **point, example/support**, and **commentary** can help you develop fluency in the essay. Remember the importance of transition sentences that create an overall feeling of cohesiveness.

Conclusion

Begin with the thesis reworded. Each sentence that follows leads toward greater generalization. Beyond just a summary, the last paragraph in the essay offers the reader an opportunity to see an extended truth about the topic. Occasionally writers will end with an effective quotation.

To Be or Not to Be...
Finding Substitutes for *Be* Verbs
• • • • •

Sometimes *be* verbs are necessary, but often a more expressive, more precise word can strengthen the meaning of the sentence, communicate more clearly the author's intentions, and provide greater diversity and more interesting discourse. The words below indicate meaning that goes beyond "being" or "existence." Look at your own rough draft for weak or overused words and determine where your diction could use some improvement. In 1906 Mark Twain wrote, "A powerful agent is the right word. Whenever we come upon one of those intensely right words in a book or a newspaper the resulting effect is physical as well as spiritual, and electrically prompt" (94). Test his belief by replacing your weak words with stronger content words until you achieve the meaning you were searching for. The examples below offer suggestions. Try making your own word bank as well.

affect	conjure	describe	integrate	prevail	secure
animate	connect	dictate	juxtapose	produce	shape
assimilate	convert	display	lead	provide	show
awaken	convey	distort	make	rank	span
become	create	endure	manipulate	reclaim	symbolize
caricature	define	establish	mold	refute	transform
carve	delineate	exaggerate	occur	regard	unveil
cease	deliver	facilitate	permeate	render	wake
change	demand	form	pertain	represent	weave
congest	depict	generate	portray	reveal	wind

Basic Writing Guide
• • • • •

The following guidelines will help the student writer become more adept with writing formal essays, especially about literature. This is only a safety net, a guide for what we sometimes call "school writing." The points below can help you understand the need for organization, elaboration, and clarity so that as you become more sophisticated writers, you can venture out and experiment with other forms while maintaining the integrity of good writing.

When writing about literature,

1. Discuss the work in present tense.

2. Avoid using first- and second-person pronouns. (I, me, we, you, etc.)

3. Use correct form for parenthetical reference for one source:
    - Indent long quotations (on left margin only).
    - Use quotations marks for dialogue only in a long quotation.
    - Include page number in parentheses (59). Do not write "page" or "p."
    - Put a period after the close of the parentheses if it is the end of the sentence.
    - Put quotation marks after the last word of the quotation. Example: "…of frailty and sorrow" (45).

4. Write in complete sentences. Avoid fragments and run-ons. The best way to correct them is to combine groups of words. More sophisticated writing contains complex sentences that contain a variety of phrases.

5. Support your thesis sentence in the body of your paper. An effective way to achieve depth as well as length in your essay is to follow this organization:
    - Make a point.
    - Support that point with an example and/or a quotation. If paraphrasing takes the place of a quotation, no quotation marks are necessary. To paraphrase, take the main idea of the quotation and write it in your own words. If the quotation is too long, but you would like to use part of it, use three periods called an *ellipsis* to indicate that words have been omitted from the passage quoted. Leave one space before and after each period.
    - Add commentary.

    Continue this procedure for as many points as necessary for adequate support of the thesis.

6. Read your draft at least three times, making necessary corrections each time. Read for fluency, clarity, spelling and punctuation, and complete sentences.

7. Follow the model given for formal essay writing. It is not the only acceptable form, but its strict guidelines ensure an essay whose organization is easily recognized.

WRITING PERSONAL ESSAYS AND MEMOIRS
● ● ● ● ●

The great scholars of writing process have reminded us from time to time that we read and write to validate who we are, what we have become, and what we can be. Today their writing continues to awaken us to the common thread that ties us all together in an archetypal way. No matter where we are in the world and what we have experienced, the quality of being human, with its collective, parallel human mythology, binds us and allows us to understand each other's joy and suffering. This ability to connect may be one of the most important reasons for reading and writing personal essays, often referred to as personal narratives and memoirs.

Writers who produce short memoirs, little snippets of their remembered experiences, reflect on the events of their past, securing the images and emotions that accompany them.

In writing about your own life, the experiences surrounding people, places, and events of importance to you, three categories can offer a number of interesting paths to explore:

- A discovery of a person, place, idea, or problem that has affected you or someone else

- An awareness of a person, place, or event of significance and the whole range of possible emotions associated with it

- A decision you or someone close to you had to make and the accompanying issues and details

In writing a personal essay, narrative, or memoir, you should try to present yourself to the reader in such a way that you disclose something significant about yourself as well as the event or person in your life that you are trying to portray. This technique, often called the writer's voice, establishes a personality that emerges from the page with every clue. When the reader finishes the essay, she has enough information to draw conclusions about how the writer thinks and feels. The secret to success is writing the essay while maintaining a balance between creating a dominant impression and not sharing too much.

So how does the writer accomplish this balance? To start with, you can give the reader an experience with which he can connect. The subject, usually a remembered event or person that is disclosed through writing, reveals not only the writer's personal experiences but also the attitude of the writer to the experience, her tone, measured out by diction and description. Figurative language, imagery, details, and anecdotes—all the tools of choice you have gained as a writer and literary critic are the resources you need to make the reader see what you see in your mind's eye as you write.

Three main parts comprise the organization of the personal essay:

1. **Introduction**: The writer begins by explaining the context of the situation or person that will be the primary focus of the writing. The context could entail the history, background, setting, attitudes, mood, or anything else connected to the environment in which the reader will see the nature of the person or event as it unfolds.

2. **The incident or person**: The writer skillfully and fluently focuses on the subject itself, whether it is a remembered incident or profile of a person. Although the essay tries to convey the significance of the person, place, or event, it also describes the details that make the subject vivid and real. The appearance, mannerisms, and way of speaking are some of the essential details for describing a person. The setting, key people, emotional responses, objects, and their descriptions are the essential details for describing an incident.

3. **Conclusion**: The writer closes the essay by reflecting on the significance of the person or event. He can summarize, return to the time of the event to share what he observed or learned, or look to the future for new possibilities. The writer has numerous choices for concluding.

Writing a personal essay can be enabling for all of us. Even though the process offers slightly different rewards for reader and writer, the outcome of the personal essay allows us both to see ourselves through the common human experiences of others. Again we look toward the wisdom of that great champion of writing Donald Murray, who says, "We write to explore the constellations and galaxies that lie within us, waiting to be mapped with our own words" (7). In the complex labyrinths of our minds and our lives, we look for solutions that will clarify and explain our existence. Thus writing, in an archetypal way, is like Ariadne's thread that Theseus follows as he not only finds his own way out of the great labyrinth but leads others out as well.

One of my favorite collections of personal narratives comes from Bailey White, whose wistful chronicles have often been heard on National Public Radio. In her first book, *Mama Makes up Her Mind*, the author shares a poignant childhood remembrance of Joe King, a horse trainer and friend, and the wisdom she gathers from that experience. She begins by placing him in a Southern setting as they watch the passing of the seasons that keep Joe King busy—the cycle of the occupants of an estate with horses and buggies to be maintained for hunting. She describes Joe King, the mentor who teaches her about horses. When the old horse Tony begins to die, Bailey White learns that the grieving process of one horse for another will prepare her for the way she will later grieve Joe King's death.

The following essay serves as a good example of a personal essay that draws the reader in with imagery and narrative style. Sasha, the writer, remembers a childhood moment with her grandfather.

Hugging the Wind

The wings fluttered in the sky as a small breeze raised the bird higher towards the heavens. This creature was now too far to be seen, but he continued to soar in the sky as I unwound the gaunt cord. Suddenly, there was a sharp tug, a sign for most that the wind was too strong to continue, but I felt a familiar ache for freedom. I realized that I could no longer seize this magnificent bird in my possession; he trusted the wind, he flew with all his heart as I cleanly snipped through the only barrier of life, a forgotten toy, to a life of hope for a desperate child in need. I prayed that this bird could find his way to a worthy little boy or girl. *I prayed that he could hug the wind.*

My first night in China was torturously painful as I tossed and turned restlessly in my bed, for my jetlagged body refused to take in even a few hours of sleep. I could see the sun desperately trying to fight through the dejected clouds of the night, but it was losing its battle as the clouds fought back with spite. I was quite surprised that even in the early morning I could hear distant train bells declare their farewells, bike chimes whispering their good mornings, and the occasional car horn screech its harsh commands. Amidst those sounds I suddenly heard the front door creak and then slam shut. I, being the curious seven-year-old that I was, scurried to the window to see who had dared to take on the early morning. I saw my grandfather dragging his feet down the dirt road, making a shuffling sound with each step he took.

I soon learned that this was his daily routine. He rose every day in the early morning, ready to take on the world, and between the times of four-thirty a.m. and one o'clock p.m., he lived in a world all his own, having great adventures in the outside world, and when he returned, he locked himself inside the solitude of his room. I yearned to be a part of that world as I, too, rose every morning at four-thirty and walked to the window, wishing, hoping that he would turn and see me, but he never did. He would continue aimlessly down the same dirt path. Feeling rejected, I would brush my hair into a messy bun and saunter down the opposite road to the town's *gong yuan*, small park. There I would sit on the clay park bench and watch enviously as the grandparents helped the squealing children raise their vibrant kites into the sky. Every time I went to the small community park, my desire for a kite grew and grew as I watched those astonishing creatures flutter in the breeze.

After two weeks of waiting by my window, my grandfather did something that made my heart leap. He didn't turn, but he said in a gruff, *dong bei* accent, "So you have been waiting for me, come on, let's get into town." I scampered out the door to meet my grandfather at the fork in the dirt road. He chuckled at my enthusiasm as he extended his hand. I grasped his rough hand as he pulled me close to him. My grandmother once told me that he smelled of chalky antacids, but at that moment, being with him, he smelled of wisdom, years of knowledge, and unconditional love. He smelled like a grandfather. We walked further down this dirt road to encounter more dirt road. I kept my eyes diverted to the ground, noticing with every long stride he took that I had to take four quick steps to keep up. He seemed so refined, so relaxed as he just continued to walk. "*Bao bao*, look!" he said suddenly, pointing to the unfathomable cerulean sea above. I was enthralled by the sight. Bright colors dotted the sky, and it seemed like a vibrant field of flowers had found a way into the heavens. Suddenly he hoisted me up on his shoulders and continued down the road, passing by farmers plowing in their fields, every bead of their sweat and every ounce of their labor creating my dinner later on that night.

"*Bao bao*, did you know that I made most of those kites?" he asked as he set me down on the ground gently and crouched down to my height. There was a gleam of pride in his eyes as he glanced up at the sky. He sighed inwardly, a broad smile erupting on his ashen face.

"Really?" I exclaimed in a shocked voice. This hidden talent of my grandfather's was so foreign to me. Actually, everything about my grandfather was foreign to me. "I never knew you made kites. Grandmother never told me that," I finished, offering myself a new sense of pride in my grandfather. I also quietly reminded myself to ask him to make me a kite before I left for Houston.

He smiled lovingly at my naïveté, but even at my tender age of seven, I could see that it was a pained smile loaded with stress and lack of self-confidence. "The kite festival is coming up next weekend and eight kites are due by then. I just don't know what I'll do, there just isn't enough time," he said to no one in particular, possibly just to remind himself that his time was slowly running out. I felt a pang of guilt as I retreated. Before his last statement I was going to beg him for a kite for the festival, but after his confession, I realized that I was never going to get a kite of my own.

"Well, it's about time to go home, don't you think? I have some work to do." He jerked me away from my thoughts as he led me back the long road home.

My grandfather locked himself in his room that day, that afternoon, and many that followed. He no longer took me on morning walks, and it seemed like he no longer acknowledged my presence. I quickly forgot about my grandfather and his kites, and being a child, I found new things to do with my cousins and other family members. My uncle would take me on long drives in the countryside, rambling on and on about his job and telling me stories about his and my mother's childhood. I felt awkward around him. He denied me many of my own thoughts, planting his own ideas in my mind. I found that when I was with my uncle, I suffered from a feeling of being trapped, and I longed to be with my grandfather. I longed to see the kites free in the sky.

Two days before the kite festival, my grandfather seemed as busy as ever. It was also the first time I saw him leave his beloved workroom. He marched out of the house mumbling about materials and colors. I waited about ten minutes, making certain that our small house was completely out of his sight, before quietly sneaking into his room. I crept in slowly, leaving the door slightly ajar behind me. I looked up to see a zoo of thrilling animals, all lifelike with facial expressions that brought my grandfather's personality to life. I slowly counted the number of kites surrounding the worktable. There were eight of them and he was done. *But why is he still working?* I thought to myself. I learned that my grandfather was one to make his life harder for himself, always a perfectionist. I was turning to leave when a dragon flying from the ceiling grabbed my attention. The piercing eyes drew me toward it, the light reflecting from it and casting an alluring shine upon it. Its long body extended to all four corners of the room, throwing a dark shadow over me. Each piece of its steady torso was connected by a thin but strong piece of twine. He looked ready to destroy the world with his fiery demeanor. At the end of his body near the tail, there was a small red envelope nearly invisible in the dim light. I warily opened the flap and slid the slender sheet of rice paper from its home. Only four words appeared in finely written calligraphy: *To my loving granddaughter.*

"Didn't I tell you not to come in this room?" I jumped hearing my grandfather's harsh tone. "Guess the surprise is out now," he said with a sigh, his tone softening.

"Is it finished?" I softly asked, tracing my finger along the rough edges of the kite.

"Not quite. Would you like to finish it with me?" he asked.

"Oh, can I?" I exclaimed ecstatically. "This is going to be so much fun!"

He placed me on his lap and removed the paint and silk from his bag. My grandfather and I spent the rest of the night joking and bringing life to a breathtaking entity. He taught me a phrase that night, a phrase that I will never forget: *bao zhi feg zou*, hugging the wind. This *chen yu*, or ancient Chinese phrase, taught me the purpose of the kite. It's not just a toy to play with, or something simply to admire. It is a sign of hope for all people around the world. The purpose of the kite festival was to give back to the community. Everyone in the city of Beijing lets loose their kites, and almost simultaneously everyone cuts their strings and sets their kites free with the hopes that when they land they will land in the hands of a little girl or boy too poor for kites or other playful things.

I realized that unlike with my grandmother or my uncle, I wasn't that different from my grandfather. We were both reserved people who enjoyed living a solitary life of silence, safe with our own thoughts and ideas. He created with his hands, letting out every thought and idea with bright colorful strands of thread, creating a one-of-a-kind being, and when it flew, no one could compete with it. That summer he gave me a gift, the gift of expression. I found that with my hands I, too, could create. When walking with him, however, there was never any lasting conversation between the two of us. The only sound was his feet dragging in the dirt, making a slight shuffling sound with every step he took.

Ten Suggestions for Writing Personal Essays

Choose one of the topics listed below or another idea you have considered. Bring your own personal narrative to the page, using the writing tools you have acquired. Perhaps your readers, too, can identify with the life experiences and emotions you have had.

- Hubris: an experience that involved excessive pride in you or someone you know

- An event that made you see your culture differently and led to a paradigm shift

- An observation or experience in nature that explains your philosophy of life

- A Latin saying that proves true today for you or life in general

- Antithesis: opposites in your own experience that seem to point to a truth about life

- Metaphor, oxymoron, hyperbole: How do these examples of figurative language remind you of people, places, or things in your experience?

- A confidence you want to share with the reader

- Humor and wit about a subject expressed ironically or whimsically or even in a self-deprecating way that is light, not so heavy that the humor becomes dark

- A graceful, poignant look at a serious topic about which you know something personally

- A real-life legend, or perhaps someone heading in that direction: one whose actions seem to make the world a better place, or at least a more interesting place

REFINING YOUR WRITING: A CHECKLIST
● ● ● ● ●

Spelling

Avoid contractions and abbreviations.

Look up any words you doubt.

Ask someone to proofread for you.

Be cautious about troublesome words: *there, their, they're*; *to, too, two*; *were, where*; *your, you're*; and so forth.

Diction

Use *a lot, too, so, very,* and *extremely* sparingly.

Avoid using first and second person pronouns (I, you, etc.) in formal analyses.

Avoid vague words such as *thing* or *nice*.

Replace the construction *there is* (or other *be* verbs) with more specific words.

Avoid calling a quotation a *quote*. Use the word *quotation*, if you must use it.

Use *different from* rather than *different than*.

Replace *be* verbs (as main verbs, not auxiliary verbs) with more specific, more interesting, more powerful words.

Use active voice verbs that let the subject do the acting, making the sentence a stronger construction, but remember there may be an occasion to use passive voice verbs when you don't know who or what is performing the action in the sentence.

Avoid clichés. Think of fresh, new words that communicate the same idea.

Avoid *due to* when you mean *because of.*

Use *fewer* when referring to numbers, e.g., *fewer students*. Use *less* when referring to amounts, e.g., *less time.*

Avoid using *I think* or *in this essay I will tell you* or *in my opinion.*

Choose fresh, new words that communicate clearly and exactly what you mean.

Sentence Structure

Write in complete sentences. Avoid fragments and run-on sentences.

Do not connect two sentences with only a comma. This structure is called a comma splice. Connect them with a comma and a conjunction (and, or but, for, nor, yet, so).

Use parallel structure (repeating words, phrases, sentences that are similar in structure and/or meaning), especially when listing items in your sentence. For example,

The Puritans punished sinners by whipping them, cropping their ears, and putting them in the stocks.

Notice each object of the preposition *by* ends in *–ing.*

Vary sentence structure and type for an interesting paper.

Combine short, choppy sentences for greater fluency, unless the effect you want is a quick staccato pace. Otherwise, try sandwiching short and long sentences together for variety.

Connect ideas with transitions between sentences and paragraphs.

Punctuation

Use a comma to separate the parts of a compound sentence.

Do not use a comma to separate the subject from the verb.

Do not use a comma to separate two items connected by a coordinating conjunction (and, but, or, nor, for, yet, so), especially a compound subject or predicate.

Use a comma to set off an introductory clause or phrase.

Use quotations marks around short works: short story, poem, article, television show, game, one-act play or song.

Use underlining or italics for a long work: book, newspaper or magazine title, three-act or five-act play, long poem.

Use quotation marks when referring to quoted text.

Do not use quotation marks for three or more lines of text quoted. Instead, indent the work quoted five spaces from the left margin, maintaining the same right margin as in the rest of the paper.

Do not use a colon after a *be* verb.

Use a semicolon between two short, closely related sentences.

Use a semicolon between items in a series only when use of commas would be confusing. For example, "I bought four green lamps; two interesting, slightly damaged porcelain birds; and a clock that chimes every fifteen minutes.

Form

Write a clear, interesting introduction with the topic sentence or thesis in a strategic position. Often this position is the last sentence in the introduction of a formal or analytical essay.

Make sure every sentence in the body supports the thesis, directly or indirectly.

Write an interesting conclusion that brings the piece to a close. Do not summarize unless this approach is truly the best one to take. Instead try drawing a conclusion, making a prediction, extending the central idea to a larger truth. Often the thesis reworded is the first sentence in the conclusion.

Remember: Content dictates form. If the assignment is to compare and contrast two items, then your paper must examine and elaborate on the similarities and differences of those items.

Perhaps, we will have to face the darkness, walk out on the moor alone at nightfall, or dive to the bottom of the sea before the old ossified ego boundaries can be shattered to make room for the dance.

Marion Woodman and Elinor Dickson
Dancing in the Flames, The Dark
Goddess in the Transformation of
Consciousness, 1977

CHAPTER 6
Rhetoric and Dialectic:

TWO ARTS IN THE DANCE OF DISCOURSE
• • • • •

What an inspiration a good speaker can be. It is quite possible for a motivating speech to make us change our minds about an issue, or even change our attitudes toward a particular person. Many years ago I volunteered to give the speech supporting Kennedy in my elementary school's Kennedy and Nixon debate. Three years later that experience led me to join the high school debate team. While I didn't know then what I do today about the psychology and the diction that form the backbone of speech making, I nevertheless have always had a fascination for the power and emotion behind public speaking.

Delivering an effective persuasive speech has a long history rooted in classic Greece. Although as a fifth grader I didn't have a very firm grasp on rhetoric, over time I developed an understanding of the methods that speakers use to evoke a desired response from an audience. Rhetoric is the art of persuasion using specific techniques in writing and speaking. Students see examples of rhetoric every day in the classroom, on television, in newspapers and magazines—anywhere that writers and speakers are using language to influence or persuade people to believe or do something the speaker deems important.

Plato (427-347 BC) condemned the rhetoric associated with a group of people called Sophists, teachers whose claim of teaching virtue seemed to rely on superficial appearances. He believed in a different approach that could produce a knowledge base more helpful to a speaker engaged in persuasion: the dialectical method.

Dialectics is a kind of discussion that enables the writer to gain insight or new information or to resolve a disagreement and come to a synthesis of opposing ideas. It is the practice of examining opinions and ideas to determine their validity or effectiveness. Simply put, an examination of an assertion plus its opposite view equals new information (thesis + antithesis = synthesis). Many students have experienced at least two methods of arriving at new information. One way is the Socratic method of discussion. The Junior Great Books program bases its examination of literature on this method. Students begin with a question or hypothesis and, through a series of questions, arrive at a contradiction, forcing them to re-examine the hypothesis as valid. The teacher, or facilitator, guides students to ideas, contradictions, and answers but does not suggest answers. Another way is keeping dialectical journals in which students analyze literature and support a number of assertions, including antitheses, made about the literature. Students read one or more pieces of literature for which they take notes, record their own responses to questions or relevant literary elements, and then draw conclusions.

Socrates used the dialectical method to examine common beliefs and then see the contradictions in them. He believed that when people realized their own ignorance, they could truly begin to search for truth as they then acquired and tested new knowledge. Essentially, Socrates was suggesting that all knowledge should be tested rather than accepted on face value.

Rhetoric is the natural complement of dialectic. It is one of two parts that fit and complete each other. The Greeks considered it the *antistrophos* of dialectic. In Book I of Aristotle's *Rhetoric*, he writes, "Rhetoric is the counterpart of dialectic" (Aristotle 95). The Greek translation of counterpart is *antistrophos*. In ancient times the Greek chorus in classic theatre danced in one direction when it sang. This movement was called the *strophe*. Movement in the opposite direction was called the *antistrophe*, which eventually indicated the speaking of the chorus as well as the singing. Dancing in different directions, this metaphor parallels the art of discourse, writing and speaking. *Dialectic finds the truth and rhetoric persuades for it.* Aristotle used dialectic in terms of discussing an issue to learn more about it or resolve it in everyday life, while he used rhetoric for practical ends, usually in a court of law or in civic or judicial affairs.

Aristotle identified three kinds of proof in the art of rhetoric:

- **Ethos** appeals reflect the character and credibility of the speaker or writer. What are the speaker's qualifications that make him experienced and believable?

- **Pathos** appeals to emotions. What does the speaker or writer say that evokes strong emotion from the audience? Think of powerful language tools: figurative language; heightened emotional language or amplification; anecdotes; allegory; parallelism and antithesis; anaphora, or repetition.

- **Logos** appeals to logic and reasoning, both deductive and inductive. What does the speaker or writer offer by way of examples that aid in drawing conclusions?

  In deductive reasoning, think *general to specific*. A conclusion follows from the stated premises, that is, statements that can be supported by evidence.

  In inductive reasoning, think *specific to general*. Specific facts or examples are examined in order to then produce a conclusion or a general principle.

  In writing a formal essay, the sentences in the introduction are often ordered general to specific, with the thesis as the last sentence in that paragraph.

The sentences in the conclusion are ordered specific to general, as the thesis introduces the paragraph and moves to a general conclusion.

Practice with this activity for using three kinds of proof:

You are trying to persuade your parents to let you do something really important to you. Write three sentences that you would say to them using the three kinds of proof:

1. Logos: a solid reason
2. Pathos: emotional support
3. Ethos: a sentence showing your character and credibility

Here is an example:

Mom, I really think you should let me go with Matt and his family to Colorado this summer. It will be a good opportunity for me to get lots of exercise when we go hiking and mountain climbing. It's been a difficult year and the time spent in nature would really give me a chance to think about my priorities before I go to high school. Besides, I'm a responsible person. You never had to tell me to do my homework or chores this year. Plus I always call you when I'm going to be late.

See how easy it is to use these famous appeals? You probably use them every day without realizing you are following in the footsteps of Socrates and Plato.

Now read these famous historical speeches and examine the rhetorical devices that identify the ethical, emotional, and logical appeals in each.

- "Give Me Liberty or Give Me Death"
  March 23, 1775
  Patrick Henry

- "I Have a Dream"
  1963
  Martin Luther King

- "Women's Rights Are Human Rights"
  September 5, 1995
  Hillary Rodham Clinton

- "Words at the Brandenburg Gate"
  Reagan's Berlin speech
  June 12, 1987
  Ronald Reagan

- "Out of Many, One"
  July 27, 2004
  2004 Democratic Convention speech
  Barack Obama

- Lincoln's second inaugural address
  March 4, 1865
  Abraham Lincoln

- "The Four Freedoms"
  January 6, 1941
  Franklin Delano Roosevelt

Terms to know and use as you read persuasive writing:

Appeals: ethos, pathos, logos

Audience and purpose: Whom is the speaker addressing? What interests and appeals to them? What qualities belonging to the audience does the speaker need to know about?

Mood: What feeling are the speaker's words creating in the minds of the listeners?

Tone: What is the speaker's attitude toward what he or she is saying?

Diction: What particular words have been selected and for what purpose?

Rhetorical devices: As you examine the literature, you will not be surprised to discover that these famous speeches and many others as well, often use the same methods in moving our hearts and minds.

> <u>Allusion:</u> In his "Give Me Liberty or Give Me Death" speech, Patrick Henry alludes to Judas's betrayal (*Chain-Reference Bible*, Matthew 26.48) in the Bible when he says, "Suffer not yourselves to be betrayed with a kiss."

Lincoln alludes to the book of Matthew in the Bible in his second inaugural address: "but let us judge not that we be not judged" (*Chain-Reference Bible,* Matthew 7.1).

Anaphora, or repetition: Hillary Rodham Clinton, in her address to the United Nations Fourth World Conference on Women, uses the following phrase consecutively seven times: "It is a violation of *human* rights when..."

Martin Luther King, Jr. uses the same rhetorical device in his "I Have a Dream" speech. He repeats "I have a dream that..." eight times.

Antithesis: Ronald Reagan employs the tension of opposites when he asserts, "As long as this gate is closed...it is not the German question alone that remains open, but the question of freedom for all mankind."

Barack Obama, in the address to the 2004 Democratic National Convention, emphasizes the unity of the country when he says, "There is not a Black America and a White America and Latino America and Asian America—there's the United States of America."

Lincoln states in his address, "With malice toward none, with charity for all..."

Parallelism: In "Women's Right Are Human Rights," Hillary Rodham Clinton illustrates parallel lives of women everywhere: "We come together in fields and in factories. In village markets and supermarkets. In living rooms and board rooms."

Reagan points out, "just as truth can flourish only when the journalist is given freedom of speech, so prosperity can come about only when the farmer and businessman enjoy economic freedom."

Irony: Reagan points out the irony of situation in Khrushchev's words, "We will bury you," with this statement: "But in the West today, we see a free world that has achieved a level of prosperity and well-being unprecedented in all human history."

Roosevelt points out in his "Four Freedoms" speech, "There is much loose talk of our immunity from immediate and direct invasion from across the seas." He then shows the irony in such thinking when he says, "The first phase of the invasion of this hemisphere would not be the landing of regular troops. The necessary strategic points would be occupied by secret agents...and great numbers of them are already here..."

Metaphor: Patrick Henry writes, "I have but one lamp by which my feet are guided and that is the lamp of experience." He talks again of feet, a synecdoche for his whole being, when he says, "Trust it not, sir; it will prove a snare to your feet."

Martin Luther King, Jr. uses the extended metaphor of banking to communicate betrayal and loss: "the bank of justice is bankrupt...there are insufficient funds in the great vaults of opportunity of this nation. And so we've come to cash a check..."

Roosevelt figuratively expresses a warning in his speech: "We must especially beware of that small group of selfish men who would clip the wings of the American eagle in order to feather their own nests."

Continue to think about the following goals as you read these famous speeches. Knowing what to look for, in terms of diction and syntax, and breaking analysis into palatable tasks can help readers have a more well-rounded understanding of the successful use of rhetoric in persuasion.

- Become familiar with three classical appeals in persuasion: logos, pathos, and ethos.
- Learn to identify and use the rhetorical devices that writers use to persuade and argue.
- Determine patterns of organization and fluency in the speeches that lead to persuasion.

CHAPTER 7

The Study of Literature

Literature gives students the opportunity to understand more about human nature and how to develop their own personal philosophy of life. By reading works of literature that span hundreds of years, students can draw their own conclusions about what makes sense to them about the world now as well as in the past. The mistakes, the successes, and the lessons from the past all contribute to a foundation of the student's concepts of life, and a way to understand recurring problems of life, enlarging our scope. Louise Rosenblatt writes, "Works of the past—the Odyssey, the Arthurian legends, Beowulf, Elizabethan drama, Victorian novels—engender a major psychological question: What are the basic human traits that persist despite social and cultural changes?" (13).

Literary terms—their denotations and connotations—are tools we use to talk about writing. Simple comprehension of what you are reading by decoding text is anything but simple. Understanding a piece of literature goes beyond pronunciation and dictionary definition of isolated words. The mystery of writing evolves from the unique diction of a writer, the literary elements that create complex stories and thoughts, and the nuance that elevates a work to a higher, more subtle level. The terms that name those elements and shades of meaning, our literary terms, help us understand and discuss the works and ultimately know how to use these tools in our own writing. The ideas that these terms represent have a long history, indicating a need for people to seek a deeper understanding of literature by naming its various elements and parts. The terms in this section can help you continue that tradition.

Diction

The words you choose to express emotions, to impart information, or to move or motivate the reader make all the difference in your success as a writer. Communication depends on diction, the words selected with the author's specific purpose in mind. For example, if I want to instruct students in the art and craft of story writing, I will focus on words that convey the wants and needs of a character. To add fuel to the plot, I'll discuss the tension stirred up by the characters, a technique that moves the plot along. As my students begin to develop their stories, they will choose words that create description and actions that lead to plausible characters who are unique rather than stereotyped, or stock. Look at the difference in the mood established in these two scenes:

> *Leaning gently out the open window, she cupped her hands around her*
> *eyes, blinded by the parade of band instruments glittering in the sun.*

> *Listlessly staring through the rain-streaked window, shut tight to keep out*
> *the cool damp air of an early spring day, she stood only close enough*
> *to gaze at the couple below.*

It is perhaps the same window in the same room on the second floor of a house, but the images constructed in the two sentences communicate two entirely different moods. The words "gently...cupped her hands...parade...band...glittering...sun" imply heightened and festive feelings. In the second sentence I chose words whose connotations might evoke a more melancholy response from the reader: "listlessly staring...rain-streaked window...shut tight...cool damp air...stood only close enough." Word choice, the most important tool of the writer, affects every other decision a writer must make.

Figurative Language

People compare certain styles of prose writing to poetry when the two forms evoke similar responses. Both rely on emotional or highly descriptive images in communicating for a variety of purposes, although poetry typically uses fewer words. Words that build images using comparison and contrast, such as metaphor, simile, oxymoron, personification, and allusion, are the tools of choice for the writer who wants to create an emotionally heightened mood or tone. Just how do these tools work? Since language is the vehicle for expressing what we think, see, and feel, more precise words that create vivid pictures can communicate a strong meaning that your reading or listening audience will recognize and interpret easily. Students often do not realize the power they gain just by choosing the right words and putting them together in a fluent way. Humans are generally sensitive creatures who respond to touch, especially the touch of memories, emotions, or snapshot images stored in the brain. If words can recreate the feelings attached to those images enough to jolt our senses, imagine the further potential embedded in those words. I know what the writer means when he compares pain to a melancholy depth or one's child to a treasure whose value grows daily, or anger to poison, an obsession to iron links, hope and joy to a frozen sunbeam, or emotional confusion to a difficult maze with no easy way out. I know what the writer means because the associations of the images she chooses are well known to me. I am susceptible to the writer's emotional punch because she cleverly taps into the meaning I have stored in those experiences with her words.

Story Elements

Everyone loves a good story with believable characters in an intriguing plot. A good story often becomes a memorable one when we can either relate to these people who have problems that mirror ours, or the characters face our worst fears for us. Maslowe (1987) tells us we have a need to belong, to fit in with other human beings, and so the need to relate to others seems to steadily tug at our selves, calling "Me too, me too!" We want to know about others' experiences and challenges, even fictional ones that can validate our own authentic selves, as well as the selves of our past and future. We are both reader and character, acting out our parts in the stories of our lives. When we weep for the characters, we do so for ourselves. When conflicts are resolved, we feel vicarious relief for the characters but also for our own restoration of balance.

Conflict, antithesis and the tension of opposites that we suffer through, provides the essential ingredient of the plot, the development of the characters' struggles to fulfill their wants and needs. The potential for tragedy lies dormant in the characters, and we understand it. Those seeds lie within us too, waiting to be sown like dragon's teeth ready to emerge from the soil, terrifying us and threatening to devour. We long for resolution, restitution, and redemption, and when the characters get it, we feel it too.

The setting of a story is more than a well-defined space that aids characters' credibility. It is all the places that we readers connect with our existence and the resulting memories. Associations are made between places and all our senses: the kitchen aromas of traditional childhood holidays; the choking death smells of a dirty meat market; the sweet and salty taste of watermelon juice that dribbles down your chin on the back porch on a hot summer evening; the sound of children on a school playground outlined by the flow of city traffic on the ground and the tall glass and metal skyscrapers rising above. We see and feel and smell and taste and hear within a setting—and we remember.

Irony

Readers expect to be surprised. They want the author to challenge their thinking and not give them something predictable. In fact, to do so is viewed by most readers as an insult to their intelligence, and for this reason, primarily, the use of irony works to the advantage of the writer and the satisfaction of the reader. While a reader can recognize the different kinds of irony that bring deeper meaning to a story, the writer works to have just the right grasp on the tool in order to keep the reader interested.

Hawthorne's story "The Maypole of Merry Mount," which you will see explained in this book, offers a good example of all three kinds of irony. The story unfolds in 1625 in the Massachusetts Bay colony of Merry Mount with the Puritan leader John Endicott destroying the symbolic center of the village, the Maypole.

In a line of **verbal irony**, he suggests his regret in having cut it down—the Maypole could have been used as a whipping post, giving the revelers one more dance around their idol. In this example, Hawthorne plays with Endicott's word *dance* to imply an image far more gruesome than the traditional, festive moves around the Maypole.

As the antithesis of the Puritans, the Merry Mount colonists live a hedonistic life with much play and little work. One couple, Edgar and Edith, begin to view life more seriously and decide to marry. Endicott, a hard man of iron, finds his heart softened by the sight of this pair and decides to spare their lives although they must leave with him and enter his community of Puritans. Before he escorts them away, he suddenly picks up the wreath of roses from the stricken Maypole and, with his own gauntleted hand, places it over their heads in a gesture of good will. His unexpected participation in even a small part of the old English custom of celebrating and dancing around the tree of the pagan goddess Cybele reveals the **irony of situation** in the story. Endicott concedes to do the unthinkable, something he earlier would never have allowed himself to do as a Puritan leader.

Finally, Hawthorne allows the reader to see the Puritans reproachfully watching the merrymakers from behind the trees in the forest as they await their opportunity to seize the unsuspecting, misbehaving colonists. Readers experience **dramatic irony** when they see the colonists' freedom coming to an end shortly before the colonists learn of their fate. A graphic way to remember this kind of irony is to think of yourself sitting in a theatre watching a play on the stage. Through the *fourth wall*, the traditional proscenium arch that frames the stage on which we watch the actors deliver the story, we become intruders of a sort, privy to information even before the characters know it. The irony is that we see their mistakes and know the price they will pay before the characters do.

Theme

Although the main idea of a story supports the theme of that work, the two elements are sympathetic but not identical, which makes them easily confused in the mind of the reader. Theme refers to the idea about life that the writer is trying to convey, and the other literary devices in the work tend to support that idea. The significance of theme is that, as a literary device itself, it draws together directly or indirectly all the other elements of a story cohesively.

Sometimes writers devote a number of pieces to working through a particular theme. Perhaps the idea about life relates closely to the author's personal journey or an issue the writer deems important or wants to explore. In nineteenth-century writer Nathaniel Hawthorne's case, the theme that appears most often in his work is *balance*, usually in this context: It is a balanced life that leads to happiness. Edgar and Edith discover this truth in "The Maypole of Merry Mount," while in a moment of dramatic irony the reader watches Endicott move closer to balance from rigid superego behavior. In "Dr. Heidegger's Experiment," the doctor who offers his four guests a second chance at youth decides in the end that old age is a necessary stage in the circle of life. Brown in "Young Goodman Brown" and Hooper in "The Minister's Black Veil" go to their graves lonely and miserable because their lack of faith and inability to forgive disturb the balance necessary to live harmoniously. In an attempt to protect his daughter from a harmful world, Dr. Rappaccini imbibes his daughter with poison so that she will be formidable to all who come near her, stripping her of any opportunity for love.

One way for students to begin to understand theme is to think of a word or phrase that summarizes the general idea about life in the story: love, revenge, justice. The next step is to write a statement that more specifically defines the idea that relates directly to the particular story: Do what is right; people have a right to have justice in their lives, no matter what the cost. Or, as the old Roman saying goes, "Let justice be done, though the heavens fall."

Symbolism

The word symbol is derived from the Greek *symbolon, symballein: sym*: together and *ballein*: to throw, which combine to mean *a throwing together*. *Symbol*, however, has come to mean something that stands for or represents another thing, a concrete representing an abstract. A tree, for example, represents life; a circle represents never-ending life, or the life/death/rebirth archetype; and fire represents both destruction and purification. We use symbols to know and express thoughts and feelings that words alone are inadequate to do. The language of symbols, therefore, transcends time and culture and even our limited spoken and written language itself.

Historically, symbols in ancient times were the realities themselves. The sun was a god, not just a symbol of a god. Metaphors have experienced the same progression from literal to figurative. If you're in "hot water," you are probably in trouble, but in earlier times, if you were in hot water or oil, you were literally experiencing a barbaric death sentence. Today, symbols permeate our everyday lives. We do not look upon symbols with the same joy and expectation, the same seriousness as our ancestors, partly because we have come to take them for granted. We see the surface of the objects and avoid the depth of thinking and emotion that were once critically important to people's existence. Manfred Lurker explains that the symbolism that once gave life to people in centuries past has today become out of date, but the "meaning of the symbol does not lie in the symbol itself but points to something else outside it" (qtd. in Biedermann ix).

Symbols encourage us to think about the complexity of reality, those things that lie beneath the surface. They contain a power that not only has maintained itself over time but also continues to affect people in ways that touch almost every aspect of our lives.

Analogy is at the heart of symbolism. Consider the parallels of the cycle of the seasons and the stages of the love motif. As autumn is the phase of darkness and death, stage three in a relationship is the untangling of problems between two people and the decision between the life or death of the relationship. The life/death/rebirth archetype is also symbolized by the waxing and waning of the moon, a familiar phenomenon.

In Hawthorne's "Dr. Heidegger's Experiment," water from the fountain of youth is a symbol of regeneration of physical life, but for Dr. Heidegger it represents regeneration of the spiritual life. At the end of his experiment he recognizes an important truth about his own life that he could not acknowledge at the beginning of the story. Hawthorne parallels with this symbol of spiritual regeneration other symbols in the story: mirror, cut glass, broken glass, sunshine, bubbles, daybreak, diamonds, and moon. The concept of analogy in symbolism serves to unify the ideas that communicate the message.

Symbols are linked together by a common rhythm. They often appear together in clusters and their placement in relation to each other is as symbolic as the symbolic function itself. According to Biedermann, symbols may function in several different ways. First, symbols can be placed alongside each other without combining meaning. Second, symbols can represent various stages in a process. Third, the proximity of the symbols can create a more complex and synergistic meaning (liv). For example, a bear (*courage*) with a bloody (*death, destruction*) crown (*power*) under his foot (*submission*) could mean the triumph of courage over the dark and destructive forces of power.

As one of humankind's greatest possessions, symbols have influenced people to express themselves in architecture, art, music, literature, religious practices, and customs and celebrations. The great cathedrals in Europe, the pyramids in Egypt and Latin America, the Greek and Roman temples and the temples of the East, the religious traditions of all cultures, the celebrations and holidays around the world, and the art, music, literature, and mythology of all people everywhere across time and place—these tangibles were "thrown together"—*sym, bolon*—with the intangible. We learned to think beyond the superficial as we recognized their meaning. We crossed the borders into universal symbolism, "throwing together" multiple levels of meaning for all of humankind.

Recurring Literary Devices in Literature

One of the most rewarding tasks in terms of real growth in the study of literature involves tracing the symbols, images, and themes through various works of a great writer. This process can result in a kind of familiarity with an author that reading only one story or one novel cannot effect. Studying several short stories and a novel by nineteenth-century author Nathaniel Hawthorne, for example, demonstrates the benefits especially well. Students can recognize recurring symbols and themes in many of his works, as well as the use of figurative language, the antithesis of light and dark in particular. The key word is *recurring*. By examining a number of his best pieces, students can verify the strength of Hawthorne's message. The biographical and historical influences, his philosophy of life and the thematic expression of it, the style and diction peculiar to Hawthorne—all of these elements and more are accessible to students who look at the scope of the writer's work rather than a single piece taken out and isolated from the body. For example, if students understand Hawthorne's use of the forest as a symbol of initiation and testing in "The Maypole of Merry Mount," they will more easily recognize this same symbol in other stories by Hawthorne, especially "Young Goodman Brown" and *The Scarlet Letter*. Each time students identify these repeated patterns, their sensitivity to the meaning of the story increases significantly. His stories also provide a palette that enables students to use several critical approaches, singly or in combination, to analyze not only Hawthorne's works but also any piece of literature.

In reality, the course of study in most schools often dictates a tightly constructed curriculum that makes applying this approach to every writer studied difficult if not impractical. In this handbook, however, you will have the opportunity to study several of Hawthorne's best short stories as well as his novel *The Scarlet Letter*. Beginning with "The Maypole of Merry Mount," you can acquire basic tools for looking at literature in general, but you can also gain ease in handling the language and style of an author whose work students in secondary schools often consider impenetrable. Perhaps cutting your literary teeth on Hawthorne will engender a smoother journey through the works by other authors.

Become familiar with the following list of literary terms so that this helpful resource will be yours when you need it. Knowing these terms gives you power as both reader and writer. You'll have at your disposal the devices that writers use to create clear and lasting images in literature and the study aids that readers use for greater understanding of the works they study in school and read for pleasure.

LITERARY TERMS
• • • • •

Allegory is a story in which people, things, and actions represent an idea or generalization about life and often has a moral or lesson.

Alliteration is the repetition of consonant sounds at the beginning of words or accented syllables.

Allusion is a reference to a well-known person, place, event, literary work, or work of art.

Anecdote is a little story about an interesting, amusing, or strange event, the purpose of which is to entertain or make a point.

Analogy is a comparison between two unlike things.

Anaphora is the repetition of words and phrases so that a pattern is created for effect.

Antagonist is a character or force in conflict with a main character, or protagonist.

Antithesis is a device in which opposites or strongly contrasting ideas are placed in sharp juxtaposition (placed side by side), creating tension.

Archetype is a universal image, character, or pattern of events that recurs throughout literature. Psychologist Carl Jung believed these images are genetically encoded and passed down to subsequent generations, so that cultures across time and geographic location would recognize them. He called this phenomenon the *collective unconscious* (Jung, *Basic Writings* 299).

Assonance is the repetition of vowel sounds without the repetition of consonants.

Autobiography is a form of nonfiction in which a person tells his or her own story.

Climax is the decisive point in a narrative or drama, the point of greatest intensity or interest.

Connotation is all the emotions associated with a word that help to give that word its current meaning.

Denotation is a dictionary definition of a word.

Denouement is the outcome of the plot of a play or story.

Dialect is the characteristic speech of a particular region or social group.

Diction is a writer's choice of words.

Didactic literature is that which instructs or presents a moral or religious statement.

Exposition is the beginning of a story, which introduces character and setting.

Fable is a brief story that is told to present a moral or practical lesson.

Falling action is the action that follows the climax leading to the resolution.

Foil is a character who serves as a contrast or challenge to another character.

Foreshadowing is giving hints and clues of what is to come later in a story.

Genre is a category or type of literature based on its style, form, and content.

Heroic couplet is two successive rhyming lines that contain a complete thought.

Hyperbole is a figure of speech using exaggeration or overstatement for special effect.

Hubris is a word derived from the Greek *hybris*, meaning "excessive pride." This excessive pride is often referred to as the "tragic flaw" which leads to the downfall of the hero.

Irony is using a word or phrase to mean the exact opposite of its literal or normal meaning. There are three kinds:

> **Dramatic irony** occurs when the reader or audience sees a character's mistakes but the character himself does not.

> **Irony of situation** occurs when the purpose of an action differs greatly from the result. A character does something that results in being the opposite of what is expected.

> **Verbal irony** occurs when the writer says one thing and means another.

Lyric is a poem, usually a short one, that expresses the speaker's personal thoughts and feelings.

Metaphor is a figure of speech that makes a comparison between two things that are basically dissimilar.

Metonymy is the substituting of one word for another that is closely related to it. (The *White House* often substitutes for the *President*.)

Meter is the patterned repetition of stressed and unstressed syllables in a line of poetry.

Mood is the prevailing feeling or emotional climate of a literary work, often developed through description of setting and development of atmosphere.

Motif is a term for an often-repeated idea or theme in literature.

Myth is a traditional story that attempts to explain a natural phenomenon or justify a certain practice or belief of a society.

Narration is a kind of writing that tells a story.

Narrative poem is a poem that tells a story.

Onomatopoeia is the use of a word that imitates a sound or suggests the meaning of the sound.

Oxymoron is a combination of contradictory terms, often two opposing words written side by side (*troubled joy*).

Parallelism is the repetition of sounds, meaning, or structure of words to point out relations between them; ideas are arranged one after another to show balance.

Personification is a figure of speech in which something non-human is given human qualities.

Point of view is the vantage point from which a narrative is told:

> **First person**: The story is told by one of the characters in his or her own words.
>
> **Second person**: It is *you* in the study of grammar but rarely used as a point of view.
>
> **Third person**: The narrator is not a character in the story but instead tells the story. It can be a *limited omniscient* narrator who tells the story from the view of one or two characters, or it can be an *omniscient* narrator who tells the story from the view of all the characters.

Protagonist is the central character of a drama, novel, short story, or narrative poem.

Resolution is the denouement or portion of the play or story where the problem is solved.

Rising action is the series of conflicts or struggles that builds a story or play toward the climax.

Romanticism is a literary movement with an emphasis on the imagination and emotions.

Rhyme is the repetition of sounds in two or more words or phrases that appear close to each other in a poem.

> End rhyme occurs at the end of the lines.
>
> Internal rhyme occurs within a line.
>
> Rhyme scheme is the pattern of end rhymes.

Setting is the time and place in which events occur in a short story, novel, play, or narrative poem.

Simile is a figure of speech comparing two unlike things through the use of the words *like* or *as*.

Stanza is a division of poetry named for the number of lines it contains. It is a unit of a poem that is longer than a single line.

Symbol is a person, place, thing, or event used to represent something else. Often a concrete object represents something abstract.

Synecdoche is a figure of speech in which the part is named but the whole is understood, or vice versa. (If I *give you a hand* with your garden, you probably will want more than my hand.)

Theme is the idea about life that the author is trying to communicate and is usually supported by many other elements or devices in the work.

Thesis is a statement of opinion that is the writer's focus or main idea that is developed in an essay.

Tone is the attitude a writer takes toward his or her subject, characters, or readers.

*Not far from Merry Mount was a
settlement of Puritans, most dismal wretches...
woe to the youth or maiden who did but
dream of a dance!...or if he danced, it was
round the whipping post, which might be
termed the Puritan Maypole.*
Nathaniel Hawthorne
"The Maypole of Merry Mount"
Twice-Told Tales, 1837

CHAPTER 8
The American Renaissance: Roots and Leaves

What was happening during Nathaniel Hawthorne's lifetime? The Industrial Revolution brought discoveries and inventions which made people's lives easier, but not without a price. Men, women, and children worked such long hours in factories and in workhouses in America and England that laws had to be made to restrict the number of hours of backbreaking labor, especially for women and juveniles. Social reformers looked into every corner of America for opportunities to root out evil. Transportation was swiftly improving on land and sea, closing the gap between people and nations, allowing countries to share in the growing wealth of knowledge and culture. People now had more time and inclination for thought and so began to express their philosophies—moral, religious, political, social, and educational—through literature and the arts. It was a renaissance of music, art, and literature for New England, as well as Europe. States were joining the Union and increasing the population as well as the power of the United States, even while the issue of slavery began dividing the nation. Toward the end of Hawthorne's life, the Civil War broke out. Southern states seceded and formed the Confederacy, abolitionists worked through their words and through the Underground Railroad to free slaves, and in 1863 Lincoln issued the Emancipation Proclamation. Hawthorne died almost a year before he would have seen the end of the war with the surrender of the Confederate States at Appomattox in 1865.

This period, called the American Renaissance, from the 1830s until about 1865, saw an awakening of expression in literature, following the Romantic Movement in England. Three groups of writers emerged: the Brahmins, the Transcendentalists, and writers of great imagination—poets and writers of fiction. Henry Wadsworth Longfellow, Oliver Wendell Holmes, and James Russell Lowell—all poets—were active professors at Harvard College, but, because they were also aristocrats educated in Europe, they based their own writing on European models. They called themselves Brahmins after a pretentious reference to the Brahmans, the highest caste of Hindu society.

Transcendentalism found its roots in the little town of Concord, Massachusetts. Its members contributed writings of great influence. They advocated reforms in church, state, and society. They fostered the abolition movement and the formation of various utopian communities, such as Brook Farm. Transcendentalism was an idealistic belief in the unity of all creation, the innate goodness of humankind, and the truth that was to be derived, not from logic and experience, but from insight. The movement resulted in a battle between the younger and older generations. Ralph Waldo Emerson, the leader of New England Transcendentalism, graduated from Harvard in 1821 and was ordained to the Unitarian ministry in 1832. He gradually turned to behavior that fueled this battle: publishing his philosophy, warning the Harvard intelligentsia against traditionalism, becoming disillusioned with the church and resigning from the ministry. Followers of Transcendentalism, however, encouraged him and joined the informal Transcendental Club. He continued to lecture, publishing his *Essays* (1841 and 1844), which included the well-known "Self-Reliance." Hawthorne welcomed the companionship of the Transcendentalists in Concord but had little interest in the philosophical approach to life. After his marriage to Sophia, Hawthorne moved his bride to the Old Manse, a house in Concord owned by Emerson. There the Hawthornes spent some of the happiest times of their life together.

Henry David Thoreau was Hawthorne's friend, as well as Emerson's friend and a fellow Transcendentalist. An essayist, poet, and philosopher, Thoreau is best known for his experiment in living out the doctrines of Transcendentalism and recording those experiences in *Walden*. Thoreau, also a Harvard graduate, was a teacher who, after traveling on the Concord and Merrimack Rivers in a canoe with his brother John, became a poet of nature. He contributed many of his essays and poems to the Transcendentalist magazine *The Dial*, edited by Emerson and Margaret Fuller. In the spring of 1845, Thoreau built a small cabin on the shores of Walden Pond on land near Concord that was owned by Emerson. He cultivated his bean rows, fished, swam, rowed, read, and wrote. He also kept a journal of his life at Walden, describing his experiment in basic living, which he published as *Walden*. Although Thoreau remained at Walden Pond for two years, midway through his experiment, he was arrested and forced to spend a night in jail. He had refused to pay taxes that supported the war with Mexico. Emerson bailed him out, and today we remember Thoreau's famous response when Emerson asked why his friend was in jail. Thoreau replied, why aren't you in *here*? It was without question a time of rebellion and reform.

The nineteenth century in America produced a number of writers of great imagination: Hawthorne's friend Herman Melville, best known for his novel *Moby Dick*; the revolutionary poet Walt Whitman, best known for his collection of poetry *Leaves of Grass*, and Edgar Allan Poe, poet and writer of fiction famous for the mysterious and macabre. Poe's most famous works include the poem "The Raven" and the short story "The Tell-Tale Heart."

DRAWING CONCLUSIONS FROM A CHRONOLOGY
● ● ● ● ●
1803-65

Just as you attempt to place your short story characters in a setting—put their feet on the ground in a clearly focused setting—it is helpful to learn about Nathaniel Hawthorne within the confines of his environment. Would Hawthorne, or any other writer, have been affected by the politics, the writers and scientists and inventors who were his contemporaries? Would he have been influenced by the art and music of the time, even the culture of the European writers, composers, and artists? When you read the chronology and complete the following activity, you will gain a more solid picture of the world in which Hawthorne lived and wrote. Adding this information to the biographical information you already have can lead to a more complete understanding of his works.

Follow these directions:

1. Read the entire chronology of 1803-65.

2. Draw conclusions about the period using these categories as a guideline:

    a. politics and government

    b. literature

    c. science and technology

    d. art and music

    e. daily life, population

3. Write a paragraph in your journal explaining your conclusions.

    Sentence 1: Topic sentence. For example, the culture of the nineteenth century in America, influenced by Europe, was marked by great change and growth as well as a flowering of the arts.

    Sentences 2-6: Conclusions drawn about the five categories.

    Sentence 7: Generalization about the entire period based on the categories.

Chronology of 1803-65

Nathaniel Hawthorne's Contemporaries and the
Events of the American Renaissance

1803	Ralph Waldo Emerson, American essayist and Transcendentalist, is born.
1804	**Nathaniel Hawthorne, American novelist, is born.** Johann Strauss, Viennese waltz composer, is born.
1805	Hans Christian Andersen, Danish poet and writer of children's stories, is born.
1806	Elizabeth Barrett Browning, English poet, is born.
1807	Henry Wadsworth Longfellow, American poet, is born. Robert Fulton's paddle steamer "Clermont" navigates the Hudson River.
1809	Edgar Allan Poe, American poet and writer of stories of the macabre, is born. Alfred Lord Tennyson, chief English poet of Victorian Age, is born. (He would be named Poet Laureate by Queen Victoria.)

Charles Darwin, English naturalist, is born.

Felix Mendelssohn, German composer, is born.

Louis Braille, French inventor of the reading system for the blind, is born.

1810   Robert Schumann, German composer, is born.

Francois Appert develops techniques for canning food.

1811   William M. Thackeray, English novelist, is born.

Franz Liszt, Hungarian composer, is born.

Jane Austen publishes *Sense and Sensibility*.

1812   Charles Dickens, English novelist, is born.

1813   Giuseppe Verdi, Italian operatic composer, is born.

Richard Wagner, German composer, is born.

The waltz dominates European ballrooms.

Jane Austen publishes *Pride and Prejudice*.

1814   The first steam locomotive operates near Newcastle, England.

The *London Times* is printed by steam-operated press.

Jane Austen publishes *Mansfield Park*.

1815   The first steam warship is the U.S.S. Fulton.

1816   Charlotte Bronte, English novelist, is born.

Jane Austen publishes *Emma*.

The English economic crisis leads to emigration to Canada and the U.S.

Richard Allen, who founded the African Methodist Episcopal Church and the
        Free African Society, is named first bishop of AME.

1817   Jane Austen, English novelist, dies.

Henry David Thoreau, American essayist and Transcendentalist, is born.

1818   Mary Shelley publishes *Frankenstein*.

Jane Austen's *Northanger Abbey* and *Persuasion* are published posthumously by
        her brother.

1819   The future Queen Victoria is born.

George Eliot (Mary Ann Evans), English novelist, is born.

James Russell Lowell, American essayist and poet, is born.

Walt Whitman, American poet, is born.

Working conditions for juveniles in England change to a twelve-hour work day.

David Napier constructs a flat-bed cylinder press for printing.

1820   Florence Nightingale, English nurse, is born.

Susan B. Anthony, American suffragette, is born.
English Romantic poet John Keats publishes "Ode to a Nightingale."
Sir Walter Scott publishes *Ivanhoe*.
The Venus de Milo is discovered.
Harriet Tubman is born a slave in Maryland.

1821   Napoleon I, French Emperor, dies.
        Faraday discovers the fundamentals of electromagnetic rotation.

1822   Percy Bysshe Shelley, English Romantic poet, dies.
        Liszt debuts in Vienna.

1823   The Monroe Doctrine closes the American continent to colonial settlements by
            European powers.
        Faraday succeeds in liquefying chlorine.
        James Fenimore Cooper publishes *Leatherstocking Tales*.
        Charles Macintosh invents waterproof fabric.

1824   Lord Byron, English Romantic poet, dies.
        Alexandre Dumas, French novelist, is born.
        The Erie Canal is finished.

1825   Johann Strauss, son of Johann Strauss and known as the "Waltz King," is born.
        Faraday succeeds in isolating benzene.
        Horse-drawn buses operate in London.

1826   James Fenimore Cooper publishes *The Last of the Mohicans*.

1827   Ludwig van Beethoven, German composer, dies.
        A water purification system is developed in London.
        George S. Ohm produces Ohm's Law defining electric current potential and
            resistance.

1828   Henrik Ibsen, Norwegian dramatist, is born.
        Jules Verne, French novelist, is born.
        Noah Webster's *American Dictionary of English Letters* is published.
        Dante Gabriel Rossetti, English poet and painter, is born.
        Gilbert Stuart, American painter, dies.
        Cap and ring spinning machines are invented.
        John Carroll begins construction of the Baltimore and Ohio RR, built in the
            U.S. for passengers and freight.

1829   Chopin debuts in Vienna.
        L.J.M. Daguerre forms a partnership with J.N. Niepce for the development of
            their photographic inventions.

James Smithson bequeaths 100,000 pounds sterling to found the Smithsonian Institute in Washington, D.C.

John Mercer Langston is born free, the first black American elected to public office; he studied at Oberlin College in 1843.

1830   Emily Dickinson, American poet, is born.

Camille Pissarro, French impressionist painter, is born.

1831   Nat Turner leads Southampton, Virginia, slave revolt, one of more than 250 documented revolts against slave owners, resulting in the strengthening of the "Black Codes" throughout the South.

Charles Darwin sails to South America, New Zealand, and Australia.

A cholera pandemic begun in India in 1826 spreads from Russia into Central Europe, reaching Scotland in 1832.

William Lloyd Garrison begins publishing the abolitionist periodical *The Liberator* in Boston.

The first horse-drawn buses appear in New York.

1832   Louisa May Alcott, American novelist, is born.

Lewis Carroll (Charles Lutwidge Dodgson), the English author of *Alice in Wonderland*, is born.

Sir Walter Scott, English poet, dies.

Edouard Manet, French impressionist painter, is born.

1833   Johannes Brahms, German composer, is born.

Alfred Nobel, Swedish inventor of dynamite and the founder of the Nobel Prize, is born.

The British Factory Act insures the inspection of working conditions in factories.

1834   Samuel Taylor Coleridge, English Romantic poet, dies.

Charles Lamb, English essayist, dies.

Edgar Degas, French impressionist painter, is born.

Victor Hugo publishes *The Hunchback of Notre Dame*.

McCormick patents a reaping machine.

Walter Hunt constructs one of the first sewing machines.

1835   Mark Twain, American essayist, novelist, and storyteller, is born.

Andrew Carnegie, American industrialist and philanthropist, is born.

1836   Davy Crockett is killed at the Alamo.

W.S. Gilbert (of Gilbert and Sullivan fame), English operatic composer, is born.

Winslow Homer, American painter, is born.

Texas receives its independence from Mexico and becomes a republic with Sam Houston as president.

1837	Nathaniel Hawthorne publishes *Twice-Told Tales*.
	Wheatstone and Cooke patent the electric telegraph.
	The U.S. Congress passes a gag law aimed at suppressing debate on slavery.
	E.P. Lovejoy, editor of an abolitionist paper, is murdered by a mob in Illinois.

1838	Georges Bizet, French composer, is born.
	Frederick Douglass escapes from slavery, founds the newspaper *The Liberator* with William Lloyd Garrison, and speaks at abolitionist meetings from 1845 to 1847.
	John Muir, Scottish-American naturalist, is born.
	Dickens's *Oliver Twist* becomes a best seller.
	Two steamers cross the Atlantic from England to the U.S.

1839	Paul Cezanne, French impressionist painter, is born.
	Charles Goodyear discovers the process of processing commercial rubber.
	Doubleday lays out the first baseball field and conducts the first game.
	The first bicycle is constructed by Scot inventor Kirkpatrick Macmillan.

1840	Thomas Hardy, English novelist, is born.
	Emile Zola, French novelist, is born.
	Claude Monet, French impressionist painter, is born.
	Pierre Auguste Renoir, French impressionist painter, is born.
	Auguste Rodin, French sculptor, is born.
	Peter Ilich Tchaikovsky, Russian composer, is born.
	Connecticut, Massachusetts, and Pennsylvania pass laws limiting the hours of employment of minors in textile factories.

1843	Henry James, Anglo-American novelist, is born.
	Robert Southey, English poet laureate, dies.
	Sojourner Truth leaves New York and travels throughout the North preaching emancipation and women's rights.
	Edward Grieg, Norwegian composer, is born.
	Dickens publishes *A Christmas Carol*.
	Elijah McCoy is born. (He was awarded patents; his oil device was most well known; the saying "the real McCoy" began with customers wanting the real thing.)
	William Wordsworth, Romantic poet, is appointed the poet laureate of England.
	Alfred, Lord Tennyson publishes "Morte d'Arthur."
	Mendelssohn's *Midsummer Night's Dream* is performed for first time.
	The S.S. *Great Britain* is the first propeller-driven ship to cross the Atlantic from Bristol.
	Congress grants Samuel Morse funds to build the first telegraph line from Washington to Baltimore.

1844   Alexandre Dumas publishes *The Count of Monte Cristo*.
        Nikolai Andreyevich Rimsky-Korsakov, Russian composer, is born.
        Friedrich Nietzsche, German philosopher, is born.

1845   Texas becomes a state.
        Poe publishes "The Raven."
        The Knickerbocker Baseball Club codifies the rules of baseball.

1846   The U.S. goes to war with Mexico.
        Famine in Ireland is caused by the failure of the potato crop.
        American dentist W.T. Morton uses ether as an anesthetic.

1847   Alexander Graham Bell, American inventor, is born.
        Charlotte Bronte publishes *Jane Eyre*.
        Emily Bronte publishes *Wuthering Heights*.
        Verdi's opera *Macbeth* opens.

        The British Factory Act restricts the working day for women and children
            between thirteen and eighteen to ten hours.
        Alexander Crummelly, well-known African American scholar, college professor,
            and preacher, works as a missionary in Liberia for the Episcopal Church.

1848   Paul Gauguin, French painter, is born.
        Communist Manifesto is issued by Marx and Engels.
        The first appendectomy is performed by Hancock.
        Gold discoveries in California lead to the first gold rush.
        Lewis H. Latimer is born. (He was an African American electrical engineer
            who continued Edison's work in lighting after his death.)
        Longfellow publishes *Evangeline*.

1849   Edgar Allan Poe dies.
        August Strindberg, Russian poet and dramatist, is born.
        Frederic Chopin, Polish composer, dies.
        Harriet Tubman escapes from slavery and leads more than three hundred slaves
            to freedom on the Underground Railroad.

1850   Robert Louis Stevenson is born.
        William Wordsworth, English Romantic poet, dies. (He was succeeded as poet
            laureate by Tennyson.)
        Nathaniel Hawthorne publishes *The Scarlet Letter*.

1851   Vincent Van Gogh, Dutch painter, is born.
        Hawthorne publishes *House of the Seven Gables*.
        Herman Melville publishes *Moby Dick*.

1852   Harriet Beecher Stowe publishes *Uncle Tom's Cabin*.
        Jan Ernst Matzeliger constructs the first machine to make thousands of pairs of
            shoes in a day.

1853   Queen Victoria allows chloroform as an anesthetic during the birth of her
            seventh child.

1854   Thoreau publishes *Walden*.
        The Republican Party is formed in the U.S.

1855   Charlotte Bronte, English novelist, dies.
        Longfellow publishes *Song of Hiawatha*.
        Walt Whitman publishes *Leaves of Grass*.
        Mary Ann Shadd is the first woman to speak at the National Negro
            Convention for women's suffrage.

1856   George Bernard Shaw, Irish dramatist, is born.
        Oscar Wilde, English dramatist, is born.
        Sigmund Freud, Austrian neurologist and the founder of psychoanalysis, is
            born.
        Massacre of Pottawatomie, Kansas: slavers are murdered by free-staters.
        Bessemer introduces the converter in the process for making steel.
        Granville T. Woods is born. (He was an African American inventor who
            patented over thirty-five electrical inventions, many of which greatly
            improved the railroad industry.)

1857   Joseph Conrad, Anglo-Polish novelist, is born.

1858   Giacomo Puccini, Italian operatic composer, is born.

1859   Washington Irving, American author, dies.
        Arthur Conan Doyle, English novelist and writer of detective stories, is born.
        Tennyson publishes "Idylls of the King."
        Charles Darwin publishes *On the Origin of the Species by Natural Selection*.
        The steamroller is invented.
        Work on the Suez Canal begins.

1860   American Christopher Sholes invents a primitive form of the typewriter.

1861   Confederate states form; Lincoln is inaugurated as the sixteenth president;
            Confederate states take Ft. Sumter on April 12—the outbreak of the Civil
            War.
        Russian serfs are emancipated.

Dickens publishes *Great Expectations*.
Pasteur introduces the germ theory of fermentation.
The U.S. introduces the passport system.

1862   Henry David Thoreau, American essayist and poet, dies.
Claude Debussy, French composer, is born.
Victor Hugo publishes *Les Miserables*.
Mary Elizabeth Bowser becomes a Union spy, gathering secrets from Jefferson
        Davis as a servant in his home.

1863   Lincoln issues the Emancipation Proclamation.
Lincoln's Gettysburg Address is delivered.
Longfellow publishes *Tales of a Wayside Inn* ("Paul Revere's Ride").
Huxley publishes "Evidence as to Man's Place in Nature."
Ebenezer Butterick develops the first paper dress patterns.
The U.S. Congress establishes free city mail delivery.
Roller-skating is introduced to America.

1864   Nathaniel Hawthorne, American novelist and short story writer, dies.
George Washington Carver, scientist and inventor, is born.
Tolstoy publishes *War and Peace*.
The first salmon cannery in the U.S. opens in California.
"In God We Trust" first appears on U.S. coins.
Norbert Rillieux receives a patent for a sugar-refining process in Louisiana.

1865   The Civil War ends with the surrender of the Confederacy on April 9 at
        Appomattox.

HAWTHORNE'S CONTEMPORARIES IN THE AMERICAN RENAISSANCE
● ● ● ● ●

HENRY DAVID THOREAU

Although Thoreau built his cabin and lived off the bounty of Emerson's land on the shore of Walden Pond in the spring of 1845, much later, in the 1970s, another writer named Annie Dillard also chose nature—the creeks and woodlands around her home in Virginia—as the context in which to examine life in its simplicity and complexity as well. When you read the selected excerpts from Thoreau's *Walden* and then from Annie Dillard's *Pilgrim at Tinker Creek*, you will see how their keen observations of nature clarify the two writers' similar insights and beliefs about philosophy and religion. Perhaps you will also begin to understand how the beliefs and philosophical ideas from the nineteenth century effected growth, new leaves on the tree, if you will, in subsequent times.

Excerpts from Thoreau's *Walden* (Signet):

Page 87, "Regularly at half-past seven…" (birds)

Page 122, "The water is so…" (clear water)

Page 155, "I was witness…" (ants)

Page 198, "Like the water…" (color of ice, water)

Excerpts from Dillard's *Pilgrim at Tinker Creek* (Harper and Row):

Page 5, "A couple of summers ago…" (frogs)

Page 7, "Cruelty is a mystery…" (mockingbird)

Page 111, "The woods were flush…" (flowers)

Page 172, "As far as lower animals…" (horsehair worm)

Page 246, "A squirrel suddenly…" (squirrel)

Page 254, "It's easy to coax…" (monarch butterfly)

Journal prompt: Think about all the elements of nature in which both Thoreau and Dillard lived and in which they devoted many hours of careful thought and observation. Spend a little time in the outdoors, perhaps looking for the same flora and fauna they found or even making some new discoveries for yourself. Your assignment is to give nature at least an hour of your time in a park or your own back garden and to take notes on your observations in your journal. Hint: Be patient. Often just waiting and watching will produce interesting results. Be prepared to use these notes later in a poetry writing exercise.

HENRY WADSWORTH LONGFELLOW

Another American Renaissance writer, Henry Wadsworth Longfellow, wrote about nature, too, and today he is known as the most popular American poet of the nineteenth century. His connection to Hawthorne, however, does not entirely relate to nature. He had been Hawthorne's roommate at Bowdoin College in Maine. At a dinner party with Hawthorne, Longfellow heard the story of Evangeline and Gabriel and later wrote the long narrative poem *Evangeline*, the story of the Acadian girl, whose real name many believe was

Emmeline Labiche. Forced to find a new home in Louisiana, the Acadians had been driven out of Canada and Nova Scotia by the British in 1755. In the confusion, Emmeline was separated from the man she was to marry and later died of a broken heart when she discovered her love married to another. Although most people believe the legend represents the typical hardships on all the French who left Canada at that time, Judge Felix Voorhies of Louisiana wrote "The True Story of Evangeline" as told to him by his grandmother who had adopted and raised Emmeline Labiche from childhood. It was the story told to Longfellow by Rev. Horace Lorenzo Conolly at the dinner party, however, that sparked his interest. In his letter to Hawthorne on February 8, 1848, Longfellow encouraged his friend to engage in a literary project on the Acadians. "It is neither more nor less than the history of the Acadians after their expulsion as well as before" (Hawthorne Collection MSS68 Philips Library, Salem).

Earlier Longfellow had published *Voices of the Night*, containing the poem "The Light of the Stars." In 1841 he published *Ballads and Other Poems*, which included the immensely popular "The Wreck of the Hesperus." Other narrative poems, *Hiawatha, Evangeline,* and *Tales from a Wayside Inn,* which includes "Paul Revere's Ride," contributed to his great success and popularity. Just as nature serves as a glass through which Thoreau and Dillard both see the mysteries of the world, Longfellow also uses nature and its abundant metaphors to communicate his beliefs. Read the following poems by Longfellow. What ideas about life are the poems communicating to the reader through nature images?

"The Tide Rises, the Tide Falls"

"Nature"

"The Sound of the Sea"

NATURE AND POETRY

Through her nature observations in the hills of Virginia on Tinker Creek, Annie Dillard suggests that, even in what may seem like a brute world, beauty can be seen as the "canary that sings on the skull," a "wholly gratuitous" beauty that asks for nothing in exchange, a gift. She writes, however, if beauty in nature exists whether we will or sense it, "the least we can do is be there" to experience it, to see it and be present to accept this gift for ourselves (Dillard 7-8). One must allow the senses to open up and be receptive to all nature has to offer. Dillard demonstrates a modern writer's attempt to observe and write about nature with the same fervor as Hawthorne, Thoreau, and Longfellow.

In your written responses to these observations, one kind of figurative language can reproduce the powerful images found in nature, the metaphor. The etymology of *metaphor* creates an image of its own:

Greek *metaphora*—change of a word to a new sense, derived from *metapherein*—to transfer, change; from *meta*—after, beyond + *pherein*—to carry

Picture the meaning of one word or phrase being carried or transferred to another word or phrase, creating a metaphorical comparison between the two. For example, one student, Betsy, wrote,

> I am the wind. I'm very inconsistent. At times I am hardly controllable, and at times I can stand absolutely still. I am not affected by circumstances that affect some around me. I can be a relief on a hot day. I can also be cold and biting.

In her metaphor, the wind, the writer transfers the qualities of wind—the movement that sometimes lacks control, the stillness of the air when the wind ceases, the pleasant effects as well as the harm it produces—to herself as a person. (Remember that personification would give human traits to the wind.) The two objects, wind and writer, have fused, creating more information about the person and thus allowing us to see another side of her.

As you read the selections by Nathaniel Hawthorne suggested in this book, you will see numerous examples of metaphor. The dominant metaphor, for example, that supports the central theme of balance in "The Maypole of Merry Mount" is the dance of life. The author ironically contrasts the dance around "the Puritan Maypole," the whipping post, with the happy, festive May Day dance. In other stories, Hawthorne's images are supported by metaphors that contribute to a sense of passion and, again, antithesis. In his novel *The Scarlet Letter*, the heroine Hester Prynne is the rose that the reader is asked to pluck, that is, to sympathize with.

Although metaphors serve the language of poetry particularly well, our everyday language is teeming with phrases and expressions that say what we mean more eloquently. Even when they have become clichés, we regard them as old friends and continue using them to express more descriptively what we mean. *Time flies, eat crow, in hot water, the last straw, fish out of water, storm out, cat out of the bag* are only a handful of the idiomatic expressions that began as metaphors. Most people don't use metaphors for poetry's sake but for the strong, colorful images they produce in the minds of both speaker and listener.

Creating Metaphors

Practice making your own metaphoric comparisons. As you write, try to extend the comparison as far as you can so that you have a number of sentences that develop an image with several components. In a paragraph of about six to ten sentences, each line should further describe the qualities of the metaphor. See suggestions below or think of a new one:

book	tree	glass
compass	rose	mirror
river	rock	glasses
snake	camera	ice
diamond	leaves	cloud
blade of grass	rainbow	silk
light	umbrella	nails
darkness	boat	iron
cheetah, tiger, cat	tortoise	water
fire	volcano	music
avalanche	wolf	storm

Start with a personal pronoun subject in either your first sentence to introduce the metaphor or your last sentence to conclude. For example,

I am a camera.

He is a tortoise.

It was a volcano.

Using Nature and Philosophy to Write Your Own Poetry

Now go back to your nature observations and select the images that could be used as metaphors for your poem. Ask yourself these questions:

- How do these images support ideas about life, my own ideas in particular?

- What do I want to say about these images?

- What ideas about life do I feel strongly about and how do I want to express them?

- What ideas are related to these images in nature that could further support my own philosophy of life?

- Which images and ideas do I want to include in my poem?

A word of caution: Don't over season your poem with too many metaphors unless your intention is to provide a string of metaphors to build up support. If you are using an extended metaphor, try not to mix up your current metaphor with other inappropriate metaphors that are not relevant. Using different metaphors in one context is often considered unacceptable. Language scholars, however, are quick to point out that Shakespeare frequently used a series of metaphors to support an idea, but his use was both grammatically correct and parallel. In *Richard II*, Act 2.1, Shakespeare writes,

> This royal throne of kings, this sceptered isle,
>
> This earth of majesty, this seat of Mars,
>
> This other Eden, demi-paradise,

This fortress built by Nature for herself

Against infection and the hand of war,

This happy breed of men, this little world,

This precious stone set in a silver sea,

Which serves it in the office of a wall,

Or as a moat defensive to a house,

Against the envy of less happier lands,

This blessed plot, this earth, this realm, this England,

This nurse, this teeming womb of royal kings,

Feared by their breed and famous by their birth.

Using Metaphors in Poetry

Read as much poetry as you can. Before you think about writing poetry, immerse yourself in many different styles and become familiar with the skills these poets use to express emotions. If "language is the serviceable clay of one's thoughts" (Oliver 16-17), you must learn about the language of poetry and how to manipulate it to communicate those thoughts. Below is a suggested list of the many good poetry collections available:

Maya Angelou, *The Complete Collected Poems*

The Complete Poems of Emily Dickenson

T.S. Eliot, *Collected Poems*

The Poetry of Robert Frost

African American Poetry, ed. Michael S. Harper & Anthony Walton

Robert Lowell, *Near the Ocean*

Edna St. Vincent Millay, *Collected Poems*

The Selected Odes of Pablo Neruda

Mary Oliver, *Dream Work*

Carl Sandburg, *Honey and Salt*

Holocaust Poetry, ed. Hilda Schiff

The Poems of William Butler Yeats

You have observed how these poets construct figures of speech from nature images in order to express a particular philosophy of life. How can you emulate these writers? If you will follow these steps for adding metaphors and other forms of figurative language to your poems, you will generate a list of images that could support the philosophical belief that you choose.

- First, write sentences that express your beliefs about the way you want to live your life. For example, in Mary Oliver's poem "Starfish," the poet tells the reader that, although it is easier to go through life without taking risks, with some effort she can face her fears and learn about and love the only life she has been given. Think about the ideals and concepts that you believe are true for you, make a list, and choose one of them for your poem.

- Divide your paper into two columns. In one column make a list of the following:

  Items of clothing

  Human actions: both calm actions and violent actions

  Parts of a house or garden

  Events in which humans engage, both positive and negative

  Things humans see, hear, smell, touch, and taste (concrete items)

  Modes of transportation

  Tools that humans use, both small and large

  Professions, jobs, or tasks in which humans engage

  In another column write nature images from both your recent and your past observations. Try to match these seemingly unlikely items in each column. Do they work as figures of speech? For example, can you put *canopy* and *green leaves* together for a metaphor, the *canopy of green*? Or how about using *needle* and *blood* with *thorns of the rose* for the metaphor, *the thorny needle of the blood-red rose*? If you have ever pricked your hand on one of those thorns, you can easily see the comparison to a needle drawing blood! Try mixing and matching your two lists until you obtain just the right images for the figurative language you might want for your poem.

Look at your list of figures of speech. Decide which ones might help you communicate your point, the philosophical belief that you have selected for your poem.

- Poets have the task of saying "a lot in a little." Using fewer words than they might use for prose, these writers go through a painstaking process of selecting just the right words and images to communicate meaning in a powerful but fresh way. At this point, review what you have written for trite ideas and expressions. Omit them and replace them with newer, more creative ones that are not overused.

- Longfellow wrote Petrarchan, or Italian, sonnets. These lyric poems contain fourteen lines written in iambic pentameter, a meter with ten alternating unaccented and accented beats. Italian poets in the thirteenth century first used this form, which was eventually named for the man who perfected it, Petrarch. Its organization should contain these stanzas:

  o Octave: first eight lines with a rhyme scheme of **abba abba**

    A question is raised.

   o Sestet: concluding six lines with a rhyme scheme of **cde cde**

   The question is answered.

If you want to try verse with meter and rhyme, you could write a Petrarchan sonnet using your nature observations. Otherwise, free verse is appropriate as well as rhyming lines without meter.

- Remember to write a title that captures the essence of your poem.

The following examples demonstrate how students can connect what they have observed in nature with their own philosophical thoughts to produce poetry. Below are two poems written by students who were part of a class that spent time in the Houston Arboretum observing nature. They considered the ideas and techniques of a number of poets and philosophers before working through several exercises using figurative language.

A Walk through the Woods
By Kelly M.

A group of crows cackle in the distance,
Their cries driving me insane.
A small wind blows through the trees
So I listen to the music of the slow, cool breeze
As it rustles the upper leaves ever so slightly.
I look up to see the sky
And watch the marathon of all the white clouds
As they outstrip each other along the vast expanse.
The fall season has painted a few leaves orange
And broken some of the old dead branches
And on the ground lies an old tree.
I look at that tree's broken branches
Still clinging to life as they try to keep
Their hoards of fading leaves.
Ravens streak between the distant trees,
Croaking in their dark, lonely way.
As I walk along the well-worn path,
I see a mourning dove waddling away,
Bobbing its head at each step.
At a crossroads, surrounded by trees and stumps,
A tiny patch of vivid green grass grows
With four white flowers, long and thin,
Beauty in a place of dark earth.
The fallen needles of the tall pine trees
Look like moss from a distance, but up close
It is easy to see what they really are.

Berries colored purple-red grow in small clumps,
A festival of color for mundane plants.
I do not wish to linger long
So that the swarming bugs do not get to me.
I hear a bird screeching its song,
A sharp, short cry of only two words.
At that moment, an ancient tree,
Its bark smooth and white and draped
With leaves in strands of green,
Looms over the canopy, dwarfing all others.
I move to a half-dried muddy creek
Next to a path less worn.
The scent of the tall pine trees
Enchants me, and I look up at the sky
But find a huge white trunk
Rising out of the earth, larger than any other.
I look up at the top and the white tree looks back,
Trunk bent with age, like a hunchback.
I want to see that tree again.
A ravine of stone walls drawn near,
Its soil long dried and hardened.
A small orange spider delicately weaves its home
Between the branches of a small bush.
A shallow marsh filled with murky brown water
And overgrown with pale green algae
Surrounds the trail on both sides.
I know I am near the end.
I come out into a clearing
And to the civilized human world;
I wish I could go back in.

Untitled

By Kellyn C.

Footsteps in the darkened mud
Running from something unknown
The sky above, a chalkboard of stars
With secrets to tell.
Teacher in the sky, do you hear me tonight?
Do you hear me amidst the dark and damp,
Kneeling in the earth,
Waiting for instructions
From a silent teacher in the sky?

Ralph Waldo Emerson

Emerson's "Self-Reliance," published in *Essays: First Series* (1841), is probably the most famous essay written by an American. In it Emerson gives his reasons for his beliefs in self-reliance and his reasoning against conformity. His ideas might remind you of some of the classical philosophers, Socrates and Plato for example. In their pursuit of wisdom, philosophers engage in investigation and inquiry of fundamental principles or of natural phenomena. Many of their beliefs become classics because these ideas transcend time, and we benefit from their enduring wisdom. Throughout history human beings have sought a greater wisdom, the greater Self as Jung called it (*Basic Writings* 151), through the counsel of sages—philosophers and poets. Emerson believed the ultimate source of truth is in ourselves. When we trust what is outside ourselves more than what is inside us, we look outside for answers, and, according to Emerson, that's where the trouble begins.

When Emerson delivered this essay as a speech to the Harvard Divinity School, it was met with strong criticism. The message, asserting the doctrine of the God within, was revolutionary. It was a risk that Emerson, following his own doctrine, was apparently willing to take. He had left the ministry a few years earlier, he had lost his young wife to tuberculosis after only eighteen months of marriage, and he was in danger of upsetting his colleagues at Harvard. Pronouncing such nonconformist sentiments could easily have jeopardized his career; writing and speaking would not have enabled him to live adequately. In light of the dangers, a man who would speak such a philosophy must stand by it.

Read the following excerpts from Emerson's essay on self-reliance. What advice can we take from his words today? Do they apply to people now in the same way that they did in the nineteenth century? How difficult is it to adhere to these ideals? Do you know people who have done so or who still do?

1. "To believe your own thought, to believe that what is true for you in your private heart is true for all men—that is genius" (150).

2. "A man should learn to detect and watch that gleam of light which flashes across his mind from within, more than the luster of the firmament of bards and sages" (151-2).

3. "Trust thyself: every heart vibrates to that iron string" (151).

4. "Whoso would be a man must be a nonconformist. He who would gather immortal palms must not be hindered by the name of goodness, but must explore if it be goodness. Nothing is at last sacred but the integrity of your own mind" (153).

5. "Good and bad are but names very readily transferable to that or this; the only right is what is after my constitution, the only wrong what is against it" (153). (Think of Shakespeare's Hamlet who said, "There is nothing either good or bad, but thinking makes it so" [*Hamlet*, II, ii, 259].)

6. "What I must do is all that concerns me, not what the people think. This rule, equally arduous in actual and in intellectual life, may serve for the whole distinction between

greatness and meanness. It is the harder because you will always find those who think they know what is your duty better than you know it. It is easy in the world to live after the world's opinion; it is easy in solitude to live after our own; but the great man is he who in the midst of the crowd keeps with perfect sweetness the independence of solitude" (155).

7. "A foolish consistency is the hobgoblin of little minds, adored by little statesmen and philosophers and divines. With consistency a great soul has simply nothing to do. He may as well concern himself with his shadow on the wall. Speak what you think now in hard words, and to-morrow speak what to-morrow thinks in hard words again, though it contradict everything you said to-day.—'Ah, so you shall be sure to be misunderstood.'—Is it so bad, then, to be misunderstood? Pythagoras was misunderstood, and Socrates, and Jesus, and Luther, and Copernicus, and Galileo, and Newton, and every pure and wise spirit that ever took flesh. To be great is to be misunderstood" (157).

8. "The sinew and heart of man seem to be drawn out, and we are become timorous, desponding whimperers. We are afraid of truth, afraid of fortune, afraid of death, and afraid of each other" (166).

9. "Let a stoic open the resources of man, and tell men they are not leaning willows, but can and must detach themselves; that with the exercise of self-trust, new powers shall appear; that a man is the word made flesh, born to shed healing to the nations, that he should be ashamed of our compassion, and that the moment he acts from himself, tossing the laws, the books, idolatries, and customs out of the window, we pity him no more, but thank and revere him—and that teacher shall restore the life of man to splendor, and make his name dear to all history" (167).

10. "Men have looked away from themselves and at things so long, that they have come to esteem the religious, learned, and civil institutions as guards of property, and they deprecate assaults on these, because they feel them to be assaults on property. They measure their esteem of each other by what each has, and not by what each is" (173).

11. "He who knows that power is inborn, that he is weak because he has looked for good out of him and elsewhere, and so perceiving, throws himself unhesitatingly on his thought, instantly rights himself, stands in the erect position, commands his limbs, works miracles; just as a man who stands on his feet is stronger than a man who stands on his head" (174).

12. "Nothing can bring you peace but yourself. Nothing can bring you peace but the triumph of principles" (174).

Journal Prompt: Think about proverbs and axioms, clever sayings that you have read or heard. What similar advice could you give to other people your age about friends, school, parents, and about the basic principles that guide your life? What would be your best piece of advice? What could you tell people about how to be happy and content? Write two or three pages in your journal. If appropriate, include a proverb that supports your point.

FROM EMERSON AND THOREAU...BACK TO PLATO

Plato is alive and well in literature, philosophy, and our everyday speech. Most students have heard at one time or another the reference to Greece and Rome as the "cradle of civilization." But what does that really mean? The ideas and words of the ancient Greek and Roman poets, playwrights, and philosophers live on in both classic and modern literature that we study in classrooms and even that we read for pleasure. Most of us don't even realize that the source of many of our expressions and philosophical ideas that we either embrace or shun come from Socrates, Plato, and Aristotle.

Plato was a young Athenian aristocrat in the late fifth century BC when he met Socrates, a powerful thinker with a strong following. When Socrates was condemned to death and forced to drink the poisonous cup traditionally known as hemlock, Plato recorded his teacher's philosophy in a series of twenty-five dialogues as well as a reconstruction of Socrates' defense before the Athenian jury that sentenced him to death. Socrates' method of lecturing was to ask leading questions, the answers to which would evoke further questioning from the master who would guide his pupils to an understanding of the logical consequences of their answers. Many students have no doubt experienced the Socratic method of discussion in their classrooms. In addition, you have already been introduced to Plato's pupil Aristotle as you learned about literary terms relevant to the writing workshop in this book. Scholars consider these three great Greek philosophers the Triumvirate: Socrates (469-399 BC), Plato (427-347 BC), and Aristotle (384-322 BC) (Sahakian, 32-7, 59). In this section, you will examine the following concepts introduced by Plato as he reconstructed Socrates' dialogues. As you look at classic and modern literature, you will be able to recall that often the roots of thought in those pieces began with Plato.

1. A cup of hemlock (from *Phaedo*)
   When a person must face an extremely unpleasant task that may
   result in his death, literally or figuratively, he might think of it as his
   "cup of hemlock" in consequence of his previous actions.

2. The ring of Gyges (from *The Republic*, book II)
   What would you do if you could be invisible at your will? Several
   writers have pondered this same question. Think about a certain Hobbit
   as well as Harry Potter.

3. Plato's cave (from *The Republic*, book VII)
   We can move from darkness into light, both literally and figuratively.
   Knowledge, experience, wisdom, and maturity are often the result.

4. A swan song (from *Phaedo*)
   In three different plays, Shakespeare refers to the final "song" of the
   dying swan as he compares the death song of three characters.

   King John, 5.7.20-4. Prince Henry to Salisbury at the death of his
   father:

   > Tis strange that death should sing.
   > I am the cygnet to this pale faint swan
   > Who chants a doleful hymn to his own death
   > And from the organ-pipe of frailty sings
   > His soul and body to their lasting rest.

   Merchant of Venice, 3.2.43-5. Portia speaks while Bassanio makes
   a decision that will either win or lose her hand in marriage:

   > Let music sound while he doth make his choice,
   > Then if he lose he makes the swan-like end,
   > Fading in music.

   Othello, 5.2.247-8. Emilia is stabbed by her husband Iago, and she
   sings to her friend Desdemona, also murdered by her own husband.

   > I will play the swan
   > And die in music.

5. "The unexamined life is not worth living." (from *Apology—Socrates' Defense*)
   Socrates questions the wisdom of the government. If not allowed to
   do that, he doesn't want to live, even in exile. Would you make the
   same decision? Is there anything that you feel so strongly about
   that you would sacrifice your life for it? Do the freedoms we
   have today offer us an alternative as we seek what we feel is just?

6. Might makes right. (from *The Republic*, book I)
   When does *right* triumph? What does *might* include? How do we define *strength*?

PLATO'S THEORY OF IDEAS

The Sophists, or wise men in Plato's day, were professional itinerant teachers who aimed at producing cleverness and efficiency rather than wisdom and goodness. Plato sought to discover the meaning of truth, beauty, and goodness.

Plato believed that everything we perceive around us is merely appearance. The true reality is the realm of *ideas* or forms from which this appearance derives. The universal realm of ideas, perceived by the mind, is unchanging and eternal. But the physical world in contrast that we perceive with the senses is in a continual state of change.

This concept leads to Plato's ethics. By concentrating on the particular, material world, all we can perceive is *what seems to be good*. With the help of reason we can gain insight into the greater universal idea of good. It is by progressing through levels of understanding that we can finally grasp the concepts of beauty, truth, and goodness.

Platonism became part of the Christian tradition through the writings of St. Augustine, which gave Christian theology a firmer intellectual foundation.

THE RING OF GYGES

It's important that you read a good translation of Plato's work rather than a writer's synopsis of the excerpts from Plato's book *The Republic*. You can examine his style, his words translated from the Greek and more clearly see what he was saying in his own way. Scott Buchanan's *Portable Plato* is a good place to begin. As Plato is instructing his student, he tells a story about a shepherd named Gyges out tending his flock who witnesses the earth opening up and revealing a bronze horse with a door, which he opens. Inside he finds a dead man with a ring on his finger. He takes the ring and puts it on his finger, realizing after sitting among the other shepherds that the ring has the power to make him invisible. Gyges soon uses this power for ill.

Plato's story of the ring of Gyges might remind you of a saying: The ethical person follows a principled life *even when no one is looking*. Plato would find it difficult to identify such a person, for he believes that, given the same set of circumstances, the just person and the unjust person would follow the same path. Scores of readers have been offended, however, by Plato's lack of confidence in the human capacity for good behavior. To express your own ideas about Plato's beliefs and gain a better understanding of what he was trying to say, write two or three pages about the following journal prompt.

Journal Prompt: If you could be invisible for a day, what activities would you engage in? Think about the things you would do if you thought no one was looking. Then think about how you behave when you think people are observing you. Why do you change your behavior? Write about your thoughts. Do you agree with Plato's message to his students in the story about Gyges?

THE ALLEGORY OF THE CAVE

Follow the text in *The Republic*, book II as Plato verbally draws the listener and the reader a picture of a cave with its fire and human contents. Or better still, use Plato's description to draw it yourself to get a good idea of the shadowy images that the prisoners interpret as reality. When the prisoners are liberated and led out into the light, they experience the pain of the sudden glare in their eyes and find it difficult to look at. Gradually, as their eyes become accustomed to the newness of light, they are able to see the world around them and to name what they see.

Journal Prompt: In your journal, write a synopsis of the allegory of the cave. Draw the cave and its prisoners to help you remember. Then write a definition for the word *allegory*: a story told on two levels, literal and figurative. Leave room in your journal (a page or two) for a response you will make later comparing the modern rendition of Plato's allegory to the famous off-Broadway play *The Fantasticks*.

YOUR PHILOSOPHY: A GIFT

Design or plan a gift you could give to a close friend or family member based on your own heritage, culture, or philosophy of life. Decide what you would like to make and list the supplies you will need. Look around for items you might already have. Be creative, resourceful, and meticulous. Begin early so your gift will reflect your time and effort. This gift, of course, wouldn't be complete without words—a written explanation or message for the recipient. To enhance the appearance of your writing, you might think about using attractive stationery, or you could make a card from construction paper, wrapping paper, or even handmade paper. Art supply stores usually have a wide array of beautiful papers, if cost is not an option. Place your beautiful card in a handmade envelope with a matching or complementary design.

Gift ideas may range from the aesthetic to the utilitarian. If you choose to give service to someone as your gift, such as doing chores or tutoring or using your talents to help someone, you will need to create a redeemable coupon for it. The coupon itself should also be an attractive work of art.

In his essay "Gifts," Ralph Waldo Emerson said, "The only gift is a portion of thyself" (361). Remember these words as you create a gift that reflects your philosophy of life, developed from your own values and principles, that you want to share with someone special.

To every thing there is a season, and a time to
Every purpose under heaven...
A time to weep, and a time to laugh; a time to
Mourn and a time to dance...

Ecclesiastes 3.1 and 4
The Bible, King James Version

CHAPTER 9

Analyzing Literature

MASTERING THE STEPS OF THE DANCE
• • • • •

The joy of reading for pleasure doesn't evolve from a strict set of guidelines or instructions for finding deeper meaning. It is a free-flowing act that occurs naturally and unencumbered. And yet, as you grow older you find teachers asking you to examine published writing, both fiction and nonfiction, with a set of criteria and a critical eye. Questions of *how* and *why* arise about the literature, and students must answer those questions in order to understand more clearly and to a greater degree what the writer's message or intentions are. This question therefore must follow: Do reading for pleasure and reading for analysis require students to take different approaches? The answer is yes. Furthermore, reading critically for analysis involves so many different skills that you will find the task more manageable if you look at individual components of writing separately. As you begin to master the steps in this dance of language, you will become more adept at analysis by using multiple approaches simultaneously. The following guide is a beginning, but each tool will soon become essential for any literary analysis you might want to do.

- **Background**: The reader looks carefully at the history, biography, and philosophy of the author and the characters.

- **Form and structure**: The reader examines genre, style and word choice, figurative language, or any part of the literary elements inside the work.

- **Psychology**: Most of us aren't prepared to psychoanalyze characters, but we can apply Freud's **id, ego**, and **superego** to gain a better understanding of characters' wants and needs.

- **Symbols and archetypal motifs**: From psychologist Carl Jung we have the terms *collective unconscious* and *archetype* (*Basic Writings*, 299). Jung believed that all people everywhere recognize certain images because they have been genetically encoded into our **collective unconscious**. Those universal images, or symbols, he termed **archetypes**. Patterns of images—sometimes with a series of events, he called **archetypal motifs**.

- **Theme**: The reader notices how the writer weaves images, symbols, and all literary elements into a thematic pattern. How do all these elements support each other and lead to a particular idea? What idea about life is the writer building toward?

HAWTHORNE'S USE OF ARCHETYPES
• • • • •

We use symbols without thinking about the origins of their meanings in much the same way that we use words without thinking of their derivations. Common usage makes us focus on the present, not the past, and so we read the surface and often miss the underlying meanings that words can bring to literature. Ideas and images unique to all human beings and their cultures across time periods may help to explain the universal quality of symbols, even if you feel unsure about agreeing with Jung's theory of the collective unconscious. Nature, the basis of mythological beliefs, offers numerous explanations of the mysteries of life and so is connected to associations we have made with color and shape and function in every part of our lives. It is easy to see how parallel myths might have originated among so many cultures at approximately the same time. Cultures may differ but in the whole of humanity, people seem to be more alike than different, and thus the explanations of their lives could easily evolve from the same abstractions. As the contemporary of Hawthorne, essayist Ralph Waldo Emerson, wrote in 1844, "We are symbols, and inhabit symbols" (*Selected Essays* 216)

Students often ask whether Hawthorne knew what he was doing when he filled his stories with symbols, or whether the large number of symbols is simply coincidental. They question the presence of symbolic language as intentional. My response to them is usually this: What does the word *coincidence* mean? Is it accidental that an author uses the same symbolic language to support similar themes throughout a body of work, especially when irrefutably strong connections between symbol and text exist? Perhaps the question begs answering only after students have read and analyzed the five short stories and the novel introduced in these chapters. If you can see the recurring symbols and archetypal motifs throughout his work, and if you can see the connections between the words that Hawthorne consciously chose to support the images and themes in his stories, you might be convinced that Hawthorne, well educated in the classics, including archetypal mythology, knew and used symbolic language intentionally and effectively. Perhaps you would be more comfortable calling them *meaningful coincidences*? The recurring symbols and themes in his work not only offer proof of Hawthorne as a writer of symbolism but also enable the student to decode a higher, more abstract level of storytelling. And if you're still not convinced, remember humans have been daily engaged in symbolic living since the beginning of recorded time.

SACRIFICE AND THE LIFE/DEATH/LIFE ARCHETYPE
• • • • •

The archetype of the seasons, or *life/death/life motif*, is a recurring image in literature. World mythology illustrates the significance of this archetype through stories of heroism and sacrifice. Although earlier cultures engaged in human sacrifice, animal sacrifice eventually replaced it, followed by the sacrifice of grains, fruit, and vegetables. In more recent times observing penance, fasting, and giving up pleasures and comforts have become a symbolic sacrifice. You can read about many different cultures and their myths, dating back as early as 2500 BC, to gain a better understanding of the similarities and differences among the various practices of sacrifice as part of their beliefs about the cycle of life/death/life.

In all mythologies a hero seeks immortality as he uses his intelligence, strength, skill, and courage on his journey. As the hero seeks accomplishment or treasure, in battle or adventure, he knows that it is honor and loyalty that guide him, even as he must deal with real and supernatural forces that threaten him. Not even the fear of death will stop her from attaining a better life for the people she loves.

The unending cyclical nature of time, of creation and re-creation, forge the foundation of world mythology. The stories that we read over and over again in every culture's mythology that deal with this life/death/life cycle are consistently about birth and maturity, innocence and experience, death and rebirth. Sacrifice plays an integral part in each mythology—in religious ceremonies, on the battlefield, and in daily life.

If you'd like to know more about sacrificial customs and how they fit into the life/death/life archetype of many world cultures, research some of the topics listed below.

Roman and Greek gods, goddesses, and heroes: Odysseus; Achilles; Heracles; Apollo and Artemis; Aphrodite, Demeter, Persephone, and Hades

British hero Beowulf, eighth century

Celtic legends of Saint Patrick

Scottish legends of Saint Columba of Iona and the Loch Ness monster

Irish hero Cuchulainn

Norse gods Thor, Loki, Tyr, Frey, Freya, and the great tree Ygdrassil

Gilgamesh of Assyria, 2500 BC: considered the first hero in literature

Chinese Taoist kitchen god, Tsao Chun; Sun Hou-Tzu, the Monkey king; Great Ten Legendary Rulers of China

Japanese legend of Izanagi and Izanami

Indian Rig Veda and the Vedic myths

Native American mythology: Nanabush and the medicine men, common stories of all aspects of nature and animals, the white buffalo calf goddess of the Plains Indians

African mythology: the myth of Two Brothers, the Dahomean Pantheon, Mbombo creation myth, common stories of the forest and animals with magic powers

THE HERO'S JOURNEY: FORSYTH'S *WHISPERING WIND*
• • • • •

The archetype of the hero begins in an ordinary world that he will later depart as he journeys to a region beyond the normal into a unique and extraordinary world. According to Joseph Campbell, the hero goes through three main stages: the departure, the initiation, and the return. In each of these stages is a pattern of events that must unfold in sequence. This hero's journey, as we have been told by Jung, is really the model that the journey of the psyche, our total being, must encounter (*Basic Writings*, 147). In other words, every person in every place and time has experienced, or will experience, this journey and the accompanying challenges and decisions and consequences along the way. The journey, which crosses time and culture, remains consistently the same story with only cultural variations (*Four Archetypes*, 50-1).

If a person can journey outward to a real place, he or she can also journey inward to the deepest recesses of the mind. Joseph Campbell writes in *The Hero with a Thousand Faces* that the first step of the hero is to "retreat from the desperations of the waste land to the peace of the everlasting realm that is within" (17). The hero must die a symbolic death and be returned, and when he or she has successfully completed this journey, the hero will have unlocked and released "the flow of life into the body of the world" (40). This is what the hero Ben Craig does in Frederick Forsyth's novella *Whispering Wind*.

Joseph Campbell summarizes the hero's journey in this way:

> A hero ventures forth from the world of common day into a region of
> supernatural wonder: fabulous forces are there encountered and a
> decisive victory is won: the hero comes back from this mysterious
> adventure with the power to bestow boons on his fellow man. (30)

Frederick Forsyth, in his modern interpretation of the mythic hero, creates Ben Craig, a hero whose annihilation of the dragon Braddock results in a better way of life for the people in Linda Pickett's world, but he also includes a shaman whose promise to the hero is fulfilled as Ben lives on in the child Linda is carrying. Although Forsyth's mythic hero story has its own unique twists on the archetypal characters and plot, you will be able to identify the parallel structure as you apply Campbell's stages to the story elements.

Whispering Wind tells a story that is spiritual on several levels. It is about compassion, friendship, romance, promises, redemption, and moral restitution, but it is also about the antithesis of love: betrayal, power, evil, and greed—all the right ingredients for the archetypal story of the hero's journey.

Stage One: The Departure

The hero knows or learns that he has a mission that he must follow, and so the adventure begins.

In Forsyth's Whispering Wind, *Ben Craig is a scout for General Custer in 1876 and is camped not far from Little Bighorn. Ben alone survives and is brought before the great chief Sitting Bull, to whom he tells his story in the Cheyenne language, taught to him as a child by Cheyenne boys with whom he hunted and played. Ben falls in love with Tall Elk's daughter Whispering Wind and takes her into the mountains, only to give her up later. Ben goes to sleep in the cave.*

Stage Two: The Initiation

The hero enters a new world where he must encounter a succession of trials. It is the archetype of the wilderness, a place of initiation and testing.

The task of the hero at this point is to reach the heart of the journey into this special world, the highest peak and the supreme part of the adventure. Many possible events can occur at this point before the hero enters the inmost cave: romance, demands, new obstacles, and new preparations.

In the deepest part of the inmost cave, afraid and discouraged, the hero faces the Ordeal in which he symbolically dies so that he is able to rise from the dead and be reborn. The hero, magically or otherwise, survives this death and eventually returns home transformed, but not yet.

The ordeal could be a real crisis of the heart, but the sacred marriage, according to Joseph Campbell, represents the hero's total mastery of life, the coming together of his multiple selves, "realized and solemnized in the symbolic adventure of the sacrifice or its equivalent" (*Mythic Image* 479). The ordeal asks the hero to face his greatest fear and by doing so moves from ego to self. The sacrificer and the victim become one, and he becomes the person he was meant to be.

The hero, having survived death and perhaps slain the enemy, now reaps his reward.

When Ben goes to sleep in the cave, the shaman lets him sleep for a hundred years, but when he rides to what he thinks is simply a fort he hasn't seen before, it is so authentic he continues to believe it is still 1876. He has actually arrived at Fort Heritage, an historic simulation designed for school children to visit and learn about history. At the gate, a group of children arrives with their teacher, Linda Pickett. He stares at her, certain she is Whispering Wind, and once again she rides willingly up into the mountains to be his wife. An avalanche of snow covers the creek and no one in the search party comes out alive to retrieve Ben or Whispering Wind.

Stage Three: The Return

The hero must undergo a final purging and purification before returning home, the place where this happens often being a cave or lodge, symbolic of returning to the womb and preparing for rebirth. The hero has made his way through all the stages and not only survived but is no longer the same person. He has grown and evolved into a better, more enlightened person with a treasure to share with others.

> *The end of the story finds Linda standing at Ben's grave with a red rose. As Linda turns to leave, the wind blows open her coat, revealing that she is four months with child.*

Although there is a twist at the end, Forsyth's hero clearly follows the archetypal motif as he makes his way through the stages of the hero's journey. A part of him returns through his now unborn child, and the treasure of his quest to be shared with others is the chance for a better life for the people who remain.

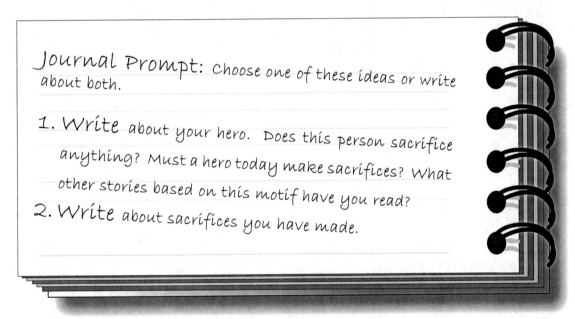

Journal Prompt: Choose one of these ideas or write about both.

1. Write about your hero. Does this person sacrifice anything? Must a hero today make sacrifices? What other stories based on this motif have you read?
2. Write about sacrifices you have made.

It is sweet to dance to violins
When Love and Life are fair;
To dance to flutes, to dance to lutes
Is delicate and rare:
But it is not sweet with nimble feet
To dance upon the air!
Oscar Wilde
The Ballad of Reading Gaol, 1898

CHAPTER 10
An Examination of Five Stories by Hawthorne

Although Hawthorne's stories may not adhere as closely as Forsyth's *Whispering Wind* to the archetypal motif of the hero's journey, they nevertheless build their plots around universal symbolism. In this chapter you will learn about not only archetypes but also four other literary elements that will provide a ready tool box for analyzing literature. In the following five short stories by Hawthorne, you will have access to several different methods of examining each work separately for a more focused look at the work, or combined to give a more comprehensive analysis. These stories are the most widely read and discussed in American high schools and universities, possibly because they represent the best of Hawthorne's skillful use of theme, symbols, and figurative language as well as his ability to tell a good story.

"The Maypole of Merry Mount"
"Dr. Heidegger's Experiment"
"Rappaccini's Daughter"
"The Minister's Black Veil"
"Young Goodman Brown"

- **Background:** How does this story reflect Hawthorne's life? How does this story reflect his philosophy of life? Does this story reflect his life and times? What do you know about the times of the characters?

- **Form and Structure:** What is the plot of the story? What kind of story is it? How does the author use language to communicate to the reader? What is the mood? The tone? Include genre and figures of speech.

- **Psychology:** Does looking at the characters' personalities in terms of Freud's id, ego, and super ego help the reader understand the characters more thoroughly? How?

- **Symbols and Archetypal Motifs**: Does the story contain archetypal characters, symbols, or motifs? What are they? How do they enhance the story? How are they related to each other?

- **Theme**: What is the theme of the story? How do all the literary elements in the story support it?

STORY #1: "THE MAYPOLE OF MERRY MOUNT"
• • • • •

Let me introduce you to the first story in our study of Hawthorne, "The Maypole of Merry Mount," by having a little fun with it. Since Hawthorne was well read in the classics and was quite familiar with the seventeenth century in both England and America, he wrote a story about a real colony in Massachusetts that was settled by colonists who left England in search of better economic, political, and religious conditions. The Puritans carried to the New World the traditions of a life similar to the one they had left in England, only now they found different hardships. The colonists who were not Puritans brought with them traditions of merriment from their native land—dancing, singing, playing games, rejoicing in their festivals and native culture—quite opposite from the Puritans. To help you become accustomed to Hawthorne's language and style, let's look at the story first as a one-act play adaptation so that you can understand the basic plot. I've also included the steps to a popular Maypole dance that you can incorporate in the play or learn just for fun. After you read the play or act it out, look at the following aids before reading and writing about this story and the four stories that follow:

> Hawthorne: A Life of Isolation, Rejection, Mystery, and Joy
> The Maypole: Past and Present
> Tree Symbolism
> Reading Assistance
> Archetypes in "The Maypole of Merry Mount"
> Literary Tools from Freud and Jung

After you read "The Maypole of Merry Mount," take the opportunity to compare Hawthorne's story with the modern play, *The Fantasticks*, which employs many of the same devices found in Hawthorne's work.

"THE MAYPOLE OF MERRY MOUNT," A ONE-ACT PLAY

• • • • •

Adapted from the Short Story by Nathaniel Hawthorne

Characters:

> **Stage Manager**
> **Priest**
> **Edith, Lady of the May**
> **Edgar, Lord of the May**
> **John Endicott, leader of a band of Puritans**
> **Peter Palfrey, a Puritan elder**
> **Colonists dressed in costumes celebrating May Day**
> **Band of Puritans following Endicott**
> **The Maypole**

Setting: The story takes place shortly after 1625 in a small colony in Massachusetts called Merry Mount, which no longer exists.

Stage Manager: (*With clipboard in hand, he walks across the stage inspecting the set, especially the Maypole, and speaking to the technicians who are offstage.*) Hey, Jim, a little more light on the Maypole. (*He waits for the adjustment.*) Perfect. Everything else seems to be okay. (*He looks stage right toward the cast.*) Are we ready to run through it again? (*Most of the cast is sitting around waiting for the rehearsal to begin. Some are standing around chatting, some are playing cards, and one is taking a nap. They all begin to move slowly toward a chest of props. One cast member opens it and begins to distribute ribbons, bells, flowers, and a vine wreath. The Stage Manager moves among them, checking to make sure everyone is in place, when he notices the audience.*) Oh, you're here. Welcome to 1625. You're in America, or at least one of its fledgling colonies in what you now call Massachusetts. Most of the history books don't bother telling you about this one. They don't want you to know about the lax morals and the gun trade with the Indians. Your teachers don't want to disillusion you with founding fathers who were, well, let's just say, less than perfect. (*He walks toward the Maypole standing up center.*) Our little play opens in the colony of Merry Mount on the wedding day of Edgar and Edith, two of its merry colonists who spend every day in celebration, usually with dancing, singing, feasting, and playing games—anything to forget their cares of early colonial life. This day is a little more solemn than usual. These two have pledged their lives to the serious responsibility of marriage. Watching on the edge of the forest, however, are the Puritans, who disdain their carefree attitude about life. The colonists haven't figured out what's in store for them yet. Until they do, let's enjoy the wedding. Hey, everyone in the group of colonists, come on out here and take your places. (*Enthusiastic colonists enter from stage right with ribbons and flowers to dress the*

Maypole, rejoicing in the day and dancing. Edith places a vine wreath around the neck of the human Maypole so that it sits on his shoulders, and the colonists thread their ribbons through it. She then places a wreath of roses in the hand of the Maypole.) Priest, are you ready? *(There is no answer. He rolls his eyes at the audience.)* Excuse me. *(He speaks more loudly.)* I said, Priest, are you ready?

Priest: *(He rushes in from stage right.)* Okay, okay. I was looking for my vine leaves. *(He takes his place to the left of the Maypole. Edgar and Edith are standing together on the right, while the colonists form a semi-circle around the Maypole. The priest speaks in a dramatic tone.)* Votaries of the Maypole! *(He walks around the circle greeting them and taking their flowers to lay them at the feet of the Maypole.)* Merrily, all day long have the woods echoed to your mirth. But be this your merriest hour, my hearts! Lo, here stand the Lord and Lady of the May, whom I, a clerk of Oxford, and high priest of Merry Mount, am presently to join in holy matrimony. Up with your nimble spirits, ye Morris dancers, green men and glee maidens, bears and wolves, and horned gentlemen! *(Several colonists mimic these creatures, some in costume.)* Come, a chorus now, rich with the old mirth of Merry England, and the wilder glee of this fresh forest; and then a dance, to show the youthful pair what life is made of. All ye that love the Maypole, lend your voices to the nuptial song of the Lord and Lady of the May! *(There is riotous uproar from the costumed colonists.)*

A Young Man: Begin you the song, reverend sir!

A Young Woman: Never did the woods ring to such a merry peal as we of the Maypole shall send up! *(Music begins to play: pipe, cithern, and viol. Colonists begin dancing around the Maypole. When they finish their dance, they clap and laugh and move back to their original places, turning to one another in happy conversation.)*

Edgar: *(He is smiling and happy, until he glances at Edith, his gloomy bride. He leaves his place among his fellow merrymakers and walks down right to be with her, taking her hands.)* Edith, sweet Lady of the May, is yon wreath of roses a garland to hang above our graves that you look so sad? O, Edith, this is our golden time! Tarnish it not by any pensive shadow of the mind; for it may be that nothing of futurity will be brighter than the mere remembrance of what is now passing.

Edith: *(She speaks in a low tone.)* That was the very thought that saddened me! How came it in your mind, too? Therefore do I sigh amid this festive music. And besides, dear Edgar, I struggle as with a dream, and fancy that these shapes of our jovial friends are visionary, and their mirth unreal, and that we are no true Lord and Lady of the May. What is the mystery in my heart? *(Edgar puts his arms around her in comfort as everyone freezes.)*

Stage Manager: *(He moves to the Maypole.)* The roses on the Maypole are beginning to wither now. Time is running out for the colonists. The light is growing dimmer, and the Puritans who have been watching secretly from the edge of the forest are preparing to destroy their colony, starting with the Maypole. Try to imagine a time around dusk. Well, in the lead is John Endicott, who makes his way to the center of the circle. You've probably heard about him from history—the Puritan of Puritans. His followers mingle around the merrymakers. (*The Puritans have been gathering behind the trees upstage and quickly surround the colonists.*)

Endicott: Stand off, priest of Baal! I know thee, Blackstone! (*He pulls out his sword and moves toward the priest.*) Thou art the man who couldst not abide the rule even of thine own corrupted church and hast come hither to preach iniquity and to give example of it in thy life. But now shall it be seen that the Lord hath sanctified this wilderness for his peculiar people. Woe unto them that would defile it! And first, for this flower-decked abomination, the altar of this worship! (*Endicott takes his sword and pretends to cut down the human Maypole. It sways and then tumbles to the ground. The stage becomes darker.*) There! There lies the only Maypole in New England! There also falls the fate of idle mirthmakers. Amen!

Puritans: Amen!

Palfrey: (*He seems to be second in command as he steps up to receive orders.*) Valiant captain, what order shall be taken with the prisoners?

Endicott: I thought not to repent me of cutting down a Maypole, yet now I could find in my heart to plant it again and give each of these pagans one other dance around their idol. It would have served rarely for a whipping post!

Palfrey: But there are pine trees enough!

Endicott: True, good Ancient. Wherefore, bind the heathen crew and bestow on them a small matter of stripes apiece, as earnest of our future justice. (*The Puritan followers take hold of the colonists, preparing to march them to their settlement.*) Set some of the rogues in the stocks to rest themselves. Further penalties, such as branding and cropping of ears, shall be thought of hereafter.

Palfrey: How many stripes for the priest?

Endicott: None as yet. It must be for the Great and General Court to determine whether stripes and long imprisonment and other grievous penalty may atone for his transgressions. Let him look to himself! For such as violate our civil order, it may be permitted us to show mercy. But woe to the wretch that troubleth our religion!

Palfrey: Here be a couple of shining ones. (*He points to Edith and Edgar, who draw closer to*

he reached the cathedral allegedly housing the remains of St. James. Coelho later wrote of his spiritual awakening in *The Pilgrimage*. *The Alchemist* has been translated into fifty-six languages and continues to be sought after for its spiritual depth. The wisdom that he passes on to his readers through this book may be part of the solution to leaving humankind a world more closely aligned to benevolence rather than betrayal. Read the wisdom of the alchemist and determine the effect these statements could have on the characters' actions in other pieces of literature you have read.

Here is the wisdom passed on from the Alchemist to Santiago:

"When a person really desires something, all the universe conspires to help that person to realize his dream" (114).

"Remember that wherever your heart is, there you will find your treasure" (116).

"Well, then, why should I listen to my heart?"
"Because you will never again be able to keep it quiet. Even if you pretend not to have heard what it tells you, it will always be there inside you, repeating to you what you're thinking about life and about the world" (129).

"People are afraid to pursue their most important dreams, because they feel that they don't deserve them, or that they'll be unable to achieve them" (130).

"There is only one thing that makes a dream impossible to achieve: the fear of failure" (141).

"When you are loved, you can do anything in creation. When you are loved, there's no need at all to understand what's happening, because everything happens within you, and even men can turn themselves into the wind" (147).

Santiago tells the sun: "That's what alchemists do. They show that, when we strive to become better than we are, everything around us becomes better, too...
Love is the force that transforms and improves the Soul of the World...when we love, we always strive to become better than we are" (150-1).

Santiago: "The Alchemist said, 'No matter what he does, every person on earth plays a central role in the history of the world. And normally he doesn't know it'" (158-9).

STUDY GUIDE QUESTIONS
● ● ● ● ●

All of the readings listed, both fiction and nonfiction, revolve around the tension found between the themes of benevolence—often turning into feelings of *esprit de corps*—and betrayal. Also included are questions that, as you read, can help you focus and think

Journal Prompt: At the begining of his book, Robert Cormier quotes Gustave Flaubert's *Madame Bovary*: "Human language is like a cracked kettle on which we beat out tunes for bears to dance to, when all the time we are longing to move the stars to pity" (242). Prior to this statement, he writes, "Whereas the truth is that fullness of soul can sometimes overflow in utter vapidity of language, for none of us can ever express the exact measure of his needs or his thoughts or his sorrow..." (242).What do you think Flaubert means? Why did Cormier choose part of the quotation for his title?

Paulo Coelho's *The Alchemist*: A Wisdom Tradition

• • • • •

Because the written word is a reflection of the stories that express human thought and behavior, what demands consideration is the wisdom of how we can cope as we deal with the darker side of our stories. In *Creating a Life*, Jungian analyst and scholar James Hollis writes,

> We make our choices through *hamartia*, a wounded vision…Hence the paradox of the tragic vision is our common condition; namely, we have made choices for which we are responsible, choices which have hurt ourselves and others, and yet we did not know we were making flawed choices at the time we made them (17).

Despite our wounded vision, Hollis adds that, "Consciousness is the gift, and that is the best it gets" (19). Perhaps the solution is in understanding what lies beneath our pain and suffering. Having this wounded vision as well as a consciousness of the condition can help us to discover how we may find harmony in ourselves and with others.

Paulo Coelho is one writer who offers that kind of wisdom through fiction. His novel *The Alchemist* takes place in Andalusia, Spain. A young man named Santiago leaves behind the world of the university seminary, where his father wants him to become a Catholic priest, to take on the life of a shepherd, traveling and exploring the world with his sheep. On his journey he meets a Gypsy woman, a wise old man who claims he is the king of Salem, and an alchemist, who give him advice that eventually leads him to the treasure he seeks.

Coelho, author of *The Alchemist*, lives in Rio de Janeiro, Brazil. After walking the Road of Santiago de Compostela in northwestern Spain over five hundred miles on a pilgrimage,

each other.) They seem to be of high station among these misdoers. Methinks their dignity will not be fitted with less than a double share of stripes.

(*Endicott rests his hand on his sword and closely surveys the couple. Edgar and Edith are downcast and apprehensive, yet they hold on to each other with mutual support and affection. Edgar puts his arm around Edith, who rests her head against his shoulder. They gaze at each other and then at Endicott.*)

Endicott: Youth, ye stand in an evil case, thou and thy maiden wife. Make ready presently, for I am minded that ye shall both have a token to remember your wedding day!

Edgar: (*He bends in supplication on one knee.*) Stern man, how can I move thee? Were the means at hand, I would resist to the death. Being powerless, I entreat! Do with me as thou wilt, but let Edith go untouched!

Endicott: Not so! We are not wont to show an idle courtesy to that sex which requireth the stricter discipline. What sayest thou, maid? Shall thy silken bridegroom suffer thy share of the penalty, besides his own?

Edith: Be it death, and lay it all on me!

(*Endicott is silent for a moment then softens his face and tone. He takes Palfrey aside to speak to him.*)

Endicott: The troubles of life have come hastily on this young couple. We will see how they comport themselves under their present trials ere we burden them with greater. If, among the spoil, there be any garments of a more decent fashion, let them be put upon this May Lord and his Lady, instead of their glistening vanities. Look to it, one of you. (*One or two Puritans exit left.*)

Palfrey: And shall not the youth's hair be cut?

Endicott: Crop it forthwith, and that in the true pumpkin shell fashion. Then bring them along with us but more gently than their fellows. There be qualities in the youth which may make him valiant to fight and sober to toil and pious to pray, and in the maiden, that may fit her to become a mother in our Israel, bringing up babes in better nurture than her own hath been. (*Puritans escort colonists off left. Palfrey takes the Priest. The Puritan leading Edgar and Edith stops as Endicott crosses to him, motioning him to go on alone. As Endicott passes the stricken Maypole, he stops, pauses to think, and then lifts up the wreath of flowers. He slowly turns to face the couple, walks over to them, and places the wreath over their heads before exiting quickly.*)

Stage Manager: (*Addressing the audience, he has stepped over the imaginary line into the play.*) Nor think ye, young ones, that they are the happiest, even in our lifetime of a moment, who misspend it in dancing around a Maypole. (*He helps the Maypole stand back up as the lights dim.*)

HAWTHORNE: A LIFE OF ISOLATION, REJECTION, MYSTERY, AND JOY
• • • • •

Hawthorne combined his strong interest in the seventeenth-century Puritans in New England and the popular cultural exemplary heroine of his own day to produce stories of redemption. At the same time, he wove his own personal autobiographical threads into his work. The rejection and isolation of *The Scarlet Letter's* Hester Prynne, for example, mirrors his own family and political rejection as well as the isolation in which he lived from childhood to his meeting with the Peabodys. Hester's redemption is Hawthorne's redemption.

In July of 1848, more than three hundred people assembled in Seneca Falls, New York, to rally for suffrage, equal pay, and a woman's right to divorce and own property. In June of 1849, with Zachary Taylor, a Whig, in the presidency, Hawthorne was fired from his position in the Custom House. He returned to Salem defeated only to contend with the death of his mother shortly afterward. The sorrow and shame of his own life, complicated by the sorrow and shame of the predicament of his society's women, he poured into characters like Hester Prynne. Hawthorne wrote darkly of the evil in the human heart (Reynolds 250).

Nathaniel Hawthorne's childhood was filled with isolation and rejection. His father, Nathaniel Hathorne, was a sea captain and the grandson of Judge John Hathorne who presided over the Salem witch trials of 1692 (Wineapple 15). His novel *The House of the Seven Gables* reflects an incident in which a curse on all Hathornes was inflicted on the family by an innocent woman that Judge Hathorne hanged for allegedly practicing witchcraft. Later in 1829 Hawthorne changed the spelling of his name to distance himself from this ancestor (Baym ix). Hawthorne's mother, Elizabeth Clarke Manning, was widowed with three children when Nathaniel was not quite four years old. The family lived with the Mannings in Salem until 1815 when Elizabeth Manning moved her family to the Manning property in Raymond, Maine. Hawthorne eventually attended Bowdoin College in Maine, making lifelong friends with Henry Wadsworth Longfellow and Franklin Pierce (Person 731). Longfellow would later become a celebrated poet and Pierce would become the nation's fourteenth president.

In 1813 Nathaniel injured his foot while playing ball at school, after which time he remained on crutches and the center of attention, even receiving tutoring at home. He spent his time reading and creating an inner world of dreaming, necessary for a boy who would become a writer of great imagination (Van Doren 10).

In 1816 Nathaniel returned to Salem to attend school, but by 1818 his family was back in Maine living in a house newly constructed by his uncle Robert Manning. By 1825 Hawthorne had graduated and returned to Salem, determined to become a writer. After having written numerous stories published singly in one magazine or another, Hawthorne's collection of *Twice-Told Tales* materialized, with less public enthusiasm than he had hoped for. Longfellow had written the review in the *North American Review,* and the two renewed the friendship that began at Bowdoin. As he began to consider his own state of loneliness as friends around him married, he wrote in a letter to Longfellow, " I seldom venture abroad till after dark…I have been carried apart from the main current of life, and find it impossible to get back again" (qtd. in Mellow 79).

Elizabeth Peabody received a copy of his *Twice-Told Tales* and by 1838 enclosed him in her circle, eventually introducing him to her sister Sophia. It was believed that Hawthorne and Elizabeth Peabody would marry, friendship being taken for courtship, but when he took a position at the Boston Custom House, he frequently called on Sophia who was visiting a friend and the romance began. Before they married, however, Hawthorne went to join the Brook Farm Institute of Agriculture and Education, an ideal community that would focus on both education and manual labor (Mellow 179-80). What Hawthorne realized after living in the commune was that he had neither the time nor the energy to write. After leaving Brook Farm, Sophia urged him to announce their engagement, which had gone on for almost three years, and in 1843 they were married and living in a house belonging to Emerson, the Old Manse, where they remained for three blissful years (Person 732).

When Hawthorne lost his job at the Salem Custom House and money was scarcer than ever, Fields offered to help him and print two thousand copies of anything he submitted. At first Hawthorne told him he had nothing, but he then handed Fields a partial manuscript of *The Scarlet Letter.* Ticknor and Fields published the book on March 16, 1850, resulting in good reviews by the critics and a reputation as an established writer. This fame, however, did not bring fortune. Although the Hawthornes were not penniless, they still lived meagerly. The publication of *The Scarlet Letter* had improved their finances, and Hawthorne began working on another book, *The House of the Seven Gables.* The Hawthornes moved about from town to town every three or four years. Ticknor and Fields continued publishing Hawthorne's stories, finding a popular and lucrative market for his retelling of classic myths for children in *A Wonder Book for Girls and Boys* (Wineapple 229).

On March 26, 1853, Hawthorne learned of his appointment by his old friend President Franklin Pierce as United States consul in Liverpool, England. Hawthorne had hopes that this new position would enable him to save enough money to return home and write unencumbered with financial troubles. Before returning to America, however, the family spent a year and a half in Italy and returned to London on June 23, 1859, with a new manuscript, *The Marble Faun,* a romance set in Rome.

On April 13, 1861, when the war between the North and the South began, Hawthorne gradually put away his writing of stories. His love/hate relationship with his country made him want to escape. He began to write essays, which Fields published in the *Atlantic,* but no more novels were to be published again. Death was everywhere. He did not know how the war was to turn out, and he was not to know, for he died the year before it ended.

Hawthorne had been suffering from several illnesses but still he asked his dearest friend Franklin Pierce to accompany him on a leisurely trip through Boston and on to New Hampshire. On May 18, 1864, the two stopped in Portsmouth to rest overnight. It was early in the morning when Pierce looked in on Hawthorne and found him dead. As soon as possible the news was taken to Sophia at the Wayside, their home in Concord. Sophia knew he had gone away to die (Mellow 577).

Sophia Peabody was Hawthorne's greatest admirer. She wrote, "I never dared to gaze at him, even I, unless his lids were down. It seemed an invasion into a holy place. To the last he was a measure to me a divine Mystery, for he was so to himself" (qtd. in Wineapple 380).

Although most of Hawthorne's contemporaries had difficulty praising the enigmatic author as a person separate from his writing, poet James Russell Lowell said, "I don't think people have any kind of notion yet what a Master he was, God rest his soul. Shakespeare, I am sure, was glad to see him on the other side" (qtd. in Wineapple 379).

THE MAYPOLE, PAST AND PRESENT
● ● ● ● ●

Dancing around the English Maypole on May Day, a great festive occasion that celebrated the coming of spring, was not a tradition in Hawthorne's New England, nor did it begin in England. Originally the pole was the sacred pine of Attis, which was carried to the Greek temple of Cybele, a mother goddess of fertility. It was Hesiod, the eighth century BC poet, who wrote of the origins of the gods, including Cybele, offspring of Zeus, who fell in love with Attis, a young man of remarkable beauty. Cybele made Attis promise that he would be forever chaste and faithful to her, but when he met and fell in love with a nymph named Sagaritis, he broke his pledge to Cybele. When she discovered his infidelity, Cybele killed Sagaritis and Attis became insane, mutilating himself. Some say that violets grew from his blood and Cybele changed him into a pine tree. Worship of Cybele was wild with dancing, singing, and uncontrollable merrymaking around the pine of Attis (Carpenter and Gula, 106-7). The entire ceremony was symbolic of renewed life, fertility, and spring. Later the Romans transported this celebration to Britain from a religious cult that had been assimilated into their culture from Anatolia, modern Turkey (Littleton 145). The rebirth of Atys (Attis) led to a celebration of the new year with dancing and occasionally blood sacrifice. A happier celebration continues to this day as May Day festivities without, however, riotous celebrating or loss of blood.

In medieval times in England, villagers met before dawn to go to the nearby woods and chop down a tall, thin pine, which they hauled in triumphant procession to the center of the town. Here they transformed this tree of Attis into a Maypole gaily decorated with ribbons the colors of the rainbow and with wreaths of flowers. Merrymaking and dancing went on all day. A May Queen presided over the crowd of masked and costumed villagers, while the Lord of Misrule insured the topsy-turvy atmosphere of the day with his pranks. This innocent May Day celebration sometimes became wild and raucous, causing the Puritans to ban the festivities in 1664. When Oliver Cromwell died and the English throne was restored to the Stuarts with the coronation of Charles II, merrymaking around the Maypole was restored as well.

In the following pages you will see steps for a traditional Maypole dance. This dance is part of the play based on the Hawthorne story, "The Maypole of Merry Mount," which is also included here. Although this story is set in 1625 in the Massachusetts Bay Colony, the celebration of the Maypole seems to have quickly died out. The powerful, authoritarian Puritans who settled in Massachusetts at that time made sure of that. Today, however, we will travel back in time to relive part of that celebration of new life as we begin our journey with the writings of Nathaniel Hawthorne.

TREE SYMBOLISM
• • • • •

How often have you read books and poems and stories, or seen movies in which a tree contributed to the setting, perhaps in some small way or even as an indispensable part of the plot? Most people never pause to analyze the tree's symbolic presence, and why should they? The pure pleasure that the beauty of the written or spoken words affords seems complete, satisfactory in itself. Psychologist Carl Jung tells us that the image goes deeper than that, however. He believed that the symbolism of a tree is basic to the mind, which knows on the unconscious level that this tree expresses some aspect of life and truth for each individual person (*Basic Writings*, 301).

Symbol scholar J.C. Cooper points to the central nature of symbolism in our lives in the introduction to *An Illustrated Encyclopaedia of Traditional Symbols*, a major resource on the subject of symbols in world mythology:

> As the Tree of Life, axial, unifying and either evergreen or perpetually renewed,
> stands at the center of Paradise and the spring at its roots gives rise to the Rivers
> of Life, so man's thought and aspiration, embodied in the myth and symbol,
> center on unity and life. (8)

In a study of Nathaniel Hawthorne's works, symbols play a critical role in increasing students' ability to understand literature in a deeper way and thereby participate in the satisfaction of the spirit. As the Transcendentalists and the English Romantic poets espoused, we know many things through intuition. Just as they put faith in their feelings, what we sometimes refer to as hunches, or gut feelings, we often obtain knowledge through a sense other than a physical one. Jungian psychology tells us that what may be at the heart of this knowledge is information genetically encoded in our collective unconscious, symbolic information we are born knowing (Hyde and McGuinness 59).

To learn more about tree symbolism, research one particular myth and produce a reflective piece of art. Below you will find topics and ideas from which to choose, but you might find it more challenging to combine similar topics related to tree mythology.

As you progress through the study of literature outlined in this book, your knowledge of symbolism will take you to higher levels of understanding and appreciation of not only the works examined here, but also of subsequent works of literature that you may read, whether for pleasure or academic study.

The Tree: A Symbol for All Cultures

It is easy to find information regarding the symbolic nature of trees and their significance to the beliefs or rituals of any culture you can name. The tree was a part of every culture's mythology, and strong evidence abounds in the literature and artwork that humanity has inherited. Even today in literature, writers use trees not just for description but also as integral parts of the story—in every story element, even as characters. The symbolism is not accidental or incidental. Writers include trees in their stories because they are ancient, time-proven symbols that carry strong meaning with their use.

Research one of the topics listed below and choose from a variety of art media for your project. Limit the size of your artwork, including sculpted pieces, to about eight by eleven inches.

Tree topics:
Tree as *imago mundi*
Tree as *axis mundi*
Tree as *omphalos* (world center, navel)
Tree as feminine principle (Great Mother)
Evergreen tree
Deciduous tree
Cosmic tree
Tree of life
> Taoist, Buddhist
> Iranian Haoma tree
> Hindu, Sumerian, Chinese, Japanese paradises with trees of precious stones
> Japanese Sa-ka-ti, Bonsai
> Mexico—Cosmic tree, agave, milk-yielding cactus with falcon
> Scandinavian—Yggdrasil ash
> Taoist peach, intertwining boughs signifying yin and yang
Tree of knowledge
> The vine and the tree of Attis (Dionysos)
> Hindu—Vishnu cuts down with his axe
Dying god on a tree
Inverted tree—magic tree
Tree of Light (heavenly tree)
> Buddhist tree at feasts of the dead
> Christmas tree
Teutonic fir tree of Woden—became Christmas tree
Sacred bird in the tree branches
Tree of Sweet Dew, or Singing Tree (Sacred Mountain) as world axis
Serpent or dragon guarding a tree
Temptation of man
Tree, stone, and altar together—microcosm

Trees as oracles
Oak of Dodona
Burning bush of Moses
Tree climbing—passage to another plane
Shamanism and myth: climbing plants or poles by which one can reach another world
Arabic: The Zodiac (fruit tree of twelve branches)
Australian aboriginal—The World Tree
Buddhist: Pipal or Bo Tree under which Buddha attained enlightenment (Sacred Center)
Great Wisdom Tree
Celtic: oak, beech, hazel, ash, yew, Druid oak, and mistletoe
Willow tree
Irish holly and yew
Gaelic rowan
Chinese peach, mulberry, plum
Formosa bamboo
The Year Tree (sun and darkness)
Cross of Christ—Tree of Knowledge as cross
Egyptian sycamore
Greek/Roman oak, palm, walnut, myrtle
Hebrew—the Tree of God
Hindu—Cosmos tree
Two trees superimposed—celestial and terrestrial
Islamic—the Tree of Blessing; spiritual blessing and illumination, light of Allah
Celestial Tree at the center of Paradise from which flow four rivers: water, milk, honey, wine

The Tree as *Imago Mundi*

It is not by mere chance that the concept of a tree can be found as a central image in many pieces of writing. Scholars who have studied world mythology explain that the connection is a natural one. Since the beginning of time humans have incorporated the tree in their religious beliefs, which offered explanations for the elements of their lives. The tree, a central figure or setting in much of literature, is sometimes referred to as the *imago mundi* (image of the world) or the *axis mundi* (center point of time and space). Important events revolve around a particular tree. When we discuss the life/death/rebirth archetype, we are reminded of the deciduous tree that regenerates itself through the progression of the seasons. Stories that parallel the seasons and the rebirth archetypes also follow a structure of ascending through life and descending into death, rising up again in rebirth. In Christian mythology, we speak of the Tree of Knowledge and the Tree of Life, and we refer to the cross as the tree on which Christ was crucified. Birds, which live in and are associated with trees, are symbolic of the soul.

"THE MAYPOLE OF MERRY MOUNT"
READING ASSISTANCE

• • • • •

You have become familiar with Hawthorne's style through the dramatic adaptation of "The Maypole of Merry Mount." You are now ready to read the short story. Study the guide below as you read in order to assist your understanding and enjoyment of a Hawthorne story that will teach you some valuable literary skills.

- Verdure: greenness, fresh green of growing things
- Mirthful: merry, jovial, festive
- Reveling: making merry, delighting in
- Venerated: looked upon with great respect, reverence
- Husbandry: farming, good management
- Fauns: rural deities in Roman mythology; human with a goat's tail, horns, cloven feet, and pointed ears
- Nymphs: in Greek and Roman mythology, beautiful maidens living in rivers, mountains, trees
- Gothic: mysterious
- Comely: handsome, good-looking
- Visage: appearance, face
- Similitude: image, form, likeness, resemblance
- Pendulous: hanging freely, loosely
- Heraldry: coats of arms
- Wampum (*wampumpeag*): small beads of shell used by North American Indians as money
- Soberer: more serious
- Revelry: boisterous merrymaking, noisy festivity
- Melancholy: sad
- Ensign: badge, symbol, flag
- Canonically: in a manner agreeable to the Bible
- Votaries: persons devoted to any pursuit
- Nimble: alert, quick-witted
- Cithern: stringed musical instrument of the sixteenth century (like a guitar)
- Viol: early violin (forerunner)
- Mummers: masked and costumed people, actors
- Discountenanced: shamed, frowned upon
- Triflers: people who engage in making light of or playing with something
- Veneration: feeling of deep respect
- Conclave: private meeting; close assembly
- Reprobate: corrupt, wicked, unprincipled person
- Precincts: boundaries, any limited area
- Magistrates: officials who enforce the law
- Scapegoat: person who bears the blame, even though he may be innocent; goat over whom a high priest confessed sins and who was then allowed to escape

- Edification: spiritual or moral improvement, establishment
- Pious: devout, religious
- Perplexed: puzzled, teased, bothered
- Affirmed: asserted, declared, pronounced
- Jurisdiction: power or right of exercising authority
- Clime: climate, tract, or region
- Posterity: succeeding generations, future
- Nuptials: marriage vows

ARCHETYPES IN HAWTHORNE'S
"THE MAYPOLE OF MERRY MOUNT"
• • • • •

Can you identify these archetypes and motifs in Hawthorne's story?

> The **archetypal woman**: the soulmate, princess, or "beautiful lady"

> **Immortality**: return to paradise; state of perfect, timeless bliss; the Golden Age—the legendary age of perfect human happiness and innocence (The age of Socrates and Plato is sometimes called the Golden Age.)

> **Life/death/life**: Life and death go together to create a balance and cannot be separated. The seasons exemplify cyclical time and therefore the cycle of life. Various tales and plays of Greek and Roman poets are responsible for the sources of mythology from which many archetypes evolved. One important source of this particular motif of life and rebirth comes from the story of Demeter. She was the goddess of seasons, the bringer of good gifts to humankind. With the powerful king of gods, Zeus, she had a child named Persephone. In secret, Zeus promised the hand of his daughter to his brother Hades, god of the underworld. One day when Persephone was picking flowers in the field, one particular flower lured her, and when she came close to it, the earth opened up and she fell into the arms and chariot of Hades. Unhappiness followed for both Persephone and Demeter. When Demeter discovered what Zeus and Hades had done, she vowed that the earth would bring forth no crops and humans would die unless her daughter was returned. Zeus finally sent Hermes to work out a compromise with Hades, who did agree to give her up but not until he had tricked Persephone into eating the seeds of the pomegranate, the fruit of the Underworld. She could now never be truly free. Persephone would spend one third of each year with Hades and two thirds of the year with her mother on earth. Thus, the seasons were created: a fruitless season and a season of abundance. With spring comes rebirth. The natural progression from the fullness of summer to harvest and then to the winter of barren fields and waiting finally brings the earth round to spring again, and the cycle continues.

Spring: This season is the birth phase, when light defeats the powers of darkness. This season also typifies the archetype of romance, or love motif.

Summer: This season represents the maturing of spring growth. It is associated with marriage, deep shades of green, the triumph phase, and entering into paradise.

Autumn: The phase of death and darkness gradually overshadows the light of summer. It is the archetype of tragedy.

Winter: Death has defeated life, and a period of darkness, chaos, and waiting for spring ensues.

➤ The **love motif** follows the life/death/rebirth pattern in both literature and life:
Stage one: One discovers the spiritual treasure of another person who becomes his or her heart's desire.

Stage two: The chase and hiding begin in an environment of hope and fear of loss.

Stage three: The lovers/friends must face problems and untangle the fragile life/death/life aspects of the relationship. This stage presents a choice, a turning point. Will the characters learn to solve stage three problems and move forward, or will their relationship die at this stage?

Stage four: The characters heal each other's wounds and learn how to trust and share.

Stage five: The characters recognize the stages and have the ability to move easily between stages three and four, healing each other, creating a harmonious life for each other.

➤ **Sacrifice**: The character makes a sacrifice that comes at great personal cost. In ancient literature, the character sacrifices to or for a god. In modern literature, the character sacrifices for a concept such as love, honor, charity, or humanity's sake.

➤ **The Shadow**: Carl Jung's term for the darker side of our unconscious self (*Basic Writings*, 316-19)

➤ **Anima**: Jung's term for the internal feminine energy in males (the passive *yin*, the feminine cosmic principle in Chinese philosophy): feminine qualities in a male that might make him nurturing, for example

> **Animus**: Jung's term for the internal masculine energy in females (the active *yang*, the male cosmic principle in Chinese philosophy): masculine qualities in a female that might give her strong leadership traits, for example (*Memories, Dreams, Reflections*, 187)

> **Persona**: the actor's mask that we show to the world, our social personality that we "wear," depending on whom we are with (*Basic Writings*, 316)

> **Tree**: life

> **Animals**
> Bear: resurrection and new life (coming out of its winter hibernation into the spring, symbol of bravery and strength; dual symbolism—evil, greed
> Wolf: dual symbol—fierceness, evil, and death on the one hand but also nurture (a wolf nurtured Romulus and Remus as depicted in Roman mythology) and valor
> Goat: masculinity, abundant vitality, superiority, light and life; dual symbol—the devil, horns, fire
> Stag: light and life (antlers/tree branches), associated with the Tree of Life, conflict of opposites—victory of good over evil

> **Number seven**: the number of the universe, of completeness; comprised of the numbers four (the number of humankind—four limbs) and three (the number of God or most perfect balance)

> **Colors**
> Green: growth, life
> Black: darkness, unknown, death, dual symbol of mourning and evil
> Rainbow: bridge between heaven and earth (seven colors—connection between three [God] and four [humankind])
> Purple: connection to blood—royalty and sacrifice
> Gold, golden, gilded: immortality, sun—masculine principle, great wealth

> **Circle, wreath**: life, totality, completeness, wholeness, recurrence

> **Eyes**: windows to the soul, all-seeing, intuition, enlightenment and knowledge

> **Hair**: strength, power, energy

LITERARY TOOLS FROM
FREUD AND JUNG

• • • • •

Sigmund **Freud** was an Austrian neurologist and founder of psychoanalysis. He is often called the father of modern psychology. Born in Moravia, in the Austrian Empire, which is now the Czech Republic, on May 6, 1865, he entered the University of Vienna in 1873 and received his degree in 1881. In 1885 he went to Paris to study mental disorders and was introduced to the idea that these disorders may be psychological. He became interested in the unconscious and neuroses and in psychosexual development, for which he developed theories. In *The Interpretation of Dreams*, he analyzes the literary characters Oedipus from Sophocles' *Oedipus the King* and Hamlet from Shakespeare's *Hamlet*. Freudian literary criticism uses psychoanalytic theory to interpret an author's work or to examine the work and construct the author's psychic life. He died September 23, 1939, in London. A well-known reference to Freud is the Freudian slip: a verbal slip that is caused by an unconscious belief, thought, or emotion.

Freud's psychic zones **id, ego**, and **superego** can be a useful tool (Guerin 120-2) as we examine in greater depth the motivations and needs that make the characters in literature behave as they do. Read the explanations below and ask yourself as you read a story, "In which zone is this character behaving? What words and actions place the character on this level?"

The Id
- Is lawless, asocial, amoral
- Functions to gratify instincts for pleasure without regard to right or wrong
- Would go to any length to satisfy its desire for pleasure
- Is not concerned with safety or well-being of others
- Has untamed passions

The Ego
- Is a regulating agent that protects the individual
- Regulates the instinctive drive of the id and its dangerous potential
- Functions in reality; attempts to maintain balance between id and superego
- Is part conscious and part unconscious

The Superego
- Is a regulating, moral censoring agent that protects society
- Is a repository of conscience and pride
- Functions to restrict morals
- Seeks perfection and represses the behavior of the id
- Often creates a sense of guilt
- Wants us to be angels

Carl Jung was a Swiss psychologist and psychiatrist whose theories were the basis of a form of literary criticism known as archetypal criticism. His work has been influential in psychiatry and in the study of religion, literature, and related fields. Born on July 26, 1875, he became a student at the Universities of Basel and Zurich, receiving an M.D. in 1902. From 1907 to 1912, Jung was Sigmund Freud's close collaborator, but he broke with Freud largely over the latter's insistence on the sexual bases of neurosis. Jung differentiated two types of people according to attitude: **extroverted** and **introverted** (*Basic Writings* 252, 269). Later he recognized four functions of the mind—thinking, feeling, sensation, and intuition, one or more of which predominate in any given person. His work in this area became the basis of modern studies of personality profiles. In an attempt to explain the source of images in dreams and fantasies, he developed the theory of the **collective unconscious** (*Basic Writings* 299-300), which states that all human beings, regardless of culture or time, recognize and understand the same images because these symbols have been genetically encoded. In Jung's terms, **archetypes** (*Basic Writings* 299) are instinctive patterns of image and behavior that have a universal character. You will often see these symbols and patterns called **archetypal symbols** and **archetypal motifs**.

According to Jung, the ego is the center of the conscious personality. He called the totality of the conscious and the unconscious the **Self** (*Basic Writings* 151). Many writers have identified the Self in a variety of ways, describing it as the concept of wholeness, the union of opposites, the bridge between man and God, the axis of the universe, the elixir of life, self-ordering chaos, and the God within. Jung believed that the first half of life is spent separating the ego from the Self and the second half of life is devoted to reuniting with the Self. Humans who experience inflated egos, he wrote, would identify with God in a destructive way. Humans who experience a severe separation from God experience alienation, as if lost in a wilderness (Edinger 11). A balance in the ego-Self relationship, a theme which runs through Hawthorne's work like an iron rod, is the way to a happy life.

Jung also wrote of the myth of the fall from paradise as the birth of consciousness. He expressed that eating the forbidden fruit from the tree of knowledge of good and evil resulted in consciousness, or knowing. Humankind moved from paradise, the unconscious state, to banishment, the conscious state (Edinger 24). Other myths parallel this story: Prometheus being punished for stealing fire from Zeus, for example. Humans in the conscious ego state are in a continuous struggle for perfect balance, which Jung called individuation.

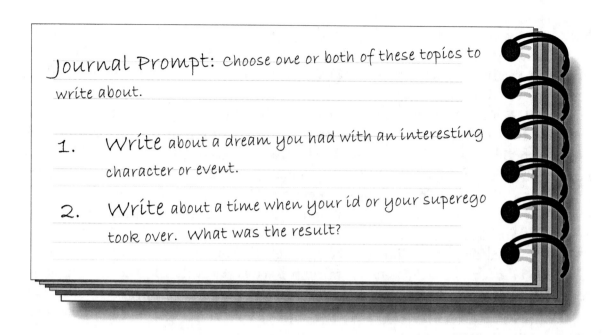

Journal Prompt: Choose one or both of these topics to write about.

1. Write about a dream you had with an interesting character or event.

2. Write about a time when your id or your superego took over. What was the result?

THE PEASCODS, A MAYPOLE DANCE

• • • • •

"The Peascods" is a typical seventeenth-century English dance and, because it is easy to learn, I have suggested this one for the play "The Maypole of Merry Mount." A good size group for this dance is eight to ten people, paired off as partners. Stand in a circle around the Maypole, if you have one, and you will begin the dance by honoring your partner with a bow or a curtsy. I have found the most agreeable music for these steps, which is authentic for the time period, is "The Buffens," from the *Watkins Ale* collection performed by the Baltimore Consort.

Follow these eight-count steps:

1. **Stand in a circle. Bow and curtsy to your partner. (Listen to the introduction.)**

2. **Chasse right around the circle with your hands held up palm to palm, connecting each dancer in the circle. (8)**

3. **Individually turn right in a circle. (8)**

4. **Chasse left with hands palm to palm. (8)**

5. **Turn left in a circle. (8)**

6. **A's go to the center and chasse right, palm to palm, in a smaller circle. (8)**

7. A's go back and turn right. (8)

8. B's go to the center and chasse right, palm to palm. (8)

9. B's go back and turn right. (8)

10. A's go to the center and clap on 4, return on 8.

11. B's go to the center and clap on 4, return on 8.

12. Repeat 10 and 11.

13. Partners move side by side right, bow/curtsy on 4, return on 8.

14. Repeat to the left side of your partner, bow/curtsy on 4, return on 8.

15. Turn in a circle with your partner, palm to palm right. (8)

16. Turn in a circle with your partner, palm to palm left. (8)

17. Entire circle moves to the center, claps on 4, returns on 8.

18. Repeat 17.

19. Chasse right with hands palm to palm. (8)

20. Turn right. (8)

21. Chasse left palm to palm. (8)

22. Bow and curtsy to your partner.

Note: *Chasse* is a step in which the feet come together in a sideways gliding move.

"THE MAYPOLE OF MERRY MOUNT": PUTTING THOUGHTS ON PAPER
● ● ● ● ●

Now it's time to write about "The Maypole of Merry Mount." The images, ideas, and symbols in "The Maypole of Merry Mount" offer the writer many opportunities for response. As you read the ideas below, think about how and why you want to delve into a subject and analyze it. Which approach to analysis interests you most, and which topic do you feel most comfortable defending? Feel free to alter any of these topics to suit your own analytical style.

- Background: How do Hawthorne's philosophy—balance leads to happiness—and his historical background with the Puritans help to explain the tone of his writing?
- Form and Structure

   Figurative language: In Hawthorne's widespread use of imagery, the dominant metaphor is dancing, e.g., partners in the dance of life, dance around the Maypole. He uses oxymoron to support the antithesis in the story and personification to give life to the Maypole. Discuss how the author uses figurative language to enhance mood, sound, symbolism, or imagery. How does figurative language lend a poetic quality to Hawthorne's prose?

   Allegory: Discuss Hawthorne's use of antithesis, e.g., light and dark, jollity and gloom, in the story. What makes the story an allegory and how does Hawthorne's use of language—antithesis or figurative language for example—support the allegory?

   Irony: Examine the three kinds of irony in the story. Write about the dominant one, or give examples of all three and show how they support antithesis, which in turn supports the theme of balance in the story.

- Psychology: Discuss the relationship of Freud's id, ego, and superego to the theme of balance.

- Symbols and Archetypal Motifs: Discuss the life/death/life archetype in terms of both seasons and the characters and their actions.

Defend the widespread use of archetypes in the story. How do the symbols, which permeate the story, enhance the writing? Discuss the relationship of the allegory to the life/death/life motif in the story. Rebirth comes with the second chance that Endicott gives to Edith and Edgar. The story opens with a kind of paradise and ends with the fall from paradise, yet Hawthorne does not dismiss the reader without a sense of rebirth. Numbers, colors, animals, seasons, even the concept of love support antithesis, conflict, and allegory. How do all these elements work together to produce meaning?

Discuss the tree as the archetype of life in the story. Apply what you know about tree symbolism to this story.

How does the life/death/life archetype support the theme of balance?

How does Hawthorne combine the archetypes of immortality and the life/death/life cycle?

Discuss the archetype of the circle in Hawthorne's narrative.

Writing Reminders:

Use effective organization.

1. State your topic in one sentence that will be your assertion, or statement that claims an idea as true or existent.
2. Write an introduction, body, and conclusion. An effective introduction contains your assertion and gives necessary information that opens up the topic to the reader. The body contains all the reasons, facts, and details that support your assertion. It also contains quoted material with documentation (page numbers). Conclusions can bring your essay to a close in several ways:
   - They can summarize the way you have supported your assertion.
   - They can summarize and draw conclusions about your assertion.
   - They can summarize and make predictions about your assertion.
   - They can summarize and show a larger truth about your assertion.

Edit your paper, both as you write and after you finish the first draft. Time may not permit you to make all the changes you might need, and so it is beneficial to start with a quick outline of your ideas so you will not need to make major changes.

Proofread your paper for any errors, especially spelling and mechanics. Be aware of the following common errors: run-ons, fragments, misspelled words, comma errors (especially not placing a comma after long introductory phrases and clauses or not using commas between parts of a compound sentence), misusing quotation marks and underlining, or italics, and discussing the story in present tense.

Remember that the overall look of your paper is important, too. Write neatly in blue or black ink or type your paper in black ink with a standard font and size.

The Fantasticks:
A Study in Archetypes
• • • • •

One of the most popular plays of the twentieth century, Tom Jones and Harvey Schmidt's Off-Broadway musical *The Fantasticks* rallies around the motif of life/death/life, or rebirth, to bring a love story of innocence and change to the audience. Having engaged in an intensive study of "The Maypole of Merry Mount," let's take a short break from Hawthorne's stories and look at the work of two modern writers whose play has much in common with Hawthorne's work. Examine how they apply the classic motifs made famous by Plato, Homer, Hesiod, Ovid, Shakespeare, Hawthorne, and a host of other writers of renown.

In 1894, when he was twenty-four years old, Edmund Rostand, a French dramatist best known for the heroic comedy *Cyrano de Bergerac,* produced his first successful play, *Les Romanesques.* It was played with modest success by the Comedie Francaise, and diminished into obscurity until it was adapted into English in 1900 by George Fleming. In the early 1940s, the revered drama teacher, Iden Payne, who was Tom Jones's mentor at the University of Texas (Jones 3), used a scene from the English adaptation called "The Fantasticks" for his graduate students. After failed attempts to put this plot in a Western setting with feuding ranch families, much like *Romeo and Juliet*, director Tom Jones and artist Harvey Schmidt began collaborating as writers.

As Tom Jones was writing *The Fantasticks,* he acquired a book by Harley Granville-Barker called *On Dramatic Method*, which told how "Shakespeare achieved a dramatic effect using a unifying palette as well as a basic theme in each of his plays" (qtd. in Jones 10), such as images of darkness or moonlight. Jones decided to make images of vegetation and the seasons the unifying imagery of *The Fantasticks*. He also mimicked Shakespeare's use of rhymed verse, blank verse, and couplets, alongside the prose.

From Thornton Wilder's *Our Town* Jones borrowed the idea of a narrator. From Goldoni's *The Servant of Two Masters*, he obtained the idea of a platform stage where actors could sit on the sidelines when not actually performing. For the idea of the cardboard sun and moon, he looked to John Houseman's production of Shakespeare's *A Winter's Tale* with its "cold moon-like first act and its sun-drenched second" (Jones 11).

Jones and Schmidt, after borrowing symbols from the best literary works, capture the theme in the words of verse spoken by El Gallo:

> Who understands why Spring is born
> Out of Winter's laboring pain?
> Or why we all must die a bit
> Before we grow again. (106)

The playwrights use the images of the seasons and growing things—vegetation, to show the change from innocence to experience, but it is El Gallo "the rooster," the narrator capable of manipulating characters, audience, and the show, who awakens people from their dream-filled sleep to take the characters from the moonlit night to the sun-drenched day. He is the catalyst that allows the boy Matt and the girl Luisa to see life and love with wiser eyes. Our journey from innocence to experience reminds us that it is the seasons that move us and every other living thing on the planet along the path of that same life/death/life cycle. We are reborn out of innocence into maturity.

In our study of Hawthorne's "The Maypole of Merry Mount," you learned about many kinds of archetypal symbols and motifs, and in our introduction to Plato you became familiar with the allegory of the cave, the image of moving out of darkness and into light. You will now use your knowledge of these symbols to examine the symbols and theme of the musical *The Fantasticks*. The focusing question is how does the play embody the life/death/life archetype?

The archetypal symbols of the seasons, romance, the mask, the rooster, the hero, and the journey, as well as the metaphor of the dance and the use of antithesis, all contribute to the heightened emotion and imagery in the play.

Pre-writing Journal Prompt: Before you embark on an essay about the richness of the language, symbolism, and theme in *The Fantasticks*, think about your own experiences with the life/death/life archetype. Write about a romantic relationship you once had, or an incident that enabled you to go from innocence to experience. Perhaps you could just write about the changing of the seasons and the relationship to your life. In this journal entry, organize your thoughts, and when you gain a clear vision about the focus of a more formal analytical essay on the play, write a first draft in your journal

STORY #2: "DR. HEIDEGGER'S EXPERIMENT"
• • • • •

Hawthorne sets his story about Dr. Heidegger in his own time, the early to mid-1800s. The doctor's skeleton and mysterious black book reveal his previous dabbling in the darker side of medicine, and even the bust of Hippocrates in the doctor's study seems to whisper, "Forbear!" Still, he decides to engage in an experiment with four elderly acquaintances and a curious sample of water he has obtained from the famous fountain of youth. In short, this water returns youthfulness to whatever living thing it touches. To add complexity to his characters, Hawthorne gives each of the four guests a shady past with subsequent unhappy lives that makes all four eager for a second chance at youth. Dr. Heidegger is just as eager to give them that chance and to observe the results. In the end what the doctor learns from the experiment is that death is an essential part of life and avoidance of it not only negates the meaning of the second half of life but also prevents the completion of the cycle of life/death/ rebirth. The four guests in their chaotic exuberance and lack of self-control break the cut glass vase, spilling the water onto the floor. Upon seeing the withered rose again, a reminder of his love long ago, Dr. Heidegger comes to recognize the importance of appreciating each stage of life for what it offers. The guests' youthfulness dissipates, and the old guests push and shove each other as they rush out the door to look for more water, doomed to repeat the mistakes of their youth.

Using these symbols to decode Hawthorne's meaning will increase your enjoyment and appreciation of his stories. Become familiar with the symbols before you read "Dr. Heidegger's Experiment," and consider the questions that follow in order to understand how these symbols enhance the text. You will begin to notice that Hawthorne uses many of the same images in his stories. Finally, use the journal prompt to think and write about a symbol in your own life.

Symbols:

- The number four: human number—four limbs
- Oak: strength, power
- Skeleton: death, mortality
- Mirror (looking-glass): truth, reality
- Bust of Hippocrates: life, reminder of the Hippocratic oath taken by doctors who agree to save and preserve life
- Black as ebony: mystery, darkness
- Center: focal point, power
- Cut-glass: reflection, refraction, transparency, purity, fragility
- Sunshine: light, life, rebirth
- Fresh, new rose: life, mystery, secrecy, passion, love
- Withered, wrinkled, dried, gray, ashen: dying, death
- Water: life, purity
- Slumber: death and rebirth on awakening
- Violets: hidden virtue, beauty, modesty
- Bubbles: transparency, emptiness, transitory nature
- Shadows: darkness, hiding, opposite of light
- Daybreak: rebirth
- Diamonds: indestructibility, refraction, light
- Moonlike: phases of the moon indicate life/death/rebirth
- Father Time: mortality
- Dance, dancing: moving to the rhythm of the universe, imitation of life
- Broken glass: death, darkness
- Butterfly: immortality, soul, life/death/life
- Withered rose: death to life, secrecy, passion

Journal Prompt #1: Use the questions to help you construct a response in your journal. Focus on one or two of the ideas below.

1. Which symbols support the theme of balance? How does Hawthorne illustrate the life/death/life archetype? How does the antithesis of light and dark support the theme?

2. Why does Hawthorne use the image of dancing? How is this metaphor appropriate?

3. Why is the image of water, in various forms, significant to the story's elements, theme, and symbolism?

Journal Prompt #2: Most of the time we take mirrors for granted, but it isn't difficult to see them as both symbol and metaphor. Before you write, take a long look at yourself in a mirror. What do you see, literally and figuratively? Take a good look, think about what you see with your inward as well as your outward eye, and write a page or two.

STORY #3: "RAPPACCINI'S DAUGHTER"

During the nineteenth century, writers in Britain and America seemed enthralled with Greece and Italy, both ancient and contemporary. Nathaniel Hawthorne actually moved his family to Italy after completing his duties at the consulate in Liverpool. *The Marble Faun*

resulted from his intense interest in this setting, but one of his most well-known stories, "Rappaccini's Daughter," is also set in Italy in the town made famous by Shakespeare's *Romeo and Juliet*, Padua.

The story is about a young man named Giovanni Guasconti who comes to Padua to attend the university. From a woman who has a house adjacent to a garden, he takes a room with a window that overlooks this beautiful and strange garden. One day he sees a young woman as beautiful as the flowers she tends below him, and he finds a way to enter the place he deems a paradise.

As you begin to think about this setting and the brief introduction to two of the characters in an archetypal way, you will be able to predict many things about the plot of the story. The reason is this: If the story follows a universal symbolic pattern, it must conform to that structure with which you already have experience. The following general information about garden symbolism will strike a familiar chord.

The garden is a symbol of earthly and heavenly paradise, the primal condition of perfect and timeless bliss. In Christian mythology, the tree of knowledge stands in the center of the garden. Adam and Eve are sent out of the Garden of Eden after they disobey God.

A walled garden, entered only with effort through a small portal that is sometimes locked, symbolizes the difficulties and obstacles that must be overcome in order to reach a higher spiritual level. The enclosed garden also symbolizes the feminine, protective principle.

Literature and art often use a garden to represent the paradise that was lost. Renaissance gardening was understood as the ultimate expression of the cultivation of life itself.

The gardener, the creator of the garden, often symbolizes the creator. Sometimes a serpent hides or simply exists in the garden, foreshadowing the impending doom.

Chinese and Japanese gardens represent perfect reproductions of cosmic harmony, designed to have a beneficial influence on harmony. The desire for balance, yin and yang, may encourage a stroll in the garden, perhaps, and reflection upon the harmony between movement and stillness.

The archetypal beautiful woman frequently appears in fairy tales as Cinderella, Sleeping Beauty, Beauty at the side of her Beast, Repunzel, the miller's daughter in the Rumpelstiltskin tale, and a host of others. She has saint-like personality traits: She is pure and kind, clever and resourceful, friendly to animals as well as humankind. Her innocence and trustfulness make her vulnerable to wicked people who intend to overpower her and harm her and take advantage of her. In the archetypal motif, the beautiful woman succumbs to danger and ultimately her own harm. She endures sacrifice through imprisonment and containment in a variety of ways and places and spells that cast her into a death-like sleep. Her fate is sometimes to wander penniless without her family or home. She is, however, also rescued and sometimes she even escapes from her circumstances before realizing her fate. Often she finds respite in a cottage in a forest before more harm is inflicted upon her. Finally in many stories her savior, usually the prince, arrives to rescue her and to bestow upon her the treasure she deserves for being so good and brave.

Many elements in this cyclical life/death/life story are symbolic, from the forest to the kiss. The beautiful woman believes she lives a good life before she is plunged into a conflict that grows more intolerable until she symbolically dies. She subsequently experiences a rebirth after mental and physical pain and suffering.

In Hawthorne's "Rappaccini's Daughter," Giovanni meets the beautiful young woman Beatrice, for whom her father Dr. Rappaccini has created a protective walled garden that she cannot leave. What he does not think to include in this protective paradise is a man, a partner for this Eve, and when the young student Giovanni appears, he falls in love with Beatrice at first glance. Dr. Rappaccini's plan is thus fulfilled. Ironically, Rappaccini believes he has given to his daughter the gift of power, the poisonous breath he has transferred from flower garden to the woman who tends the garden, and yet it is the very thing that makes her most miserable and ultimately leads to her death. Beatrice proclaims her freedom before she leaves on her journey to another paradise. This brutal episode communicates a truth—an ancient way of causing the self to pay attention. A woman's meaningful life can be robbed from her unless she holds onto or retrieves her basic joy and worth. The story calls our attention to the traps and poisons that the archetypal woman must face. Beatrice craves love from other people, but in order to complete the balanced life/death/life motif in the story, she must drink the antidote to the poison, which, to the poisonous Beatrice, is ironically toxic. In the fairy tales the prince rushes in to save the beautiful lady. In "Rappaccini's Daughter" Beatrice saves herself. Only through death can she cast off the poison inflicted by her father and the venomous words of Giovanni and find her own paradise.

The love, sacrifice, and savior motifs add depth and consistency to the story and contribute to the archetypal lost paradise, but the author adds his own twists to give the story that unique Hawthorne style and also, as the reader comes to expect, the theme that it is balance in life that leads to happiness.

Again, take a look at the symbols and their universal meanings below and become familiar with them before you read "Rappaccini's Daughter." Then answer the questions that invite you to consider the symbols in the context of other literary devices, and finally, write about the symbols in your own life using the prompts given.

Symbols:

- Window: opportunity
- Marble fountain: strength in life
- Center: power
- Water: life
- Purple: sacrifice
- Serpent: temptation, evil, regeneration
- Vertumnus (God of changing seasons, of flowers and fruit): life/death/rebirth
- Black, gray: darkness, shadow, unknown
- Gloves: protection
- Mask: persona, hiding of a face
- Adam: first man
- Gems/jewels: hidden treasures of knowledge or truth
- Kiss: breath of life, token of peace and good will, contact with a holy object, betrayal

- Night: darkness, death
- Flower: feminine principle, innocence, fragility, paradise when in a garden
- Maiden: innocence
- Morning: rebirth, the dawn of a new day
- Wine, Lachryma Christi (an Italian wine meaning Christ's tears): sacrifice
- Wall: protection, separation
- Eye: window to the soul
- Chameleon: in Christian mythology, Satan in disguise
- Butterfly ("winged brightness"): soul, rebirth
- Gold: masculine principle, the sun, paradise
- Music: harmony, felicity
- Door, portal: hope, opportunity, passage
- Sphere, circle: life, cycle of life/death/rebirth
- Sunshine: light, life
- Shrub growing wild, forest: initiation and testing
- Path: journey
- Rubies: dignity, zeal, love, passion, longevity
- Dawn: rebirth
- Four: humankind
- Whiteness: purity, innocence, simplicity, redemption
- Mirror: truth, self-realization
- Spider/web: weaving one's destiny
- Heart: love, passion, wisdom of feeling, center of life
- Lightning flash: revelation, enlightenment
- Dark cloud: concealment, gloom
- Silver vial: feminine principle, healing waters

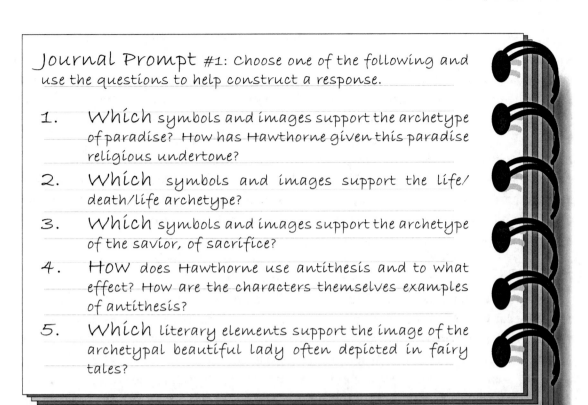

Journal Prompt #1: Choose one of the following and use the questions to help construct a response.

1. Which symbols and images support the archetype of paradise? How has Hawthorne given this paradise religious undertone?

2. Which symbols and images support the life/death/life archetype?

3. Which symbols and images support the archetype of the savior, of sacrifice?

4. How does Hawthorne use antithesis and to what effect? How are the characters themselves examples of antithesis?

5. Which literary elements support the image of the archetypal beautiful lady often depicted in fairy tales?

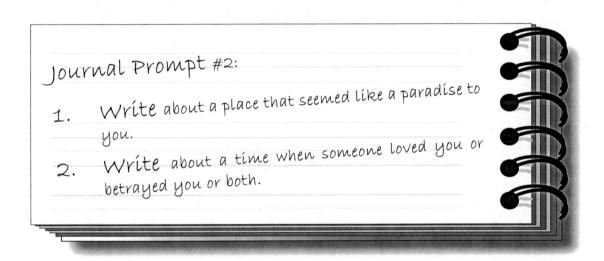

Journal Prompt #2:

1. Write about a place that seemed like a paradise to you.

2. Write about a time when someone loved you or betrayed you or both.

STORY #4: "THE MINISTER'S BLACK VEIL"

• • • • •

Hawthorne's character Reverend Hooper exemplifies Jung's shadow in the story "The Minister's Black Veil." Although Hawthorne wrote his story unaware of Carl Jung's explanation of that powerful dynamic that we take with us wherever we go, he perceived the idea of repressed guilt and fear that plagued humankind. Reverend Hooper embodies that idea, and Hawthorne has this character cover his face with a black veil as the emblem of that secret sin for which he suffers guilt, fear of rejection, and longing for atonement. Jung believed that the shadow is the unconscious aspect of our psyche, or total being, into which we hide that which makes us uncomfortable (*Basic Writings*, 319). Hawthorne writes that even Hooper's sermons refer to "secret sin, and those sad mysteries which we hide from our nearest and dearest, and would fain conceal from our own consciousness" (103). The minister's veil, Hawthorne says, "seemed to hang down before his heart, the symbol of a fearful secret between him and them" (107). The veil symbolizes his shadow, the secret sin that overpowers his life and prevents him from developing any close relationships with the people in the town, even his own beloved Elizabeth, the woman he is to marry. Yet in the end on his deathbed, Reverend Hooper has still not come to terms with his shadow, instead projecting it on to his parishioners. As he looks around at them in the final hours, he declares that he sees a black veil on every person gathered around his deathbed.

Inevitably, the shadow comes to possess qualities opposite to our outward appearances, or masks, that we put on, which Jung called the persona. That persona seems to balance the antisocial characteristics of the shadow, which we keep out of sight. We normally do not try to offend others with hostility, anger, or inappropriate and rude behavior. When that inner regulating agent that wants us to be good makes us keep those feelings buried in our shadow, we usually submit to it. We like maintaining an accepted position in society, at least on the outside, but unconsciously, deep in our shadow, other things are taking place: repression, denial, projection, paranoia, and all kinds of complexes. Jung says, however, that to own one's shadow is to become responsible for it. In C.G. Jung's *Letters*, volume 1, he writes,

> It is a very difficult and important question, what you call the technique of dealing with the shadow...First of all, one has to accept and to take seriously into account the existence of the shadow. Secondly, it is necessary to be informed about its qualities and intentions. Thirdly, long and difficult negotiations will be unavoidable. (qtd. in Hoffman 84)

In "The Minister's Black Veil," Reverend Hooper demonstrates with the outward sign of the cloth covering his face that he accepts and takes seriously his secret sin, but to what extent he knows what to do with it except to be miserable isn't clear. With Hooper there are no negotiations, and unfortunately, as Jung pointed out, "We cannot change anything unless we accept it. Condemnation does not liberate, it oppresses" (qtd. in Hoffman 151). Hooper goes to his grave an unhappy old man who continues to condemn not only himself but also everyone around him.

In this story, Hawthorne's use of symbolism is sparse, but the images he uses are powerful. Look for these symbols as you read the story:

Symbols:

- Black, darkened: secrecy, gloom
- Veil: secrecy, hiding
- Gloomy shade: darkness, ignorance, gloom

- Circles: life/ death/life
- Wine: sacrifice
- Looking-glass: truth, self-realization, self beyond the mask
- Earth's black veil: projection of darkness onto humanity
- Woven with threads: weaving one's own destiny
- Wind: vital breath of the universe, power of the spirit that sustains life
- Shaded candlelight: light concealed, covered, not accepted
- Heart as a prison: feelings locked away and not recognized
- Lifting of the veil: freedom, acceptance, joy
- "on every visage, a Black Veil": projection of sin, secrecy, shadow on humanity
- Veiled corpse: death without acceptance of the shadow

Jung's Shadow Theory in "The Minister's Black Veil"

Although Hawthorne predates Jung by eleven years, he seems to perceive Jung's ideas as if the two had been contemporaries. The elements embodied in the shadow theory clearly describe much of Hooper's behavior. Several questions may come to mind as you look at Jung's interpretation of the shadow. Does Hooper use the veil to represent his shadow, or does his veil take on the role of the superego, punishing the minister for his secret sin? Why does Reverend Hooper insist on an outward display of his shadow? What makes the reader think of *hiding* and *displaying* at the same time when the two actions seem antithetical? What theme is Hawthorne communicating?

Anthony Stevens, a Jungian scholar trained at Oxford University, co-authored the book *Freud & Jung* with Anthony Storr. Read the following points he makes that help identify the phenomenon that Carl Jung believed all human beings possess. Use this information to enhance both your reading of and your written response to "The Minister's Black Veil." Look at each point and determine how these ideas might apply to the Reverend Hooper.

- The shadow is the darker side of our unconscious selves.
- We take the shadow with us wherever we go as a dark companion. We try to ignore it, but it constantly reminds us of its presence.
- The culture of the shadow is everything we have been taught to avoid because someone thinks it is bad or evil.
- We all keep our shadow out of sight in order to be good and win the approval of someone important to us.
- Being "good" and behaving within the law or established rules could be an act of submission to our superegos, which expect us to act like angels.
- Jung believed that the fear of being rejected causes us to feel guilty. We therefore long for forgiveness, atonement, and reconciliation. We want to be punished in order to speed up the process of making things right again.
- We use repression, suppression, denial, and projection as defense mechanisms in

dealing with the shadow.

- Shadow projection involves paranoia when one's own hostile feelings of persecution are disowned and projected onto others.
- The shadow complex is tinged with feelings of unworthiness.

In his book *Why Good People Do Bad Things*, James Hollis explains that the shadow contains all the things that are "an affront to what we consciously wish to think of ourselves" (30). The fear we have of others discovering our weaknesses, mistakes, and actions that would humiliate us, Hollis believes, derives from our earliest insecurities that remain with us forever. Although Hawthorne was unaware of depth psychology, his intuitive nature as a writer allowed him to put his character, the Reverend Hooper, in this common human framework of dealing with the shadow in a way that, despite its symbolism, we can understand and identify in ourselves.

Journal Prompt #1: After reading the story and the information about Jung's shadow theory, consider the following questions to synthesize your understanding, and then write about one.

1. What is it that Reverend Hooper does not want to face?

2. Does he project it onto others?

3. Is the purpose of the veil to hide something, or to declare something? If not, why do you think Hooper wears it for the remainder of his life, even when it means losing Elizabeth?

4. How does Hooper cope with "secret sin"?

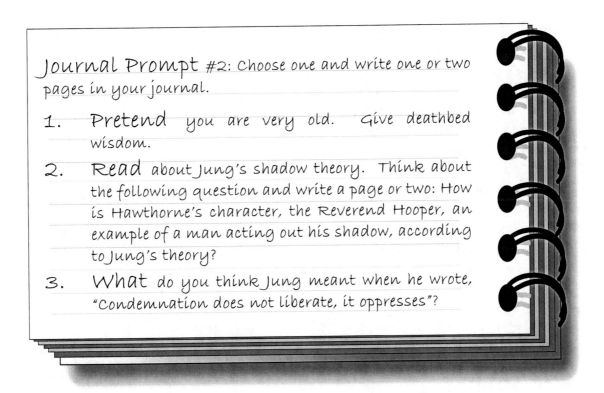

Journal Prompt #2: Choose one and write one or two pages in your journal.

1. Pretend you are very old. Give deathbed wisdom.

2. Read about Jung's shadow theory. Think about the following question and write a page or two: How is Hawthorne's character, the Reverend Hooper, an example of a man acting out his shadow, according to Jung's theory?

3. What do you think Jung meant when he wrote, "Condemnation does not liberate, it oppresses"?

STORY #5: "YOUNG GOODMAN BROWN"

• • • • •

You have already been introduced to the literary concept of the allegory with Plato's cave from *The Republic*. You recall that an allegory is a symbolic story in which characters, their actions and environments are embodiments of abstractions. In Hawthorne's "Young Goodman Brown," the elements of the story support the characters and actions that remind us of moral qualities. Even the name Goodman Brown implies something about his moral fiber: He is a good man whose surname Brown symbolizes the earth—he is a man of the earth, and in the story he could easily represent all men who try to live a good but imperfect life. Yet in Christian mythology the color brown implies spiritual death, which the reader will come to understand by the end of the story.

"Young Goodman Brown" opens with the title character kissing his young wife Faith goodbye as he sets off from his home in Salem Village and walks into the forest for one last journey into sin. When he returns, he says, he will cling to Faith's skirts and follow her to heaven. Hawthorne outlines a clear allegorical tale from the beginning. Along the journey of his life, this average man depends on his spiritual faith to lead him in the direction toward heaven, and even if he yields to temptation and sin, he can always lean on his faith and be all right, so he thinks. What Brown doesn't count on is that his wife Faith also journeys into the forest for a night with the devil, and, upon spying her pink ribbons caught on a branch, becomes convinced he has lost her, which means he has lost his spiritual faith. When he sees her face to face in the forest at the convocation of lost souls, which includes even the most pious of the village, he implores Faith to look up to heaven and regain her goodness. He suddenly finds himself alone, making his way out of the forest and back to Salem Village, wondering if it was all a dream. As he looks around, everything seems unchanged as Faith runs happily to greet him on the path, but to Brown everything has changed. He now trusts no one. One is reminded of Shakespeare's Hamlet who, in act II, scene 2, says, "There is nothing either good or bad, but thinking makes it so" (*Hamlet*, II, ii, 259). Because Goodman Brown thinks the entire community has given itself over to the devil, including his wife Faith, he lives the rest of his life as if it were so—lonely, miserable, and distrustful.

A large number of symbols support the allegory in "Young Goodman Brown." The symbols actually enhance each other so effectively that it is easy to understand why Hawthorne chose the words and images he did. Take a look at them prior to reading so that you can increase your awareness of the images in this highly archetypal story. Following the reading are questions to consider, a journal prompt, and a chart for you to complete that can clarify the sequence of events in both the literal and figurative levels of the allegory.

Symbols:

- Brown: earth, spiritual death
- Pink ribbons: faith, the color white (purity, innocence) combined with red (passion)
- Dreary road: difficult journey
- Trees: life
- Forest: place of initiation and testing
- Staff: tree, life
- Black snake: darkness, evil
- Fellow traveler: archetypal companion to the hero
- Journey: life
- Path: journey
- Dew: water (life), morning (rebirth)
- Gloomy hollow of the road: difficulties and trials of the journey
- Branch of maple, boughs: (tree symbols) life
- Faint gleam from sky: hope
- Wilderness: initiation and testing
- Looked up to the sky: hope
- Blue arch: heaven
- Stars: hope, light, struggle against forces of darkness
- Black mass of cloud, cloud of night, dark cloud: darkness, concealment, gloom
- Fire, blaze: destruction
- Dark wall of the forest: difficult, gloomy separating initiation and testing
- Altar: sacrifice
- Four blazing pines: destruction of human life
- Red light: sacrifice of life
- Sudden gleams of light: hope
- Roaring wind: violence in life
- Rushing streams: violence in life

- Howling beasts: violence
- Loftier flame: violence and destruction
- Smoke wreaths: transitory life, illusion of life
- Fire on the rock: destruction
- Shadow of the trees: dark side of life
- Blazing rock: destruction, sacrifice
- Veiled female: concealment
- Canopy of fire: widespread destruction
- Sheet of flame: destruction
- One mighty blood spot: mortal sin, critical sacrifice
- Basin with water reddened by light or blood: sacrifice, life in danger

Journal Prompt #1: Choose one of the following to write a response in your journal.

1. HOW does Hawthorne use both symbolism and the concept of antithesis to support the theme of balance?

2. WHY do you think Hawthorne used a circular story structure?

3. WHO are the allegorical characters in the story? What is the moral message that Hawthorne is trying to deliver?

4. WHY does it not matter if the story was a dream or reality?

ALLEGORY IN HAWTHORNE'S "YOUNG GOODMAN BROWN"
• • • • •

Directions: An allegory is a story that is told on two levels, a literal one and a figurative or symbolic one. The characters and their actions represent ideas or generalizations about life. Below you will see the story retold on the symbolic level. Read each event in the story carefully and determine the literal events that actually correspond to the symbolic ones. Fill in the blanks and include page numbers from the text. Note: Although the word *man* is used for the symbolic level, Hawthorne obviously is referring to people of both genders.

Level 1 – Literal

1._____

2._____

3._____

4._____

5._____

6._____

7._____

8._____

9._____

10._____

11._____

Level 2 – Symbolic

1. Man bids his faith farewell as he casts it aside for a journey into sin.

2. Man says he'll return to his faith and trusts that it will get him into heaven after a night of sin.

3. Man meets temptation. It doesn't seem strange or harmful, but when the person who represents temptation informs him he is late, the man explains that his faith made him uncertain about his decision. His conscience hurts.

4. Man, accompanied by his sin, journeys deep into the realm of testing his faith.

5. Man's conscience has been jolted and he is having second thoughts. He wants to return to his faithful, moral life, and yet he continues walking closer to sin.

6. Man discovers his long history with sin and is disillusioned.

7. Man claims he will not lose his faith.

8. Man's faith is tested when he sees his role models as sinners.

9. Man holds on to his faith, but his temptation temporarily gives him strength.

10. Man's faith is tested again when he is disappointed in misconceptions. He sees he was wrong in his perceptions of goodness.

11. Man now believes his faith is gone.

12._____

13._____

14._____

15._____

16._____

12. Without his faith, man gives himself over to sin, no longer resisting temptation.

13. On the perimeter of sin and temptation man still has a glimmer of hope that his faith will protect him.

14. Man must examine his own faith and see it for what it really is, an illusion.

15. Man suddenly relies on his faith to pull him out of trouble at the last minute.

16. Man is never able to regain his faith again and dies a spiritual death.

Journal Prompt #2: Write about an unusual dream you once had. Describe a character or a place in your dream in as much detail as you can remember. Jung tells us that our dreams may be associated with the current happenings in our lives. Can you think of any connections between your dream and your life at the time?

THESIS SENTENCES FOR WRITING ABOUT
HAWTHORNE'S SHORT STORIES
● ● ● ● ●

After reading the five short stories by Nathaniel Hawthorne listed below, choose one story to analyze in a three- or four-page essay in your journal. Gather ideas from the section on Hawthorne in this chapter, as well as your own journal writing.

Stories:
- "The Maypole of Merry Mount"
- "Dr. Heidegger's Experiment"
- "Rappaccini's Daughter"
- "The Minister's Black Veil"
- "Young Goodman Brown"

Sample Thesis Sentences:
These are suggestions. You may create your own using the ideas below as a model.

1. In Hawthorne's "The Maypole of Merry Mount," the use of antithesis, especially images of light and dark, supports the life/death/life archetype.
2. In Hawthorne's "Dr. Heidegger's Experiment," three symbols—the rose, water, and the butterfly—support the theme of balance. (You can choose other symbols as well.)
3. In "Rappaccini's Daughter," Hawthorne shows how Beatrice's sacrifice contributes to the archetype of paradise lost.
4. Hawthorne's character the Reverend Hooper exemplifies Jung's shadow theory in the story "The Minister's Black Veil."
5. Hawthorne uses symbolism, antithesis, and allegory to create a story that focuses on the human perception of good and evil in "Young Goodman Brown."
6. In "Rappaccini's Daughter," Hawthorne creates characters, setting, and plot that suggest the archetype of paradise and paradise lost.

Remember: Adhere to all the elements of good writing that you have learned. Refer to the section on writing at the beginning of your handbook as well as the essay-writing guide for "The Maypole of Merry Mount."

SYMBOLIC ILLUSIONS
● ● ● ● ●
Artistic Representations in Hawthorne's Stories

Films and filmmaking are a significant part of our culture. How do you suppose human beings discovered that pictures could move? A very simple explanation is the creative response you can make in this activity. At this point you have read several stories by Hawthorne and you have a clear picture about his use of symbolism. For this art project, you will combine symbols you have studied and the simple essence of moving pictures. Follow the directions below.

Materials needed:
cardboard or poster board cut in a 2 ½ inch disc
two pieces of string ten inches long each
fine-point black pen or marker
colored markers
scissors

Directions:
1. Choose two symbols from any of Hawthorne's short stories. Make sure they have a connection to each other in the story.
2. In your journal, plan your drawing of two symbols strategically placed so that their proximity to each other also creates meaning. For example:
   Side one: a tree with its shadow
   Side two: a star shining over the shadow of the tree
   Twirling the disc creates the illusion of one picture: a tree shadowed with a star illuminating the shadow. Meaning: There may be a dark side to life, but the light of the spirit struggles against the forces of darkness.
3. Make your first drawing on notebook paper so you can see through the paper to line up the two symbols. Note: the symbol on the back of the disc should be inverted.
4. Try out several different combinations of images that together create a symbolic statement.
5. Make a tiny hole on each side of the disc, insert a piece of string in each side, and knot it. Holding the string with both hands, twirl it. Observe the images coming together.
6. Your final product should be a finished disc and a statement, which you have written in your journal with your original plans. Share these with another person and let her try to interpret the meaning of your combined symbols.

If we throw ourselves into the flames of desire
and then dance with her in the refining fire,
how will our everyday lives be changed?
                    Marion Woodman and Elinor Dickson
                    Dancing in the Flames, 1996

CHAPTER II

The Scarlet Letter

You have sampled the best of Hawthorne by studying five of his most highly regarded short stories. Some scholars believe there is no better author than Hawthorne for getting a straightforward introduction to symbolism in literature. You can now take that introduction and apply it to the novel that gave Hawthorne his greatest recognition not only in his own time but also in modern times as one of the most significant pieces of literature in America today. *The Scarlet Letter*, therefore, is a novel to be studied in neither a cursory way nor an independent way. This chapter will help you to organize a guided study of the novel, accompanied by opportunities to write, discuss, and create. Before you read the book, take a look at the supplementary material that can make reading this nineteenth-century novel, which at times seems to contain archaic language, more enjoyable as well as easier to read.

KEEPING A JOURNAL
• • • • •

The following reading assignments can help you divide the book into more manageable sections:

1. Chapters 1-3
2. Chapters 4-5
3. Chapters 6-8
4. Chapters 9-10
5. Chapters 11-12
6. Chapters 13-15
7. Chapters 16-18
8. Chapters 19-20
9. Chapters 21-22
10. Chapters 23-24

Read the assigned chapters and write at least two pages in your journal on the topics listed below. Choose a different topic for each of the ten journal entries on the basis of which one seems most suitable for those chapters. You'll want to stay as close to the novel as possible in your discussion, so include textual references often, and remember to write page numbers after each quotation.

Topics:

1. **Character analysis:** Uncover the details about how the character acts and thinks, and what he or she says and does. What words and images contribute to the characterization?

2. **Figurative language:** How does Hawthorne use the tools of metaphor, simile, allusion, personification, and oxymoron?

3. **Archetypal motifs and symbols:** What universal symbols does Hawthorne use in developing characters, plot, and theme?

4. **Conflicts:** Address the three basic conflicts in the novel: private vs. public, the differing views about the letter, and the conflict between Hester and the Puritans (defiant individual vs. repressive society).

5. **Autobiographical connections:** How much of Hawthorne's life seems similar to the character Hester's?

6. **Psychological zones of id, ego, and superego:** How are the characters acting out of each of these zones?

7. **Antithesis:** How does the tension of opposites contribute to the development of the conflict?

8. **Historical influence on the writing:** Hawthorne wrote and published the novel in the mid-nineteenth century in a setting of social reform. How does *The Scarlet Letter* reflect the problems or the reforms of Hawthorne's day?

9. **Theme:** What ideas about life in general is Hawthorne trying to communicate?

10. **Moral ambiguity/moral relativism:** What makes the characters or the situations not clearly right or wrong? How is morality in the novel relative to the reader's interpretation as well as the characters' interpretations?

11. **Irony:** How does the author use words or situations to mean the opposite of their literal meaning? Specifically, what examples of dramatic irony, irony of situation, and verbal irony can the reader identify in the novel?

CONFLICT IN *THE SCARLET LETTER*
• • • • •

Have you ever had a secret that you kept to yourself, or maybe that you told to a trusted friend? The nature of secrets touches the human need to share a burden in the framework of privacy. That privacy, however, can quickly be destroyed by betrayal, the releasing of the carefully, or perhaps loosely, guarded information by the one entrusted with it. As a result, what is deemed private clashes with the act of making it public and enduring the consequences that follow. In *Hawthorne, a Life,* Brenda Wineapple writes, "Characters bound together by love and hate keep one another's secrets" (212). In *The Scarlet Letter*, Hester, Dimmesdale, and Hester's husband, who now calls himself Chillingworth in order to hide his identity, all keep secrets from the Puritan community about the nature of their relationships with each other. Sometimes revealing the secret is the only way to lift the unbearable burden that destroys its host, yet exposing the secret causes pain and suffering. Such is the case for these three characters in Hawthorne's novel.

People often look at the same sight or situation but, because of different value systems, have contrasting opinions. These value systems, which form as a result of experiences, education, moral influences, and personality, lead people to make decisions that affect their lives and the lives of people they touch. In *The Scarlet Letter* every character brings a different perspective to the letter *A,* which Hester must wear as her punishment for adultery, and through the passage of seven years time, the meaning of the letter changes. What influences the change in the interpretation of symbols and images? In the novel, when Pearl is seven years old, the people of the village cannot remember the original meaning of the letter. They now say it means *angel* and *able*.

Since the beginning of recorded history, the conflict between the defiant individual and the repressive society has facilitated progress. It is the one who believes in the necessity of change that renders the current laws and traditions obsolete by the act of rebellion. It is the higher law that replaces manmade law in acts of civil disobedience, and it is the desire for justice that challenges the powers that would deprive individuals of their personal human rights. Hester Prynne refuses to be manipulated by a society whose authority would strip her of having a right to privacy, of raising her child in her own way, of living in a community with respect and dignity, of loving in the light of redemption and healing.

ANTITHESIS IN *THE SCARLET LETTER*
• • • • •

Antithesis, the tension of opposites, wraps itself around the novel, encompassing everything about the plot, characters, imagery, and symbolism in order to support the theme of balance. Each chapter offers evidence of those opposites—light and dark, young and old, ugly and beautiful, love and hate, private and public, forgiveness and revenge, and a host of others, as you will see below. Try to focus on these examples and you will understand more clearly how Hawthorne guides his readers through the conflicts.

Chapter 1: the rose bush vs. the prison

Chapter 2: the Puritan women vs. Hester

Chapters 3, 4: Hester vs. Chillingworth (young/old, ugly/beautiful, forgiving/vengeful)

Chapter 5: Chillingworth as healer vs. Chillingworth as destroyer (throughout book)

Chapter 6: Pearl vs. Puritan children

Chapter 7, 8: Hester vs. the Puritans

Chapters 9, 10: Dimmesdale as man of God vs. Chillingworth as Satan

Chapter 11: private vs. public, truth vs. deception

Chapter 12: the scaffold at night vs. the scaffold during the day

Chapter 13: Hester as adulteress vs. Hester as *angel* and *able*

Chapter 14: forgiveness vs. revenge

Chapter 15: love vs. hate, good vs. evil

Chapter 16: forest vs. town, forest as initiation and testing vs. forest as refuge

Chapter 17: Hester and Dimmesdale: private vs. public, love vs. shame

Chapters 18, 19: Hester as lover vs. Hester as mother

Chapter 20: Dimmesdale's temptation vs. Dimmesdale's resolve

Chapters 21, 22: Hester's hope vs. Hester's fear

Chapter 23: Dimmesdale's private shame vs. his public shame, life vs. death, hope vs. disappointment

Chapter 24: Hester as outcast vs. Hester as mentor and guide

MORAL EXEMPLARS IN HAWTHORNE'S WRITING
• • • • •

You have read about the cultural conditions of the nineteenth century in the chronology of 1803 to 1865. These events created a popular kind of heroine that David Reynolds, American Renaissance scholar, terms the **moral exemplar**. Two kinds of female characters—the angel and the practical woman—emerged from the pages of American literature that appeared to reflect the social and economic affairs of the country (Reynolds 342).

What was happening politically, economically, and socially that would cause writers of fiction to produce these exemplary characters? Politically women were uniting, writing, and speaking out to get the vote and secure more rights, including freedom from slavery and the tyranny of white men over black female slaves. Key reform movements—anti-prostitution, anti-seduction, temperance, antislavery, and prison and asylum reform—attempted to right the wrongs of working-class women who were brutalized by their situation, especially the exploitation by the men for whom they worked. A new kind of literature grew out of these conditions that illustrated a heroine, the practical woman, who eked out a meager existence while frequently struggling to combat unfair treatment and attempts at seduction by employers with harmful motives. Many of these characters were seamstresses. Hawthorne's heroine Hester Prynne's only means of survival is by her needle, embroidering and making clothes for people in the community.

While most people in the nineteenth century recognized the onerous burdens of the American homemaker, they praised her for the ease with which she bore her lot in life. From this image came the **practical exemplar**, whose good works and cheerful acceptance of hard work won her high esteem, even from those who contributed to her plight. The general consensus about the American working-class woman of the century was that she had a special capacity to endure misfortune. Fortitude, independence, and spirit gave her mental and physical strength to tackle her duties and survive. It was said that she could cope with the kinds of hardship that would drive a man to desperation.

The second kind of exemplar evolved from a society with a moral struggle between men and those women who had fewer rights and could be taken advantage of. The belief that women were the morally weaker sex and needed more protection and guidance than men was a belief perpetuated by the Puritans and still existed to some degree in Hawthorne's time. His character Endicott in "The Maypole of Merry Mount" exhibits this attitude when he tells Edgar, "We are not wont to show an idle courtesy to that sex which requireth the stricter discipline" (124-5). Even Jonathan Edwards's Calvinistic gloom that promised uncertainty and fatalism could not create despondency in the cheerful exemplar. She was an angel who reconstructed a faith of love and kindness, even as Calvinism separated her, and all humankind, from God with their image of His terrifying power to send humankind into the fires of hell at His whim. The moral exemplar preferred a benign God, and in literature she was often more respected and valued than male clergymen. The fallen woman, another female victim character who appeared in the literature of moral reform, was described as a woman who sinned, often as a result of male seduction over which she had little control, but, through a life of penitence and good works, she redeemed herself in the eyes of the community. The sacrifice she made for this redemption was often a life of loneliness.

Hawthorne was aware of the literature that preceded and set the stage for both "Rappaccini's Daughter" and *The Scarlet Letter*, whose heroines are both moral exemplars. Hester Prynne in *The Scarlet Letter* is both moral and practical exemplar, and she rises above the patriarchal Puritan society to such an extent that she redeems herself and supplants her secret lover Arthur Dimmesdale. He collapses under the weight of his moral weakness as she stands tall and strong on the scaffold with the daughter of their illicit relationship by her side.

METAPHORS IN *THE SCARLET LETTER*
• • • • •

Think about what is being compared in the metaphors on the left. Write their literal meanings on the right in the blank provided—what is being implied, not stated, in the comparison. Page numbers refer to the Penguin Classics edition of the novel.

Writing Figuratively…	Writing Literally…

- "the black flower of civilized society" (45)   _____

- "writhing horror twisted itself across his features" (56)   _____

- "pile up their misery upon the heap of shame" (71)   _____

- "ugliest weeds of the garden were their children" (85)   _____

- "made her the very brightest little jet of flame that ever danced upon the earth" (90)   _____

- She "had been plucked by her mother off the bush of wild roses, that grew by the prison door" (99)   _____

- "He dug into the poor clergyman's heart, like a miner searching for gold" (113)   _____

- "black weeds have sprung up out of a buried heart" (115)   _____

- "high mountain peaks of faith" (124)   _____

- "Walking in the shadow of a dream" (129)   _____

- They "had made a shrine for him in their white bosoms" (133)   _____

- "The three formed an electric chain" (134)   _____

- "iron link of mutual crime" (139)   _____

- "messenger of anguish" (222)   _____

- "well-spring of human tenderness" (141)   _____

- "All the light and graceful foliage of her character had been withered up by this red-hot brand" (142)

  _____

- "secret sting of remorse" (145)

  _____

- "constant shadow of my presence!" (150)

  _____

- "truth of red-hot iron" (151)

  _____

- "marble image of happiness" (154)

  _____

- "holy whiteness of the clergyman's good fame" (159)

  _____

- "disease of sadness" (160)

  _____

- "with a deep utterance out of an abyss of sadness" (170)

  _____

- "this brook is the boundary between two worlds" (182)

  _____

- "honeysweet expressions" (182)

  _____

- "infectious poison of that sin" (194)

  _____

- "the wine of life" (198)

  _____

- "blackest shade of Puritanism" (202)

  _____

- "labyrinth of misery" (213)

  _____

- "shower of golden truths (216)

  _____

SYMBOLISM IN _THE SCARLET LETTER_
• • • • •

Many of the symbols that Hawthorne uses in the five stories preceding _The Scarlet Letter_ will seem familiar to you. A Jungian approach to an examination of the archetypes will enable you to see the continuity of Hawthorne's imagery, the thread that connects the characters in their search for retribution and redemption. Hawthorne often uses the same symbols to communicate the themes of antithesis and balance. Consider the symbols below that add depth to his story and think about the richer meanings that develop as a result of their associations with each other as well as their support for the other elements of the story.

1. **Pearl**: Hester appropriately names her child Pearl, associated with the life-giving power of the great mother and the pearl of great price. The pearl as sphere and circle represents birth and rebirth. Its biological essence indicates the union of fire and water, its whiteness innocence, purity, and humility.

2. **Meteor**: The shooting star upon which Hester, Pearl, and Dimmesdale gaze reminds the reader of the forces of the spirit struggling against the forces of darkness.

3. **Thread**: It is no coincidence that Hester uses her needle and thread to create her destiny, for the thread of life weaves human destiny. The thread holds life together in unity and continuity. In mythology, it is said that the thread passing through the sphere of the pearl is an *axis mundi* (the center of the world around which all things revolve).

4. **Rose**: Hawthorne asks the reader to pluck the rose growing outside the door of the prison, through which Hester will pass, for the very reason that it represents perfection, the mystery of life, silence, and secrecy. Yet the rose also supports the theme of antithesis: life and death, time and eternity, innocence and passion. Being a flower, the rose is a paradise symbol, a garden of timeless perfection.

5. **Mirror**: The water in the brook reflects, as a mirror does, the truth, self-realization, and therefore wisdom and self-knowledge.

6. **Brook**: Similar to a stream or river, the brook reminds one of a journey from one state to another as in a rite of passage, from one bank to another across the river of life or death.

7. **Forest**: Dimmesdale walks daily through the forest, and Hester meets him there to ask his forgiveness and to make plans for their future. Thus, the forest becomes a place of initiation and testing, of unknown perils and darkness, of secrets. Entering a forest indicates the loss of spiritual insight and therefore the loss of direction and purpose. Hester meets Dimmesdale in the forest to set things right again and to rekindle their love. For her the forest is also a place of nurture, refuge and rebirth.

8. **Three**: Hester, Dimmesdale, and Pearl represent the family—mother, father, and child. Strength and balance of the triangle show the power of the number three. It manifests its power in the beginning, middle, and end; birth, life, and death; past, present, and future; and the three phases of the moon. The reader must also remember the triangle of Hester, Dimmesdale, and Chillingworth, joined by their interrelated connections to each other.

9. **Circle:** Throughout the novel Hawthorne refers to circles enclosing, protecting, or isolating, and he uses the sphere as both world and pearl. The circle symbolizes life, death, and rebirth.

10. The **paths** from the prison to the scaffold, from Hester's cottage to the town, and from the town into the forest depict the different journeys in the lives of the characters.

11. The letter *A* in the sky as well as the letter on Hester's bosom and on Pearl's is, at the outset, Hester's cross to bear, yet the gold threads that form an *A* on a scarlet background weave a different destiny for Hester, as during those seven years the *A* comes to mean *able* and *angel*.

12. **Square:** The house that contained Hester Prynne was square, an enclosure which represents permanence and stability.

13. **Black flower:** In this instance, black is the color of darkness, shame, humiliation, and sadness. A flower, symbol of the feminine principle, often represents fragility, innocence, and hope. The combination of *black* and *flower* suggests the tension of opposites in a story filled with antithesis.

14. **Shadow:** This negative principle is the antithesis of the sun and often represents darkness and its concomitant symbolism.

15. **Dancing** indicates movement to the rhythm of the universe, and the different motions of the dancer represent the different reasons for the dance.

16. **Light** and **sunshine** represent life, truth, knowledge, and the divinity.

17. **Wellspring, water:** Water is the source of all life, able to cleanse and purify. Immersion indicates death and rebirth. Diving into water represents the search for the secret of life and of the unconscious.

18. **Hair** loosened depicts freedom, since hair in general represents strength and energy. Hester, her hair tucked into a cap, goes into the forest to meet Dimmesdale with hopes of declaring truth and love and plans for a future together. When Dimmesdale reciprocates her hope, Hester takes off the cap and lets her beautiful hair flow freely about her shoulders. Pearl's response upon seeing her mother changed insists on Hester's return to her former self. It is only when Dimmesdale accepts Pearl publicly that the conflict will end, and so Hester puts her hair back under her cap and waits.

19. **Hand:** The hand signifies power, strength, blessing, transmission of power, or healing.

20. **Kiss:** The kiss is a token of good will, affection, and reconciliation, though some believe that it also signifies betrayal because of the kiss that Judas gave to Jesus.

21. **Blood** on the withered leaves reminds the reader of the natural juxtaposition of life and death.

22. The **burial ground,** a major landmark in the town, is often referred to in mythology as the womb of the earth mother who welcomes the body back to the earth and shelters it. It is a sacred and final resting place of the dead.

23. "ON A FIELD, SABLE, THE LETTER *A*, GULES" (*The Scarlet Letter* 228):
    field: the background in a coat of arms (also known as the sphere or domain in which something takes place or can be seen)
    sable: the color black (gloom and doom)
    gules: the color red (passion, love, sacrifice)

SAMPLE JOURNAL RESPONSES
• • • • •

The journal essays that I ask students to write for *The Scarlet Letter* reflect the eleven topics listed as well as the model you learned about in chapter 5. Students write one short essay for each of ten clusters of chapters using the structure point-quotation-commentary one time for each body paragraph and the traditional introduction ending in the thesis sentence and conclusion beginning with the thesis reworded. Below are two student samples.

Chapters 4-5
The Effect of Figurative Language in *The Scarlet Letter*
By Thomas D.

Figurative language is a device used in pieces of writing to enhance and better describe items in details. Using figurative language in writing gives the reader better tools to picture the image in his or her mind. Many writers use metaphor, simile, allusion, personification, and oxymoron as tools to accomplish this task. In chapters 4-5 of *The Scarlet Letter*, Nathaniel Hawthorne effectively uses a combination of simile, metaphor, and personification.

Simile is a comparison to two unlike things, and Hawthorne uses one to describe the effect of the Indian drink that was administered to Hester.

"…a recipe that an Indian taught me, in requital of some lessons of my own, that were as old as Paracelsus. Drink it! It may be less soothing than a sinless conscience. That I cannot give thee. But it will calm the swell and heaving of thy passion, like oil thrown on the waves of a tempestuous sea" (67).

Hawthorne is comparing the soothing powers of the Indian remedy to throwing oil on waves on a sea because oil doesn't mix with the water so it helps quell it as the remedy calms Hester.

Like a simile, a metaphor also compares two objects and Hawthorne uses it to compare Hester's mark of infamy to an inescapable hold. "The chain that bound her here was of iron links, and galling to her inmost soul, but never could be broken" (72). This comparison describes Hester's punishment, the branded letter *A* on her bosom and how it is linked to Hester in a way that will not release her from its imprisonment.

Personification adds great detail to an object by giving it human qualities to help understand what it is really doing, such as in the description of Hester's cottage on the peninsula. "A mystic shadow of suspicion immediately attached itself to the spot" (73). Hawthorne gives life to the shadow by describing the suspicion of Hester and her infant child inside the cottage, away from the other villagers and children who are too young to understand the troubles Hester is going through.

By combining the three literary devices into his work, Hawthorne gives the reader a better image while reading through figurative language. Using the combination of images gives greater depth to the story and assists the reader in deciphering the image that the author is trying to depict. By adding detail with figurative language, the story keeps the reader interested and encourages him to continue reading.

Chapters 1-3
Antithesis in Nathaniel Hawthorne's *The Scarlet Letter*
By Raissa L.

Antithesis is often used as figurative language to enhance or add tension. This juxtaposition also serves to contribute to the conflict from the tension created. Writers often use antithesis as a mechanism to advance the development of the conflict. In Nathaniel Hawthorne's *The Scarlet Letter*, antithesis is utilized to supplement the development of the conflicts of private vs. public, the differing views about the letter, and the conflict between Hester and the Puritans.

Both Dimmesdale and Chillingworth prod Hester in different directions, with one urging her to confess her sins and the other telling her to keep her sins secret.

> " If thou feelest it to be for thy soul's peace, and that thy earthly punishment will thereby be more effectual to salvation, I charge thee to speak out the name of thy fellow-sinner and fellow-sufferer!" (62)

Reverend Dimmesdale, Hester's lover, tries to persuade Hester to speak the name of the father of the baby, while her husband, Chillingworth, tells her to keep quiet, creating a conflict around whether Hester should keep her sin private or make it public.

Hester does not see the scarlet letter in the same way as the rest of the village does, for instead of seeing it as shame and disgrace, like the townsfolk, she sees the letter as a symbol for love. "Why, gossips, what is it but to laugh in the faces of our godly magistrates, and make a pride out of what they, worthy gentlemen, meant as a punishment?" (51). The people of the town see the beautiful scarlet letter as an act of defiance and pride, when it should have been worn in shame. The differing views of the letter cause tension.

In the repressive society of the Puritans, Hester becomes a defiant individual rebelling against all the standards.

> But on one side of the portal, and rooted almost at the threshold, was a wild rose-bush, covered, in this month of June, with its delicate gems, which might be imagined to offer their fragrance and fragile beauty to the prisoner as he went in, and to the condemned criminal as he came forth to his doom, in token that the deep heart of Nature could pity and be kind to him. (46)

This rose bush symbolizes Hester in the fact that it stands strong in a dismal environment, just as Hester retains her individuality, making tension grow between her and the Puritans.

The conflicts in this novel are developed through several examples of antithesis used throughout the book. Even though she lives in an oppressive society, Hester manages to keep private her sin and retain her individuality instead of publicizing her sin and conforming to the rules. Throughout her ordeals she also keeps a rosy view on the scarlet letter when it is thought that it should shame her. Such rebellions as Hester's are powerful tools and have often changed the world for the better, as is the case with Gandhi in India.

CHAPTER SYNOPSES FOR *THE SCARLET LETTER*

• • • • •

Reading chapter synopses does not take the place of reading the chapters themselves. The inclusion of summaries here offers you another aid in comprehending the many facets of this nineteenth-century masterpiece. As you read, you begin your study of the novel in a more prepared way—knowing about the basic plot, allowing you to focus on more complex elements.

Chapter 1: Hawthorne describes the prison, the community, the people, and the rose bush.

Chapter 2: Townspeople are gathered around the jail, waiting for Hester Prynne to come out. The women speak about her in angry tones. Hester emerges with her baby to stand on the scaffold.

Chapter 3: Hester recognizes a man in the crowd—a small man, intelligent looking with a physical deformity. He recognizes her also and asks a townsman why she is on the scaffold. Reverend John Wilson speaks to Hester and urges Dimmesdale to make her confess the name of the baby's father. He does. She refuses. Hester is led back to prison.

Chapter 4: The stranger, Roger Chillingworth, is Hester's long-lost husband. He has become a physician of sorts and ministers to the needs of Hester and the baby inside the prison. They talk and he makes her promise to keep his identity secret. He swears he will find out the name of the father of the child.

Chapter 5: Hester is released from prison. Instead of leaving Boston and returning to England, she chooses to stay in a small cottage by the shore. She supports herself and her child by doing needlework for the people in the town. She begins to sense that the scarlet letter enables her to know the "hidden sin in other hearts" (78). She begins her lonely existence of isolation, rejection, and torment.

Chapter 6: Hawthorne describes Pearl and how she grows up. Hester dresses Pearl in beautiful clothes. He says she is "wild, desperate, defiant" (82). Hester imposes a tender but strict control over her. Pearl is a born outcast; she has no one to play with. Both mother and daughter are excluded from society. Pearl learns to play by herself and becomes imaginative and creative. Pearl becomes aware of the letter. She says, "I have no Heavenly Father" (88) when Hester tells her who made her.

Chapter 7: Hester goes to see Governor Bellingham to give him a pair of gloves he ordered and, more importantly, to speak up for her cause. The Puritans aim to take Pearl away from her, thinking Pearl would receive better nurture elsewhere. The governor's house is luxurious.

Chapter 8: Hester sees Governor Bellingham with John Wilson, Arthur Dimmesdale, and Roger Chillingworth, who now lives with Dimmesdale and cares for him as his physician. Wilson examines Pearl's knowledge of the Christian faith. Pearl gives a response that shocks the Puritans, and Bellingham decides Pearl must be removed from Hester's care. Hester pleads for Pearl and begs Dimmesdale to plead for her also. He delivers an impressive speech, which moves the governor. Pearl takes his hand and lays her cheek on it. Dimmesdale lays his hand on Pearl and kisses her brow before a suspicious Chillingworth. Hester may keep Pearl.

Chapter 9: Dimmesdale and Chillingworth have many intellectual, philosophical discussions as they become friends. Because of Dimmesdale's failing health, Chillingworth lives with him in order to take care of him. They move into the house of a widow of good social rank. People begin to suspect that Dimmesdale is haunted by Satan in the guise of Chillingworth.

Chapter 10: Chillingworth is suspicious of Dimmesdale, but Dimmesdale trusts no one except Chillingworth. In a conversation, both men discuss the public and private nature of sin. Dimmesdale says only God will know the secrets of a human heart and Chillingworth believes that idea is deceptive. A false show cannot be better than "God's own truth" (116). Pearl sees Chillingworth and tells her mother to come away from the old Black Man who has "got hold of the minister already" (118). They discuss the mystery of Dimmesdale's illness and Chillingworth rushes out. While Dimmesdale is sleeping, Chillingworth opens the minister's shirt and sees something on his chest, the revelation of which makes him ecstatic.

Chapter 11: Arthur Dimmesdale feels bitter hatred for Roger Chillingworth but tries to get rid of the ill will he has toward him. Dimmesdale, meanwhile, grows in popularity as the community holds no one in higher esteem. He longs to tell them the truth, but he can't. Hawthorne says that he "loathes his miserable self" (126) to the extent that Dimmesdale practices self-abasement, fasting, and keeping vigils. In his secret closet "under lock and key, there was a bloody scourge" (126). One night he discovers a way that he might find peace.

Chapter 12: At midnight Dimmesdale leaves his house and goes to the scaffold in the town and ascends the steps to the platform. He shrieks aloud, but no one comes. They cannot see him on the dark platform. John Wilson passes him but does not see Dimmesdale. He calls out to Pearl and Hester, also passing on their way home from Governor Winthrop's deathbed. He asks them to climb the steps and stand with him. They do. Pearl asks that he stand with them on the scaffold the next day. He replies no, but he will on "the great judgment day!" (134). Suddenly a meteor lights up the sky. Pearl points across the street to Roger Chillingworth, who helps Dimmesdale home. The next day the sexton returns Dimmesdale's black glove that he found on the scaffold, saying "Satan dropped it there..." (138).

Chapter 13: Hester's own transformation is more apparent, and the town's attitude toward the scarlet letter changes their label of her from *adulteress* to *able*. She has an austere look in her dress, hair hidden completely in a cap. She believes passion and tenderness have gone from her life. She does, however, resolve to meet her former husband and try to rescue his victim, Dimmesdale.

Chapter 14: Hester meets Chillingworth in the forest as he is gathering herbs. He tells her of the council's consideration of allowing Hester to remove the letter. She replies they have no power to do so. If she were worthy, it would fall off. He comments, then, on the beauty of the letter. Instead of returning his good will, she accuses him of causing Dimmesdale to "die a living death" (149). He says he has done no evil, that he had no choice. He could have exposed Dimmesdale, but he wants the minister to suffer even more by Chillingworth's own hand. Hester says she must reveal him to Dimmesdale. He tells her to do what she must.

Chapter 15: Hester declares her hatred for Chillingworth. She wonders how she could ever have been persuaded to marry him. She even thinks that the marriage was her "crime to be most repented" (154). Still in the forest, Hester summons Pearl who is playing by the sea. Pearl has constructed a green *A* of her own. When Hester asks her why her mother wears the letter, Pearl replies, "It is the same reason the minister keeps his hand over his heart!" (156). In all of Pearl's questioning, Hester finds that she cannot tell her the truth. Pearl, nevertheless, continues to ask about the letter. Hester, annoyed, warns her not to tease her or she will put her in the closet.

Chapter 16: Hester plans to warn Dimmesdale about Chillingworth. She and Pearl set out for the forest since she knows he walks there daily. Pearl wanders off to play in the forest so that Hester can talk to Dimmesdale. Soon Hester sees him on the path, again with his hand over his heart.

Chapter 17: Hester calls out to Dimmesdale and he is surprised to see her. They greet each other, asking warmly how each has fared these seven years. As they talk, Hester finds the right moment to tell Dimmesdale how and why his friend Chillingworth is his worst enemy. He sinks to the ground, burying his face in his hands and proclaims that he cannot forgive her. She throws her arms around him, pressing him to her: "Thou shalt forgive me!...Let God punish! Thou shalt forgive!" (169). He does forgive her, and they sit side by side, hand in hand. Dimmesdale is worried that Chillingworth will now strengthen his revenge. Hester reassures him and says he must no longer live with Chillingworth. She then reveals a plan: They should leave Boston together and the three sail back to England and begin a new life.

Chapter 18: Dimmesdale now has hope. The world looks brighter than before to him and he agrees to sail with Hester. They agree not to look back on the past. Hester removes the scarlet letter and throws it on the other side of the brook. She calls Pearl to come and greet Dimmesdale and for him to meet Pearl for the first time as her father. Pearl hears her mother's voice and returns slowly and cautiously when she sees Dimmesdale.

Chapter 19: Hester assures Dimmesdale that Pearl will love him dearly. Dimmesdale confesses that Pearl has caused him much alarm and that his "heart dreads this interview, and yearns for it!" (181). When Pearl comes closer to them, she becomes distressed that Hester has taken off the letter. Hester tells her to look near her feet and fetch the letter she has thrown. Pearl refuses and Hester goes to the brook, picks it up, and fastens it to her dress. Pearl is satisfied and knows her mother now. Dimmesdale kisses Pearl's brow, and she runs to the brook to wash it off. While she is playing, Hester and Dimmesdale make their plans for the future.

Chapter 20: Dimmesdale leaves Hester and Pearl in the forest and makes his way back to town. He thinks about the Election Sermon he is supposed to preach in three days. He encounters three parishioners: a deacon, an old widow, and a young woman. With each meeting, Dimmesdale is tempted to say and do rude and blasphemous things. Dimmesdale wonders if he made a contract with the fiend in the forest and signed his name in blood. Once he reaches his home, Dimmesdale goes up to his study. Chillingworth knocks on his door and asks if Dimmesdale needs his medicinal aid. Dimmesdale refuses it but remains civil to him. When Chillingworth leaves, Dimmesdale flings his sermon into the fire and begins a new one.

Chapter 21: Hester and Pearl go to the marketplace for the New England holiday marking the Election Sermon. A crowd has gathered to see the procession of the governor and magistrates, ministers, and soldiers. When Pearl asks if Dimmesdale will be there, Hester explains that he will but he will not greet her, nor should she greet him. Pearl does not understand why. Meanwhile the commander of the Bristol ship stops to tell Hester that he has yet another passenger on the ship, a surgeon. It is Roger Chillingworth who will be traveling with them. Hester looks at Chillingworth and beholds a "smile which...conveyed secret and fearful meaning" (214).

Chapter 22: Hester and Pearl are in the marketplace watching the procession of soldiers, magistrates, and Dimmesdale. Hester realizes that Dimmesdale has changed his mind and that no real bond between the clergyman and herself exists. Pearl recognizes Dimmesdale as the man who kissed her in the forest, and Hester chides her to be silent. Mistress Hibbins holds a conversation with Pearl and Hester. She knows about the forest meeting and about Dimmesdale's keeping his hand over his heart. Hester stands beside the scaffold to listen to Dimmesdale's sermon inside the meeting house. The commander sends a message to Hester by Pearl: Chillingworth will escort Dimmesdale to the ship.

Chapter 23: Dimmesdale has given his most eloquent sermon. The crowd rushes out of the church into the marketplace. Hester is still standing by the scaffold. Dimmesdale marches through the street, stopping at Hester and Pearl. He beckons them to come to him. Pearl runs to him and clasps her arms about his knees. Hester moves slowly. Chillingworth rushes forward and takes Dimmesdale's arm. Dimmesdale tells Chillingworth it is too late. Dimmesdale asks Hester and Pearl to join him on the scaffold, where he finally confesses his guilt. He reveals what townspeople later recall as his own version of the letter and then collapses. Chillingworth repeats, "Thou hast escaped me!" (221). Hester asks Dimmesdale if they will be together in heaven, but Dimmesdale says it is vain to hope. He dies.

Chapter 24: People speculate on what they really saw on the minister's breast and how it got there. Chillingworth dies within the year, leaving much of his fortune to Pearl. Hester and Pearl disappear, but years later Hester returns to the cottage and begins ministering to the needs of the women in the town. Pearl sends Hester gifts from Europe, and Hester is seen embroidering a baby garment. Hester never removes the scarlet letter. When she dies, one tombstone is erected for both Dimmesdale and Hester, with a space between them.

THE SCARLET LETTER ESSAY:
WRITING, EDITING, AND REVISING
● ● ● ● ●

At this point you have read *The Scarlet Letter*, you have kept a detailed journal of ten short essays in an intensive study of the novel, and you are now ready to write a longer analytical essay. Again, you will make an assertion about the novel and attempt to prove it with textual support. I have included in this chapter a study guide, sample essay topics, an essay-writing guide, and models to assist you in this endeavor. The most helpful activity I know, however, is actually taking each draft of your essay at various levels of completion and sitting down with your teacher or another person, one on one, and editing together. The key word is *time,* which seems to be a rare commodity for most of us, but if you and your teacher or a parent or friend can work together, your knowledge of essay writing will increase exponentially with this one-on-one help. When you use this approach, the product can be far superior, and the fear of attacking an assignment that can seem insurmountable suddenly becomes palatable. Below you will find suggestions for editing that go beyond correctness to address refinement as well.

1. Be careful with <u>be</u> verbs. Use them only if necessary, but don't use them because you don't want to think of more exact or powerful words. Also try to avoid them in passive voice constructions. Active voice gives a stronger grammatical construction.

2. Avoid using the word <u>this</u> except as a demonstrative adjective. The pronoun reference is not clear. <u>This</u> could refer to too many things in the previous sentences.

3. Avoid using the words <u>there</u> plus any <u>be</u> verbs. Example: *There is a doctor in the novel who treats Hester in her prison cell.* This sentence simply states the existence of a character, a cursory treatment of Chillingworth when you know the writer could say much more about him.

4. Avoid first and second person pronouns in a formal essay, e.g., I, me, my, you, or your.

5. Use textual support. Choose passages carefully. Sometimes you will want to quote a long passage, but do this sparingly. Your teacher wants to know how *you* write. Use correct punctuation for parenthetical references. Remember to indent the entire long passage that you are quoting—three or more lines. No quotation marks are needed for long quotations except for dialogue.

6. Write clearly. If you don't know what your sentences mean, your reader certainly won't. Use transitions between ideas for greater fluency and cohesiveness throughout your essay.

7. Elaborate and support each main point in the body. Follow the format of point-example-commentary for every point in the essay. Invest the time it takes to write an effective opening and closing.

SUGGESTED ESSAY TOPICS
● ● ● ● ●

Directions: Choose a topic and work it into a clear thesis sentence that indicates the focus of your essay. Follow the guidelines given for writing an essay.

1. How is Hester Prynne's struggle with the repressive patriarchy of Puritan society a microcosmic view of the struggle of the women's movement today?

2. The key to understanding many forms of human behavior may be to understand the spiritual nature of human beings. How does understanding the spiritual nature of the characters help us to understand their behavior in *The Scarlet Letter*?

3. How is *The Scarlet Letter* a "tale of human frailty and sorrow" (46)?

4. How does Hawthorne's use of imagery (figurative language) enhance and support the development of characterization and plot in *The Scarlet Letter*?

5. How is Hawthorne's use of antithesis central to the development of the various conflicts in *The Scarlet Letter*?

6. Pearl's role in *The Scarlet Letter* is a "messenger of anguish" (222). How does Hawthorne develop this role that fuels the plot?

7. Why is the archetypal approach to analyzing *The Scarlet Letter* an effective one?

8. How is *The Scarlet Letter* a story of betrayal?

9. How is *The Scarlet Letter* a story of redemption? You might try combining numbers 8 and 9.

10. Autobiographical strands exist in *TSL* between Hester and Hawthorne. What is the common thread between them, and how does Hawthorne develop it in the novel?

11. *Moral relativism* implies that each individual has a different or unique interpretation of what is moral, relative to what the individual believes. Discuss how morality is relative in *The Scarlet Letter* to Hester's and Dimmesdale's personal interpretation of their own behavior in the novel.

12. Why and how does Hawthorne use irony in *The Scarlet Letter*?

13. **Moral ambiguity** is a term used to describe a situation in which a rigid code of right and wrong does not seem to be applicable. Does Hawthorne lead the reader to experience a feeling of moral ambiguity when he asks the reader to pluck the rose by the prison door—to accept Hester's morality—in chapter 1? What circumstances might make the morality of Hester's crime ambiguous, not clearly right or wrong?

LOOKING AT STUDENT MODELS
● ● ● ● ●

The following essays exemplify student writing that meets the criteria for excellence. The first piece you will read is a thoughtful look at symbolism in *The Scarlet Letter* with textual support and good analysis. Stacey has organized her thoughts well, beginning with her thesis sentence, and she moves smoothly through a discussion of three major symbols in the story. Her effective use of parenthetical reference to cite sources adds to the clarity of her paper while the use of transitions between sentences and paragraphs contributes to the fluency. The writer elaborates on and explains each point with careful attention to word choice. Finally, she closes her paper by returning the reader to the beauty as well as the usefulness of symbols as tools for understanding literature and life.

In the second piece of student writing, Kyle examines Hawthorne's use of antithesis, a literary device that strengthens the conflict in the story. In this paper, the writer shows how, using stark contrasting words, images, and actions, Hawthorne creates the tension of opposites that surrounds three particular conflicts in the novel. Again, each paragraph clearly supports the thesis that the student asserts at the beginning of his paper with well-constructed sentences, textual support documented with parenthetical reference, and he closes his paper effectively with generalizations about the use of antithesis.

Example 1:

Symbolizing Struggles of the Spirit

Over time, many objects and ideas have become symbolic to humans throughout the world. Because they extend into the inner thought and emotions of each individual rather than simply relating to the literal world, the use of these symbols allows people to find greater significance in the literature that they read. Through his many short stories and novels, Nathaniel Hawthorne shows mastery of the art of symbolism as his plots and characters move along this higher level. In *The Scarlet Letter* Hawthorne uses symbolism to give Hester Prynne's character and actions deeper meaning.

One of the most important symbols found in *The Scarlet Letter* is the rose. Hawthorne uses the rose to represent Hester, for the rose's symbolism explains her character and many of her actions and conflicts. The rose represents both earthly passion and heavenly perfection and completion. Similarly, the Puritan society sees Hester as a model of sinful passion, for she has committed a crime for love. However, Hester defies the repressive Puritan society by showing that she is a good-hearted, capable woman. The rose also represents silence, secrecy, and paradise, showing the conflict of private versus public life and the conflict between Hester and the harsh Puritan society. The placement of the rose throughout *The Scarlet Letter* adds much significance to Hester's choices. Hawthorne places a rose bush outside "the black flower of civilized society" (45), the prison from which Hester emerges.

> On one side of the portal, and rooted almost at the threshold, was a wild rose-bush
> covered, in this month of June, with its delicate gems, which might be imagined
> to offer their fragrance and fragile beauty to the prisoner as he went in, and to the
> condemned criminal as he came forth to his doom, to token that the deep heart of
> Nature could pity and be kind to him. (45-46)

The rose-bush is again found in Governor Bellingham's garden. The roses lead to the conclusion that Hester is inseparable from the town and community in which she sins and receives her punishment. Through the symbolism of the rose, the reader better understands Hester Prynne.

Another major symbol found in *The Scarlet Letter* is thread and embroidery. Thread represents the course of life and human destiny. Hester uses her skills in the art of embroidery to make her letter a beautiful decoration rather than a mark of shame.

> On the breast of her gown, in fine red cloth, surrounded with an elaborate embroidery and fantastic flourishes of gold thread, appeared the letter A. It was so artistically done, and with so much fertility and gorgeous luxuriance of fancy, that it had all the effect of a last and fitting decoration to the apparel which she wore. (50)

By embroidering her letter, Hester begins to change the meaning of the letter from a stigma to a display of love and ability, thus strengthening the conflict between the spirit and the letter. Hester also uses needlework to support herself by embroidering the clothes of the townspeople. In this way, she creates her own destiny rather than letting the repressive Puritan society rule her life by trying to punish her and make her live in ignominy and infamy by wearing the scarlet letter. Hester also takes part in the conflict between the Puritan's patriarchal society and the matriarchal society that she supports. Hawthorne presents her embroidery as an act of defiance, for it becomes a sign that she is not a weak victim of society, as the Puritans attempt to make her, but a strong, able woman. Hester uses needlework to make clothes for Pearl. In doing so, she begins to have a role in Pearl's destiny. Because the thread passing through the sphere of the pearl represents an *axis mundi*, Pearl finds a natural attraction to the glimmering gold embroidery on her mother's scarlet letter and helps change the townspeople's treatment of Hester. For example, she protects her mother from the Puritan children who attempt to throw mud at Hester as she passes them while they play at the side of the road. Thread also represents unity. Hawthorne's use of the symbolism of thread adds to the reader's understanding of the plot and characters, for it explains the links between Hester, Pearl, and the Puritans and the changes between Hester and society.

Hawthorne uses the strong symbolism of the meteor at a climactic point in *The Scarlet Letter*. The meteor represents the struggle between the forces of the spirit and the forces of darkness. Dimmesdale finally climbs onto the scaffold, although not yet in public. He calls to Hester and Pearl, and the three stand together on the scaffold. As they do, a bright meteor lights up the night sky.

> So powerful was its radiance, that it thoroughly illuminated the dense medium of cloud betwixt the sky and the earth…And there stood the minister, with his hand over his heart, and Hester Prynne, with the embroidered letter glimmering on her bosom, and little Pearl, herself a symbol, and the connecting link between those two. They stood in the noon of that strange and solemn splendor, as if it were the light that is to reveal all secrets and the daybreak that shall unite all who belong to one another. (135)

During the appearance of the meteor, Chillingworth beholds the scene of Dimmesdale on the scaffold. As Hester, Dimmesdale, and Pearl stand with the meteor flashing through the darkness, they stand as one united spirit fighting against the society and their meaning of the letter. They become the light struggling to overcome the darkness of Chillingworth's plots to crush and break them. Hawthorne combines the powerful symbolism of the meteor with the powerful scene of the three united spirits of Hester, Dimmesdale and Pearl to create a strong vision that makes the reader become sympathetic with their struggles. With this understanding of the conflicts of the spirit versus the letter and the matriarchal versus the patriarchal society, one can gain a close understanding of Hester Prynne.

Through the use of symbolism, Nathaniel Hawthorne reveals a higher level of Hester Prynne's struggle against society, thus allowing the reader to gain a better knowledge of the plot and characters of *The Scarlet Letter*. Hawthorne's symbolism is strong in all of his stories and makes a great impression on the reader as he further understands the powerful ideas that Hawthorne presents. Because Hawthorne's stories and novels are often allegories, interpretation of the lives of his characters through symbolism allows people to better understand life itself.

Example 2:

Antithesis and Conflict
in Hawthorne's *The Scarlet Letter*

Sometimes the most obvious conflicts in life come from, and get their strength from, antithesis. Whether the conflict revolves around the balance of power between men and women, the idea of pride versus humility, or simply white and black pieces on a chessboard, antithesis draws conflict by its very nature. Nathaniel Hawthorne knew a great deal about this truth because of his life experiences and the conflict between the proud Hathornes and his family during his childhood. In *The Scarlet Letter*, Nathaniel Hawthorne uses antithesis to show the various conflicts of the book.

The first major conflict of *The Scarlet Letter* addresses the power struggle between matriarchal and patriarchal ideals. Hester's brave defiance of a stern government of men who want to repress the thoughts coming from her more revolutionary side represents this conflict and its many aspects.

> [Hester] assumed a freedom of speculation, then common enough on the other
> side of the Atlantic, but which our forefathers, had they known of it, would
> have held to be a deadlier crime than that stigmatized by the scarlet letter. (143)

Hawthorne uses antithesis to make this point even clearer by contrasting Hester's youth and beauty to the old, stern men of Puritan Boston. In the first chapter, Hawthorne compares the beautiful rose by the prison door to the ugly building next to it, using it as an analogy to Hester's struggles. Some antithesis exists in the character of the magistrates themselves, as Hawthorne tells the reader that though they "were doubtless, good men, sage, and just" (60), their gender and age make them the least worthy to judge an erring woman's heart. Despite their dislike for Hester's crime, the governor and magistrates wear fine clothes made by Hester, further deepening the antithesis provided by the story. In chapter 8, when Hester confronts the governor over Pearl's custody, the luxuriance of the governor's palace contrasts sharply with Hester's plain garb. Throughout *The Scarlet Letter*, Hester must step forward for herself and all freethinking people everywhere.

The fight between Hester's meaning for the scarlet letter and the one assigned to it by the Puritans represents the second conflict in the book. This conflict presents itself in the transformation of Boston's view of Hester, from a sinner to a saint. The scarlet letter originally stands for Hester's crime, but Hester reverses its purpose by making it out of fine thread and endowing it with a beauty that, along with her kindness and goodwill toward the people of Boston, gives her an image of an angel instead of an adulteress.

> She was self-ordained a Sister of Mercy; or, as we may rather say, the world's heavy hand had so ordained her, when neither the world nor she looked forward to this result. (141)

When Hester goes to Governor Bellingham's palace, an indentured servant new to Boston thinks that the letter *A* denotes some kind of high status, and in a way, he guesses correctly. Many times Hester refuses to take off the letter, knowing that it represents both a reminder of her sin and a symbol of her rebirth and contrition.

The unending struggle between public life and private life takes the focus in the final conflict of *The Scarlet Letter*. Secrets exist everywhere and in every character, most of all in Dimmesdale, who lies to the world and to himself. This conflict first starts when the magistrates and Dimmesdale question Hester about the father of her child and she refuses to reveal his identity. This conflict also goes on a much deeper level, as the public views Hester as a terrible person, but she knows that what she did was out of love. Hester and Pearl's lives from the beginning fill with conflict and antithesis because of the seemingly flawless child coming from a sinful birth. Also, Hester and Pearl's natures contrast so much that a stranger would have difficulty telling that they were of the same bloodline.

> Pearl was decked out in airy gayety. It would have been impossible to guess that this bright and sunny apparition owed its existence to the shape of gloomy fray; or that a fancy, at once so gorgeous and so delicate as must have been requisite to contrive the child's apparel, was the same that had achieved a task perhaps more difficult, in imparting so distinct a peculiarity to Hester's simple robe. (198)

Dimmesdale and Chillingworth both have many secrets about themselves and their actions, secrets that somehow draw Dimmesdale to Chillingworth together though they are mortal enemies. Neither of them can reveal their secrets until the end, when Dimmesdale dies and finally tells the world of his sin, while at the same time escaping Chillingworth's malice.

Throughout *The Scarlet Letter*, characters face conflicts filled with antithesis. Nathaniel Hawthorne drew many of his ideas about antithesis from his own life experiences, especially those as a child. He knew that antithesis and conflict are inseparable and consequently wove them together in every story. Because antithesis adds greater depth to the conflicts, it forms for readers a clearer image of what is really happening, both inside and out.

THE ART OF QUILT MAKING IN AMERICA
• • • • •

Women have always engaged in producing art, but our society has traditionally viewed female art as a craft rather than an art. In a patriarchal world, women artists have gone unrecognized and have often been discouraged and prevented from creating certain kinds of art. For hundreds of years, women were owned and supervised by men—fathers and husbands—and so women devoted their skill and talent to needlework, which they used to educate their daughters, especially through samplers, and provide for the warmth of their families through quilt making.

Women made quilts using three techniques: pieced, appliqué (also known as patchwork), or the use of quilting stitches alone on a solid color background. Cold winters demanded that all females old enough to hold a needle engage in needlework, in particular, quilt making. Girls learned to use their needles before they were taught to read, and most became skilled enough to produce at least twelve quilts by the time they were engaged to be married. Individuals designed and sewed the decorative top of the quilt and enlisted other women to help with the quilt stitches that held the top, padding, and back together, further adding design and beauty to the quilt. Quilting often provided a social life for women, even though women were sometimes very particular about selecting women skilled with their needles to help finish their quilts.

The quilting bee afforded rare opportunities for women to assemble for conversation and friendship. This all-day event ended with husbands, brothers, and friends joining the hostess for supper and dancing. Contrary to common belief, colonial women actually had very little time and available natural light for making quilts. From tending gardens and farm animals to candle and soap making, women performed many duties before sitting down in the evening to work on quilting.

Nathaniel Hawthorne's heroine Hester Prynne rescues herself from the patriarchal Puritan society of seventeenth-century Boston through her needlework. She supports herself by trading her skills of sewing and needlework for the goods she needs to survive, alone without a husband or family and with a daughter to raise and educate for seven years. Her beautiful needlework gains her favor with both men and women in the community, even those with the most power and authority. Her charity with her skill and her willingness to help others actually change the meaning of the badge of shame she must wear for her adultery and the child she bears as a consequence. By the close of *The Scarlet Letter*, the people of Boston declare to one another that the letter *A* Hester Prynne wears on her breast stands for *able* and *angel*.

Throughout world mythology, symbols of thread, needlework, and weaving create stories of destiny. The Greek poet Hesiod told stories of the three Fates, called *Moirae* in Greek and *Parcae* in Latin, who gave humankind at birth the powers of good and evil. *Moira* is the Greek word for lot, share, and destiny. The first Moira, Clotho, spun the thread of life, the second, Lachesis, gave each person a certain length of string, and the third, Atropos, cut that thread, bringing about the end of life.

Both Hawthorne and Hester appear to take on the role of the Fates. Hester embroiders her letter with flourishes of gold on scarlet, taunting the Puritans yet at the same time preparing them for the beautiful embroidery she will do for them. She continues to draw them in with her skillful work as she changes the way they perceive her, and when at the end of her life she has created her own destiny, the thread is cut and she is buried near the man she loves, the father of her child Pearl.

MAKING A PAPER QUILT
USING SYMBOLS
● ● ● ● ●

The following creative response to the novel is the design and production of a quilt square, one piece of a large quilt that will be constructed to show the symbolism in *The Scarlet Letter*. Remember as you design each piece of this appliquéd quilt the skill of the colonial woman and the heroine who controlled her own destiny through her needle and thread.

Preparation
1. Choose five symbols from the handbook, your journal, or the book itself that you think are related to each other as well as the novel.
2. Construct a design with these five symbols that show their connection to each other, placing them strategically to show their relationship. Their placement will be as meaningful as the symbols you have selected.

Materials
1. One six-by-six-inch sheet of white construction paper or heavy art paper
2. Colored construction paper
3. Glue, scissors, paper clips for gluing tiny pieces, black yarn for tying the squares together

Directions for Making Quilt Squares
1. Write the colors you need on your design sheet. Get the glue, scissors, a quilt square, and the construction paper you need.
2. Cut out the symbols and place them on your quilt square. Do not draw or write on the construction paper. All details must be cut out of paper and glued in place.
3. On the back of your finished square write a short paragraph explaining what the symbols mean and how they are connected to each other.
4. If you alone are designing the quilt, make enough quilt squares for the size quilt you want.

Directions for Making a Quilt
1. Punch holes in each of the four corners of each square.
2. Cut four- to six-inch pieces of black yarn.
3. Connect all squares by tying them together with the yarn. The yarn must pass through four holes at a time and then be tied in a bow in order to secure each piece to the quilt.

As I continued teaching, it became apparent that the experience of movement connected to feelings generates long-buried and unknown emotions and images. When these emotions and images are expressed through movement, we dance. And when these dances are connected to our lives, they bring about dramatic release and change in our will to live.

Anna Halprin
Dance as a Healing Art, 2000

CHAPTER 12
Modern American Literature

The canon of modern American literature spans decades of turbulent times in our history, each decade uniquely important in its contribution to the depiction of Americans as a people and a nation. Reading the literature from and about each period enriches our lives. It not only adds to an enlightenment and understanding of every subsequent literary period, but it also provides clues that help to explain just how and why we arrived at this place where we now live and work and play.

Although you may have a favorite writer or piece of literature from one particular period, taking a look at literature highlighted from several periods may be beneficial to adolescent readers in building a foundation for thinking and writing and connecting various authors and their ideas. I have selected poetry and prose from the Harlem Renaissance as well as from African Americans who began writing in the late 1930s and '40s. Although *To Kill a Mockingbird* was published in 1960, the novel reflects author Harper Lee's childhood reminiscences as well as the stirrings of Hitler's rise to power in the 1930s. A good segue for students who will be moving into nonfiction writing about the atrocities of labor camps and detention centers during World War II is a novel by John Knowles, *A Separate Peace*, which gives the reader an adolescent view of the war from a distance.

Writing flourished in Harlem as black American educators, philosophers, and writers of poetry and prose encouraged a changing literary scene. In this section you will study the poetry of Harlem Renaissance writers Langston Hughes, Countee Cullen, Claude McKay, and Paul Dunbar. Born during the Harlem Renaissance but not considered part of this movement, are Gwendolyn Brooks and Maya Angelou, whose extraordinary work in poetry and prose you will discover here.

The poignant story of families living in the South during the depression of the 1930s, Harper Lee's Pulitzer Prize winning novel *To Kill a Mockingbird* is a story in which students can see a number of themes that mirror humanity in every decade: race, class, and gender prejudice; courage; growing up; education; boundaries; isolation; and illusions. Harper Lee intertwines these themes with the other elements of the story to produce a book that endures.

John Knowles sets *A Separate Peace*, a story of friendship, maturation, and self-acceptance, at a New England boys' prep school during World War II. What makes this story a good one that teenagers continue to read is its universal theme: the hardships of the rites of passage from boy to man. His use of symbolism enhances characterization, setting, and plot and offers students a good story with opportunities to increase literary analysis skills.

Lorraine Hansberry's play *A Raisin in the Sun,* set in the 1950s, looks at the human condition and choices people make while struggling to become the people they were meant to be, despite racism and economic disadvantage. With realism and pathos and a sense of humor, too, Hansberry allows the audience to see the members of the Younger family overcome their obstacles through love and pride.

All the pieces of modern American literature in this section support the basic theme of the chapter titled "Heritage of Humanity." These readings ask you to analyze the pieces thematically with less emphasis on a formalistic approach. As you refer to the ideas of three psychologists—Carl Jung, Abraham Maslow, and Lawrence Kohlberg—you will consider concepts that may help to answer this question: What is America's heritage regarding humanity? Have Americans inherited a widespread benevolence, perhaps even a feeling of *esprit de corps*, and are we passing it on to future generations? Or have Americans succumbed to the temptation of betrayal, all too easily handed down in habits of greed and selfishness? Or are Americans sitting on the fence confused about which path to take? Three decades of literature will help build a foundation for discussing these questions and their possible answers.

THE HARLEM RENAISSANCE
AND BEYOND
● ● ● ● ●

The Harlem Renaissance

A literary surge of a different kind came to fruition after World War I. A renaissance of creativity and energy among black American writers took root in the ghetto of Harlem in New York City in the 1920s. Starting around 1910, this section of upper Manhattan witnessed a migration of African Americans from the South, making it the largest community of its kind in the nation. It was one of the centers of innovation in jazz, and the prolific new writers who lived there helped to give this literary movement its name. It was called the Harlem Renaissance, significantly altering the character of literature for African American writers who no longer tried to imitate white writers but created a new style that encouraged confidence and racial pride. The poems, stories, and novels of these authors explored black life and culture in a sophisticated way.

Below you will see listed many of the major figures in this movement whose writing we will be exploring.

Alain Locke: Teacher, writer, and philosopher, Locke graduated from Harvard University and was the first black Rhodes scholar, studying at Oxford from 1907 to 1910. He served as head of the department of philosophy at Howard University in Washington, D.C. His many works include nonfiction books about black achievement in America.

He is remembered as the leader of the Harlem Renaissance. His work includes the following:

The New Negro
Four Negro Poets
Frederick Douglass, a Biography of Anti-Slavery
Negro Art—Past and Present
The Negro and His Music

James Weldon Johnson: A lawyer, poet, novelist, and anthologist of African-American culture, Johnson was admitted to the bar in 1897 and began practicing law in Atlanta, Georgia. He and his brother began writing songs and made their way to the Broadway stage in 1901, writing more than two hundred songs for the stage. He later held diplomatic posts, taught at Fisk University in Nashville, and wrote poetry. His books include

Fifty Years and Other Poems
Book of American Negro Poetry
American Negro Spirituals
God's Trombones
Along This Way
Autobiography of an Ex-Colored Man

Claude McKay: In 1928 this Jamaican-born poet and novelist wrote what was considered during his time to be the most popular novel by an African American, *Home to Harlem.* He attended Tuskegee Institute and Kansas State Teachers' College. His writing was considered the most militant of the Harlem Renaissance, displayed in two volumes of poetry, *Spring in New Hampshire* in 1920 and *Harlem Shadows* in 1922. He lived abroad successfully and continued to produce short stories, poetry, articles, and books.

Countee Cullen: Easily winning academic honors, especially in poetry, during his early school years, Cullen attended New York University and Harvard University, where his poetry attracted wide acclaim. His first collection of poetry *Color* earned him the reputation of one of the finest poets of the Harlem Renaissance. After he published *The Black Christ and Other Poems* in 1929, he taught in the New York City public schools until the end of his life.

Langston Hughes: After attending Columbia University, Hughes took menial jobs while continuing to write poetry. As a busboy in a hotel in Washington, D.C., he put three of his own poems beside the plate of American poet Vachel Lindsay in the dining room. The next day, newspapers around the country reported the discovery of a new poet, and he was given a scholarship to Lincoln University in Pennsylvania. His first two books were published before he graduated in 1929. Some of his books follow:

The Weary Blues
Fine Clothes to the Jew
Not Without Laughter
Mule Bones (a play with collaborator Zora Neal Hurston)
The Ways of White Folks
A Pictorial History of the Negro in America
The Book of Negro Folklore
Street Scene (opera)
The Panther and the Lash

Wallace Thurman: Editor, critic, novelist and playwright, Thurman moved to Harlem in 1925 and became the managing editor of the black periodical *Messenger.* His contributions to the Harlem Renaissance involved editing publications that encouraged black writers. He also wrote a popular play, *Harlem,* in 1929. That same year he published his first novel *The Blacker the Berry: A Novel of Negro Life.* He is best known for his novel published in 1932, *Infants of the Spring.*

Arna Bontemps: This writer also published poetry in the famous black periodicals of the mid-1920s, *Opportunity* and *Crisis.* He published what scholars consider to be the final work of the Harlem Renaissance, the novel *God Send Sunday.* Countee Cullen and Arna Bontemps collaborated to dramatize the novel in 1946, and it became *St. Louis Women.* He is also known for his many nonfiction books for children and his edited anthologies of other black American writers.

Paul Dunbar: Best known for his verse and short stories written in black dialect, Paul Dunbar was one of the first black writers to attain national recognition with a large popular audience. His work is often set in a pastoral Pre-Civil War South. His volumes of poetry include *Oak and Ivy, Majors and Minors,* and *Lyrics of Lowly Life.* He was only thirty-four when he died, yet he published four collections of short stories and four novels in addition to his collections of verse.

...and beyond:

Maya Angelou: Although this writer was born at the end of the period known as the Harlem Renaissance, she also explored the themes of economic and racial oppression by drawing heavily on her personal experiences. Her autobiographical work, *I Know Why the Caged Bird Sings,* won recognition for her in 1970, and in 1981 she received a lifetime appointment as Reynolds Professor of

American Studies at Wake Forest University, Winston-Salem, North Carolina. In 1993 she was invited to compose and deliver a poem for the inauguration of President Bill Clinton. Other works include the following:

Gather Together in My Name
The Heart of a Woman
All God's Children Need Traveling Shoes
Just Give Me a Cool Drink of Water 'fore I Diiie
And Still I Rise

Gwendolyn Brooks: Born in 1917 in Topeka, Kansas, this American poet was the first black poet to receive a Pulitzer Prize. Published in 1949, *Annie Allen* is a collection of poems about a black girl growing up in Chicago. Her novel *Maud Martha*, published in 1953, uses this same theme. Brooks' other works include

A Street in Bronzeville   *Winnie*
The Bean Eaters   *Children Coming Home*
Selected Poems
In the Mecca
Primer for Blacks
Young Poets' Primer
To Disembark
The Near-Johannesburg Boy, and Other Poems
Blacks

Journal Prompt: Read the poems listed below and choose one to write about. Identify the most effective features of the poem: symbols, figurative language, irony, antithesis, theme, sound, and rhyme. Listen to the jazzy blues of the 1920s and 30s, especially the haunting lyrics of Billie Holiday's "Strange Fruit." How do these literary tools contribute to the themes of betrayal, loss, intolerance, injustice, freedom, sacrifice, isolation, hope, and despair?

Langston Hughes: "Mother to Son," "Cross," "Theme for English B"

Countee Cullen: "Saturday's Child," "Incident," "Scottsboro, Too, Is Worth Its Song"

Claude McKay: "If We Must Die," "The White House"

Paul Dunbar: "We Wear the Mask," "Sympathy"

LINDY HOP:
A DANCE FOR HARMONY AND HEALING
● ● ● ● ●

In the late 1900s, millions of Southern African Americans migrated north looking for an easier way of life, a life free of the burdens that racial tension, injustice, and poverty created. What transpired was a movement that made freedom its trademark—in the literature, as we have seen in the writers of the Harlem Renaissance, but also in their music and their dance.

In the world of white social behavior of this period, dancing was formal and learned. The movement of blacks into New York City's neighborhood of Harlem, together with the growing enthusiasm for swing music, produced lively new dances. They were characterized by a kind of freedom that allowed dancers to let go and improvise, to move their bodies in a way that in the 1920s white people considered suggestive. They took the popular swing-out steps, improvised, and a new dance was born—the Lindy Hop. It was fast, athletic, and even sometimes airborne. The dance took its name when pilot Charles Lindberg "hopped" across the Atlantic to Paris in a solo crossing in his plane the Spirit of St. Louis on May 21, 1927.

Whites and blacks upset the segregationists of the time by dancing the Lindy Hop together in popular dance halls. The Savoy Ballroom occupied one city block at Lenox Avenue and 140th Street in Harlem. Although nightclubs and stages showcased the dancing of this jazz age, the center of the new dances, particularly the Lindy Hop, was the Savoy.

Frankie Manning, one of the lead dancers at the Savoy, performed worldwide with Whitey's Lindy Hoppers as well as his own troupe, the Congaroo Dancers. In the late 1950s when the popularity of swing music began to fade, Manning left dancing for thirty years. He later returned as swing dancing re-established interest, and at the age of eighty began teaching the Lindy Hop to a new generation. Many people, young and old and of every ethnicity, began learning from his easy instructional videos.

Ernie Smith, a white dancer who remembers whites and blacks together crowding the dance floor at the Savoy, made this observation, "When cultures don't freely mingle, they get weird ideas about each other" (*Dancing*). It has been said that you know who you are when you dance, when you allow yourself to move freely and unrestrained to the beat of the music you feel in your body and heart and soul. While therapists today subscribe to the theory that dancing heals both the body and the mind, the Lindy Hoppers of the 1920s were already practicing a cultural healing through dance. African Americans created a dance out of their heritage that drew both whites and blacks together in harmony.

Journal Prompt: Write about your own personal experiences with dancing: a school dance, a recital or performance, or perhaps an unusual experience you had with dancing. How did dancing make you feel? What "rules" of behavior change when you dance?

HARPER LEE'S *TO KILL A MOCKINGBIRD:* TEXT AND FILM

• • • • •

Although the novel *To Kill a Mockingbird* was published in 1960, Harper Lee set her story in the Depression years of the early 1930s. Because little social progress had taken place since the writers of the Harlem Renaissance, change was slow in coming for African Americans. The Civil Rights Act had not been signed into law, and discrimination existed as an arduous and oppressive way of life that would not be assuaged for more than thirty years. In the 1960s large demonstrations occurred, riots erupted, militant movements began, and civil rights workers were murdered. After the law was passed in 1964, the movement shifted toward changing attitudes of white people and creating a more equitable life for all citizens, regardless of race. In writing *To Kill a Mockingbird*, Harper Lee said she had one story to tell, and she never wrote another book. She relied on remembrances of her childhood growing up in the 1930s as well as the controversial account of the Scottsboro Trials in 1931 in which nine black youths were unfairly indicted on charges of having raped two white women in a freight car passing through the state. In a series of trials all nine were found guilty, receiving either life in prison or the death penalty. Between 1937 and 1976, the charges were dropped and those who had fled were pardoned. This incident may have suggested the parallel tragedy of Tom Robinson who is also unjustly accused of raping a white woman.

In the early 1960s, Texas playwright and screenwriter Horton Foote wrote the screenplay for Harper Lee's Pulitzer Prize winning novel *To Kill a Mockingbird*. Gregory Peck starred as Atticus Finch and won an Academy Award for his portrayal as the Southern lawyer, a hero to his family and his community. The film won other Academy Awards, even though, as often happens when books are turned into films, several of the subordinating characters were eliminated: Aunt Alexandra, Francis, Uncle Jack, and Dolphus Raymond, to name a few. Some interesting parts of the action were also cut: Jem's destruction of Mrs. Dubose's camellias and his subsequent reading aloud to her as the old woman weans herself from her addiction. Despite the changes, Horton Foote also won a Pulitzer Prize for the screenplay of *To Kill a Mockingbird*. Watching the film version after reading the novel gives you additional exposure to a classic story and introduces you to the work of two important writers.

In this chapter you will find a study guide with questions that can help you achieve greater depth in your understanding of *To Kill a Mockingbird*. Read the questions before each group of chapters. Once you have finished the novel, you will see more clearly the ways in which more modern writers use figurative language, antithesis, themes and archetypal motifs.

Through your own experience with writing short fiction, you learned how important it is for a writer to develop characters' wants and needs. Psychologist Abraham Maslow's years of research resulted in a theory that he termed a hierarchy of needs (1987). He believed all people have certain basic and certain higher needs that are interdependent for harmonious living. When one lower need is not met, a person cannot meet a higher need. In this chapter you will find an explanation of those needs. Apply them to the characters in *To Kill a Mockingbird* and discover how useful Maslow's ideas can be in explaining why characters, as well as people in real life, behave the way they do.

Finally, we will look at the work of another psychologist, Lawrence Kohlberg (1981), who conducted research studies at Harvard's Center for Moral Education. Kohlberg, also a developmental psychologist, looked at how people progress in their moral reasoning. He believed that human beings move through six stages of moral development, one at a time from elementary school age to adult, and that only through experience with moral dilemmas could an individual move up to the next level. The characters in *To Kill a Mockingbird* offer numerous moral dilemmas for the reader to examine. Read about the six levels of moral development and determine where each character resides along the continuum. This information should provide more insight into the motivation that drives the characters' actions.

Journal Prompt: Choose one of the following to write about: 1. an incident in your relationship with parents or siblings, 2. a memorable adventure with a friend or group of friends, 3. an injustice you experienced over which you had little or no control.

To Kill a Mockingbird,
A Study Guide
● ● ● ● ●

Before you read Harper Lee's *To Kill a Mockingbird*, consider these questions and ideas not only after reading but also before in order to read with more insight into the novel.

Chapters 1-5

1. In the first three paragraphs of chapter 1, what three events in the lives of Jem and Scout Finch does the narrator attribute to Jem's broken arm? Why do you think those events might be important?
2. How is Dill Harris a catalyst in the story? How does he move the plot along?
3. Who is the malevolent phantom? How and why has he become a legend? What is the truth about him?
4. From the children in her room, what opportunities does Miss Caroline have to learn about class? What does the reader begin to learn about class prejudice?
5. How do these characters cope with isolation: Boo, the Radleys, Scout, Dill, the Ewells, Miss Caroline, the Cunninghams, Atticus?
6. How do the children's activities reflect the culture of the 1930s?
7. How do summer and autumn support the archetype of the seasons?

Chapters 6-10

1. Which characters perpetuate the myths of race and gender? Who are the objects of those myths?
2. How does Harper Lee support these themes: gender prejudice, change, boundaries, friendship, racial prejudice, justice, and courage?
3. The author uses images and symbols: moonlight, the gate, the Radley's ramshackle house, white shirt bobbing, the knothole, darkness, the fence, curtains, oak tree, street light, shadow, gray, broken pocket watch, knife. What is she trying to accomplish? Why does she use these particular images?
4. How is the mad dog scene an example of foreshadowing?
5. How does the author create a scene of antithesis even though the community works together when Miss Maudie's house burns?
6. Why does Harper Lee juxtapose images in characterization, setting, mood, tone, events in the plot, and themes? What overall feeling or image is she trying to create?

Chapters 11-15

1. What is Cal's reason for having two ways of talking? What element of the story does this "modest double life" (125) support? What do the children learn from Cal?
2. What do Atticus and Alexandra mean by "gentle breeding"? (133). How do their interpretations differ? How does Alexandra perpetuate the myth of Southern

womanhood?

3. Describe Atticus as a parent. How would you rate him and why?

4. In chapter 11, Atticus says, "It's when you know you're licked before you begin, but you begin anyway and you see it through no matter what. You rarely win, but sometimes you do. Mrs. Dubose won, all ninety-eight pounds of her" (112). How does this statement seem a paradox? Does this philosophy also describe Atticus?

5. In chapter 14 Dill runs away. How are his actions related to the actions of Boo Radley? What is Harper Lee trying to show?

6. Which characters embody the theme of innocence? How does the author develop that theme in terms of story elements and word choice?

7. What mature understanding of friendship and loyalty does Atticus seem to have? Do you think Atticus is naïve or realistic?

8. In chapter 15, as well as several other chapters, the author uses images of light. Why is this symbolism effective?

9. In chapter 15 Harper Lee shows different kinds of strength. Which kind prevails in this chapter?

Chapters 16-25

1. What does Bob Ewell show about himself in this testimony?

2. How is Mayella isolated? How is she being used to perpetuate the myth of Southern womanhood?

3. Explain the symbolism of Atticus unbuttoning his vest.

4. Based on testimony, what do you think actually happened between Mayella and Tom and Mayella and her father?

5. What do you think Atticus is really saying in his closing remarks?

6. Why does Dill say, "I think I'll be a clown..."? (216).

7. In chapter 23, why does Jem think Boo Radley wants to stay inside and not come out?

8. In chapter 25, how does Scout explain Mr. Underwood's editorial about the senseless slaughter of songbirds? Why do you think the narrator says, "...in the secret courts of men's hearts Atticus had no case"? (241).

Chapters 26-31

1. How does Scout define democracy? How does Miss Gates explain the difference between the U.S. and Germany politically? Does Miss Gates appear to be hypocritical?

2. What three things happen in October that foreshadow the end of the book?

3. What is the irony in Mrs. Merriweather's conclusion about the Mrunas?

4. In chapter 29, do you think the author's description of Boo is appropriate for him?

5. Why does Atticus think Jem killed Bob Ewell?

6. Why does Heck Tate have a switchblade? Who do you think the owner is?

7. Why does Heck Tate want to cover up Bob Ewell's killer? Why does Scout compare this cover-up to shooting a mockingbird?

8. How is the archetype of seasons explained in chapter 31?

9. Why does Harper Lee have Atticus read *The Gray Ghost* to Scout at the end? What final words does the author have to say about innocence, friendship, and illusions?

Discuss

1. The myth of Southern womanhood
2. Parenting in each of the four families: Finch, Cunningham, Ewell, and Radley
3. Courage, as shown by Dill, Scout, Jem, Mrs. Dubose, Atticus, Boo, and Tom
4. Cowardice, as shown by the town, the Ewells, and Dolphus Raymond
5. The symbolism of the tree and seasons
6. The theme of growing up, moving from innocence to experience
7. Illusions, things that are not what they seem to be
8. Justice and equality
9. Influence of the 1930s

Maslow's Hierarchy of Needs
• • • • •

Abraham Maslow (1987) is an American psychologist who established a widely accepted theory that human beings are motivated by needs that must be satisfied in a particular order. He believed that violence and other evil deeds occur as a result of people not getting their needs met. Furthermore, certain basic needs had to be met before people could reach out and help others. Finally he believed that all needs had to be met before a person could be considered "self-actualized," that is, a mature person who has developed over time a healthy, positive sense of self-worth and contentment with his or her life.

The most basic needs begin at the bottom of his hierarchy, the physiological needs, while self-actualization, at the top, denotes that all needs have been met and the individual is happy and satisfied with life. Hence, this person can behave unselfishly towards others in a much broader way.

Maslow's hierarchy can be a helpful tool in examining the motives of characters in literature, but, as one student wisely pointed out, not everyone always fits so neatly into tight little categories. Their circumstances dictate a different mentality. Furthermore, the categories are fluid, not rigid, as they apply to unique situations and personalities at the time. Death of a loved one, for example, often affects one's feelings of stability. A person who at one stage of life may be experiencing a strong sense of self-esteem—all's right with the world—could find himself with quite different needs as he copes with that tragedy.

Characters in fiction reflect that reality. Applied to Harper Lee's *To Kill a Mockingbird*, Maslow's theory can help the reader to understand the wants and needs of the characters and, thus, their motives. For example, perhaps Mayella Ewell has a troubled family life and no friends because her need for safety and stability has not been fulfilled by her abusive father. Another character, Dill Harris, runs away from home to the safe haven of the Finches. Atticus

Finch, the figure of the archetypal father, lives a self-actualized life even when tragedy strikes. His ability to respond to grief indicates his high level of wisdom and strength.

Lawrence Kohlberg's
Stages of Moral Development
● ● ● ● ●

Lawrence Kohlberg was also an American psychologist who became famous for his work in moral education and development at Harvard University from 1968 to 1987. According to Crain (118-36), Kohlberg believed that moral reasoning develops through a process of six stages that lead to ethical behavior, and his observations convinced him that individuals become more adept at responding to moral dilemmas as they progress from stage one to stage six.

Any one of us has the capacity to respond in one stage of moral development and yet, in the next moment, act out of a different stage. We choose to behave in stages that fit our particular circumstances at the time. For example, you may follow human-made laws of society established by government (stage four) but later behave in such a way that will benefit your own best interest, a kind of reciprocity with a friend who might do something for you (stage two). And who hasn't behaved in an especially appropriate way in order to gain approval from someone (stage three)?

You don't need a background in psychology to observe characters in literature and decide where the motivation for their behavior lies. In applying Kohlberg's stages to the moral and ethical behavior of the characters in *To Kill a Mockingbird*, the reader has yet another tool for a more complex analysis of the literature. Because characters in literature reflect real human behavior, they too can exemplify Kohlberg's stages of moral development. Scout Finch considers losing Atticus's good opinion of her a serious situation to avoid (stage three). Sheriff Tate, at the end of the novel, makes the decision to break the law and cover up a crime for the benefit of the one man who protects the children from the vicious attack of Bob Ewell and who does "this town a great service..." (276). Although he is probably acting out of what Kohlberg called social contract, stage five, he could actually come close to the sixth and highest level of moral development called principled conscience. Tate breaks the law when he realizes the existence of a higher law that protects Boo Radley from any more harm.

All paths lead to the same goal: to convey to others what we are.
And we must pass through solitude and difficulty, isolation and
silence, in order to reach forth to the enchanted place where we
can dance our clumsy dance and sing our sorrowful song—but in
this dance or in this song there are fulfilled the most ancient rites
of our conscience in the awareness of being human and of believing
in a common destiny.

Pablo Neruda (1904-73)
Toward the Splendid City, upon
receiving the Nobel Prize, 1971

CHAPTER 13

Heritage of Humanity: Esprit de Corps, or Betrayal?

In chapter 7 you read a play and then the story "The Maypole of Merry Mount" by Nathaniel Hawthorne. Although the author saw himself as a writer of romance and not history, he nevertheless implies accurately the righteousness of the Puritan settlers in the Massachusetts Bay Colony and their lack of tolerance for all others, including the Indians. What historians tell us is that the English Puritan settlers saw the Indians as savages. When they left England to travel to America, they left a country that had recently suppressed the Irish, massacring thousands of the Irish "savages." The dehumanization resulted from the colonists' association of Indians with the devil, in much the same way they viewed the Irish. In 1611 theatergoers in London were told that in Shakespeare's *The Tempest*, Caliban, whose characteristics were similar to the American Indian, was a vile devil who had to be isolated from the preferred race.

The Puritans in Hawthorne's stories are the same kind of English colonists who believed the New England Indians were savages who could not be redeemed. They massacred thousands of them, and thousands more died from the diseases these Europeans brought with them to the New World. They justified so many deaths by saying they were God's way of making land available for the chosen people. The death of the Indians, they say, was a sign from God that the land now belonged to them. In *The Tempest*, Prospero enslaves Caliban, whom the English would have identified as an Indian, and isolates him on another part of the island. One historian, Richard Takaki, suggests that "*The Tempest* can be approached as a fascinating tale that served as a masquerade for the creation of a new society in America" (25). If so, what this says about the English Americans is that they were once again drawing the line between the civilized and "the other." As history played out this story several hundred years later, the American people eventually pushed the Indians onto reservations, preventing them from moving forward and living harmoniously in their own way.

Will the legacy humankind leaves to future generations be one of *esprit de corps*—a spirit of loyalty that unites us and encourages us to help one another—or will it be one of betrayal, caused by greed and indifference to human suffering and need? We often speak of the desire for world peace in a casual, facetious manner. Is it because we really don't believe in our hearts that it is attainable? Always in search of life's answers, social scientists point to ethnic, cultural, and class differences as the agents that divide us and prevent the world from reaching a point of compromise and conciliation. We read and hear about and even sometimes view aghast via television and internet any number of barbaric events that raise man's inhumanity to man to shocking, unimaginable extremes.

Literature, that great mirror of all life as writers see it, has become the outlet and essentially a reflection of this struggle, and so it is through our writing and our reading that we have an opportunity to change the outcome of our inheritance. Perhaps if we see ourselves in this mirror often enough, we may choose a synergistic life in which helping others concomitantly improves the quality of our own lives. In the epistle dedicatory to the play *Man and Superman* (1903), George Bernard Shaw writes,

> This is the true joy in life, the being used for a purpose recognized by yourself as a mighty one; the being thoroughly worn out before you are thrown on the scrap heap; the being a force of nature instead of a feverish selfish little clod of ailments and grievances complaining that the world will not devote itself to making you happy. (203)

In this chapter we will look at novels, short stories, autobiographies, poetry, and articles that will help us understand the nature and responsibility of this legacy. Following the descriptive information about the pieces of literature are questions students can consider and discuss. The culminating activity asks you to state an assertion about one of the issues and support it with the literature you have read.

The heritage and culture projects in this handbook are natural accompaniments to your examination of the heritage of our humanity.

STUDY GUIDE TERMS
● ● ● ● ●

Scholars who study human behavior attribute the conflict between kindness and hatred largely to the distress that comes from fear of *the other* and the subsequent inability to tolerate people and things that are different. The reasons for this intolerance vary, but research shows that the more tolerance for ambiguity we have, the more we can accept and understand the mysteries of life, of which the other plays an important role. Is the answer to harmony, therefore, simple compliance? No, but an understanding that certainty is not always possible, that a gray area exists, may be the antidote to our anxieties about life's many conflicts. The following terms may be helpful in discussing the short stories, books, and plays that you will be reading as well as the films you will be viewing.

The other: people who have ideas that conflict with yours; also, the conflicting ideas themselves

Ambiguity: quality of being uncertain, indefinite, open to interpretation (adjective: ambiguous)

Moral ambiguity: thinking that something is neither good nor bad but somewhere in between: "Good" and "bad" are open to interpretation, depending on the circumstances.

Tolerance for ambiguity: acceptance of uncertainty or lack of clarity, acceptance of what one does not understand fully and completely

Esprit de corps: the close bond or common spirit of a group often devoted to a cause

Shadow: according to Jung, the darker side of our unconscious selves

Individuation: according to Jung, becoming the individuals we were meant to be (similar to Maslow's highest level in the hierarchy of needs, self-actualization)

Compliance: agreement to go along with someone else's wishes or decisions regardless of one's own wishes or needs

Righteousness: quality of being morally right or thinking of oneself as morally right and often morally superior

Ego: the part of the psyche that is conscious and most directly controls thought

Archetypal warrior: one who is willing to commit to a value higher than his own ego's needs

Paradox: a statement that seems contradictory on the surface but nonetheless may be true

Antidote: an agent that counteracts an injurious or harmful effect

HERITAGE OF HUMANITY QUESTIONS
• • • • •
Discussing the Issues

1. Does the legacy of humanity involve a choice between *esprit de corps* or betrayal? Why? Is there a middle ground?
2. Is this choice affected by a state of moral ambiguity?
3. How does an act of civil disobedience support the side of *esprit de corps*?
4. Do rules of civility change in war time?
5. Do power and greed override honorable behavior?
6. Which is more honorable: *esprit de corps* or betrayal?
7. Is friendship always fragile, able to be broken easily?

8. What makes one person adhere strongly to the bonds between human beings and others succumb to the weakness of betrayal of other human beings?

9. When one betrays others, does he betray himself? All humankind?

10. What does helping one person do to the whole of humanity? (Mother Teresa)

11. Why is it so difficult to adhere to the state of *esprit de corps*?

12. Why does betrayal seem patriotic to some?

13. Is humankind's nature one of benevolence or hatred?

14. How does Jung's shadow theory contribute to our understanding of betrayal?

15. How does Jung's theory of individuation explain our achievement of *esprit de corps*?

16. How can people achieve tolerance for ambiguity?

17. What makes an individual resist a request of compliance with something he doesn't accept?

18. What ego needs affect your choices in loyalty and betrayal?

19. Is betrayal just a matter of opinion or perspective, or is there a universal code or principle on which all people agree?

20. Is the code of "an eye for an eye" a result of betrayal or justice?

21. Should we be looking more at the big picture, or at the individual person?

22. When does *esprit de corps* become betrayal? Does *esprit de corps* always result in doing good?

23. When is it appropriate to view yourself as belonging to humanity, not just to a country or a group?

24. Can we define betrayal as going against your group for a higher cause?

25. When does tolerance for ambiguity become complacency? (Complacency is the comfort zone we are in that makes us avoid doing what we should do. It is a feeling of acceptance of the way things are, even when they are morally wrong.)

READINGS
● ● ● ● ●

1. Title: "Guests of the Nation"
   Author: Frank O'Connor
   Form: Short story
   Setting: Ireland during or shortly after the Easter Rebellion, around 1919
   Synopsis: Two young Irish soldiers, having been assigned the task of guarding two British soldiers in a farmhouse, become friends with their captives. They play cards, discuss politics and religion, and help with the chores. Unexpectedly they receive word that two Irish soldiers have been executed by the British and must therefore respond in kind.

Journal Prompt: Choose one of the following to write about.

1. DOES duty to country have no limitations?
2. When do human beings have value as a commodity?
3. What are people willing to do to the other?
4. Why do you think the Rules of the Geneva Convention, the international humanitarian laws in armed conflict, were signed in 1949? If they had been signed before the story began, how would the plot have changed?

2. Title: "The Heathen"
Author: Jack London
Form: Short story
Setting: Tahiti, Borabora, Australia, and various South Pacific islands during the late 1800s
Synopsis: An American pearl buyer is saved by a Pacific Islander when their ship breaks up in a storm. The white man and the brown-skinned native named Otoo become best friends until they participate in the ceremony of the exchanging of names and make their bond permanent. Otoo's loyalty to his friend saves his life a second time.

Journal Prompt: Choose one of the following to write about.

1. TO what extent will a person go for friendship?
2. HOW does viewing yourself as a part of humanity contribute to your capacity for friendship?
3. What is the difference between friendship and obsequious behavior toward another person?

3. Title: *To Kill a Mockingbird*
    Author: Harper Lee
    Form: Novel
    Setting: Macomb, Alabama, 1932
    Synopsis: Two stories intertwine around the Finch family who live in the midst of the Great Depression. The father, Atticus Finch, a lawyer in this small Southern town, agrees to defend Tom Robinson, a black man unjustly accused of raping a white woman. At the same time, the Finch children, Jem and his younger sister Scout, spend countless hours trying to discover the identity of their reclusive neighbor Boo Radley. The characters cross lines of race, class, and gender, not only to help each other but also to save their lives.

> Journal Prompt: Choose one of the following topics, apply it to the novel, and write at least three pages in your journal using textual support (two to four quotations), citing your page numbers with parenthetical references.
> 1. Maslow's hierarchy of needs
> 2. Kohlberg's stages of moral development
> 3. One of these tools: antithesis, symbolism, irony, theme, imagery
> 4. Historical references
> 5. Moral ambiguity or moral relativism
> 6. Freud's id, ego, and superego

4. Title: "The Enemy"
    Author: Pearl S. Buck
    Form: Short story
    Setting: Japan, 1940s during WWII
    Synopsis: Prior to WWII, a Japanese doctor received his training in the United States, where he met his Japanese wife who also was a student. One morning in Japan, after the war begins, the doctor and his wife find a wounded American sailor washed up on the beach outside his house. Faced with a dilemma, he must decide whether to adhere to his nationalistic loyalty and let the sailor die, or abide by his American training to save all lives and heal the man.

Journal Prompt: Choose one of the following to write about.

1. Explain how the author Pearl Buck uses diction and imagery to show the theme of brotherhood in the story "The Enemy."

2. Explain how the author creates a sense of moral ambiguity through the development of the character Sadao Hoki.

3. HOW is tolerance for ambiguity an asset for the characters in the story?

4. What was the irony in defining people as friend or foe in the story?

5. Title: *Farewell to Manzanar*
    Author: Jeanne Watatsuki Houston and James D. Houston
    Form: Autobiography
    Setting: Long Beach, California in 1941 and Manzanar internment
    camp in Owens Valley California, 1942
    Synopsis: Jeanne Houston recalls her life with her family after all the Japanese living in America during WWII were relocated to internment camps. Houston describes the fear, the indignation, and the financial loss forced on a group of Americans whom the government labeled as potentially dangerous.

Journal Prompt: Choose one of the following to write about.

1. What has America learned from the relocation of the Japanese during WWII?

2. Why is the relocation an incident that could repeat itself today?

3. What makes an entire nation afraid of "the other"?

6. Title: *Night*
    Author: Elie Wiesel
    Form: Autobiography
    Setting: Sighet, Transylvania, 1941-43

Birkenau, Auschwitz, and Buna—Nazi concentration camps, 1944-45

Synopsis: Elie Wiesel, winner of the 1986 Nobel Peace Prize, relates his experience of peaceful life in Sighet, Transylvania, until rumors spread about Nazi terrorism. Soon, he explains, life as his family and friends remember it disintegrates as Jews are torn from their homes and sent to work camps and extermination centers. Wiesel describes the nightmare of trying to survive under impossible conditions.

Journal Prompt: Choose one of the following to write about.

1. What can the world learn from Elie Wiesel about surviving the most heinous kind of betrayal?

2. What can Jung's shadow theory tell us about that kind of betrayal? Does understanding the shadow help you understand betrayal?

3. If we have learned from the Holocaust, why is the betrayal of humanity, "homo homini lupus," still happening in the twenty-first century?

7. Title: *Man's Search for Meaning*
   Author: Viktor Frankl
   Form: Autobiography and nonfiction book on logotherapy
   Setting: Concentration camps of Auschwitz and Dachau, 1944-45, WWII
   Synopsis: Psychiatrist Viktor Frankl writes about his experiences in Nazi concentration camps and the positive approach he developed to help himself and his fellow prisoners survive. Today his ideas are known as logotherapy, a way to transcend suffering and find meaning in life.

Journal Prompt: Viktor Frankl believed that survival depends to a great extent on the quality of one's response to the things that threaten survival. How does having a choice to love or to hate a person or a thing, even one's enemy, make a difference in living or dying? How does autonomy contribute to one's attitude about life?

8. Title: *A Separate Peace*
Author: John Knowles
Form: Novel
Setting: New Hampshire private boys preparatory boarding school, 1942, WWII
Synopsis: Two boys, roommates in an exclusive New England prep school, learn how to live harmoniously with themselves, with each other, and with the events of WWII hanging over their heads—but not without a price.

Journal Prompt: Choose one of the following to write about.

1. Why is it so difficult to face the truth in times of trouble?

2. Some people believe humankind's inherent bestiality is a manifestation of the shadow. Do you support this idea? Explain.

3. Why is sending young men and women to war a necessary evil?

9. Title: "The Coup de Grace"
    Author: Ambrose Bierce
    Form: Short story
    Setting: Civil War battlefield
    Synopsis: An officer happens upon a friend who is wounded. Although the dying man cannot speak, his eyes ask for mercy. Will his friend be able to deliver a merciful death?

Journal Prompt: choose one of the following to write about.

1. Can the rules of civility apply in wartime? How?

2. Is it possible to betray another person for a higher cause?

3. Is mercy killing ever benevolent?

4. What is the moral ambiguity of war?

10. Title: *A Raisin in the Sun*
    Author: Lorraine Hansberry
    Form: Play
    Setting: Chicago, 1950s
    Synopsis: A black family struggles to overcome issues of generation, race, gender, and education. It is about conflicts that too often destroy individual fulfillment. Ms. Hansberry takes her title from Langston Hughes' poem,

    What happens to a dream deferred?
    Does it dry up
    Like a raisin in the sun? (qtd. in Hansberry, 3)

Journal Prompt: Choose one of the following. Write three or four pages in your journal, including three to four quotations from the play with parenthetical references.

1. How do the characters' wants and needs (dreams) motivate them throughout the play?

2. How does the playwright use antithesis to create tension and advance the plot?

3. How is each character trying to understand his or her own identity as well as the identity of others in the play? Who is misunderstood and what is the outcome? Is the misunderstanding resolved?

4. Discuss betrayal in the play.

5. How is Mama, the matriarch of the family, the catalyst for change? How difficult are the changes? Discuss the nature of change in the play.

6. What is the moral responsibility of the adults in the play?

7. Why does this family not have *esprit de corps* throughout the play? Do they ever obtain it? Explain.

8. How is the Younger family like any other American family? (Scout Finch in *To Kill a Mockingbird* says there's only one kind of people.)

9. Would you consider the ending a happy ending or not? Explain.

10. How is Beneatha's nickname *Alaiyo* symbolic of the social reform of which this character is a significant part?

11. What is the symbolism of the house and of sunlight, Mama's plant, and the joy of planting and growing flowers at the new house?

12. What does Lindner really mean when he says, "We don't try hard enough in this world to understand the other fellow's problem" (117)? How does this ironically relate to the entire play?

13. How does Walter "come into his manhood" (151)? Why does Mama compare it to a rainbow?

11. Title: "The Veteran"
    Author: Frederick Forsyth
    Form: Short story

Setting: London, modern times

Synopsis: A shopkeeper witnesses a brutal beating on the sidewalk across the street. Two thugs beat and kick an old man and leave him to die, which he does later in a hospital. Despite an eye-witness account, a well-known barrister wins their freedom in court, but there is a twist at the end. The old man was a veteran of World War II and he had comrades.

Journal Prompt: Choose one of the following topics, apply it to the story, and write at least three pages in your journal using textual support (two to four quotations), citing your page numbers with parenthetical references.

1. Honor over justice

2. Ego needs: How do they influence loyalty and betrayal?

3. Can betrayal be defined as going against the group to adhere to a higher cause?

4. Is the code "eye for an eye" a result of betrayal, or justice?

5. How is the retribution in the story morally ambiguous?

6. When are people called upon to save or help others, and when must people do their duty, even when it means destroying others? What is duty?

7. Read John Donne's "Devotions upon Emergent Occasions" (1624) Meditation XVII. How could his advice about humankind's connectedness explain Vansittart's decision?

12. Title: *Whispering Wind*
    Author: Frederick Forsyth
    Form: Novella
    Setting: Montana, 1876 and 1976
    Synopsis: Ben Craig, a young scout working for the U.S. government, is sent to aid General Custer in his dealings with the Indians. What he sees is intolerable to him and he disobeys orders. A young Cheyenne Indian girl is captured after her village is plundered and all the women and children are massacred while the men are away. He leaves with Whispering Wind, the young woman, and begins a journey that takes him into another lifetime.

Journal Prompt: Retribution can be defined as something given in recompense, such as punishment or reward. On your own journey through life, what have you learned about the connections between retribution and loyalty, and retribution and betrayal?

13. Title: *Tunes for Bears to Dance To*
    Author: Robert Cormier
    Form: Novella
    Setting: A small town in America after WWII
    Synopsis: Eleven-year-old Henry and his family move to a new town after the accidental death of his brother Eddie. He meets Mr. Levine, the only person in his family to survive the Holocaust, after following him from the "crazy house" to the social center where Mr. Levine does wood crafting. Henry has a part-time job working for a grocer named Mr. Hairston, whose hatred for people exacts a harsh price that becomes a dilemma for Henry. Mr. Hairston asks Henry to destroy Mr. Levine's hand carved village for an attractive price. Will Henry be bullied into betraying his friend?

critically about some complex issues. Be sure to take notes in your journal.

Readings:

The Alchemist
"Guests of the Nation"
"The Heathen"
To Kill a Mockingbird
"The Enemy"
Farewell to Manzanar
Night
Man's Search for Meaning
A Separate Peace
"The Coup de Grace"
A Raisin in the Sun
"The Veteran" (a story in Forsyth's *The Veteran*)
Whispering Wind (a novella in Forsyth's collected stories *The Veteran*)
Tunes for Bears to Dance To

Questions:

1. Who is "the other" in each story?
2. How does the character's level of moral development make a difference in each story?
3. Would you consider any of the characters to be archetypal warriors? Explain.
4. How is tolerance for ambiguity an asset for the characters? How does moral ambiguity increase the difficulty of righteousness for the characters?
5. What is the price for compliance in the stories?
6. Do the rules of civility change in any of the stories? How and why?
7. How can Jung's shadow theory contribute to our understanding of the betrayal in the stories?
8. How can you apply Freud's id, ego, and superego to the characters for a better understanding of their actions?
9. See the guide "*Esprit de Corps*, or Betrayal?" on page 188 for more general questions to consider.

Some of the most powerful poetry ever written has emerged from suffering. Poets who experienced the atrocities of the Holocaust and the decades of racial hardships in America add another perspective in answering the question, "Will future generations inherit benevolence and goodness, or a world full of hatred and betrayal?" Two good resources are Hilda Schiff's compilation *Holocaust Poetry* and Michael S. Harper and Anthony Walton's *African American Poetry*.

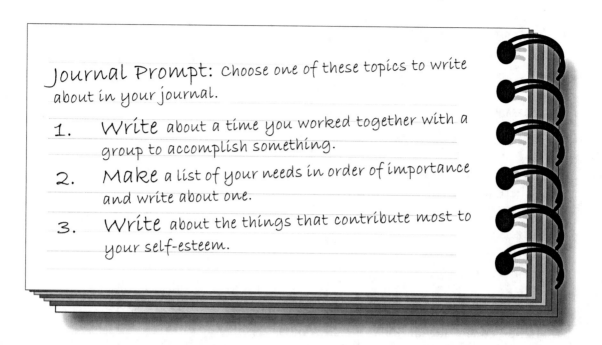

Journal Prompt: choose one of these topics to write about in your journal.

1. Write about a time you worked together with a group to accomplish something.

2. Make a list of your needs in order of importance and write about one.

3. Write about the things that contribute most to your self-esteem.

LEARNING ABOUT OURSELVES AND OTHERS
• • • • •

Unless you are a first-generation resident or citizen of the United States, you might not give your heritage or culture a second thought. Perhaps you have never asked your parents about your ancestors or your origin. Think about this. If our daily lives are going to be affected by growing immigration and what the media call "the changing face of America," then it is essential that we learn about ourselves and each other and how to respect the traditions and values of groups of people in order to live peaceably and productively in our schools, our communities, and our world. On the next page you will find fifteen reasons for looking more closely at the heritage and culture of your family as well as the people in the world around you.

Why learn about other people? Because doing so…
- Makes us see an image of a culture as positive.
- Helps us understand how and why people are the way they are.
- Helps us appreciate our lives now.
- Helps connect us to our past, to learn from others and pass information and pride down to future generations.
- Makes us feel good to know there are others like us.
- Reinforces what we know about ourselves.
- Helps us find similarities between generations in order to compare the present with the past.
- Gives us a reference and helps us to see what worked before.
- Helps us to understand how to carry on our own cultures.
- Enables us to see our heritage through other people's eyes.

- Helps us to appreciate our lives and our environment.
- Gives us role models to build self-esteem and allows us to identify with others.
- Opens our minds to other cultures, expanding our choices.
- Helps us relate to the problems and solutions in literature.

Journal Prompt: Think about a time when you had an opportunity to learn about another person's culture. Was it at a traditional celebration, an outing with friends, a class discussion, or a school-sponsored event such as an athletic or scholastic competition? Whatever the setting describe what you learned about the experience and the people involved. Did you also learn anything about yourself? Write a page or two in your journal.

Reading fiction and nonfiction can open our minds to different points of view. When we are not exposed to other ideas, habits, customs, or perspectives, we have a tendency to hold fast to our own way of thinking and behaving as the *best* way. The result can be destructive, even devastating. These feelings of superiority can create and perpetuate a condition of fear that stifles open-mindedness, rendering harmony almost impossible. The novel *A Separate Peace* focuses on teenagers who must face two worlds, one engaged in a war and the other sheltered by a New England preparatory school that protects boys from the war but not from the conflicts arising from the differences among each other and the battles raging within themselves.

What brings people together in friendship, and what kind of bestiality destroys their relationships? This novel about youthful rites of passage in the early 1940s offers one answer. Consider the following questions before you read to gain more depth of understanding. Then after reading, use them as a springboard for discussion and writing about the complex problems and solutions of people trying to live as harmoniously as they can.

FRIENDSHIP AND BESTIALITY IN JOHN KNOWLES'S
A SEPARATE PEACE
• • • • •

Chapters 1-5

1. Where is the novel set? Why do you think the setting might be important to the plot?

2. Who are the main characters? Start gathering mental notes: Will these characters remain static (unchanging) throughout the story, or will they be dynamic (changing)? Who is telling the story?
3. What is the significance of the trip to the beach? Why does the author include this scene?
4. Why does the author have Gene and Finny identify with each other?
5. Why did Gene jounce the limb?
6. Why can't Finny accept the fact that Gene made him fall?
7. Make note of the figures of speech that the author uses to enhance the imagery in his story—metaphor, simile, allusion, personification.

Chapters 6-7
1. In chapter 6 Gene says, "If you broke the rules, then they broke you" (66). What do you think this may foreshadow?
2. What is the nature of the bitter rivalry between Gene and Finny?
3. Why does Gene vacillate between being Finny and being himself? How is this behavior part of the overall conflict?
4. Who are the two casualties of the war at Devon?
5. How does figurative language contribute to the author's imagery in these chapters?

Chapters 8-13
1. Why does Finny claim there is no war, that it is just a lie? What is the truth about Finny?
2. Why does the author make Leper the one who speaks the truth? How is Leper's role ironic? How does Gene think Leper's illness will work to his advantage?
3. What does it take for Finny to forgive Gene for jouncing the limb and causing his fall?
4. Why does Finny die?
5. How does the author use language to enhance the imagery in these chapters?

Chapter 13 (additional focus)
1. Gene says, "…they reminded me of adolescents" (188). How does the statement summarize the novel?
2. How could Gene be certain of only two people?
3. Gene says, "…wars were made instead by something ignorant in the human heart" (193). How does he know this now? Would knowing this have made a difference in his relationship with Phineas?
4. Does Gene admire Phineas in the end? How do you know?

Chapter 13 (additional focus)
1. How was Phineas the embodiment of peace?
2. Explain the irony in this statement: "I was ready for the war, now that I no longer had any hatred to contribute to it" (195).
3. If Gene believed his war ended at Devon, why does he enlist?
4. Some literary critics have identified the story of Phineas and Gene as the savior archetype. What would cause people to see the connection to this archetype?
5. If Gene believed he was at war at Devon, why does he often refer to Devon as peaceful?

Journal Prompt: Write about a personal experience you have had, or about someone you know has had, with one or more themes in *A Separate Peace*: friendship, anger, change, man's bestiality, irony, moral ambiguity, youth enlisting or being drafted and going to war.

Journal Prompt: This journal assignment now offers you an opportunity to consider all of the pieces you have read and all of the tools that enable you to delve deeply into the inner workings of the characters: the philosophy, the psychology, and the literary devices that authors use to construct round, believable characters. Carefully consider the question posed below and write your answer in your journal.

In his poem "Man Was Made to Mourn," the Scottish poet Robert Burns called cruel bestiality "man's inhumanity to man" (123), from the famous Latin expression, "Homo homini lupus"—man is a wolf to man. Reflect on these words as you answer this question: If humankind possesses this inherent bestiality, is it possible to attain any degree of peace and harmony?

In your writing refer to Maslow, Kohlberg, Freud, Jung, Plato, Emerson, and any other thinkers you have read to help you arrive at some conclusions. You will want to draw upon the vast literary resources you have accessible as well, especially the ones you have read in this chapter, but feel free to use any other pieces of literature that support your answer.

MANDALAS AND LABYRINTHS
● ● ● ● ●
The Mandala

In this chapter you have used reading and writing to help you perceive your place in the world, especially in light of your own heritage and culture, and to compass the new journeys you will inevitably begin. You learned how finding where you fit in can also contribute to your own harmony with others who are like you but also different from you. Yet another way to recognize your true feelings and strive for greater balance in life is through art. In school you are asked to use the left side of your brain to read, write, calculate, and analyze, but the right hemisphere dominates artistic endeavors and adds balance through harmoniously using both sides of the brain. Designing a mandala can give you the opportunity to express your artistic side while centering yourself.

To create your own mandala, which in Sanskrit means *circle*, draw a simple circular pattern that can enclose your favorite images, or try to replicate some of the more complex wheels and circles by creating your own intricately patterned designs. Several sources that highlight the ancient art of mandalas are available in books and on the internet, but you can just as easily make up your own design.

In Jungian psychology, the Self (the inner deity or *imago Dei*) is expressed by the mandala, a circle with a center and a square or cross or another design that results in quaternity, expressing the quality of wholeness, or the four functions that Jung identified as thinking, feeling, sensation, and intuition (Edinger 265). The division of the circle into four sections contributes to a sense of peacefulness for the person meditating on the mandala.

Mandalas exist at the root of all cultures. Historically they have had greater attention in earlier times, so much greater that people considered them an ancient Eastern tradition for meditation and spiritual healing, even though the Gothic rose windows and medieval labyrinths of great European cathedrals provide stunning examples of mandalas as well. Regardless of the time period, the mandala drawings are believed to be an attempt by the artist to recognize and assimilate unconscious knowledge. Many believe that constructing and meditating on the mandala can bring about self-healing properties for people. As the artist creates or the viewer gazes at the circle, she turns her focus inward and allows herself to find the balance of her own center. If you want to meditate using the mandala you have created to relieve stress or just relax, sit comfortably with your circle at eye level. Concentrate on it, allowing your mind to wander but also drawing it back to the center each time. Do this for twenty minutes, and approach all those tasks waiting for you with renewed energy.

The Labyrinth

Another kind of mandala is the circular labyrinth. The ancient Greeks told several versions of a story about a maze-type labyrinth built by King Minos to contain the Moon-Bull, also called the Minotaur. As the story goes, this creature is the offspring of his wife and a bull given to him by Poseidon. At first, Poseidon asks Minos to sacrifice the bull to him, but

Minos can't bring himself to kill it. Angry at Minos's refusal, Poseidon creates in the king's wife an irresistible attraction to the bull, and the result is a monstrous offspring that Minos must hide away in an impossible labyrinth. The bull-human is pacified only with the blood sacrifice of fourteen young men and women who are put into the labyrinth with him. A young man named Theseus, son of Aegeus, tells his father he can no longer stand for this slaughter and will volunteer to go into the labyrinth as a victim. He intends to slay the monster. As the victims are parading before the crowd, the daughter of Minos, whose name is Ariadne, falls in love with Theseus and discovers a way to save his life. She goes to Daedelus, the designer of the labyrinth, and he tells her the way to escape. Before Theseus enters the labyrinth, she gives him a ball of thread and tells him to attach it to the opening of the labyrinth and unwind it along the path so he can retrace his steps. Theseus does this, slays the Minotaur, and escapes the labyrinth, leading the others out as well. True to his promise, Theseus marries Ariadne and takes her with him on his ship to return to his father. In his joy, Theseus forgets to raise the white sail and as he enters the port, Aegeus sees the ship's black sails hoisted, a sign of his son's death to the Minotaur. Grieving for his son, his father then casts himself into the sea, hence the name of the Aegean Sea. At least two other stories exist about Ariadne. One says she becomes ill and dies on shore, and the other tells of Theseus's betrayal to her as he lies to her and sails away without her (Hamilton 152-3).

In medieval times, the labyrinths were designed on the floors of churches, in gardens, or simply with circles of stones or hedges in grass or pebbles. They were often used in religious rituals or by pilgrims to walk and meditate or even to crawl through as an act of penance. Christians sometimes referred to the journey through the labyrinth as the road to Jerusalem, the medieval pilgrimage route. It was easy for them to adapt the Greek myth of Theseus to their own religion, Theseus becoming Christ slaying the devil and the guiding thread of Ariadne identifying Mary who makes Christ's task on earth possible. Dancing through the labyrinth was sometimes incorporated into the ritual, the priests tossing a ball that represented the sun in the life/death/life seasons archetype. Even now women sometimes dance through the winding circuit of the labyrinth with ribbons and scarves in their hands, connecting each to the other in a symbolic re-enactment of the threads that create their own destinies. Today many houses of worship, and even individuals, have designed labyrinths that the public can use for walking and meditating. One of the more well-known labyrinths is located on Wall Street in New York City, where city dwellers can walk and meditate on their lunch breaks. Find out where the nearest labyrinths in your own city are and plan to visit one for a relaxing, meditative walk.

Since ancient times, the labyrinth, much like the mandala, has been used as a tool for meditating and returning to a balanced state. For students today whose lives are full of the stresses of tests, homework, and other responsibilities that may seem medieval at times, just tracing your finger slowly through the winding path of the labyrinth's circuit can bring relief. Perhaps the inward journey to the Self can offer the strength and sense of harmony you need. Draw your own simple seven-circuit labyrinth, or use the eleven-circuit labyrinth popular in medieval times as a tool to help you relax, always keeping in mind the symbolism and the stories that have given the labyrinth its deeper meaning.

Both the seven-circuit and eleven-circuit labyrinths are based on symbolic numbers. Seven is the sum of three—the number of perfect balance, or God—plus four—the number of humankind. Thus the sum of three plus four is the union of God and human beings, or heaven and earth. The journey down the one-way path to the center is symbolic of a return to the Center, or paradise, regained only through the winding path that moves close to the center and then away from it again and again until the pilgrim finally reaches the center of the labyrinth.

The eleven-circuit labyrinth has additional numeric symbolism. The most famous and well-preserved medieval labyrinth at Chartres Cathedral in France contains four quadrants, each having eleven paths, or circuits. The walk through this labyrinth begins with the pilgrim entering the first quadrant:

Quadrant one: The pilgrim walks three paths.

Quadrant two: The pilgrim continues the circuit but enters quadrant two and walks two paths.

Quadrant one: As the pilgrim walks on, she returns to the first quadrant and walks four paths.

Quadrant two: The pilgrim continues the journey entering the second quadrant again and walks three paths.

Quadrant three: The pilgrim now enters the third quadrant and walks three paths.

Quadrant four: The pilgrim enters the fourth quadrant and walks four paths.

Quadrant three: As the pilgrim continues walking the circuit, he returns to the third quadrant and walks three paths.

Quadrant two: The pilgrim returns to the second quadrant and walks three paths.

Quadrant one: The pilgrim returns to the first quadrant and walks four paths.

Quadrant two: The pilgrim moves to the second quadrant and walks three paths.

Quadrant three: As the pilgrim moves nearer the end of his journey, he completes three paths.

Quadrant four: The pilgrim moves to quadrant four and walks four paths.

Quadrant three: Just as the pilgrim walked two paths close to the beginning of the journey, she walks two paths as she is close to the center.

Quadrant four: In the last leg of the journey, the pilgrim walks three paths.

Center: The pilgrim reaches the image of the rose at the center of the labyrinth.

Notice the numbers *eleven*, *three*, *two*, and *four*. World mythologies, the ancient stories of people and their cultures throughout time, teach us that these numbers hold meanings that were relevant to the people who first constructed the labyrinths and the people who later used them in their sacred rituals. Because *eleven* represents sin, peril, and the difficulties of life, it is appropriate that one must travel eleven circuits to reach the Center, or paradise. Along the way, the pilgrim travels paths in sets of *three* and *four*, with *two* sets of *two* paths. Remember that the sum of *three* and *four* represents the union of heaven and earth to these pilgrims, while the number *two* symbolizes duality, opposites, reflection, God and man.

CELEBRATING CULTURAL DIVERSITY:
TOUCHSTONES
• • • • •

Reading literature about our many heritages and cultures connects us to our past and helps us better understand the places we establish in our own little microcosms as well as in the larger world of all peoples. Reading keeps our family stories alive and teaches us how to preserve our own cultures while developing sensitivity to the cultures of others. We learn from literature how to live with joy and sorrow and, ultimately we hope, with dignity.

In this chapter you examined a world view of literature and its reflection of the heritage of the past, present, and predicted future of our humanity. In a more personal reading list of your devising, you can research your own unique answers to this question: "How can literature clarify and strengthen what I know and feel about my heritage and culture and where it is leading me?" It is a natural inclination to choose reading material that suits your own needs and tastes, whether fiction or nonfiction, and this choice alone helps to identify your composite culture. Consider the range of possible literary works that identify who you are: picture books, cartoon books, poems, song lyrics, short stories, folklore and fairy tales, magazines, newspapers, nonfiction books, novels, plays, and essays. Think about how you are connected to this literature. You choose pieces because they are strong reminders of your thoughts, ideas, actions, memories, and hopes and dreams. Brainstorm a short list of the pieces of literature that readily come to mind as favorites that have had a specific impact on your microcosmic view of life and another list that we'll call *Touchstones*.

The concept of a *touchstone* as an exemplary model in literary criticism was first proposed in 1880 by Matthew Arnold in "The Study of Poetry." In geologic terms, a touchstone is a hard stone used to evaluate the purity of a piece of gold, which is determined by striking the gold against the stone and observing the mark left there. Applied as a metaphor, touchstones are those poems and passages in great literature against which we can measure the excellence of lesser-known pieces, even our own writing, and see what mark they leave on the hearts and minds of their readers. For Arnold those literary touchstones came from the words of Homer, Dante, Shakespeare, and Milton.

To compile a *Touchstones* list for yourself, consider writing that exemplifies what you consider the very best, the epitome of description or expression in a variety of categories: love, hate, terror, courage, isolation, boundaries, transformation, revenge, humor, depression, insanity, sadness, joy, greed, confidence, mystery, manipulation. The list seems inexhaustible. The object is to gather together the best examples, in your opinion, from not only classic and modern literature but also literature that represents many cultures. The more representative titles you can assemble, the more exposure you will have to the quality that you as a writer are trying to produce.

When you have made your list, choose one of your favorites and complete the directions below for a culinary celebration of life and literature.

THE TASTING PARTY
• • • • •

Food brings people together in celebration and commemoration of the important moments of our lives. Although you may never have considered throwing a party to celebrate the literature you have studied in school, think about the stories you have loved throughout your life, maybe even in your classrooms. What a richer world we have today because of them. So bring on the food and let's celebrate! Choose a piece of literature that either *mentions* a food item that has significant relevance to the writing or that *reminds* you of the food of your heritage or culture. Follow these five steps:

1.   Find a recipe for the food item.
2.   Write a paragraph of five or six sentences explaining how this food item relates to the writing and also how the writing and food item both relate to you.
3.   Type the paragraph and recipe using the form given and compile it with your friends' or classmates' recipes or put together a collection of just your own recipes. Your one-page recipe and explanation will be part of a memorable literary-based cookbook, literally *food for thought!*
4.   If you're doing this as part of a classroom activity, bring your prepared food item to class on the day of the tasting party. Make only what the recipe calls for, not enough for twenty-five servings. Everyone should receive just a taste.
5.   Use the model below for your recipe page:

Title of book: *Curious George Goes to the Hospital*
Author: Margret Rey and R.A. Rey
Dish: Banana Pudding
Presented by Allison Y.

When I was little, the Curious George books were my favorite books because they were about a lovable monkey who has adventures and gets into a lot of mischief. I was always curious about everything, just like Curious George, and I tried to have adventures like his. I was raised to ask questions and be curious, so I can really relate to the Curious George adventures. My banana pudding dish relates to the book because George's favorite food was bananas. He was a monkey and ate bananas all the time, and my banana pudding reflects that. Also, the color yellow represents Curious George's owner's hat, which was yellow.

Banana Pudding

Ingredients:

48 vanilla wafers

2 medium bananas sliced

1 package vanilla pudding and pie filling

1 T. butter

2 ½ cups milk

whipped cream

Line bottom and sides of an 8-inch square or 1 1/2 – quart baking dish with vanilla wafers. Combine pudding mix, milk, and butter in a saucepan. Cook and stir over medium heat until mixture comes to a full boil. Remove from heat. Layer slices of banana over wafers, then add a layer of pudding. Repeat layers of wafers, bananas, and pudding. Chill for about three hours, or until firm. Serve with whipped cream or topping, and garnish with banana slices.

Renaissance intellectuals conjured up visions
of the universe as a great cosmic dance...
Stephen Greenblatt
The Norton Shakespeare, 1997

CHAPTER 14

The English Renaissance: The Dance of Shakespeare

Students begin the literary study in this book with an intensive look at Nathaniel Hawthorne's short story, "The Maypole of Merry Mount." A lesser-known story, it nevertheless serves as an early introduction for the skills and background for Shakespeare's *Twelfth Night*. The Hawthorne story's characters are vagabonds, street performers, perhaps those from the Elizabethan underworld, disillusioned English transported to America by their desire for a better life. In the seventeenth-century Massachusetts colony of Merry Mount, which was dissolved quickly by Miles Standish and the Puritans, echoes of life in Shakespeare's England reverberate. Students can produce the Hawthorne story as a play, and six months later return to Shakespeare's English to study and perform scenes from *Twelfth Night*.

Years ago I thought teaching Shakespeare to middle school students would be a formidable task undertaken with some academic risk. Could thirteen-year-olds get it? Would they be able to synthesize background, language skills, and life experiences necessary for understanding and appreciating Shakespeare's plays? It took a warm and memorable summer evening's performance of the Houston Shakespeare Festival's *The Taming of the Shrew* to make me realize how much my students might enjoy learning about Shakespeare if they could do it through studying and performing scenes from the plays. I chose to start with a comedy, *Twelfth Night, or What You Will,* not only one of my favorites but also the one that many scholars believe to be his best comedy. Beyond the necessary introduction to the period and the little we know about Shakespeare's life, the culminating activity would be the performing of scenes selected and prepared by the students, from opening the text to blocking movement on a stage.

The unit of study spans about nine weeks, but as all Shakespeare enthusiasts know, it could go on indefinitely with a study of the language that characterizes the Elizabethan culture, the conventions of Shakespearean comedy, and, of course, the verse and meter itself. Familiarity with background contributes to the ease of following a film of *Twelfth Night* as students stay close to the text. I use a Folger Library edition based on *The First Folio*, pausing frequently to analyze and point out examples in the play. Students are then ready to select scenes, memorize lines with appropriate blocking, and perform these scenes for an audience.

Everything you know about Shakespeare will have an effect on your performance, but there is one key element that classically trained actors know. It involves hidden clues to what scholars believe Shakespeare might have intended actors to do when they spoke their lines. Shakespearean actors have training in **verse speaking**. Without knowledge of how to speak lines of the plays that Shakespeare wrote in iambic pentameter, rhymed couplets, and prose, students are just reading words on a page.

Because Shakespeare is in vogue now among an audience more diverse than ever, American students have some familiarity with his plays. The years 1995 to 2006 brought to movie-going audiences a modern *Romeo and Juliet, Ten Things I Hate about You (The Taming of the Shrew), Scotland, PA (Macbeth), O (Othello), and She's the Man (Twelfth Night)*. While high schools continue to require the study of four plays, many middle and even some elementary schools have begun to include Shakespeare in their curriculum. Why so early a start? What is the appeal that demands his inclusion in schools across the nation, both public and private? The supporting evidence is convincing. Every new reading or exposure brings readers closer to Shakespeare's meaning. Perhaps four hundred years later, with "the voices of many mirrors" (Bloom 15), Shakespeare can still teach us the truth about human nature. Bloom says Shakespeare invents "ways of representing human changes, alterations not only caused by flaws and by decay but effected by the will as well..." (3). Harrison adds that Shakespeare is "the most universal of all because he is the wisest...he can understand and sympathize more than other men. He can see the whole picture of humanity and recreate it so that men of every kind, country, creed and generation understand" (3). When we read or see Shakespeare, we find our own experiences and so we use his words to express our own emotions more aptly. Second only to the Bible in quotations is Shakespeare. The more we read, the more we understand the plays and ourselves as well. The study of Shakespeare is the most valuable because we are able to see our own lives as part of universalism—we can find ourselves in his plays.

Elizabethan life was rich with words. Shakespeare's plays, sonnets, and poems illustrate his mastery of common language which "runs the gamut from fools and rustics to kings and fairies" (McCrum and MacNeil). The Elizabethans borrowed 12,000 words from other languages, and Shakespeare alone coined over 1,500 words. Compared with the Puritans of his day who relied on only about 8,000 words—the language of the Bible—Shakespeare's plays reflect the use of about 34,000 words. Aside from everyday speech, equally important to a study of Shakespeare is a close look at the heightened language of the plays. Van Tassel, a successful Shakespeare acting coach and director, believes "Unless you make the effort to discover what the language is saying and doing, and then have the skills to read that language correctly, your Shakespearean characterization will be unsuccessful" (7). An audience who can't understand what is being said will nod off. Speaking skills supercede development of characters and background information. Only after a speaker applies verse speaking skills are those elements helpful in making the reading or acting as complete and truthful as possible.

Exposing middle school students to as much as they can handle about reading and performing Shakespeare's plays affords an advantage for students in two ways. First, Shakespeare is "the fixed center of the Western canon" (Bloom 3). Bloom turns to Samuel Johnson's words: "We owe Shakespeare everything...Shakespeare has taught us to understand human nature" (qtd. in Bloom 3). In what might be the definitive philosophy on the teaching of English in America, *Literature as Exploration,* Louise Rosenblatt completes the connection: "...the human experience that literature presents is primary...The reader seeks to participate in another's vision—to reap knowledge of the world, to fathom the resources of the human spirit, to gain insights that will make his own life more comprehensible" (7). If students can relate to experiences from literature, they will be able to validate more easily experiences from their own past. In studying Shakespeare, students grow, and while they understand his plays better, they also see themselves in the largeness of Shakespeare's characters, the representation of human beings at their best and worst—at whatever stage the students are in at the time they read the plays.

Middle school students should study Shakespeare for a second reason. Americans fall behind the British in reading and acting Shakespeare, not because Americans lack the proper accent. Elizabethan speech, as Peter Hall points out in *The Story of English,* was a rough, unrefined language closer to American speech today. Rather, the British believe that beginning their training with the heightened language of Shakespeare will enable them to do any kind of acting after that. Even British school children read Shakespeare and see many performances. Studying Shakespeare's plays with middle school students, using methods that are age appropriate gives students an earlier preparation for four years of Shakespeare in high school. What they can bring to text analysis, characterization, and background will better guarantee their success with subsequent plays.

Teaching Shakespeare clearly gives students the kind of language study they deserve, but then why is *Twelfth Night* a good choice for students? It doesn't take an intensive study of the plays to discover that many scholars, critics, and directors believe that *Twelfth Night* is the greatest of all of Shakespeare's comedies, although it may not be the individual favorite. Bloom tells us, "Like all the other strongest plays by Shakespeare, *Twelfth Night* is of no genre...but in its own very startling way it is another 'poem unlimited'...One cannot get to the end of it, because even some of the most apparently incidental lines reverberate infinitely" (227). Jenkins adds that *Twelfth Night* is the greatest comedy because of its success with romantic love, symbolizing "the mind's aspiration towards some ever alluring but ever elusive ideal" (140). Although Shakespeare borrowed this romantic love plot "from the story of Apolonius and Silla and Barnabe Rich's *Farewell to Military Profession* (1581) and ultimately from a comedy performed in Sienna in 1531, *Gl'Ingannati"* (Howard-Hill xiv), its mellow happiness, its zany spiritedness, its irony and metaphor and the resilience of its characters make it a superb choice.

In *Twelfth Night,* Shakespeare complicates the plot with tangled relationships that engage in the revelry that the title suggests. The holiday of Twelfth Night is the Christmas finale, twelve days after Christmas when boisterous merrymaking and revelry turn wisdom and responsibility into a Feast of Fools, presided over by Festus, or the master of ceremonies. In earlier times for twelve days people could indulge their fantasies and release their cares, but when it was over, their lives returned to the seriousness of hard work. Twelfth Night, however, is a holiday of hope, the archetype of the life/death/life cycle. After the dead of winter comes the rebirth of spring; after darkness there is light and joy. Such is the re-enactment of Shakespeare's characters in *Twelfth Night*. Bloom tells us that "Everyone…is mad without knowing it" (226). The Duke Orsino is sick with love, pining for the Countess Olivia, who uses the mourning of her brother as an excuse not to see him. The pretentious Malvolio, Olivia's steward, is full of self-love and ambition, believing that Olivia can love him. Olivia's cousin Sir Toby Belch is a drunken parasite whose feelings of revenge cause the manipulation of Malvolio's humiliation and downfall. The foolish Sir Andrew Aguecheeck becomes Toby's easy victim as his weakness allows him to be duped into believing that he, too, can be loved by Olivia. The twins Sebastian and Viola, each believing the other has drowned in a shipwreck, fall too easily in love themselves—Sebastian with Olivia and Viola with Orsino. But the power of love in this play must succumb to the revelry of Twelfth Night. Viola, from the beginning, disguises herself as a boy so she may serve in Orsino's court as Cesario, who quickly becomes his confidant. Orsino sends Cesario to woo Olivia for him, and according to the topsy-turvey world of Twelfth Night, Olivia, unaware of the disguise, gives up her mourning to fall in love with Cesario. Sebastian, Viola's twin, wins Olivia only because she believes him to be Cesario. They marry in the haste dictated by Twelfth Night insanity, as do Toby and Maria, who is Olivia's lady-in-waiting, followed by Orsino who discovers his beloved Cesario is Viola, whose convenience as a woman allows him to have "share in this most happy wrack" (278; 5.1.l.). It is Feste, however, at the end of the play, who helps the audience across the boundary of revelry to the serious light of a new day.

During our study of Shakespeare and the Elizabethan period, students can participate in a simulation of Elizabethan life, including the Twelfth Night celebration with "St. George and the Dragon" followed by wassail and cake, in order to understand the words and phrases and cultural context of the times. The festival begins with a welcome wassail song, the guests lifting their glasses of apple cider and toasting the tree in the center of the room and finally pouring the remaining cider in the tree tub. Following this ritual is the selection of the King and Queen of the Bean, chosen when a boy finds the bean in his piece of cake and the girl finds the pea in hers. Mummers will perform the traditional play of St. George who must fight a powerful evil dragon who is scourging the land.

An introduction to Shakespeare and *Twelfth Night* through discussion and film will enable students to connect the text to influences of Elizabethan life. Imagine trying to interpret Shakespeare's play when over 250 references to Elizabethan life are not accessible to you. When you understand the puns and the interaction between characters who speak of pitch, viol-de-gamboys, bearbaiting, fivefold blazon, galliards, and "carrying his water to the wise woman" (110; 3.4.l.), you overcome a critical barrier to understanding meaning. A combination of research, discussion, simulation, guest speakers, and lessons on verse speaking accompany an intensive study of *Twelfth Night*, followed by the culminating activity of student productions of three- to five-minute scenes from the play.

WATCHING, READING, AND DISCUSSING *TWELFTH NIGHT*
● ● ● ● ●

Students today will find it easy to apply Shakespearean convention, what we know about Elizabethan culture, and knowledge of verse speaking with a little guidance. If you prefer a more Hollywood-looking version of the play, I recommend the Trevor Nunn version of *Twelfth Night*. Its appeal to more modern audiences who have only a little experience with Shakespeare is the advantage for a wider range of audiences. Another good film version is the BBC and Time-Life Films versions. Follow them with a reliable book—the New Folger Library *Twelfth Night* is a good one. The application of situations, events, and character types in this play to students' lives in the twenty-first century can reinforce the universality of Shakespeare's writing. As you follow the play with the film, pause to consider the following questions:

1. Do people today engage in betting on brutal entertainment similar to bearbaiting?
2. Do people today become lovesick over unrequited love?
3. Do people grieve over the loss of a loved one in the same way as people in Shakespeare's day?
4. Is excessive drinking still a problem for people today?
5. Do you know people in society who use people for their money?
6. Are naïve people taken advantage of today in the same way that Andrew was?
7. Have you ever helped a friend get the girl/guy *you* wanted?
8. Have you ever known someone who was conceited and self-righteous?
9. Do you know someone who has fallen in love with someone who was unavailable?
10. Have you ever been chastised for being rowdy?
11. Have you ever been at a party that got out of control?
12. Have you ever played a mean trick on someone?
13. Do stand-up comics still rely on word play, puns?
14. What is the history of man's treatment of the mentally incompetent? Do we still put people in a "dark house"?
15. How do we use jewelry symbolically today?
16. Do people today still engage in duels?
17. How can our emotions play tricks on us? Why is this a universal human trait?
18. Why do people today still sacrifice so much for love?
19. Why can love distort a person's ability to reason?
20. Do you think the feeling of being reunited with a loved one has changed since Shakespeare's day? Why or why not?
21. Do people today still blame their behavior on conditions related to the moon (midsummer madness) or blood or organs (liver, heart)?
22. Do we still blame our conservative nature on the Puritans?
23. Are singing and dancing important parts of almost all cultures today?

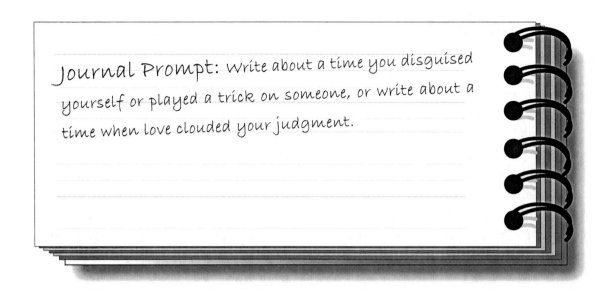

Journal Prompt: Write about a time you disguised yourself or played a trick on someone, or write about a time when love clouded your judgment.

WHO IS SHAKESPEARE?

• • • • •

Despite the number of books and articles and films written and produced about Shakespeare's life, the truth is we have only scant information actually documented about the life of William Shakespeare. For years scholars have attempted to disprove the authenticity of the author. Who really wrote the plays, poems, and sonnets? Was it Marlowe? Edward de Vere? Francis Bacon? Or was it a woman—Elizabeth I? How could it be that a sixteenth-century man would know so much about the heart of a woman, as this author certainly did? Perhaps the name of the playwright matters less than the fact that we have the plays, that they really do exist for our entertainment and enlightenment.

Tradition crowns William Shakespeare the greatest writer in the history of the English language. Whoever he was, we do know a little about the life he probably led. He lived at a time when a devastating plague wiped out huge portions of the population. He probably attended a Latin grammar school where he learned from a horn book the alphabet and the Lord's Prayer. Boys of seven learned their Latin from William Lily's book, and a typical school opened with devotions—a reading from the Bible, singing of a psalm, and prayer. He would have also attended lower school and studied classical drama and upper school, studying Ovid, the Bible, the Book of Common Prayer, and logic and rhetoric from Aristotle. Simple texts like Aesop and Cato from a Latin phrase book would have contributed to a moral education, which was an important part of Elizabethan education and life. An examination of Shakespeare's plays points to the Bible and the Book of Common Prayer as significant influences on his writing. He made allusions to forty-two books of the Bible, probably as a result of regular required attendance at church and study of the Bible and Prayer Book. He would have heard the words all his life. The Bible was the most common and most discussed book of the day. The best seller, especially the Genevan Bible, was a handy size, inexpensive, and written in English, not Latin. The Bible provided the foundation of popular culture; everybody had to go to church or be fined.

Images of daily life, work, and travel have a widespread role in his plays: images from the kitchen, the garden, out of doors, sports, animals, the river, the hills, as well as other parts of Europe, especially Italy. Dramatic entertainment was common all over England in the inn yards and later in the theatres.

In addition to Holinshed's *Chronicles* of the history of England, published in 1587, Shakespeare didn't have to look far to find fodder for his historical and political plots. In 1587 Elizabeth I executed her cousin Mary Queen of Scots, who was trying to claim the throne by declaring that Elizabeth was illegitimate. Elizabeth's mother, you remember, was Anne Boleyn, one of several of Henry VIII's wives he took in hopes of producing a male heir. In 1588 Philip II of Spain launched the Spanish Armada against the English in hopes of overthrowing the Protestant Elizabeth and placing himself, a Catholic, on the throne. England experienced twenty years of conflict with Spain. The English continued their attempts to subdue the Irish by the Earl of Essex, who in 1601 led a revolt against Elizabeth and was later tried for treason and executed. Guy Fawkes was arrested for trying to blow up the House of Lords during James I's opening of Parliament. It was a time of turbulence but also peace and cultural change, a great renaissance. Shakespeare was concerned with the importance of unity and good government and the consequences of chaos and anarchy.

We know that Shakespeare, the man, had little formal education, probably no more than grammar school. Scholars who believe someone other than Shakespeare wrote the plays believe only a man with a university education could have done it, men such as the University Wits, Thomas Lodge, Thomas Kyd, Lyly, Peele, Greene, Marlowe, and Nashe.

In 1576 permanent theatres were established in London. A cross section of society made up his audience, rich and poor, educated and illiterate. Everyone could afford to go to the theatre. The Elizabethan audience, however, was far more educated by ear and memory than we are today. An actor might be asked to memorize lines very quickly and perform in several plays in one week. James Burbage built the first permanent playhouse in 1576. Before this, players performed in yards of inns, often coaching inns. Burbage borrowed the money to build the theatre out in the fields beyond Bishopsgate. Later the theatre was demolished and the materials were used to build the Globe on the south bank of the Thames. Written documents indicate that Shakespeare the man was one of the owners of the theatre.

Although theatres were drawing bigger crowds than the churches, which angered the Puritans, it was the plague that forced the theatres to close temporarily. Elizabeth loved the plays and refused to give in to the opponents. In response, however, the government formed the Queen's Company in 1583. Twelve of the best players from other companies were selected to wear her livery as her servants and to prepare plays for her recreation at Christmastime and Shrove-tide.

As for diction, Shakespeare appeared to be influenced in his writing by Thomas Wilson's *Arte of Rhetorique*. Wilson believed that practice was more important than theory. He used three rhetorical devices in particular: *descriptio* (names and descriptions in a series), line-for-line exchanges that would have been suitable for taunts and banter, and amplification, which piled up speeches with vivid metaphor and heightened emotions. Shakespeare was a borrower of phrases, images, and plots—all greatly improved upon by his pen.

His stock devices and conventions have made his plays beloved: the girl dressed as a boy, the noble band of outlaws, the sheltering forest, the exile from court, the girl talking over her lover with her maid, the lovesick young man brooding over love, the songs in the comedies with the dance at the end, and the two kinds of clowns or fools. The wise clown offers advice if not sanity to the characters in the play, and the rustic clown, who is not very bright, adds humor.

After the plague came to London and shut down the theatres, Shakespeare the writer produced two poems dedicated to his patron, the Earl of Southampton: *Venus and Adonis*, 1592, and *The Rape of Lucrece*, 1593. After 1603 the Puritans gained power and plays were strictly forbidden in some towns. In London, boys began to fill the roles that men previously had. Remember, no women were allowed on the stage. Many theatres went indoors and were private. Shakespeare and his friends bought one of these indoor theatres called the Blackfriars but continued to produce plays across the Thames in the Globe as well. In 1611, after the production of *The Tempest* at court, Shakespeare the man returned to Stratford to New Place, his new home, and retired. The Globe burned and was rebuilt. In 1616 Shakespeare died and was buried in Holy Trinity Church in Stratford-upon-Avon.

Heminges and Condell, two fellow actors and friends, collected Shakespeare's thirty-six plays and published them in the *First Folio* edition in 1623. Whoever this writer may be, the writer of the Shakespeare plays had a rare point of view full of philosophic wisdom at a time when groups like the Puritans were imposing their own stifling and relentless brand of perfectionism on others. Shakespeare expressed a more temperate and balanced mixture of good and evil from which one might learn tolerance and wisdom.

SHAKESPEARE'S POEMS AND SONNETS
• • • • •

Shakespeare also wrote long poems and sonnets. On April 18, 1593, his long poem *Venus and Adonis* was entered for publication and dedicated on the title page of the book to Henry Wriothesley, Earl of Southampton and Baron of Tichfield. The Earl of Southampton was at this time nineteen years old and regarded as a young man of considerable promise. He was conspicuous among the queen's courtiers for his beauty and intelligence. Southampton was also wealthy and could possibly offer a poor poet a living if this poet dedicated his work to him, which is what Shakespeare did. Scholars have concluded that Southampton showed the writer considerable favor. On May 9, 1594, Shakespeare's second long poem, *The Rape of Lucrece*, was entered for publication with another dedication to Southampton. Because of their immense popularity, these poems established Shakespeare's reputation as a poet, even though they were regarded as improper.

The first volume of Shakespeare's sonnets published in 1609 is known as *Q*, from its quarto size, and is one of the most famous and mysterious books in the history of publication. It contains 154 sonnets as well as a narrative poem of 329 lines in 47 stanzas, entitled "A Lover's Complaint." Some critics have refused to acknowledge this poem as Shakespeare's, which again underscores the man and his life as an enigma.

What is a sonnet? The first kind of sonnet is the *Italian*, or *Petrarchan*, as you learned when you read about Longfellow in the American Renaissance, and the second kind is the

English, or *Shakespearean*. The English sonnet has four divisions: three quatrains and a rhymed couplet. The typical rhyme scheme for the English sonnet is **abab cdcd efef gg.**

In his 154 sonnets about love, Shakespeare addresses a young man in the first 126, a dark woman in the next 26, and writes about Cupid in the last two. Critics have tried not only to identify the man and the woman, but also to determine if the poems reveal Shakespeare's personal feelings about them. Again, if scholars are uncertain about the authenticity of the *playwright* Shakespeare, the *poet* remains an enigma as well. The world would do well to remember, we still have these works of genius regardless of the name of the writer.

SHAKESPEARE'S PLAYS
• • • • •

Shakespeare's plays have been classified by scholars as history, tragedy, comedy, and romance—a combination of tragedy, comedy, and romance. Below you will find a classification of the plays of Shakespeare the playwright with the approximate date each was written.

History
Henry VI, Part II (1590)
Henry VI, Part III (1590)
Henry VI, Part I (1590)
Richard III (1592)
Richard II (1595)
King John (1596)
Henry IV, Part I (1597)
Henry V (1598)
Henry VIII (1612)

Tragedy
Titus Andronicus (1593)
Romeo and Juliet (1594)
Julius Caesar (1599)
Hamlet (1600)
Othello (1604)
King Lear (1605)
Macbeth (1605)
Antony and Cleopatra (1606)
Coriolanus (1607)
Timon of Athens (1607)

Comedy
The Comedy of Errors (1592)
The Taming of the Shrew (1593)
The Two Gentlemen of Verona (1594)
Love's Labour's Lost (1594)
A Midsummer Night's Dream (1595)
The Merchant of Venice (1596)
Much Ado about Nothing (1598)
As You Like It (1599)
Twelfth Night (1599)
The Merry Wives of Windsor (1600)
Troilus and Cressida (1601)
All's Well That Ends Well (1602)
Measure for Measure (1604)
Two Noble Kinsmen (1612)

Romance
Pericles (1608)
Cymbeline (1609)
The Winter's Tale (1610)
The Tempest (1611)

A Chronology: Shakespeare in The Elizabethan and Jacobean Periods
● ● ● ● ●
1536 – 1616

The years outlined in this chronology offer a picture of the events that surrounded and included Shakespeare and his contemporaries. It was a time of rebirth for all of the arts and for science, technology, language, and philosophy and religion. It is no wonder that the world's greatest writer emerged from such a setting.

1536	Anne Boleyn is sent to the Tower and executed. An act of Parliament declares the authority of Pope void in England. Michelangelo paints *Last Judgment* on the altar wall of the Sistine Chapel.
1558	Elizabeth succeeds Mary.
1559	Elizabethan Prayer Book (*Book of Common Prayer*)
1560	Beginnings of Puritanism in England (1550-1660)
1564	**Shakespeare is born.** **Christopher Marlowe is born.** Galileo is born. Michelangelo dies. The Royal College of Physicians, London, is empowered to carry out human dissections.
1590	Edmund Spenser: *The Faerie Queene*, books 1-3 **Shakespeare: *Henry VI*, parts 1 and 2**
1591	**Shakespeare: *Henry VI*, part 3**
1592	The plague kills 15,000 people in London. **Shakespeare: *Richard III, Comedy of Errors***
1593	Christopher Marlowe is reputedly killed in tavern brawl. London theatres are closed because of the plague. **Shakespeare: *Titus Andronicus, The Taming of the Shrew***
1594	**Shakespeare: *The Two Gentlemen of Verona, Love's Labour's Lost, Romeo and Juliet***
1595	Sir Walter Raleigh explores three hundred miles up Orinoco River.

The English army finally abandons the bow as a weapon of war.
Shakespeare: *Richard II, A Midsummer Night's Dream*
The first appearance of heels on shoes

1596   Edmund Spenser: *The Faerie Queene*, books 4-6
Galileo invents the thermometer.
Tomatoes are introduced in England.
The first water closets, designed by Sir John Harington, are installed at the
    Queen's Palace, Richmond (toilets).
Shakespeare: *King John, The Merchant of Venice*

1597   The Second Spanish Armada leaves for England, scattered by storms.
An English Act of Parliament prescribes sentences of transportation to
    the colonies for convicted criminals.

1599   The Globe Theatre, Southwark, London, where Shakespeare's
    plays are performed, is built.
Shakespeare: *Julius Caesar, As You Like It, Twelfth Night*
Edmund Spenser dies.

1600   The Earl of Essex, tried for misdemeanors in Ireland, loses offices at court.
Shakespeare: *Hamlet, The Merry Wives of Windsor*
The English East India Company is founded; its initial capital is 70,000
    pounds.

1601   The Earl of Essex leads a revolt against Elizabeth I, is tried for treason, and is
    executed.
Shakespeare: *Troilus and Cressida*

1602   The Spanish army, after landing in Ireland, surrenders to the English at
    Kinsala.
Shakespeare: *All's Well That Ends Well*

1603   Elizabeth dies and is succeeded by her cousin James VI of Scotland as James
    I of England and Ireland
Sir Walter Raleigh, arrested for suspected complicity in a plot to de-throne
    James I, is tried for high treason and sentenced to imprisonment in the
    Tower of London
There is a heavy outbreak of the plague in England.

1604   **Shakespeare: *Measure for Measure***

1605	Guy Fawkes is arrested in the cellars of Parliament, accused of trying to blow up the House of Lords during James's opening of Parliament (the Gunpowder Plot). Cervantes' *Don Quixote I* is published. **Shakespeare: *King Lear, Macbeth***
1606	Guy Fawkes and fellow conspirators are sentenced to death. **Shakespeare: *Antony and Cleopatra*** Galileo invents the proportional compass. The Virginia Company of London, granted a royal charter, sends 120 colonists to Virginia.
1607	**Shakespeare: *Coriolanus, Timon of Athens*** Jamestown, Virginia, the first English settlement on the American mainland, is founded.
1608	The King's Men, a London actors' company, play at Blackfriars Theatre. **Shakespeare: *Pericles*** Galileo constructs an astronomical telescope. Captain John Smith: "True Relation of Virginia"
1609	**Shakespeare: *Cymbeline*** Henry Hudson explores the Delaware Bay and the Hudson River. Tea from China is shipped for first time to Europe by the Dutch East India Company.
1610	**Shakespeare: *A Winter's Tale*** Ben Jonson: *The Alchemist*, comedy The Stationer's Company begins to send a copy of every book printed in England to Bodleian Library, Oxford.
1611	Parliament is dissolved by James I. George Chapman completes his translation of Homer's *Iliad*, begun in 1598. **Shakespeare: *The Tempest*** An authorized version of the Holy Bible, the King James Bible, is published. William Byrd, John Bull, Orlando Gibbons: *Parthenia*, a collection of music for virginals **Shakespeare: *Henry VIII***
1612	The last recorded burning of heretics in England occurs.
1613	Fire destroys the Globe Theatre.

Thomas Bodley, English diplomat and scholar, dies, leaving the bulk of his fortune to Bodleian Library, Oxford.

1614   Sir Walter Raleigh: *The History of the World*
        Glass industry in England is developed.
        North American Pocahontas, an Indian princess, marries John Rolfe.

1615   Cervantes: *Don Quixote*, part 2
        George Chapman completes his translation of Homer's *Odyssey*.
        Inigo Jones becomes England's chief architect.
        Galileo faces the Inquisition for the first time.

1616   **William Shakespeare dies.**
        Sir Walter Raleigh is released from the Tower to lead an expedition to
            Guiana in search of El Dorado.
        Richelieu becomes the Minister of State for Foreign Affairs and War in
            France.
        The works of Ben Jonson, the first folio edition of its kind, is published.
        Galileo is prohibited by the Catholic Church from further scientific work.
        John Smith: *A Description of New England*

SHAKESPEARE AND ELIZABETHAN LIFE
● ● ● ● ●

Now is your chance to wander back in time to the streets of London, or maybe a small village in Warwickshire, or perhaps a farm in Sussex or a fishing village on the coast. You can enhance your understanding of the plays by creating a simulation of life during the reign of Elizabeth I and the period of time marked by enormous popularity for the theatre.

Research is essential, and when you have chosen an area to study and the information you need, you can work alone or, if you are in a classroom setting, with a partner or group of students to write a scene that replicates a day in the life of an Elizabethan. Here's the plan:

First, choose a topic and the characteristics of the person you are going to play. Some considerations include gender, age, and station in life. Are you a farmer, a sailor or soldier, a courtier, an entrepreneur, a trader, a scholar, a shop keeper, or are you part of the nobility?

Next, research one of the following categories as it would apply to your character.
    Daily life in the city
    Daily life in the countryside or sea shore
    Religion and morality
    Education
    Crime and punishment

Government
Entertainment: sports, theatre, music and dancing
Science, inventions, medicine
Weddings and funerals
Food and dining habits
Economy: jobs, wages, cost of living

Finally, write a three- to five-minute script in which your characters speak from their own station in life in the context of the topic you have researched. As students in the audience watch the plays, they can keep a diary of what they witness in the voices of their own invented Elizabethan characters. You can record private events from the plays as hearsay, gossip, or news from other sources, and then share your journal accounts of what you saw and heard that day as an Elizabethan.

CELEBRATING TWELFTH NIGHT
• • • • •

In Shakespeare's day, Elizabethans celebrated Christmas for twelve days up to Twelfth Day, or January 6, which Christians also call Epiphany or Three Kings Day. These holidays marked a time of revelry and boisterous merrymaking, a Feast of Fools by which conventional, normal behavior could be suspended for a time. In a seemingly topsy-turvy world, the master became the servant, disguise and masques were organized by the Lord of Misrule, and comic madness flourished. Pranks and deceptions were allowed up until the twelfth day. The day that followed this holiday season would be a return to the normal day of hard work and the seriousness of life. For twelve days, people could indulge their fantasies, and the end of this celebration brought a kind of sadness. But on the evening called Twelfth Night, the Christmas finale was the most glorious celebration filled with contests, plays and disguises, and great feasting. Twelfth Night was one of the most magnificent of winter holidays, celebrated since medieval times.

The festival began with a man chosen as the leader who performed the welcome wassail song, followed by the selection of the King and Queen of the Bean. Usually two Twelfth Cakes were baked. Inside one the baker placed a single large dried bean, and when the cake was served to the men only, the finder of the bean became King of the Bean. Inside the second cake the baker placed a large dried pea, and when this cake was served to the women, the finder of the pea would be named Queen. If only one cake was made and the man found the pea, he could choose the queen, and if the woman found the bean, she could choose the king. Together they presided over the festivities, deciding on the songs and games. They even sometimes assigned the merrymakers silly tasks, all in fun, of course. The revelers wassailed a fruit tree, walking around the tree in a circle and lifting their glasses to toast the tree and each other. After circling the tree several times, the wassailers poured the remaining cider around the roots of the tree for good luck.

Mummers performed the traditional holiday play, their favorite being a scene about St. George defeating evil.

You will find everything you need here to begin planning your own Twelfth Night celebration: recipes for wassail, lamb's wool—another favorite Twelfth Night beverage—the famous cakes, an English country dance, and a play in which St. George slays the dragon.

RECIPES FOR A TWELFTH NIGHT CELEBRATION
• • • • •

WASSAIL

Ingredients

> 1 gallon apple juice
> 2 oranges
> 2 lemons
> 1 lime
> 1 tablespoon cloves
> 1 tablespoon allspice
> 2 cinnamon sticks
> 1 quart water
> 1 cup sugar

Directions

1. While the water is heated to boiling, cut the lemons and oranges and lime in half, squeezing the juice into a separate bowl. Set aside. Put the skins and pulp of the fruit into the boiling water, add spices, and simmer for one hour.

2. Remove the cinnamon sticks, a few cloves, and allspice. Set aside for later. Use a slotted spoon to remove the citrus peels and pulp and remaining spices. Return the cinnamon sticks and saved spices to the water. Add apple juice and return to heat.

3. When mixture comes to a boil, remove from heat and add the squeezed citrus juice and sugar. Simmer for another ten minutes and serve. Makes twenty one-cup servings.

LAMB'S WOOL

Ingredients

> 6 apples, cored
> 2-8 tablespoons brown sugar
> 2 quarts sweet apple cider
> 1/8 teaspoon nutmeg
> ¼ teaspoon cinnamon
> ¼ teaspoon ground ginger

Directions

1. Roast the apples in a baking pan at 450° F for about an hour, or until they are very soft and begin to burst. You can also peel the apples and boil them until they are soft and flaky. You may leave the apples whole or break them up. Set aside.

2. In a large saucepan, dissolve the sugar a few tablespoons at a time in the cider, tasting for sweetness. Add the spices and bring to a boil. Simmer for 1-15 minutes.

3. Pour the liquid over the apples in a large punch bowl and serve. Makes eight one-cup servings.

TWELFTH CAKE

(For Beginners)

Ingredients

   3 cups all-purpose flour
   5/8 cup currants
   ¾ cup golden raisins
   1 1/3 cups mixed candied peel, shredded
   1 cup butter
   5/8 cup brown sugar
   1 tablespoon molasses
   3 eggs
   ¼ cup milk
   ¼ teaspoon allspice
   1 ¼ teaspoon ground cinnamon
   1 dried pea
   1 dried bean

Directions

1. Cream together butter and sugar.
2. Add the eggs, one at a time, beating thoroughly after each addition.
3. Warm the molasses and milk and add them to the butter, sugar, and eggs, beating briskly.
4. Sift a little of the flour over the fruits, to prevent them from falling to the bottom of the pan.
5. Sift together flour and spices and mix into batter, stirring lightly.
6. Fold in fruits.
7. Line bread tin with waxed paper. Pour in mixture and hide a bean and a pea in the batter. Bake in a slow oven (250° F) for 2-2 ½ hours.

TRADITIONAL TWELFTH NIGHT CAKE

(For more advanced cooks)

Ingredients

¼ cup white rum (The alcohol cooks out.)
½ cup golden raisins
½ cup currants
3 tablespoons diced citron
2 tablespoons diced candied orange peel
1 cup sweet butter
¾ cup sugar
4 eggs
2 tablespoons milk
½ teaspoon almond extract
3-3 ½ cups flour
1 teaspoon cinnamon
½ teaspoon nutmeg or mace
½ teaspoon allspice
½ cup slivered blanched almonds
Grated rind of one lemon
1 dried pea
1 dried bean
Almond Icing

Directions

1. Combine rum with raisins, currants, and candied fruits. Let soak one hour.
2. Drain, keeping the fruit and rum in separate bowls.
3. Cream butter with sugar until light and fluffy.
4. Add eggs one at a time. Beat well each time.
5. Add milk, almond extract, and two tablespoons of the saved rum.
6. Sprinkle a little of the flour over the fruits until lightly coated.
7. Sift remaining flour with spices, and mix.
8. Fold in fruits, nuts, and grated lemon rind. Mix well.
9. Put batter into a buttered nine-inch round cake pan or loaf pan. You may line the bottom of the pan with waxed paper first if desired.
10. Insert the dried bean on one side of the batter and the dried pea on the other.
11. Bake in a preheated 275° oven for two hours or until a tester inserted comes out clean. When cake shrinks away from the sides, put on a rack and let cool completely. Ice and let harden overnight.

ALMOND ICING

    2/3 cup ground blanched almonds
    ½ cup sugar
    ¼ cup sweet softened butter
    ¼ cup milk (For adults, tradition calls for ¼ cup white rum.)
    2 egg yolks
    1-2 drops almond extract

Combine ingredients and beat strongly using a wooden spoon. Mixture should be a creamy light yellow and soft. Spread over a cool cake. Let harden overnight.

RE-ENACTING ST. GEORGE AND THE DRAGON
• • • • •

Few English monarchs enjoyed political power *and* the love and devotion of English society. Elizabeth I was such a queen. From an impoverished country torn apart by religious strife, she created the Golden Age of English history. Perhaps it is true that, as a woman, she remains a mystery, but as a ruler she was regal, stately, cultured, and well educated. She reputedly spoke five languages fluently. She played the virginals, and she loved plays and masques. She loved to hunt and she loved to dance. Elizabeth converted England not only to the religious state of Protestantism but also to the political state of most powerful and prosperous country in the world.

Edmund Spenser must have shared in the English adoration of Elizabeth. Written some time between 1590 and 1599, his highly nationalistic epic poem *The Faerie Queene* was dedicated to the honor of England, Protestantism, and Elizabeth I, who appears in the poem as Gloriana, the Faerie Queene. In the poem, Una, the daughter of the king of a nearby kingdom, travels to the court of Gloriana to beg for assistance. A terrible dragon is scourging the rulers and their subjects, holding them hostage in their own land. Gloriana sends the Redcrosse Knight to slay the dragon and save the village, which he does. The king shows his gratitude by offering the knight his daughter's hand in marriage and the inheritance of the kingdom. The Redcrosse Knight becomes St. George, the savior and patron saint of England. It is no coincidence that *George* is derived from the Latin *geo*, meaning earth or farmer of the earth, a symbol of the common man. Therefore, every man could attain sainthood and follow in the footsteps of St. George.

During the reign of Elizabeth, it was traditional for the English to celebrate the twelve days of Christmas that began December 26 and ended January 6. On the evening of January 6, or Twelfth Night, which was also called Epiphany—Three Kings Day—the favorite entertainment would include a play about the story of St. George. Sometimes it would show him fighting a fierce, evil knight, but often the actors would tell the story of how the knight rid the countryside of a terrible dragon. You can recreate this holiday scene by re-enacting the heroic Redcrosse Knight fighting the dragon and saving the kingdom for Una and her family. If finding a dragon costume proves too difficult, do what my students did. We found a dragon mask with long flowing hair attached, put a gray sweat suit on our dragon, and enhanced the look with gray gauntlets and a long matching dragon-like tail that a capable seamstress made. The fire that he breathed was a large piece of red chiffon fabric that he waved around at appropriate moments. It was a quite satisfactory suggestion of ferocity. Celebrate the defeat by wassailing the trees and shrubbery nearby, saving some to enjoy with your Twelfth Night cakes.

SAINT GEORGE AND THE DRAGON
● ● ● ● ●

The Adventures of Una and the Red Cross Knight

Adapted from
Edmund Spenser's *The Faerie Queene*

Characters:

Narrator	Queen
Una	Messenger
Red Cross Knight	Villagers
Dwarf	Wise man
Dragon	Wise woman
Watchman	A mother
King	

Narrator: A gentle knight clad in mighty arms and silver shield was bound upon a great adventure that the great Gloriana, Queen of the Fairies, had given to him. And on his breast a bloody cross he bore. Upon his shield the like was also scored for sovereign hope, which in his hand he held. He longed to prove his courage in her honor in battle brave upon his foe, a dragon terrible and stern.

A lovely lady walked beside him fair, but under a black cloak hid she a heavy heart. So pure and innocent as her little lamb she was till that infernal fiend forewasted all their land. To avenge her mother and father, the good king and queen of that far kingdom expelled from their home, had she traveled to the court of Gloriana to beg assistance from a brave knight.

Behind her far away a Dwarf did lag bearing her bag of needments on his back, and angry Jove a hideous storm of rain did pour while this fair couple sought to shroud themselves in vain.

Many days passed and many dangerous challenges did they face, but as their journey approached the end, the lady Una, daughter of that noble king and queen, with hearty words her knight she began to cheer.

Una: Dear knight, as dear as ever knight was dear, ye suffer all these sorrows for my sake, but heaven beholds the tedious toil ye for me take. Now are we come unto my native soil. Here haunts that fiend who does his daily spoil. Therefore, be at your keeping well and ever ready for your foe to fell. The spark of noble courage now awake and ye evermore shall be renowned above all knights. Lo yonder is the tower in which my parents dear for dread of that huge fiend imprisoned be.

RCK: Lady, stand aside and to that hill draw near, from whence ye might behold that battle proof and ye be safe from danger. The ground beneath us has begun to shake and soon the dreadful dragon before us will appear.

Una: (*She turns and walks out of harm's way but close enough to watch. She speaks softly, invoking the Muse.*) O gently come into my feeble breast. Awake the God of war that this brave knight his godly arms may blaze.

Dragon: (*The dragon draws near roaring and rears up to frighten the knight. He flaps his wings as a show of force. He moves his tail around and claws at the air to show how fierce he is. He opens his mouth and displays his teeth as smoke and fire issue out.*)

RCK: (*He quakes in fear yet runs at the dragon with his spear, but the dragon's hide is too tough to pierce. RCK falls to the ground but gets up quickly. The dragon picks up RCK and hoists him into the air as if to carry him away, but he struggles and the dragon puts him down. With his spear, RCK wounds the dragon under his left wing. The dragon howls and rages. He grabs at the air with his claws and shoots forth fire from his nostrils. He hurls his tail about and knocks RCK down. RCK tries to strike the dragon again but to no avail. The dragon cannot use his left wing. He brays loudly and sends fire from his mouth, which scorches the face of the RCK, who, seared, removes his helmet and arms.*)

Narrator: Faint, weary, and sore, this Red Cross Knight desired death. He fell to the ground into the waters of a healing spring whose powers restored the knight.

When Una saw her hero from afar struck by the monstrous dragon and lying on the ground, she fell to her knees with folded hands and began to pray. All night she watched, not once would she lie down, but praying still did wake and waking did lament.

Una: (*On her knees praying. She then walks to RCK to see how he is recovering.*)

RCK: (*RCK arises healed and refreshed. He strikes the dragon's head with his sword and wounds his skull.*)

Dragon: (*Roaring in pain, he tries to destroy whatever is in his way. He pierces RCK's shoulder with his claw that goes through his shield.*)

RCK: (*RCK takes his sword and chops off the dragon's tail until only a stump is left.*)

Dragon: (*He is outraged and gathers himself up with his uneven wings and falls upon RCK's shield, grasping it tightly.*)

RCK: (*He chops off the paw closest to him.*)

Dragon: (*He spews forth huge flames and smoke.*)

RCK: (*He moves back away from the fire of the dragon and again falls down beside the tree of life, laden with red apples.*)

Narrator: In all the world there was never to be found so goodly a tree, laden with apples rosie red, the tree of life, and from it flowed, as from a well, a stream of balm. Life and long health that gracious ointment gave, and deadly wounds could heal and rear again, which did from death the knight save.

When gentle Una saw the second fall of her dear knight, who wearied of long fight, again she stricken was with sore affright and for his safety she devoutly prayed.

RCK: (*RCK rises healed and ready to resume battle. He approaches the dragon whose mouth is open to swallow him. RCK takes his sword and runs it through the dragon's mouth and kills him.*)

Dragon: (*He falls down and groans.*)

RCK: (*He falls back and looks at the slain dragon trembling and tired.*)

Una: (*She slowly approaches RCK and the dragon. She holds her hands up as if in prayer and then bows low to RCK in thanksgiving.*)

Watchman: (*He speaks from afar.*) The dragon, he is slain! He is dead! Peace to all!

King: (*The king and queen, the court, and people of the village all come out to see the slain dragon.*)

Villagers: Let us rejoice! From eternal bondage are we now released. (*They lay laurel branches at the feet of the RCK.*) Victory and peace in all our land! (*Everyone marches past, bowing to RCK as their patron and savior. Maidens dance with flower garlands and timbrels—bells or tambourines. When they come to Una, they put a green garland on her head. Some run to look at the dragon.*)

Wise man: (*He speaks to a child.*) Do not touch the beast! Some lingering life may yet remain within his hollow breast.

Wise woman: Or in his womb might lurk some hidden nest of many dragonets!

A mother: (*She warns her child.*) Stay! How can you tell but that his talons may yet scratch or rend your tender hand?

King: (*He goes to RCK and offers him gifts of ivory and gold, bowing to him and shaking his hand, embracing and kissing his daughter.*)

Come to my palace and with trumpets and with Clarions sweet. The joyous people will sing. On costly scarlet of great name we will sit and feast and hear these tales of strange adventures and of perils sad.

Narrator: And so it was that they were quenched with meats and drinks of every kind. With great pleasure, mixed with pitiful regard, did the King and Queen listen to the Red Cross Knight's tales of fortunes cruel, and all the while salt tears ran down every hearer's cheek.

King: Dear son, great have been the evils which ye bore. For never living man, I believe, of so sore a sea of deadly dangers been distressed. Now that ye are safe and well arrived, let us devise of ease and everlasting rest.

RCK: Ah, dearest Lord, of ease or rest I may not yet devise. For by the faith I am bound straight back to return to that great Faerie Queene, and her to serve six years in warlike state. Therefore I crave pardon, till I there have been.

King: Unhappy falls that hard necessity, the troubler of my happy peace, but since that bond ye cannot now release, as soon as the term of those six years shall cease, ye then shall hither back return again, the marriage to accomplish vowed betwixt you twain, which I long to perform. I did proclaim that who so killed that monster should have mine only daughter for his wife and of my kingdom heir apparent be. Therefore, by due desert of noble chivalry, both daughter and kingdom I yield to thee. (*He turns to one of his court.*) Call forth my daughter Una.

Una: (*She comes forth, her dark cloak removed, revealing a lily white garment, fresh and beautiful. She bows low to the knight. The knight is about to speak.*)

Messenger: (*He comes running in, bows to the king, and hands him a letter.*)

King: (*He takes the letter and opens it.*) What have we here?
(*He reads the letter aloud.*) "To thee, most mighty king of Eden fair, her greeting sends in these sad lines addressed, the woeful daughter and forsaken heir of that great Emperor of all the West, and bids thee be advised for the best before thou thy daughter link in holy band of wedlock to that new unknown guest. For already has he given his right hand unto another love and to another land. To me, sad maid, he was pledged long time before, and sacred pledges he both gave and had. Therefore, since mine he is, withhold, O sovereign prince, your hasty bond with him. For truth is strong, her rightful cause to plead and shall find friends, if need requireth so. So bids thee well to fare, thy neither friend nor foe. *Fidessa*."

Knight, what means these bloody vows and idle threats? Let nought be hid from me, though ought to be expressed. If in yourself, Sir Knight, you faulty find or wrapped in love with another be, with crime do not cover it, but disclose the same.

RCK: My Lord, my King, be nought hereat dismayed till well ye hear what woman doth upbraid me with breach of love and loyalty betrayed. It was in my mishaps as thitherward I lately traveled that unawares I strayed out of my way through perils strange and hard. There I did find, or rather I was found of this false woman, that Fidessa, most false Duessa who by her wicked arts and wily skill too false and strong for earthly skill or might, unawares me wrought unto her wicked will and to my foe betrayed, when least I feared ill.

Una: (*She steps up to verify his speech.*) O pardon me, my sovereign Lord, to show the secret treasons which of late I know to have been wrought by that false sorceress. She only it is that did throw this gentle knight into so great distress, that death him did await in daily wretchedness. And now it seems that she hath sent this crafty messenger with letters vain to work new woe by breaking the band betwixt us twain. Wherein she hath used this false footman, cloaked with simpleness, whom if ye please for to discover plain, ye shall him Archimago find, the falsest man alive.

King: (*He speaks to his guards.*) Search this traitor false and bind him straight. (*They remove his cloak and find him to be Archimago, the evil magician.*) Lay him in the dungeon and bind him hand and foot with iron chains and with continual watch do warily keep. (*He turns to RCK.*) Dear knight, to you I do renew my promise. With mine own two hands, I the holy knots do knit, that none but death forever can divide. (*He places the silken cord around their hands.*)

Villagers: (*The people sprinkle all the trees with wine and begin to bring out trays and baskets of food. They perfume the air with spices and play music and dance.*)

Narrator: Great joy was made that day of young and old and solemn feast proclaimed throughout the land. Thrice happy man the knight himself did hold, possessed of his lady's heart and hand. Her joyous presence and sweet company in full content he there did long enjoy. Yet swimming in that sea of blissful joy, he nought forgot how he had sworn unto his Fairie Queene back he would return, the which he shortly did and Una left to mourn. And now whenever the story is told time and again, the people long to hear how the brave Red Cross Knight became Saint George, the savior and patron saint of England.

> *When you do dance, I wish you*
> *A wave o' the sea, that you might ever do*
> *Nothing but that.*
>
> William Shakespeare
> *The Winter's Tale, IV, iii, 140*

HOBOKEN BRAWL:
AN ELIZABETHAN CIRCLE DANCE
● ● ● ● ●

Music: "Hoboken Brawl" played by The Broadside Band, *Songs & Dances from Shakespeare*

Steps: (twenty-eight four-counts)

(The key to success in this dance is to shuffle the feet rather than pick them up to move in any direction.)

1. Bow and curtsy and take the girl's left hand.

2. Move in a circle: step, step, step, hop. Continue around for six four-counts.

3. Move backward one four-count.

4. Drop hands and circle away from your partner with two four-counts.

5. Move in a circle four four-counts.

6. Boys move to the center and bow facing outward.

7. Girls circle five four-counts.

8. Girls retrieve the boys and they move together in circle three four-counts.

9. Move backward one four-count.

10. Boys turn the girls to the center of the circle and they curtsy to one four-count.

11. Boys move in a circle to five four-counts.

12. Boys turn the girls to the outside of the circle. They bow and curtsy to each other.

VERSE SPEAKING: SHAKESPEARE'S STAGE DIRECTIONS
● ● ● ● ●

Now that you've learned more about the history and traditions surrounding Shakespeare and the Elizabethans, you're ready to focus on the language of the plays. In this section you will find information about the iambic pentameter, the rhyme, and the prose of Shakespeare's plays that give the actors the necessary information about how to speak the verse. Although the playwright did not include the kinds of stage directions we see in plays today, he did give the actors subtle clues within the text that tell them how to deliver their lines.

Verse Speaking: Scanning the Text

Elizabethans devised iambic pentameter for their plays because this meter is as near to ordinary speech as possible. Shakespeare used this form with greater freedom than any other writer of the period, allowing him to make the writing as formal or as colloquial as he wished. Students can learn verse speaking skills and practice scanning scenes from *Twelfth Night*. Practice using these four skills with your lines: supporting the final word in each line, emphasizing the stressed words or syllables, separating the thoughts with phrasing, and breathing only at punctuation points (Van Tassel 89).

Students can become familiar with the following literary terms and keys to verse speaking in preparation for scanning the text:

1. meter: inner rhythmical structure of a line consisting of a relationship between stressed and unstressed syllables

2. iamb: a metrical foot consisting of two syllables in an unstressed, stressed pattern
3. pentameter: five metrical feet of ten syllables per line
4. blank verse: unrhymed iambic pentameter
5. scan: to score syllables indicating unstressed and stressed
     Ex.: "The quality of mercy is not strained." (Begin with the unaccented syllable *the*.)
6. scansion: the process of scoring syllables in a metric line
7. phrasing: breaking the metric line into individual thoughts by using caesuras when punctuation is absent
8. caesura: a short sense pause, marked // which does the following:
     a. allows words to be understood
     b. places focus on a word or phrase following it
     c. slows the language down
     d. separates phrases and allows the listener to hear one at a time
9. short line: a metric line with fewer than five feet, calling for a pause
10. shared line: a metric line with fewer than five feet, calling for completion by one or more speakers with no pause in between
11. enjambment: the thought or meaning implicit in the line which may run from one metric line to the next
12. elision: contracting two words or syllables into one
     Ex.: Elide "raven" to "rav'n" spoken as one syllable.
          Elide "even" to "e'en" spoken as one syllable.
13. rhymed couplet: two lines of verse that rhyme
     Scenes in the plays often end with a rhymed couplet as a kind of end punctuation for the scene.
14. trochaic foot: a stressed followed by an unstressed syllable (as in <u>older</u>)
15. spondaic foot: two stressed syllables (as in <u>heartbreak</u>)
16. long lines: Shakespeare uses variants of iambic lines for emphasis.
     Alexandrine: six metrical feet (iambic hexameter) usually with a caesura after the third foot. The thought cannot be contained in just five feet. The Alexandrine also creates balance.
17. trimeters: three feet lines (not short lines) used for emphasis

Verse Speaking: Some Guidelines

The advice from the experts on verse speaking says, unlock the verse, and you unlock the plays. The meter "provides the emotional pulse of the speech" (Berry 53) as well as Shakespeare's own directions to the actor. Linklater suggests that each end word is "a springboard that propels the thought or feeling onto the beginning of the next line" (156) and prepares the listener for what comes next. These experts agree that students must read Shakespeare out loud before they can understand it. They have to know the rules of meter and form in order to make choices about how to use the verse, to understand Shakespeare's intentions. When Patsy Rodenburg coaches actors, she tells them, "I want you to respect the line energy, its start, middle and end, but I also want the sense of the words to travel through each line...you must, throughout this exercise, breathe and think the whole text" (202). When working with the text, students will beat out a whole iambic pentameter speech and indicate where the stressed and unstressed syllables are. Students should follow these guidelines.

1. Regular verse lines often indicate the character's control over a situation.
2. Feminine endings indicate weakness or uncertainty.
3. Some regular metric lines break the rhythm. Some words hold more thought or content than others and should therefore be stressed instead of unstressed. Ex.: From *Romeo and Juliet*,
   Chorus:
   "From ancient grudge break to new mutiny" (Prologue, line 3).
   (A trochaic foot is formed because *break* is stressed and *to* is not in that foot.)
4. Some words must be elided to keep the rhythm. Ex.: "heaven" to "heav'n" (one syllable)
   Stress the last words in the line. Don't pitch the end of the line down.
5. In an enjambment, don't breathe at the end of the line. Keep going until the punctuation. Remember to lift the pitch on the final word of the line.
6. You must pause at the end of a short line long enough to complete five feet.
7. Think about why characters change from poetry to prose or vice versa. Determine how to play the characters from this discovery.
8. Don't breathe until the end of a metric line. (You may take a short breath on a caesura if necessary.)
9. Pick up a shared line quickly.
10. The structure of the line influences the shape of the scene. Shakespeare gives stage directions in the verse.
11. Always play to the rhyme. Rhyme exists as a kind of punctuation (the audience will remember it), as comedic effect, and as a way of portraying innocence.
12. Always lift the ends of lines. Supporting the last word makes the meaning of the word specific, not general, and therefore memorable. The audience will think more about it.
13. Characters sometimes speak in prose when they
    a. have lost control
    b. are ordinary people
    c. are characters who act unwise
    d. are speaking in an earthy way or are in an earthy relationship
14. Shakespeare uses variants of iambic lines for emphasis.
15. Long lines express
    a. heavy or turbulent emotions, terror, or madness
    b. humor or symmetry in comedies
    c. strength
16. Characters who speak verse do so to show respect or love or other noble feelings of depth.

Verse Exercises Using Scenes from *Twelfth Night*

Students can learn to use the verse as Shakespeare may have intended, not only to enhance the beauty of the lines, but also to unlock meaning and receive direction regarding interpretation of the lines.

1. Van Tassel (2000) suggests an exercise called "Kick the Box" to help students support the final word in each metric line. For this exercise you need a small cardboard box. On the beginning sound of the last word in each line, the student will literally kick the box. This physical action accompanies the "explosion" of the word stressed by the actor, and as Rodenburg emphasizes, those end words complete a thought and end the journey, even if "the energy of the thought might go into the next line or lines" (201). Linklater also reminds students to beware "falling inflections" (131), a downward inflection of the voice on the word at the end of the metric line. She believes the cause of this problem is the dying of the thought and that the cure lies first in the revival of the thought contained at the end of the line. Our culture has conditioned us to believe the second half of our sentences are redundant and therefore often ignored. Loyalty to Shakespeare's verse lies in extending the energy both in thought and voice to the end of the line. The following two scenes offer opportunities to practice stressing the end of the line.

> Act 1, sc. 4, lines 10-46 (Viola and Orsino)
> Act 5, sc. 1, lines 345-411 (Orsino, Malvolio, Olivia)

2. Scansion: Students should score, or mark, the unstressed and stressed syllables in each metric line using a *breve*, the symbol that is similar to the mark used to indicate that a syllable has a short vowel sound, for unstressed syllables, and the *accent* mark to show that a syllable is stressed. Use the two scenes that follow for practice. You may also identify other variations in the verse: short lines, shared lines, irregular lines, and feminine endings, for example. See "Verse Speaking: Scanning the Text."

> Act 1, sc. 5, lines 250-318 (Olivia, Viola, Malvolio)
> Act 5, sc. 1, lines 46-95 (Viola, Orsino, Antonio, First Officer)

3. Phrasing: A break within the five-foot line usually comes after the second or third stressed syllable, sometimes coinciding with punctuation and also a break in thought. This pause actually separates the thoughts by urging the actor to stop momentarily as the "word holds and lifts for a fraction of a moment before it plunges into the second half of the line" (Berry 59). Voice coaches, however, agree that this pause is negotiable and depends on the interpretation of the line. At any rate, this break, called a caesura, shows the separation in thought on paper with the use of double diagonal lines, //, where the pause should go. You can use these two scenes to practice marking and using caesuras.

> Act 2, sc. 4, lines 1-47 (Viola, Curio, Orsino)

4. Breathing: Some voice coaches insist on speaking seven lines of blank verse on one breath, some allow a breath at the end of a line, and some allow breaths at the caesura. Who is right? The answer seems as varied as the individual answering it and may be connected to the actor's interpretation. Most, however, agree on some basic guidelines. Breathe at punctuation marks: take a full breath at a period or colon, pause at a comma or semicolon. Voice coaches usually suggest continuing without a pause for an enjambment, or a line whose thought runs over into the next line, and also in the middle of a line for a caesura. Well-trained actors learn correct posture and breathing habits from the outset. Rodenburg's key tip about speaking on stage or before the public is this: "Breathe. Take breath when you speak. Many of us under stress of speaking publicly do exactly the opposite and stop breathing just when we need it most…The trick is to keep breathing as you speak" (39). Practice breathing with these two scenes.

> Act. 2, sc. 4, lines 86-137 (Orsino and Viola)
> Act. 5, sc. 1, lines 219-291 (Sebastian, Orsino, Antonio, Olivia, Viola)

5. Antithesis: Understanding opposites relies on understanding the content and quality of language. Shakespeare creates both tension and balance in his use of antithesis, swinging the actor and listener from side to side both emotionally and intellectually. Rodenburg states the importance of attending to the antitheses in the verse lines: "The actor must remember that drama is about debate and constant struggle. There is rarely a rest between opposing forces" (204). Renowned voice coach Cicely Berry (1992) advises the actor to understand that in order to catch the attention of the listener, he/she must attend to the weight of the words: the length of the vowels and consonants and the number of syllables in the word. This involves enunciation and stress, but also pacing—slowing down and not hurrying to speak the words too quickly. You can identify the examples of antithesis in the following scene and then practice speaking the lines with attention to the sound and meaning of the words that create the antitheses.

> Act. 3, sc.1, lines 100-172 (Viola and Olivia)
> (Find 10-12 examples of words or phrases placed against
> each other to show opposites.)

Rhetorical Devices in *Twelfth Night*

Classical rhetoric was of great interest to philosophers who used its process to discuss the relationships among language, truth, and morality. Aristotle in particular wrote of the uses of rhetoric, and Roman rhetoric developed a process of speech composition broken into five categories:
1. invention: analyzing and researching the speech topic
2. disposition: arranging the material into an oration

3. elocution: fitting the words to the situation
4. pronunciation or action: delivering the speech
5. memory: lodging ideas within the mind

By Shakespeare's day, rhetoric was reduced to style mainly, known for its prettily turned phrases. In his book *William Shakespeare*, A.L. Rowse tells us that Thomas Wilson's *Arte of Rhetorique* had a marked influence on Shakespeare's writing, and readers now can easily identify three rhetorical devices found over and over in his plays. Examples from *Twelfth Night* follow. As students read the play, they will be able to find many more examples.

1. *Descriptio* lists names or descriptions in a series.
    (*Twelfth Night* act 1, sc. 3, l. 55)
2. *Line for line exchanges* are suitable for taunts and banter.
    (*Twelfth Night* act 1, sc. 5, l. 221-9)
3. *Amplification* refers to piling up speeches with vivid metaphor.
    (*Twelfth Night* act 1, sc. 1, l.1-15)

Conventions and Stock Devices

Students reading Shakespeare's comedies can identify conventions and stock devices that appear frequently. Many of the ones listed below contribute to the humor and enjoyment of *Twelfth Night*.

1. The girl dressed as a boy
2. The noble band of outlaws
3. The sheltering forest
4. The helpful friar
5. The exile from court
6. The girl talking over her lover with her maid
7. The girl dressed as a page who pleads her lover's suit with her rival
8. The lovesick young man, brooding over love
9. The songs in the comedies and the dance at the end
10. The two kinds of clowns: the wise clown who is generally a court jester and a sophisticate and the rustic clown who means well but is not very bright

Performing Scenes from *Twelfth Night*

Choose one scene to scan, or score, and read from the following scenes from *Twelfth Night*. Students should mark unstressed and stressed syllables, breaking the lines into feet and then marking the stresses, two syllables comprising one foot with a soft and a stressed syllable in each foot. When you read a line, you will place emphasis on the stressed syllables. The scenes that you scan could be the scenes that you will use in your final performances.

1. Act 1, Scene 4, lines 10-46 (Orsino and Viola)
2. Act 1, Scene 5, lines 238-end (Viola and Olivia)

3. Act 2, Scene 2, lines 17+ (Viola)
4. Act 2, Scene 4, lines 1-55 (Orsino and Viola)
5. Act 2, Scene 4, lines 89-137 (Orsino and Viola)
6. Act 3, Scene 1, lines 1-69 (Fool and Viola)
7. Act 3, Scene 3, lines 1-54 (Sebastian and Antonio)
8. Act 3, Scene 4, lines 341-404 (Orsino's officers and Antonio)
9. Act 4, Scene 1, lines 46-70 (Toby, Sebastian, Olivia)
10. Act 4, Scene 3 (Sebastian and Olivia)
11. Act 5, Scene 1, lines 96-181 (Viola, Orsino, Olivia)
12. Act 5, Scene 1, lines 219-91 (Sebastian, Viola, Orsino, Olivia)
13. Act 5, Scene 1, lines 326-392 (Malvolio, Olivia)

TWELFTH NIGHT:
PREPARING THE TEXT FOR ACTING
● ● ● ● ●

You are ready to begin looking at scenes from *Twelfth Night* for the purpose of acting in front of an audience. Following these steps will help your final presentation to evolve more smoothly.

Once you and your partner have selected a scene to enact, you will want to prepare the text in two ways: first, by coming to a clear understanding of the meaning of the lines and what Shakespeare was trying to say, and second, by making yourself aware of verse-speaking skills to deliver the lines using clues that scholars believe Shakespeare intended his actors to use.

- Look at each line in your scene. Use all information available to determine what you think the character is saying. Rewrite each line in your own modern language and jargon. Use necessary resources to arrive at an appropriate and close meaning of the text. Learn to pronounce all words correctly, and look up the meaning of any unfamiliar words in a dictionary. Once you have transposed your entire scene, run through the lines with your partner or group, using appropriate inflections, tone, volume, and emotion.
- Once you are satisfied with the level of meaning and delivery, go back to the original text. Maintain the inflections, tone, volume, and emotion that you established before.
- Review the verse-speaking guide and find examples in the scene you selected.
- Decide whether your lines contain meter or prose. If your lines contain meter, mark the unaccented and accented syllables. This procedure will help you to identify short lines, shared lines, and elisions.
- Rehearse the lines by yourself, working on verse-speaking skills, volume, pacing, and interpretation.
- Sit down with your group and block your scene, i.e., decide on stage movement and mark it in your script.
- Rehearse the scene with blocking, making changes when necessary.

- Decide how you will costume your scene. Shakespeare's plays have been set in many different time periods. Will you keep it in the Elizabethan period, or will you choose another setting?

We dance round in a ring and suppose,
But the Secret sits in the middle and knows.
Robert Frost (1874-1963)
Published in 1942

"CIRCLE DANCE": A MODERN VIEW OF SHAKESPEARE
• • • • •
Dancing around the Madness of *Twelfth Night*

"Circle Dance" is a short two-act play that mirrors the zany plot of Shakespeare's comedy *Twelfth Night*. Although some of the characters and events have been altered to accommodate a modern high school teen culture, their basic traits remain intact, as do their actions, a testament to the universality of Shakespeare's plays. Events that were not suitable to replicate are now represented symbolically or metaphorically. For example, in *Twelfth Night*, Viola and Sebastian are twins who are separated after being shipwrecked, each believing the other has perished. Modern audiences might find it difficult to accept the same fate, as well as the disguise that confuses Sebastian for Viola, in a play about teenagers. Therefore, in "Circle Dance," Joe drenches his sister-like best friend Lucy with a barrage of water balloons, and Lucy reciprocates with a vase of water thrown in his face. In a sense, they "drown" their relationship and the battle between long-time friends results in a subsequent separation and temporary demise of friendship.

As for the disguise, Lucy does not pretend to be a boy, as Viola does in Orsino's court, to gain the attention of Dave Orson. She uses her wits to become the mystery contributor to the school newspaper for which Dave is editor-in-chief. She is wise beyond her years, and her philosophizing in her "Battle of the Sexes" articles soon attracts the attention of the teenagers in need of advice at Thomas Knightly High School.

They are bewildered but intrigued by their own naïve attempts at love, a slow dance that seems to spin out of control as the play moves toward its finale.

Each character in "Circle Dance" retains something of his or her counterpart in Shakespeare's version. Maria Hernandez loves revenge, a good scheme, and Toby Milch. Toby is obsessed with food, especially snacks wrapped in plastic, but he too loves revenge, especially on Malcomb Hightower, the antithesis of Toby. The name Hightower should give the reader a clue about his connection to Shakespeare's Malvolio. Malcomb, comfortably operating in his superego, sets himself above the average student with his love of academics and his sense of righteousness, both taken to an extreme. Andy Andrews, III is Sir Andrew Aguecheek. A follower who is easily manipulated, Andy wants what the others want, to be loved, but the only way he knows how to get it is to submit to Toby's extortion: a portion of his weekly allowance in exchange for the promise of a date with Olivia, which never quite materializes. The character Olivia closely resembles Shakespeare's beautiful young Olivia who seems to have it all, including a string of hopeful suitors who want to share in her good fortune. Although Frank Greene, a member of the newspaper staff, does not have the breadth of character that Feste does in *Twelfth Night*, his one catalytic act of unveiling Lucy's disguise as the mystery writer elevates him to a Feste-like level. His role is absolutely essential in moving the plot to its resolution.

The title that suggests the image of dancing in a circle is both symbolic and metaphoric. Dancing in a circle implies magic—conjuring and creating and protecting what is enclosed. Love, after all, is the theme and worth protecting, whatever the cost. The dancers, moving to the rhythm of the universe, create the archetypal circle of life, death, and rebirth. What follows all our attempts at love is the hope for a rebirth of the spirit. One either holds on to the pain of loving and languishes in it or is transformed by the redemptive, healing power of the experience. Yet the metaphor of dancing in a circle can also express movement that goes nowhere, perhaps taking one back to the place of beginning rather than advancing ahead. The madness of the dance in all its chaos spins like a top. It is the "whirligig of time [that] brings in its revenges," as Feste concludes in *Twelfth Night* (5.1.399-400) .

In the end, the play is not meant to be a reflection of the darkness of Shakespeare's play. "Circle Dance" offers instead an expose on both the strengths and weaknesses of the human spirit as well as the tension that ironically does not repel but serves as a magnet to draw people together in love and friendship.

Circle Dance

A Play in Two Acts

Synopsis of Scenes

The action of the play takes place in three locations, the bedroom of Lucy Viola, the newspaper office of Thomas Knightly High School in Houston, Texas, and the high school commons.

Act I
   Scene 1: Late afternoon, the day before school starts in August in Lucy's bedroom
   Scene 2: Afternoon, opening day of high school, in Lucy's bedroom
   Scene 3: Next day in the school's newspaper office
   Scene 4: Later that day in the commons
   Scene 5: A week later in the newspaper office
   Scene 6: Friday afternoon in the newspaper office

Act II
   Scene 1: Monday morning in the commons
   Scene 2: Next afternoon
   Scene 3: Saturday night
   Scene 4: Monday morning after the dance in the newspaper office

Characters:
Lucy Viola: freshman girl at Thomas Knightly High School
Joe Sabatini: freshman boy and Lucy's best friend and next-door neighbor
Maria Hernandez: Lucy's friend and Toby Milch's new girlfriend
Dave Orson: senior at Knightly and editor-in-chief of the school newspaper *The Knightly News*
Frank Greene: senior at Knightly and newspaper staff reporter with a humor column
James and Michael: freshman JV football players and Joe's buddies
Olivia Carmichael: freshman at Knightly and Lucy's friend
Toby Milch: senior at Knightly and Olivia Carmichael's cousin
Andy Andrews, III: freshman at Knightly who follows Toby Milch around
Malcolm Hightower: senior valedictory hopeful at Knightly
Robert, Will, Ben, Alicia, and Sandra: newspaper staff reporters
Veronica Perez: dance instructor at Dance Studio One

Act I

Scene 1

Lucy is lying on her bed talking on the phone. Her bedroom does not appear to be the typical frilly bedroom of a pretty high school girl. No pinks, no ruffles, no lace—it looks more like a dorm room with posters of Betty Friedan, Edna O'Brien, Sylvia Plath, and Albert Einstein. A computer is situated on her desk while books and magazines are scattered and stacked in every other available space. A vase of fresh flowers seems somehow out of place. One might be tempted to call it clutter, but clothes and shoes and other accessories are neatly put away. With the exception of a mug sitting near the computer, no dishes with half-eaten meals lie about. The room gives the impression of a scholarly haven. It's late afternoon, the day before the first day of the new fall semester at Thomas Knightly High School.

Lucy: Why do you say guys can't be friends with girls? I can be friends with a guy. I don't have a problem with that. (*She listens.*) But....but...(*She listens.*) Okay, okay, so there might be a little tension, but nothing two people can't deal with. Not everyone is attracted that way, you know. I read this article in *Seventeen* the other day about guys and girls being attracted to the way they smell. Can you imagine going around sniffing people to see if you like them or not? (*She giggles.*) Hey, where are you? I'm hearing an echo. (*Joe opens her door; he's on his cell phone.*) A-a-a-ah! (*She falls off the bed in surprise.*)

Joe: Wha-a-a-t?

Lucy: Don't you knock?

Joe: Knock? (*The term seems foreign to him.*) It's just me. We're like...you're like my sister.

Lucy: And you *have* a sister. Do you barge in on her, too? I mean, I could be naked? (*He leaves, closes the door, and knocks.*) Go away. (*He comes in and just stands there. She turns her head to look at him.*) Oh, are you still here? I told you to leave. You're really getting on my last nerve, Joe.

Joe: A-a-w-w. (*He pretends to be hurt.*) Okay. No more talk about girls trying to be friends with guys.

Lucy: (*She sits up and faces him.*) Okay, you can stay. (*She asserts her argument one more time.*) But try to see my point. Guys need to see girls as...Oh, I don't know, maybe in the same way they see other guys. I mean, like people, not the opposite sex but like another human being, just someone they can talk to.

Joe: Too complicated. Guys don't wanna talk. They just want things easy. Give 'em something they can fix quickly, without any hassles, so they can be normal again.

Lucy: Normal? You gave up *normal* years ago.

Joe: (*He frowns.*) Play fair.

Lucy: Look, the real problem with guys is that they don't understand what a girl needs. If they would just talk more, they would know. She doesn't want you to fix anything. She just wants you to listen.

Joe: Talk more? How can I talk more if I'm supposed to be listening? (*He smiles now, as if this is entertaining.*) Besides, I am listening.

Lucy: Not now, dummy. I mean when she has a problem, when she needs someone to listen. You know, a shoulder to cry on.

Joe: Oh, no. No, no. (*He picks up a stool, blocking Lucy as if taming a lion.*) Not crying. I can take anything but that.

Lucy: Don't be a wimp. What if she's counting on you? Are you going to just walk away and leave her sobbing…alone? As usual, we're going in circles again. Getting nowhere. It's like they say, can't live with them, can't live without them.

Joe: *Them* could also be girls, you know. I could say the same thing, you know. Anyway, you think too much…just let things happen. Can I borrow your nail clippers? (*He looks at his nails.*) My mom won't let me eat with the rest of the family 'til I cut 'em. (*He takes on a sarcastic tone.*) She's threatening to put my dinner on the floor next to Winkie's bowl.

Lucy: Let's see. (*He holds up his hands.*) Gross. At least cats are supposed to have claws. Yours look more like Freddy Kruger's. (*She picks up the clippers off her dresser.*) Here. (*She holds on to the clippers.*) I want them back. (*He starts to leave but turns around.*)

Joe: I like 'em this way. I can scratch better.

Lucy: Go home.

Joe: Look, Lucy, you don't understand guys any more than we understand you. Don't say I said this, but guys are Neanderthals. They like things simple. You Jane, me Tarzan. They see the opposite sex as fish in a large pond waiting to be caught with the right bait. (*He starts to frame a picture with his hands.*) Look, this is how I see it. (*He speaks playfully now.*) Here she comes swimming by in bright blue with little silvery things all over and one of those soft wavy tails....

Lucy: Enough, Fish Man.

Joe: Or maybe a cute little catfish with whiskers.

Lucy: We had catfish for dinner last night.

Joe: What? You don't like my little fish story? You're the one who likes all that literary stuff. Besides, my little fish story is...symbolic. You like symbolism. In fact, everything's really symbolic, even sports—oh, yeah, *sports symbolism.* I like that. (*He uses his macho football voice but also tries to make her laugh, which isn't working.*) Conquest. Victory.

Lucy: Okay. This is too much. This discussion is over. Goodnight, Joe.

Joe: Oh, yeah, and here's something else you need to think about. I have a news flash for you. Say the word *friendship* and you've just given a guy the kiss of death.

Lucy: *We're* friends...and no one's dead yet. (*She mutters. She's tired of this discussion.*) Yet.

Joe: (*He hesitates.*) That's different. You and I, we.... (*He smiles.*) We played together in your wading pool half-naked when we were three, we gave each other chicken pox when we were six, we got our first zits together right before the eighth-grade dance. We're only three days apart. We could have been exchanged at birth. You look a little like my sister, you know.

Lucy: Enough, Joe. (*She sighs.*) You're hopeless and I'm tired. Go home. I need to get my sleep. Tomorrow is the first day of school and I'm not going to show up with circles under my eyes.

Joe: Oh, come on, it's not hopeless. Just accept it. Guys and girls can't be friends because neither of 'em wants to be!

The phone rings. She picks it up.

Lucy: Hi, Olivia. What's up? (*She turns to Joe.*) See you later. (*She speaks back into the receiver.*) Hey, did you get the dress?

Joe: Who's that? (*Joe grabs a magazine and sits in a comfy chair near the bed.*)

Lucy: Really? What's it like?

Joe: What's *what* like?

Lucy: (*She looks in Joe's direction, perplexed.*) I'm sorry, what'd you say? Who's going out with Frank Greene? You're not serious. Why would she do that? The guy's Looney Toons!

Joe: Maybe she just likes cartoon-y kinda guys. Why do you always have to get involved? Anyway, who's Frank Greene?

Lucy: (*She turns to Joe.*) Will you stop! (*Joe shrugs, flops on the floor and begins reading one of Lucy's magazines.*) No, no, sorry, Olivia. I was just trying to stop Joe from interrupting me. No, you don't know him. He's only my next-door neighbor who came to borrow nail clippers and IS NOW LEAVING. (*Joe frowns but gets up to go. He pats Lucy's head on his way out.*) No, you do NOT want to meet him. He's not your type. Besides, he's got some weird, chauvinistic ideas about guys not being able to be friends with girls. (*She listens.*) Him? Please. I assure you there's nothing going on in that department. (*She listens again.*) Well, that's different. He's my neighbor….He's like my brother.

Curtain

Scene 2

Lucy opens the door slowly and trudges in looking forlorn. Her hair is stringy and wet, plastered to her head and face. She looks as if she has been caught in a rainstorm, but the sun is shining. She sits down in front of a dressing table and looks in the mirror, picking up a strand or two, then giving up. She plops down on her bed and stares above her. There is a knock on the door.

Lucy: If you've come to apologize, forget it. You're dead meat, Sabatini! History, you hear?

Maria: (*She peeks her head in the room slowly.*) It's me. Maria. Your mom said you were up here. (*She looks at Lucy's hair.*) Whoa! What happened to your hair! Did you just get out of the shower?

Lucy: Yes. I stick my head in the shower whenever I'm mad. You should try it.

Maria: Really? (*Lucy glares up at her.*) Oh…well, what are you so mad about? (*She plops down on the bed.*) First day back must have been a disaster. What happened? Didn't you get the classes you wanted?

Lucy: I'm gonna kill him. I'm gonna write in bright red marker on every stall in every girls' bathroom at school: "For a good time, call Joe Sabatini…852-7441."

Maria: (*She gets up and walks over to Betty Friedan and sits on the stool a short distance from Lucy.*) Lucy, I haven't seen you this mad since Toby Milch demolished your birthday cake an hour before your party. You wanted to smash his face into the rest of the cake but you just kept screaming at him. I'll never forget that day. You can really scream loud. Poor guy. He just stood there in shock.

Lucy: (*She sits up.*) What is it with these guys? You want to like them. You need to like them. They're even likeable most of the time. You can't eliminate them from your life—you need them. But then they go and do something so incredibly stupid and you wonder if they aren't aliens come to destroy the world, or worse, stay and take over.

Maria: (*She speaks sheepishly.*) So what did Toby do this time?

Lucy: (*She sighs.*) It wasn't Toby this time. It was Joe.

Maria: Joe Sabatini ate your birthday cake?

Lucy: Maria, remember? (*She picks up a strand of wet hair.*) My hair? My *wet* hair?

Maria: (*Maria looks puzzled.*) Oh. Joe Sabatini did something to your hair? I thought you said….

Lucy: Okay, sit down. (*Maria sits on the edge of the bed.*) Whole story: Joe Sabatini and his new jock friends were leaning over the second floor railing with water balloons after school today. I got ambushed, Maria. By four water-filled latex bombs. Three really. I think this poor, unsuspecting kid behind me got the other one.

Maria: (*She starts to laugh uncontrollably. Lucy gives her a look.*) Sorry. It's just so….The thought of it is so funny. I love water balloons. Last summer my cousins were here from Beaumont and we sneaked up behind these really buff lifeguards at the pool and we really let 'em have it. Were they mad! We ran so fast Jason almost lost his trunks. They tried to keep us out of the pool for two weeks, but we snuck back in. (*She is whining.*) It was really hot last summer. So, you didn't take a shower?

Lucy: (*She mutters to herself.*) Is everyone insane? (*She looks at Maria, trying to make her understand.*) I feel totally betrayed. Joe Sabatini may be stupid sometimes, but he's also my oldest friend. We go back a long way, and I can't believe he would do this to me. He humiliated me. How can I ever face all those people again. Everyone was laughing at me. I had to leave school like this. Riding the bus is bad enough, but with everyone staring and asking the same question over and over?

Maria: (*She tries not to laugh.*) Well, there's only one thing to do. Get back at him and make it really good. (*She is getting excited.*) Want some help?

Lucy: (*She falls back on her pillow.*) As much as I'd like that right now, I just can't do it. Besides, I'm through with him. He's as good as gone. I'm not even going to waste my time. (*She grumbles.*) Even though he still has my nail clippers…and my Spanish dictionary…and my tennis racquet. The guy's a leech. I wonder how he's going to manage without me.

Maria: So, how was your first day? (*She looks away, not waiting for an answer.*) Mine was so-o-o good. (*She giggles.*) I was almost late to my first-period class. I think I'm in love.

Lucy: (*She sits up, feigning a spark of interest in her voice.*) Oh, yeah? Who's the lucky guy? Do I know him?

Maria: Hmmm, actually, you do. I've known him for years, too. I used to think he was such a dork, and he always had his hand in a bag of chips, but, Lucy, he's so-o-o cute now. Over the summer he put something in his hair, I think. Anyway, he's so-o-o cool now.

Lucy: Well, who is this Romeo?

Maria: Um, it's …well…it's Toby. Toby Milch.

Lucy: (*She pauses, looking at Maria, trying to fathom what she has just heard.*) You're kidding, right?

Maria: No, but, Lucy, wait till you see him. He's so-o-o cute.

Lucy: Whatever makes you smile, Maria…. (*She turns and rolls her eyes. There is a knock at the door. Lucy looks but doesn't move.*) Don't answer it. (*The knocking continues. Maria starts toward the door. Lucy puts her hand up to stop her.*)

Joe: (*He speaks from the other side of the door.*) Lucy? I know you're in there. Your mom said you were. Open up, ple-e-ase? I need to talk to you. I'm sorry. Really. I'm really, really sorry. (*There is no sound.*) Lucy, don't do this. You're my best friend.

Lucy: (*She jumps up, picks up the vase, throws the flowers on the bed, and opens the door.*) If you think this is how best friends treat each other, great. Now, it's my turn. (*She throws the water from the vase in his face as Maria gasps.*)

Maria: Cool.

Curtain

Scene 3

Lucy opens the door to the office of the school newspaper, The Knightly News. *The room looks like a typical classroom-turned-newspaper-office, with tables, computers, soda cans, pizza boxes, old newspapers, empty coffee mugs, and other clutter. She is clearly here for the first time, as she looks around a bit unsure of herself. Two boys rush around busily from their computers to tables of papers. Another boy is sitting at a table reading copy. Dave, the editor-in-chief, sits at a computer, staring straight ahead. No one notices her come in.*

Lucy: Excuse me. (*She waits. There is no reply. She speaks again, louder.*) Excuse me. Is this where you apply to work on the newspaper staff?

Dave: (*He stops his gaze to turn his head in her direction. He looks her over before speaking.*) Did you register for journalism?

Lucy: No, I'm afraid it wasn't offered at a time when I....

Dave: (*He swivels his chair to face her.*) You're a freshman, aren't you?

Lucy: Yeah, how did you know?

Dave: (*He gets up and walks toward her with his hands in his pockets, taking advantage of his senior status.*) Freshmen can't sign up for journalism or the newspaper. You should know that. Can you write?

Lucy: I *like* to write.

Dave: Well, Miss I-Like-to-Write Freshman, I hope you can write better than some of these Bozos around here. We've got three good writers on this paltry staff and about fifteen mediocre ones, *when* they show up on time, and I could occasionally use a sub. Can you cover a story? Do you know what to look for? Do you have the guts to run with a lead and stand by it?

Lucy: Well, I don't know, but I'm not afraid to speak what's on my mind.

Dave: What's your name, little fishy?

Lucy: Little fishy? (*She laughs, amused at his attempted put-down.*) It's Lucy. Lucy Viola.

Dave: Look, Lady Violet....

Lucy: Viola.

Dave: Don't confuse having a mouth on you and having the guts to dig out facts for a story.

Lucy: (*She is getting defensive now but preparing to play the game.*) I'm not sure about mouths and guts, but I do have brains and fingers and I can even make them work together.

Dave: (*He smiles at being challenged.*) Well, well. If you can make your brains *and* fingers work as well as your mouth and guts, I might be able to use you. What have you written?

Lucy: (*Opening her notebook, she gets out a sheet of paper with writing on it.*) I brought a sample.

Dave: (*He scans the pages quickly.*) Not bad, not too bad. (*He tosses pages at her.*) You can fill in as backup. Can you stay after school? Do you have transportation? Can you cover something at the last minute?

Lucy: Yes, no, yes.

Dave: Listen, you're an okay writer and I can probably throw something your way, but right now we don't need anybody else. (*He starts back to his chair. Lucy follows him.*)

Lucy: I can pick up. You know, stack things, keep things in order, make coffee.

Dave: Rule number one: DON'T...TOUCH...ANYTHING! All right, listen. Here. (*He hands her a dollar bill.*) Get me a Coke, no sissy Diet Coke, either. Just regular

Coke, got it? (*She nods, takes the money, and starts to leave. A boy comes through the door waving a British flag. It's Frank Greene who writes a humor column for the Knightly News.*)

Frank: (*He waves his flag in Lucy's face.*) Hello, mates.

Dave: What's with the Union Jack, buddy?

Frank: (*He feigns an English accent.*) I pinched it off the Queen of Hearts, ol' chum.

Dave: A-a-w-w, sweet. Hey, Frank, meet Lucy, fresh off the boat, our latest fish. She's gonna fill in when some of these goof-balls around here can't get their articles done, so you better be on your toes or you just might find her writing YOUR column.

Frank: (*Back to his old self, he glares at Lucy.*) No way.

Dave: She's going for cokes now. Anybody want one? (*Two reporters wave him off.*)

Frank: (*He slips back into the accent.*) A spot of Sprite, please. (*He reaches into his pocket for change, hands it to Lucy, who leaves to get drinks.*)

Dave: (*He grabs the flag.*) Frank, shut up and put the flag down. Anyway, where'd you get it?

Frank: Seriously, this hot new freshman girl was handing out flags to the best-looking senior men on campus. I got this one. You know how freshmen girls can't resist us senior men.

Dave: So you've paid a visit to the Model UN booth in the commons, huh, Frank? (*He chuckles.*)

Frank: No kidding, man. The girl at the booth was so hot. I haven't seen that much talent the three years I've been here. I couldn't take my eyes off her face. And then she smiled at me, man. I thought I was gonna….

Dave: Yeah? What's her name? (*He is getting interested.*)

Frank: You think I don't know, but I'm not stupid. I looked at her nametag. OLIVIA….

Dave: I thought you couldn't take your eyes off her face. Olivia what?

Frank: Olivia Who Cares? What does it matter to you anyway? I saw her first.

Dave: I need a date for the fall newspaper dance. Something nice attached to my arm would be just right.

Frank: Oh, no you don't, you traitor. She's mine. I saw her first.

Lucy: (*She walks back into the room with two sodas.*) Saw who first?

Dave: Our man Frank here is a prime example of good investigative reporting, Lucy. He's sniffed out a story. Seems like there's a. . . something exciting at the Model UN booth down in the commons that needs checking out. I think we should go downstairs and investigate the....uh...capital of Bolivia. (*They start to rush toward the door.*)

Lucy: Oh, you mean Olivia.

Dave: (*He stops suddenly.*) You know her?

Lucy: Olivia Carmichael. We went to the same school last year. She's a good friend of mine. She's running the Model UN booth downstairs and then she's coming over to my house later.

Dave: (*He shuts the door.*) Lucy, Lucy, Lucy. I knew you were going to be good for this paper. What do you know about this girl? Give it to me in one minute or less.

Lucy: Five-two. Green eyes. Long brown hair. Good grades....

Dave: Okay, that's enough. Let's go. Frank, gimme that flag.

Dave leaves, followed by Frank and two reporters.

Lucy: (*Looking around, she realizes she is alone.*) I can't believe it. I'm a reasonably smart person. Will I ever understand guys? Are the laws of attraction not based on any logic at all? When a guy is interested in a girl, what makes him lose rational behavior? Where's the rule book that explains how to get it back? Why doesn't somebody teach us this stuff before it's too late? (*She sits at a table, opens her journal, and begins writing. She picks up the book and reads aloud.*) "The Peace Process: The Impossible Dream?"

Curtain

Scene 4

Joe and several members of the junior varsity football team walk toward a table in the commons in the center of the school. At a table up left is Toby Milch, his new girlfriend Maria Hernandez, and a new freshman, Andy Andrews, who seems to be following Toby around. At a third table Malcomb Hightower, a well-known candidate for valedictorian of the senior class, sits with his head in a book, apparently studying. Every now and then, however, he looks at his calculator and then glances quickly in the direction of the Model UN booth. Olivia Carmichael is standing behind a table, and close observation reveals that he is more interested in Olivia than the calculus on which he appears to be working. The sign behind her reads, "Join Model UN today! Find your international voice here." Flags of different nations adorn the table.

Joe: (*He walks in with a coke in his hand laughing, apparently at a joke from James and Michael, two of Joe's new football friends accompanying him.*) That's a good one, man. Hey, I bet you haven't heard this one. Okay, see there's this guy and he stops at this farmhouse after he's been walking for about three days and…. (*He stops when he sees Olivia at the booth. James and Michael sit down at a table up center.*)

James: So he's been walking for three days and then?

Joe: (*He leans over to talk to Michael.*) Who's the goddess?

Michael: I dunno. Let's ask her. (*He gets up and swaggers over to her table.*)

Olivia: Hi. Would you like to sign up for Model UN? It'll be lots of fun. You get to represent the nation you choose. Here, you can look over this information and….

Michael: So…your name is Olivia. Well, Olivia, I'm here to sign up for Bolivia. (*He laughs and looks at his buddies, who join in the laughter.*)

Olivia: Bolivia? You're making fun of me? Look, if you're not interested in joining Model UN, fine. But don't come over here and waste my time.

James: Ooo, she's so cute when she's mad!

Joe: (*He walks closer to the table.*) Hey, look, he was just playing around. He didn't mean any harm. (*Olivia gives him a look that says, "Oh, really."*) C'mon, guys. Give her a break. Hey, Olivia. I'm Joe. Help us out here. We're just dumb guys who don't know anything about Model UN, and I guess (*He looks at James and Michael.*) less about how to approach a girl. What's it all about?

Olivia: Approaching a girl, or Model UN?

Joe: (*He laughs.*) Touché. Let's start with Model UN.

Olivia: Well…. (*Hesitant, she takes a pamphlet and slowly unfolds it without taking her eyes off Joe.*) Our organization is just a smaller version of the UN. Global issues are addressed and…. (*She begins to show him the information. He pays close attention. Michael and James are bored. They walk over to the snack bar. In the meantime, at a table down left, another conversation is taking place.*)

Toby: Sure, I know her. That's my cousin Olivia. Why?

Andy: I think I'm in love. She's so beautiful she makes me want to cry.

Toby: No girl will ever make me cry. Onions make me cry. Not having money for food makes me cry. (*He opens a bag of chips without looking.*) Oh, look, onion rings. (*He takes a bite.*)

Andy: What I wouldn't give to go out with that girl. Every guy would go insane when they saw me walking into the dance with her.

Toby: Oh, yeah? Well, for a small fee, I might be able to arrange something. Like a reciprocal agreement, know what I mean?

Andy: A what?

Toby: Didn't they teach you anything in eighth grade? It's like you scratch my back and I'll scratch yours. (*He waits for the light to come on in Andy's eyes.*) I can help you out, man, for a little cash-ola.

Andy: Oh, man, you gotta be kidding. (*He's now very interested in this proposition.*) What! I'll do it, whatever it is. Name your price. Are you serious?

Toby: I don't know. I am running a little low on the green stuff these days. A guy's gotta eat, ya know. How much allowance do you get every week?

Andy: Uh, well…. (*He thinks about it a moment.*) I've been getting $50 a week, but I have to buy my lunch, so that really only leaves me about $25 for….

Toby: That's good. First payment will begin…now.

Andy: (*Andy digs in his pocket for the money.*) All I have is a ten.

Toby: (*He reaches for the bill.*) That'll do.

Meanwhile Malcolm has been listening to the conversation. His interest in Olivia is more than casual.

Malcolm: (*He walks up to table where Toby is sitting. He speaks to Toby.*) I heard what you said. In a civilized society of ethical people, a transaction such as this one constitutes a crime. (*Trying to be righteous, he comes across as sarcastic.*) I believe this illegal behavior is called extortion. But the real crime, gentlemen, is the damage done to this girl. (*He looks over at Olivia, still busy with Joe.*) One has only to observe the situation to recognize how this spotless, blameless model of perfection has been tainted by the evil mind of one who would stoop so low as to trade her favor for…money. You disgust me! You'd be wise to drop this transaction, or others will know about this, if you understand my meaning. (*Malcolm walks back to his table, his head held high, picks up his books and calculator, and exits the commons, leaving Toby, Maria, and Andy speechless. When Malcolm is gone, the three burst out laughing.*)

Maria: WHO DOES HE THINK HE IS?

Toby: Somebody just elected him president.

Andy: President? Of what?

Maria: Well, he could be president…of the math club. (*They laugh.*)

Toby: No way. Without his calculator, he can't even add and subtract. He sure can't count. If he could, he'd know how outnumbered he is. Out-numbered, get it! (*He laughs.*)

Andy: Huh?

Toby: It's a joke, man. (*Toby rips open another bag of chips.*)

Andy: Oh.

Maria: Listen, I've personally had enough of his attitude. He sees himself as better than everybody else. It's getting so bad that you wonder if he snoops around trying to catch people making mistakes or committing crimes just so he can set everyone straight and make himself look good. Like he's captain of the Nice Squad. He needs somebody to put him down in a big way—so much that he'll never bother anyone again.

Toby: Yeah. Yeah, that's right. So what? What do you suggest, my little Cheeto? (*He puts the Cheeto to her lips and then stuffs it in his mouth.*) Lay it on us.

Andy: Yeah…lay it on us. (*Toby gives Andy a puzzled look.*)

Maria: It's pretty clear he's hung up on Olivia, right? What if he was made to believe she liked him, too?

Toby: Oh, sure. How's that gonna happen? Girls like Olivia don't give guys like Malcolm the time of day.

Maria: What if he *thinks* she likes him?

Toby: He'd be dreaming.

Maria: Exactly. We create the dream. Here's my plan. We write a letter to Malcolm making him think it's from Olivia.

Toby: Remember this guy is gonna be valedictorian. He's not stupid. He'll know it's not her handwriting.

Maria: No problem. She's your cousin. Can't you get close enough to get a sample of her handwriting? It won't take me long to copy her style. Leave it to me.

Toby: All right! I'm beginning to get the picture and I like it. So what are you going to say in this letter? Tell us, tell us!

Maria: Well, you know the newspaper dance is next Saturday, right? Chances are he doesn't have a date. We'll make him think Olivia wants him to take her.

Toby: Is that it?

Andy: Yeah. Is that it? (*Toby claps his hand over Andy's mouth. Andy slouches back into his chair.*)

Maria: No, wait for it. Here's the best part. In the letter Olivia will say she's wearing a bright yellow dress, and wouldn't it be perfect if he wore a matching suit. Oh, yes, and her favorite flower is the sunflower. And he should probably wear one, too. In his lapel. The guy worships her so much he'll do anything she says without question. At the end of the letter, we'll say she has to be at the dance early, but he can meet her by the punch bowl at nine o'clock.

Toby: Brilliant, my honey bun! (*He takes a bite of the pastry he's just unwrapped.*) Start writing!

*Andy tries without success to open a bag of chips of his own. Dave and Frank come rushing in, spot Olivia, and Dave freezes. All he can do is mutter, "**Oh-h, y-e-a-h!**"*

Curtain

Scene 5

It's the next day in the newsroom. Dave gathers his staff around him for an announcement.

Dave: Okay, everyone. Listen up. Bigsby, get over here. All right. You guys have really been slow on the ticket sales for the dance. We don't have a rich benefactor, you know. We need to meet our goal to keep this paper running. Ads aren't bringing in enough to cover the costs, (*There are groans from the staff.*) which brings me to the news of the day. We're going to announce to the student body on Friday a dance contest. Since the theme of this year's dance is *Fiesta!* it's going to be a Latin dance contest. (*There are more groans.*)

Robert: Hey, boss, I can't dance. No way I'm getting out on that floor.

Dave: To supplement the income from ticket sales, there will be a small entry fee. I'm making it mandatory that all staff members enter. We've got to show 'em a good example.

Will. No, man. You really don't wanna see me get out there and make an idiot of myself.

Ben: You're already an idiot, William. (*Will swats at Ben, missing.*)

Dave: I've thought about that. Which is why, starting tomorrow afternoon, you'll show up here for complimentary lessons. You've got three free hours of instruction to learn how to make your feet move. Hips, too, from what I can gather.

Alicia: Dave, you gotta be kidding.

Sandra: That's great! My boyfriend and I go out dancing at this salsa club every Friday night. Sign me up.

Will: But I have a date Friday.

Dave: Cancel.

Will: Right. She's not gonna like this. Can I bring her with me?

Dave: Okay. Just SHOW UP. Lucy, you're not officially on the staff, but I expect you to be here, too.

Lucy: Sure. Cha, cha, cha.

Dave: Oh, yeah, one more thing. Someone put an envelope in Mr. Morris's box yesterday with my name on it. (*He holds up the envelope and pulls out sheets of paper.*) Folks, I think we've got ourselves a little mystery writer, and it's pretty good. I'm thinking about printing it, even though we don't have a by-line.

Sandra: What's so good about it?

Alicia. Yeah. What makes this one so great? I have a few pieces we haven't run yet. Use one of mine for a change.

Dave: Stop writing about Paris Hilton's latest boyfriend and I might.

Sandra: Let me get this straight. You're going to print an article written by someone you know nothing about?

Dave: Yeah, I know, but it's a fresh look at an old topic, the battle of the sexes. Nobody ever loses interest in that, and with the dance coming up, it's the kind of thing people want to read about. I really want to run it. I know it's ultimately my decision, but does anyone have any fierce objection to printing it?

Will: Don't you think that's taking too much of a risk? I mean, what if it's a set-up? What if Morris himself wrote it?

Dave: Morris wouldn't do that. He's too ethical and he wants the paper to succeed. And, okay, maybe there are some risks, but it's a better piece than I've gotten from any of you in quite a while. Frankly, we're losing our readers and we're barely covering our expenses. We need something to light a fire under 'em again. I'm doing it. Lucy, I'm assigning you to proofread it. Edit if necessary. (*He hands the piece to Lucy, whose mouth drops open.*) I want it tomorrow morning at 7:30 so I can run it in the next issue. All right, you guys, get outta here and get those articles finished. I want them in the morning before school…in this box. See you tomorrow. Oh, yeah, and remember our dance lesson tomorrow after school.
(*Everyone leaves. Lucy pulls out her notebook, looks around, gets sheets of paper out, slips them into the box on Dave's desk, and quickly exits.*)

Curtain

Scene 6

In the newsroom Dave and the staff have pushed tables and chairs back to make space for a dance floor. He's brought in a dance instructor for the afternoon, and salsa music is playing. The staff sits around the room nervously watching and waiting. A few stragglers enter and join the others.

Dave: Okay, you guys. Gather 'round. This is Veronica Perez from Dance Studio One, and she's agreed to spend three hours teaching you some basic steps. (*He looks at Veronica.*) Ready?

Veronica: Hi, everyone. Call me Ronnie, okay? It's nice to be here. We're gonna grab a partner and make a big circle around me. You're gonna learn the basic steps for the salsa, that Latin beat of love! First, just watch what I do and then we'll try it together. Okay, hold your partner like this. (*She demonstrates with Dave who doesn't have a partner. Everyone watches. Lucy looks around for a partner. They're all taken. She decides to dance by herself.*) Okay, kids. Now let's salsa! Ready? Watch my feet. Off we go! (*Ronnie notices Lucy doesn't have a partner and drags Dave over to her, putting them together to practice.*) That's it. Now remember your footwork and your hip motion. You got hips, now wiggle them!

(*The partners practice. Most are struggling to remember the steps but some are just trying to make their feet work. One couple seems a bit stiff, no hip action. Another couple has too much movement. Lucy and Dave seem to be experiencing a little success. Ronnie shows Dave how to turn Lucy so that his arms are around her as they face the front. Everyone on stage freezes. Dave closes his eyes and smells her hair. They have stopped. Lucy turns slowly to face him and they stare into each other's eyes for a moment before they break apart. Lucy rushes over to the chair to retrieve her purse.*)

Lucy: I have to go now. Sorry... (*She looks at her watch.*) ... have to go. (*She runs out the door.*)

Curtain

Act II

Scene 1

The second act opens in the commons. It is Monday, the week of the dance. Students who have congregated begin talking about the event. At a table up center are Toby, Maria, and Andy. At another table down right are Olivia and Lucy, and at a third table down left are Dave, Frank, Will, Robert, and Sandra. The next issue of the paper is out and people are reading. In fact, all you can see are newspapers covering everyone's face. The hot topic is, of course, the mystery writer. Dave is gloating over the success.

Toby: Hey, Orson, 'bout time you gave us something worth reading.

Andy: Yeah… (*He pauses before going on, looks at Toby, and shrinks back.*)

Maria: Who's the new mystery writer, Dave? (*Dave smiles but says nothing.*) Come on, you can tell us.

Dave: You know I can't reveal my sources. (*Lucy starts to leave; Olivia pulls her back into her seat. She is clearly interested in the conversation.*)

Olivia: It has to be a girl.

Dave: (*He turns to look at her.*) What makes you so sure of that?

Olivia: Trust me. Guys don't know that much about relationships. Besides, the writer uses details. Guys don't do that. They generalize.

Dave: (*He gets up and walks two steps to the table next to him.*) I have to disagree with you. (*Lucy looks at Dave but says nothing.*) Think about all the journalists who write every day. What percentage are men? Do you think only women can observe and write about details? More men than women have won the Pulitzer.

Olivia: And what percentage has written about relationships? (*Dave pauses, unable to respond quickly. He's mesmerized by her as she gets up and faces him.*) Face it. Women have the advantage of default behavior, thousands of years of tribal clanship, the millennia of women discussing relationships over cook fires after a long day of gathering nuts and berries.

Dave: (*Looking out to the audience, he is perplexed and confused.*) What?

Toby: (*He has put* The Knightly News *down to listen. He speaks to the audience.*) That's it? Thousands of years gathering nuts and berries makes women experts on relationships? Yeah, I guess that says it all. Feed us and we're yours.

Maria: Here, have another honey bun...honey bun! (*Toby obliges her by taking a bite.*)

Dave: (*He gets up again and crosses to Olivia.*) Hey, look, uh...Olivia, right? (*She nods.*) Why don't we continue discussing this over a frappuccino down the street?

Olivia: Sorry. I promised Lucy I'd study with her at the library this afternoon. (*Lucy puts her paper down, smiles, and nods her head.*)

Dave: (*He glances at Lucy, frowning.*) Okay, well how about the dance Saturday night?

Olivia: Sorry again. I've got a date.

Dave: Oh. Who with?

Olivia: Joe Sabatini. He's a freshman football player. JV quarterback.

Dave: Well, good for you. If you change your mind, give me a call. (*He walks back to his table and talks to Frank.*)

Lucy: (*She looks at Olivia, astonished.*) Joe Sabatini plays football now? You know him? (*The agitation in her voice grows.*) You're actually going to the dance with that deceiving water-balloon bombing traitor?

Olivia: Calm down! It's just a date. Aren't you being a little hard on him? What did he ever do to you?

Lucy: Olivia, don't you remember the first day of school when Joe and his jock friends ambushed me on the landing with water balloons? Remember on the phone when my neighbor Joe came over to borrow nail clippers and I said you didn't want to meet him. Being a bit hard on him? Oh, as far as I'm concerned Joe Sabatini doesn't exist. He's a non-entity.

Olivia: And why exactly didn't I want to meet him?

Lucy: He's not your type.

Olivia: Lucy, I'm crazy about him. He is SO my type. He's so cute and so sweet. I can't believe we're talking about the same guy.

Lucy: I thought I knew him. (*Her tone is softening now.*) The thing is…the thing is, he was my best friend. I mean, there could never be any romantic involvement, but we literally grew up together. Our parents have been best friends since we were babies. We've always lived next door to each other and well, we've been like brother and sister. He taught me how to ride a bike when no one else would help me. (*The anger is returning to her voice.*) But what he did to me—I'm not sure I can forgive him….

Olivia: Oh, Lucy. I wish you could be friends again. He really seems like such a nice guy. He just made a stupid mistake. Guys *do* that, you know. Besides, I know a secret. (*She leans in toward Lucy and glances around her for eavesdroppers.*) You know that mystery writer Dave Orson was talking about? The one who wrote that great article we all loved on the battle of the sexes and making peace and everything…. (*She looks at Lucy as if she has just had a revelation.*) Hey, maybe you should read it again. It might help you with Joe.

Lucy: Yeah, what about it? (*She frowns.*)

Olivia: I know who it is.

Lucy: (*She is getting uncomfortable.*) You do?

Olivia: Yes. It's Joe Sabatini. (*She unfolds her newspaper and finds the article.*) Look at this. (*She shows Lucy a paragraph.*) That theory about people being attracted to each other's smell—I never heard that until Joe told me about it—on the telephone last weekend. That was before the paper came out, Lucy. I know it's him. It has to be.

Lucy: You've been talking to him on the phone?

Olivia: Lucy, have you been listening to anything I've said?

Lucy: Okay, but didn't you just tell Dave that you thought the mystery writer was a girl?

Olivia: I was just trying to throw him off. Joe's the one guy who really understands what a girl needs. (*She takes her mirror and lipstick out and begins to apply it.*)

Lucy: (*She puts her head in her hands.*) Oh-h-h-h-h.

Olivia: Oh, my gosh! It's four o'clock. We gotta get out of here if we're going to study. I have to be home by seven. (*They quickly gather up their backpacks and exit. Lucy's notebook slips out and remains on the floor by her chair. The snack bar manager wipes the table, picks the journal up off the floor and lays it on the table. With some interest, Frank walks over to the table, picks it up and looks at it, then looks at the door, and opens it. He begins reading.*)

Frank: (*He is still reading.*) Well, whadya know!

Curtain

Scene 2

The scene opens on the next afternoon in the commons. Toby, Maria, and Andy are sitting at a table.

Andy: Look, I can't stay here any longer. You said you could get me a date with Olivia, but she won't even look at me. She gives all her attention to that Joe guy and none to me.

Toby: Be patient, my man. She's just being a woman. You know how they like to play hard to get. It's all in the chase. I heard her tell Lucy that she wished they could be *friends* again. If you ask me, she's waiting to meet her prince. Eh, Prince Andrew, heh, heh, heh.

Andy: Do you really think so?

Toby: Would I lie to you?

Andy: (*He looks at Toby like he is finally catching on, but hope prevails.*) Okay, but I can't wait forever. The dance is only a few days away.

Toby: That's the spirit! (*He slaps Andy on the back*) Hey, listen, my good friend, I'm a little short of cash and the feedbag's empty. Can you spare me, say, a five? (*Andy reluctantly digs in his pocket and produces the bill.*) Thanks, pal. I'm working for you. (*He gets up to go to the snack bar to spend his new cash.*)

It's lunch time. Dave and Lucy enter and walk toward the snack bar to buy sandwiches and chips.

Dave: Olivia will listen to you. Please talk to her for me. Tell her how great I am. Lie if you have to. (*Lucy laughs. They sit down at a table down right.*) Look, we've become good friends. I'm really glad you walked into the newspaper office that day. You're one of the best writers we have and you're only a freshman. (*She gives him a warning look that says he's going too far.*) Okay, so you're old for your age. But my point is we get along and you know me. Talk to Olivia and tell her she should go out with me.

Lucy: (*She is getting serious now.*) But what if she just can't? I mean, say there's a girl who has the same feelings for you that you have for Olivia. What would you say to her? That no matter how you feel, you'll put your true feelings aside and go out with her anyway? Just because she likes you? It doesn't work that way, Dave. It *shouldn't* work that way. Relationships—and that includes friendships—should be based on mutual respect and trust. And being a perceptive listener! (*Dave looks as if he is searching his memory for something. He begins looking through the newspaper for the answer.*)

Dave: Where have I heard that before? Didn't I just read that somewhere?

Lucy: (*Quickly guiding him to another point, she takes the paper away from him and folds it up, realizing she must divert his attention from the clue she has carelessly tossed him.*) Well, if you've just read it, why didn't you listen to it? The fact is the media has been trying to pound this into guys' heads for the last decade, at least. Don't you watch *Friends*?

Dave: (*He sighs.*) Okay. I guess you're right. Maybe I'm not supposed to take anyone to the dance. Like fate, huh.

Lucy: Oh, come on. (*She puts her hand on his shoulder in mock comfort.*) It's not that bad. I'm going by myself, too. If you're lucky, I'll ask you to dance. You know, salsa, that Latin beat of love! (*Mocking the dance instructor, they begin to dance around the room laughing.*)

Curtain

Scene 3

The dance is under way in the commons. Balloons, streamers, colorful paper flowers, and piñatas adorn the room. Rock music plays as couples dance. When the music stops, Dave finishes his dance with Lucy and walks with her to the punch bowl.

Dave: Thanks, Luce. You're really a good dancer. (*He pours her a cup of punch.*) You can write, you're really smart, you're cute—for a freshman (*He playfully pats her head*) and you can dance. So why don't you have a boyfriend?

Lucy: Who says I don't?

Dave: Oh. Well, where is he? You've never mentioned having a boyfriend. I just assumed....

Lucy: Things are seldom what they seem.

Dave: So, what's he like?

Lucy: About your age.

Dave: No good. You need to date a freshman. That's the mistake all freshmen girls make.
         They're flattered when senior men want to date them, but when they take the bait
         and go out with seniors, who eventually graduate, it takes a long time for these girls
         to get back into the dating pool. Be smart, Lucy. Date a guy your own age so you
         can spend your senior year together and not end up like me, without a girlfriend to
         do things with. I mean, like tonight for example. Look at all these couples who've
         been together. They can count on someone to be there for them.

Lucy: What have you been doing all this time? Chasing illusions?

Dave: You know something, sometimes you act like you're really old. You're starting to
         sound like my mother, and it's scary.

Lucy: I read a lot. (*She changes the subject.*) Look, Dave, you're the editor-in-chief of the
         school newspaper. That's no small thing. You got early acceptance into Yale while
         other people were playing the social scene. You were doing what you had to do to
         get to the top.

Dave: Well, you know what they say. It's lonely up there. (*There is an uncomfortable
         silence as they look at each other.*)

*The door opens and Malcolm Hightower walks in. He is wearing a yellow suit and
has a bouquet of large sunflowers in his hand. There is a smaller sunflower in his lapel. He
walks over to the punch bowl looking at his watch. He then spies Olivia and rushes over to her.
Gradually all of the students look in his direction and laugh. It appears the only one he sees is
Olivia.)*

Malcolm: Hello, Olivia. Here I am. You look beautiful. (*He hands her the flowers, which
         she takes reluctantly.*) But I thought you were going to have on a yellow dress. (*He
         looks at his own bright yellow outfit.*) To match my suit. (*Olivia is speechless. He
         looks at Joe and it dawns on him that she is with him. He leans in to speak to her.*) I've
         come here to be with you. Why are you with him?

Olivia: Malcolm, thank you for the flowers. That was so sweet, but I don't know what you mean. What are you talking about—yellow dress? (*He pulls the letter from his coat pocket and hands it to her.*) I'm here with Joe. Joe is my date. (*She reads the letter. When she looks up, she sees Toby doubled over in laughter.*) Oh, no. Malcolm, I'm so sorry. (*She walks toward Toby, holding the letter up.*) I get it. You did this, didn't you. You wrote this. Why?

Toby: (*He backs up like a coward.*) Hey, I didn't write it. Maria did. (*Maria hits him on the arm. He winces.*)

Olivia: Out of my sight, you brute. (*Although the music continues, many of the couples have stopped dancing.*) Do you think of no one and no *thing* but yourself and food? Why do you think you can take advantage of people and hurt them like this? I'm really disappointed in you, Toby. After that embarrassing cake incident at Lucy's, you promised you would stop. Sometimes I'm sorry to be related to you.

Toby: It's no big deal. You're overreacting. We were just having a little fun.

Olivia: I'm sorry, Malcolm. (*Toby has stopped laughing. He and Maria exit with Andy following behind them. Toby finally pushes Andy away. Andy moves over to a table and sits by himself.*) I'm sorry, Malcolm. (*He is looking sad and bewildered.*) I didn't write this. I would never have done this to you.

Malcolm: (*He takes the flower from his lapel and throws it on the ground. He starts to leave but turns around for one last word.*) Oh, don't you worry. I'll have my revenge on the whole lot of you. (*He exits.*)

The dance has temporarily halted as the spectacle with Malcolm ends. Dave goes to the mike to make an announcement.

Dave: Okay, everyone, the judges are ready with their decision. (*He opens the envelope and looks at the card.*) The winning couple in the first annual Newspaper Ball Latin dance competition is….Olivia Carmichael and Joe Sabatini. Congratulations! Come on up and receive your trophies. (*Olivia and Joe excitedly step forward. Dave hands them their prize and the crowd applaudes.*) And now, if music be the food of love, play on…. (*The music resumes, a slow dance this time, and Olivia and Joe begin the dance. Frank rushes up to the mike.*)

Frank: Hold on, everyone. We've got another surprise announcement. (*The music stops and there is a buzz from the crowd.*) Several weeks ago, the newspaper staff received the first of its feature articles on the battle of the sexes. It caused quite a stir and for a while everyone wanted to know who the mystery writer was. Well, my friends, tonight I'm going to let you in on the secret. *The Knightly News* mystery writer with the olive branch is…drum roll, please (*Lucy moves toward the door.*) our very own little freshman…Lucy Viola! (*Everyone gasps, surprised at the information, but they applaud as if another award has been bestowed. Olivia and Joe both exclaim to each other,* "**Lucy?**" *Lucy has already made her escape.*)

Olivia: I'm going after her. (*She looks at Joe and heads for the door.*)

Joe: Wait, I'm coming with you! (*They exit together.*)

Curtain

Scene 4

The curtain opens on the newsroom. It is late afternoon. Dave is sitting at his computer, but his feet are up on the desk, his hands behind his head. He seems far away. Lucy opens the door slowly. She enters and walks quietly over to a table to retrieve the journal Frank has left for her.

Dave: (*He quickly looks up to see Lucy has come in and turns back around.*) You could have told me.

Lucy: (*She stops at the table and answers. She can't look at him.*) Could I really? You mean you would have published the controversial articles of a freshman girl you didn't know? (*She turns and walks toward Dave.*) Wasn't it because there was an air of mystery that you used them and kept on printing them? Wasn't that the real reason? I wanted to tell you, but then things got out of hand and I…I just couldn't. I was afraid you wouldn't like me any more. I thought you'd throw me out of the newspaper and I….

Dave: Lucy….

Lucy: Don't. It's okay. I'm quitting. I won't be back. I just came to pick up my journal.

Dave: (*He gets up and moves toward her.*) No, Lucy. Don't go. You don't have to quit. I don't want you to leave…. I mean, you're one of our best writers. You *are* the best writer. You're looking at editor someday.

Lucy: I'm so embarrassed. Why did Frank have to announce it at the dance? Why did he have to say anything at all? I felt so…foolish.

Dave: Foolish? You ended up having a hugely popular column that woke everybody up. No, not foolish. More like…brave. As for Frank, I don't know. You know Frank. He likes getting attention. He knew something no one else did and for a moment he had a little power. I have to say, I was pretty surprised. I actually thought the mystery contributor was Joe Sabatini, that guy Olivia was with Saturday.

Lucy: (*She is surprised.*) Why? Why him?

Dave: I guess because he was new on the scene and he was with Olivia. When she insisted it was a girl writing the column, I thought she was trying to cover up for Joe.

Lucy: Well, that Joe guy is my next-door neighbor. I've known him all my life. He's like my brother. He can't even write his own essays without my help. The weird thing is, Olivia thought it was Joe, too, so maybe she did think she was protecting him. In a way I understand. Joe and I have argued endlessly about relationships. It's scary, but now that I think about it, we probably do say the same things, maybe even use the same words. Sometimes even the same philosophy. All that time, I thought we disagreed about everything. We've been really good friends for so long; maybe we're too close. You know how people in families feel so safe with each other that they argue all the time? Anyway, thanks to Olivia, we're friends again.

Dave: Friends again?

Lucy: (*She laughs.*) It's a long story.

Dave: So why aren't *you* with Joe?

Lucy: He's like my brother. The thought of kissing Joe would be, well…like kissing the back of my hand.

Dave: Here, let me see. (*He takes her hand and studies it with mock seriousness. Then, to the surprise of both of them, he kisses it.*) Hmmm. Not bad.

Lucy: (*Feeling suddenly shy, she laughs awkwardly.*) Right. Well, I have to go now.

Dave: What about the paper?

Lucy: I don't know.

Dave: You could continue the column—"The Battles of the Sexes: Peace in the War Zone." (*He grabs the Union Jack and starts waving it.*) What do you say?

Lucy: It wouldn't be the same with a by-line.

Dave: Things change.

Lucy: I'm not so sure. What's that saying? "*—plus c'est meme chose, plus ca change.*"

Dave: The more things change, the more they stay the same, right?

Lucy: Something like that.

Dave: Lucy, you might not have put your name on it, but you were honest about a lot of what you said. This whole attempt at relationships is such a game. Nobody fully understands the rules, but an unknown came in—a freshman girl, and gave a little insight to some kids in desperate need of advice. At least you gave them something to think about. You can't stop now.

Lucy: Can I think about it?

Dave: Sure. The paper goes out on Friday. (*She nods and walks to the door but hesitates as if she doesn't really want to go.*) Hey, listen, the staff's meeting at Tony's this afternoon to celebrate "fiscal success." (*He grabs his backpack to go.*) We're in the black again. Wanna come? (*She pauses and looks at him. He holds out his hand. She looks at him briefly and then takes it. They head for the door.*) Now, about that line from Betty Friedan. You might want to rethink using those feminist tactics of yours. . . (*Lucy groans. They exit and the battle continues. . . .*)

Curtain

ANNOTATED BIBLIOGRAPHY OF SHAKESPEARE SOURCES

In addition to biography, commentary on the plays, and verse speaking, I have collected a number of titles of books, pamphlets, videos and CDs that students may use in their research on Elizabethan life.

Arnold, Janet. *Patterns of Fashion, c. 1560-1620.* New York: Macmillan, 1985.

Good illustrations of Elizabethan costumes.

Barton, John. *RSC in Playing Shakespeare.* London: Methuen, 1984.

Informative conversations on verse speaking with members of the RSC.

Berry, Cicely. *The Actor and the Text.* New York: Applause, 1992.

An incredibly wonderful handbook for verse speaking (and more) written by the voice director of the Royal Shakespeare Company.

Bloom, Harold. *Shakespeare, the Invention of the Human.* New York: Riverhead, 1998.

Not entirely unbiased commentary on the plays, but an enlightening introduction. The title indicates the genius of Shakespeare and why we love him.

Brook, Peter. *The Empty Space.* New York: Touchstone, 1968.

A book about the theatre itself written by a former director of the RSC. He addresses four classifications: Deadly Theatre, Holy Theatre, Rough Theatre, and Immediate Theatre.

Gibson, Rex, ed. *Cambridge School Shakespeare: Twelfth Night.* Cambridge: Cambridge UP, 1993.

Includes commentary and activities specially designed for students.

Gordon, Richard. *The Literary Companion to Medicine.* New York: St. Martin's, 1993.

Informative essay on Elizabethan medicine.

Graham, Rob. *Shakespeare, a Crash Course.* New York: Watson-Guptill, 2000.

Everything you've always wanted to know about Shakespeare, sort of, with lots of photographs and drawings with a humorous look at what we think we know about Shakespeare. It's a small picture book with great graphics.

Grun, Bernard. *The Timetables of History*. New York: Simon, 1991.

Useful guide to art, music, literature, philosophy, science, technology, and daily life during the Elizabethan and Jacobean periods.

Harrison, G.B., ed. *Shakespeare, Major Plays and the Sonnets*. New York: Harcourt, 1948.

Old, out-of-print book, but its background information on Shakespeare's England is excellent.

Hearn, Karen, ed. *Dynasties, Painting in Tudor and Jacobean England 1530-1630*. New York: Rizzoli, 1996.

Art in Shakespeare's day, completely portraiture, with popular miniatures.

Howard-Hill, T.H. Introduction. *Twelfth Night*. By William Shakespeare. The Blackfriars Shakespeare. Dubuque, Iowa: Brown, 1969.

An edition of *Twelfth Night* with ample footnotes and an excellent introduction that includes information on Shakespeare's life, language, and the printing of his plays as well as a discussion and text of the play.

Kennedy, Judith. "Popular Dances of the Renaissance." Talent, Oregon: Judith Kennedy, 1985.

A booklet and an accompanying audiotape with clear instructions for twelve English Renaissance dances. The instruments that play the music on the audiotape are copies of the early Renaissance instruments, including the viol de gamba. Produced by members of the Oregon Shakespeare Festival.

Linklater, Kristin. *Freeing Shakespeare's Voice: The Actor's Guide to Talk the Text*. New York: Theatre Communications, 1992.

Subtitled "The Actor's Guide to Talk the Text." An excellent, well-written guide that covers language, verse and prose, and the roles and responsibilities of an actor.

McCrum, Robert and Robert MacNeil. "Muse of Fire," *The Story of English*. MacNeil-Lehrer Productions/BBC, 1986.

This video covers the Age of Exploration, as the English of the Bible and of Shakespeare came to the New World.

Onions, C.T. *Shakespeare Glossary*. Oxford: Clarendon, 1986.

A book that offers readers immediate and practical assistance with words in Shakespeare's plays that only the Elizabethans would have used and understood.

Paston-Williams, Sara. *A Book of Historical Recipes*. London: National Trust, 1995.

Traditional favorites of Elizabethan cooks.

Quinton, Alfred Robert. *Stratford-upon-Avon and Shakespeare's Country*. Sevenoaks, Kent: Salmon, 1995.

Lovely watercolors and descriptions of Shakespeare's Warwickshire.

Rodenburg, Patsy. *The Actor Speaks: Voice and the Performer*. New York: St. Martin's, 2000.

Another essential guide not only for verse speaking but also for speaking and interpreting the language of Shakespeare in general. Well written, easy to follow.

Rosenblatt, Louise M. *Literature as Exploration*. NY: Noble, 1978.

A definitive philosophy of the teaching of English, then and now.

Rowse, A.L. *Shakespeare the Man*. New York: St. Martin's, 1988.

A revised edition of his book *William Shakespeare*. I liked the older edition better—more details—but really because I read it first and found it intriguing. Not for those who believe Marlowe wrote the plays.

Rowse, A. L. *William Shakespeare*. New York: Pocket, 1965.

An older edition of *Shakespeare the Man*. Rowse is a literary historian with a passion for Shakespeare. What makes this book unique is that he states with serious confidence who he believes to be the dark lady and the young man of the sonnets. Interesting read, unless you believe Marlowe wrote the plays.

The Royal Shakespeare Company. "Rehearsing the Text," *Playing Shakespeare*. Princeton, NJ: Films for the Humanities, 1990.

John Barton directs Judi Dench and Richard Pasco in act 2, scene 4 of *TwelfthNight*, focusing on the necessity of skills in verse speaking.

The Royal Shakespeare Company. "Speaking Shakespearean Verse," *Playing Shakespeare*. Princeton, NJ. Films for the Humanities, 1990.

Members of the RSC give a workshop on styles of verse speaking.

Rosenblum, Joseph. *A Reader's Guide to Shakespeare*. New York: Salem, 1987.

A resource for basic information on Shakespeare as a man, dramatist, and poet.

Salgado, Gamini. *The Elizabethan Underworld*. Phoenix Mill, Great Britain: Wrens Park, 1999.

Interesting focus on crime and punishment, poverty, and the mentally ill in Elizabethan England.

Shakespeare, William. *The First Folio of Shakespeare, the Norton Facsimile*. Ed. Charleton Hinman. New York: Norton, 1996.

A full-size photographic facsimile of the thirty-six plays compiled by John Heminges and Henry Condell. Because the first folio originally was printed two pages at a time, with corrections and changes made each time, no two folios are identical. The late Charleton Hinman invented a device he called the Hinman Collator which, by superimposing images of apparently identical pages, produced finally a corrected state of the entire folio text. Norton has included line numbering in the margins for easy use. A fascinating and beautiful book to be treasured.

Shakespeare, William. *The Norton Shakespeare*. Ed. Stephen Greenblatt, et al. New York: Norton, 1997.

The complete works of Shakespeare, plays and poems, with scholarly articles about his life, stage, and writing.

Shakespeare, William. *Twelfth Night*. The New Folger Shakespeare Library. New York: Washington Square, 1993.

An edition that includes introductory information about Shakespeare's life, theatre, publication of his plays, an introduction to the play, textual notes, and an article by Catherine Belsey. I chose this particular text for use in the classroom with students because of its excellent annotations.

Shakespeare's Globe Theatre Restored: Much Ado about Something! Venice, CA: TMW Media Group.

A video documenting University of California, Berkley students producing *Much Ado about Nothing* on the stage of the Globe Theatre in London.

Spain, Delbert. *Sounded Soundly: The Verse Structure and the Language*. Santa Barbara: Capra, 1988.

A close, scholarly, sometimes difficult to read examination of the elements of verse speaking.

Strong, Roy. *The Renaissance Garden in England*. London: Thames, 1998.

The art and the importance of gardens in the lives of the Elizabethans.

Van Tassel, Wesley. *Clues to Acting Shakespeare*. NY: Allworth, 2000.

Acting coach/director gives specific information and exercises for verse speaking.

Warren, Roger and Stanley Wells, eds. *The World's Classics: Twelfth Night, or What You Will*. Oxford: Oxford UP, 1994.

Excellent appendix on the music in the play as well as a very good introduction.

Wells, Stanley. *The Cambridge Companion to Shakespeare Studies*. Cambridge: Cambridge UP, 1986.

Good collection of essays on a wide variety of subjects regarding Shakespeare.

Sources of Early Music

All of the CDs listed below contain music played by musicians and scholars who have used copies of Renaissance instruments in the recordings in order to produce a sound as close to the time period as possible.

Baltimore Consort. *Ladyes Delight*. Dorian Recordings, 1991.

Baltimore Consort. *Watkins Ale*. Dorian Recordings, 1991.

The Broadside Bank. *Songs & Dances from Shakespeare*. Saydisc Records, 1995.

The New York Consort of Viols. *Music of William Byrd*. Lyrichord, 1993.

The New World Renaissance Band. *Where Beauty Moves and Wit Delights*. Nightwatch, 1993.

Phyfe, Owain with L'Ensemble Josquin. *Sweet Was the Song*. Nightwatch, 1995.

Rutter, John and the Cambridge Singers. *Olde English Madrigals and Folk Songs at Ely Cathedral*. American Gramophone, 1984.

*The art of dancing stands at the source of
all the arts that express themselves first in
the human person. The art of building, or
architecture, is the beginning of all the arts
that lie outside the person; and in the end
they unite.*
Havelock Ellis
The Dance of Life, 1923

CHAPTER 15

A Classical Approach to Word Study

Reading and participating in language can lead to the acquisition of a larger vocabulary, and becoming aware that Latin and Greek roots make up the underpinnings of much of our language can enhance that endeavor. These roots provide the key to understanding many words in the English language and the rich contributions these classical languages have made. In fact, memorizing them means being able to recognize familiar meanings in words that were previously unknown to you, thereby increasing exponentially the power of your vocabulary. Have you ever wondered how these classical word parts evolved into the English words that you use and read every day? Before you begin your study of Latin and Greek roots in this handbook, it is important to learn about the contributions made by the Romans in the gradual assimilation of Latin words into the English language.

Although the first Roman invasion of the British Isles took place in 55 BC under the authority of Julius Caesar, it was not until AD 43 that an army of 40,000 men, ordered by Emperor Claudius and led by Aulus Plautius landed on British shores and stayed for a while, subjugating eleven British tribes. Over a period of forty years the Romans subdued these various tribes and remained there for almost four hundred years. They left physical evidence of great progress: the founding of Londinium (London), villas adorned with beautiful mosaics, and the hot baths that remain in the city of Bath in southwestern England. They left great walls built for protection, some of which still stand today: one circling the city of York, another one seventy-two miles long known as Hadrian's Wall also in northern England, and a thirty-two-mile wall built to protect the farthest boundary in Scotland.

While the northern frontier in Scotland proved difficult and fierce, the Romans in southern England prospered with the amenities of a peaceful life. Many Britons adopted Roman culture and customs, evidenced by a society complete with orderly governments, temples, public squares, villas, bath houses, shops, amphitheatres, and good roads. Stone blocks with iron fastenings, however, have been discovered by archeologists in Cheshire, suggesting gladiatorial games, the bloodiest of Roman traditions.

In AD 410, however, news from Rome indicating a crumbling Roman empire led to the decision that it was time to pack up and go home. But they left behind many words that named the details of their way of life: camp, street, village, villa. The inhabitants of Great Britain, Celtic tribes, had been invaded, their land had been turned into a Roman province, and they had been expected to learn Latin. They didn't, but they incorporated and used many Latin words in their own language.

More than 150 years later the Romans left behind a new religion called Christianity. In AD 597, St. Augustine, a missionary sent to convert Anglo-Saxons to Christianity, baptized Ethelbert, the Saxon king of Kent.

In 1066, William the Conqueror from Normandy invaded England and established French, which had evolved from Latin, as the dominant language. Ancient Greek words came in alongside Latin, which bore many similarities to Greek. Early British scholars at Oxford and Cambridge studied Latin and Greek and borrowed words as needed in their writings on philosophy, literature, science, and religion.

Despite the Romans' advanced way of life, most of the British people did not assimilate Roman culture. Latin did not replace Brittonic as the dominant language just as French did not take hold during the reign of William the Conqueror. The influence of Latin clearly left its mark, but Roman influence was more successful through the church. By the close of the fourth century, Christianity had replaced the old Celtic gods.

And so it is that another language besides Latin evolved in the now English-speaking world. But the language that was cultivated, first by Roman invaders, then by the Roman Christian missionaries, and eventually through the Latin-based French, is the richly diverse language we have inherited as our own today.

LATIN AND GREEK ROOTS: IMPROVING VOCABULARY
• • • • •

This approach to building a better vocabulary is systemic, feeding your understanding of words at the roots so that the plant—you and your ability to use the language articulately—will flourish and grow. This unit is organized by the root and its meaning, the vocabulary word and its meaning and etymology (origin and meaning), additional words that stem from this same root, and a sentence with context clues for each word. This knowledge of roots gives you the tools you will need for gaining word attack skills, while using the words in sentences gives you essential practice for improving construction and elaboration in writing.

Now, let's write! Combine your knowledge of sentence construction with the underlined vocabulary word to produce a complex sentence. Remember, you can build good sentences using any of the tools below. See the section on five-minute grammar for more information on these grammatical structures.

- Prepositional phrases
- Appositive phrases
- Participial, gerund, and infinitive phrases
- Noun, adjective, and adverb clauses
- Absolute phrases

1. **ager** (Latin: field, country)
   <u>agrarian:</u> (ager) relating to land or agriculture
   (agriculture, peregrine, pilgrim)

   His <u>agrarian</u> interests, which led him to a career in farming, began with a summer job on his grandfather's farm ten years ago.

2. **amare** (Latin: love)
   <u>enamored:</u> (in + amor) filled with love and desire; charmed; captivated
   (amour, amorous, amateur, paramour)

   <u>Enamored </u>with the old Scottish castle and its secrets of a long history, she wandered in and out the rooms and down the narrow stairs, almost hoping for a surprise.

3. **anthrop** (Greek: man, human)
   <u>philanthropy:</u> (Greek philein—to love and anthropos—man) a desire to help humankind as indicated by acts of charity; love of humankind
   (misanthrope, anthropology, anthropomorphism, anthropozoic)

   Lovejoy's <u>philanthropy</u>, especially toward well-meaning people whose fortunes had turned sour, often resulted in the redemption of not only failing businesses but also the families who ran them.

4. **arkhein, arch** (Greek: to rule, begin)
   <u>archaic:</u> (arch) belonging to an earlier period; ancient

   The <u>archaic</u> vocabulary, sentence structure, and style of classical literature often prevent readers from giving many good books a chance to prove themselves worthy of the reader's time and effort.

   <u>archetype:</u> (archetypon, from arche and typos, from typtein—to strike) the image's original pattern or model; in Jungian psychology and in literature, a way of thinking that has been inherited from experience and remains in the consciousness of the individual (collective unconscious of all people), genetically encoded and passed down in understanding and recognition from one generation to the next; universal symbol or motif

   Even though Jenny couldn't accept the theory that symbols have been genetically handed down to subsequent generations, she agreed that all people recognize the <u>archetype</u> of the circle of life.

(monarch, patriarch, matriarch, hierarchy, architect, archives, archeology)

5. **biblion** (Greek: book, papyrus, scroll)
   <u>bibliophile:</u> (biblio + phil—to love) a person who loves books
   (bible, bibliography, biblioclast, bibliomania, bibliophage, bibliophobe)

   James Murphy, a self-proclaimed <u>bibliophile</u> from his early teen years when he came to love books, became the highest bidder in the history of the auction house for a first edition copy of *Ivanhoe*.

6. **capere, cept** (Latin: to seize, lay hold on, contain)
   <u>inception:</u> (in + cept + ion—noun-forming suffix) beginning; outset; commencement
   (accept, deceptive, exception, perception, interception, precept, receptacle, susceptible)

   From its <u>inception</u>, the plan to recover water from the cloud-covered mountains in the tiny country of Lesotho and pump it into its semi-arid neighbor South Africa seemed the only viable solution.

7. **citare, cit** (Latin: to set in motion, urge)
   <u>incite:</u> (in + cit) to stir up; to rouse; to spur on; to instigate
   (cite, citation, recite, recitation, recital)

   The six young men, planted by the terrorists to <u>incite</u> fear in the country, lost their lives when the bomb they were planting accidentally detonated early.

8. **chronos, chron** (Greek: time)
   <u>chronicle:</u> (chron + icle—relating to) record of events in time order
   (synchronous, synchronicity, chronological, chronogram, chronic, chronometer)

   Cleaning out the attic that spring revealed a number of treasures, in particular my great-grandmother's diary, the <u>chronicle</u> of her life in the mid-nineteenth century.

9. **credere, cred** (Latin: to believe, trust)
   <u>credulity:</u> (cred, credulous + ity—state or condition) easiness of belief; lack of doubt
   (credit, creditable, incredible, credence, credentials, credenza, accredited, discredit, miscreant)

The governor's <u>credulity</u>, built upon the rock of years of honesty and integrity, easily won him another term in office.

10. **decem, deka, dec** (Latin decem, Greek deka: the number ten) <u>decathlon:</u> (Greek deca + athlon—contest) an athletic contest in which each contestant takes part in ten events (December, decade, decimating, Decalogue; duodecim became the word *dozen*)

In preparation for the state academic <u>decathlon</u> that week, the students watched classic movies and visited several museums to learn information for the pop culture portion of the competition.

11. **dorm** (Latin dorm: sleep)
<u>dormant:</u> (Latin dorm—sleep + antem—performing) inactive, asleep, in a period of waiting
(dormitory, dorm, dormer, dormancy, dormouse—slumber mouse)

The idea for building a magnificent, highly efficient city underground lay <u>dormant</u> in the scientist's mind for forty years, at which time he unveiled his magnum opus with the publication of his book.

12. **durare** (Latin: to harden)
<u>obdurate:</u> (obdurare + ate—adjective-forming suffix) hardened and unrepenting; not giving in readily; stubborn; obstinate; inflexible
(endure, durability, duration, during, duress)

The teacher earned his <u>obdurate</u> reputation from a series of inflexible assignments, but the crowning irony of his life occurred when he was replaced by a first-year rookie with no experience and far less knowledge than he.

13. **facere, fic, fice** (Latin: to make)
<u>artifice:</u> (ars—art + fice—to make) skill; ingenuity; trickery; craft; artful device
(artifice, artificial, beneficence, beneficial, beneficiary, certificate, deficit, difficult, edifice, efficient, magnificent, office, orifice, proficient, sacrifice, specific, suffice, superficial)

When genuine talent used for the good of humankind is replaced by the <u>artifice</u> of men with self-serving agendas, progress often takes a step backward.

14. **forma** (Latin: shape, figure, image)
<u>conformity:</u> (Latin conformare—to conform; con—with or together + form + ity—noun-forming suffix) compliance in form and manner; resemblance; harmony

(reform, formation, malformation, deformed, formal, formality, format, formula)

Crystal's idea of <u>conformity</u>, established by parents who had participated in every aspect of the hippie movement of the 1960s, was to agree to wear clothes in most public places.

15. **genus** (Latin: birth, race)
<u>genocide</u>: (gen + cide—killing) deliberate destruction of a racial, political, or cultural group
(general, generation, generate, engender, degenerate, generous, generic, genre, gender)

Although <u>genocide</u> in many African countries has been going on for decades, it either receives little or no coverage by the media or is considered by the rest of the world as a way of life that cannot be disturbed.

16. **gignoskein, gnos** (Greek: to know)
<u>prognosis</u>: (pro—before + gnosis—knowing) a forecast; a judgment in advance concerning the probable course of something, often an illness; a prediction

When the student council met to discuss the <u>prognosis</u> of the school's numerous dress code violations, they proposed a mandatory uniform that all students would be required to wear.

<u>incognito</u>: (in—not + cognos—known) in disguise, in an assumed identity
(gnosticism, agnostic, diagnose, prognosticate)

When the president delivered his address to the nation, no one suspected he was actually a Russian spy <u>incognito</u> and that the actual American leader had been kidnapped.

17. **graphein, gramma** (Greek: to write or draw)
<u>epigram</u>: (epi—upon + gram—to write) concise, witty, pointed poem or statement
(telegram, sonogram, gram, kilogram, centigram, grammar, gramophone)

Using the diamond in her wedding band, Sophia etched a wife's <u>epigram</u> to her beloved Nathaniel on the windowpane of the Old Manse.

18. **krinein, crit** (Greek: to distinguish, separate)
<u>criterion</u>: (Greek kriterion—a test, from krinein) a standard of judging; any established law, rule, principle, or fact by which a correct judgment may be formed; plural form criteria
(critic, criticize, critical, hypocrite, crisis)

Over time the <u>criteria</u> for judging the superior feat of an athlete change with the ever increasing ability of the body to exceed its limitations.

19. **levare, lev** (Latin: to lighten, lift, or raise)
<u>alleviate:</u> (ad—to + lev—lighten) to remove in part; to lessen; to mitigate; to make easier to be endured
(elevate, lever, leverage, levity, levitate, levy, relevant, relieve)

With the arrival of labor-saving devices and electronic inventions, the average person in the modern world has been able to <u>alleviate </u>drudgery in favor of more leisure time.

20. **locare, loca** (Latin: place)
<u>allocate:</u> (al—towards + loc—place + ate—make or cause) to set aside or divide for a specific purpose
(local, locate, dislocate, locomotion, localize)

When the owner of the company returned from Iraq, he <u>allocated</u> a portion of his profits for prosthetic devices for children caught in a war whose politics and tragedy they were too young to understand.

21. **loqui, locu** (Greek: talk, speak)
<u>loquacious:</u> (loqu—talk + ous—full of) talkative
(colloquial, grandiloquence, circumlocution, ventriloquist, soliloquy, eloquence)

The <u>loquacious</u> patrons of the theatre received taps on their shoulders and a polite request to leave when their conversation continued into the second act of the play.

22. **mainesthi, mani** (Greek: rage, madness)
<u>maniacal:</u> (mania + al—relating to) wildly insane; raving
(manic, maniac)

Upon learning that the dictator required everyone in the tiny country to memorize the book he had written on threat of imprisonment or worse, the journalist called him <u>maniacal</u> and subsequently went into hiding for a year.

23. **mater** (Latin: mother)
<u>matriarch:</u> (mater + arch, Greek and Latin root—rule, ruler) mother or mother figure who rules a family or tribe
(maternal, matron, matrix, alma mater, metropolis)

Although no birth certificate could be produced, the old <u>matriarch</u> claimed she was 110 years old, ruling over her large family with the clarity and shrewdness of a younger woman.

24. **meninisse, mem** (Latin: remember)
<u>memento:</u> (memento—remember) anything serving as a reminder or souvenir (remember, memorize, memory, memorial)

A small religious icon, a picture of the Virgin and Child framed in gold, served as the <u>memento</u> of his past and a reminder of the good fortune of his present.

25. **mittere, mise, miss, mit, mitt** (Latin: send)
<u>intermittent:</u> (inter—between + mitt—send + ent—adjective-forming suffix) periodic; ceasing at intervals; stopping and starting at intervals
(admit, admissible, admission, commit, compromise, demise, dismiss, emit, intermission, missile, omit, permit, premise, promise, remit, submit, transmit)

The <u>intermittent</u> laughter of the television audience coming in waves from the set in the adjacent apartment kept Marcy awake for what seemed like hours.

26. **morph** (Greek: form, shape)
<u>metamorphosis:</u> (metamorphosis: meta—over + morphe) the change of form, shape, structure, or substance, especially by magic or sorcery
(morph, morphology, morphogeny, morphous, anthropomorphic)

In order to teach Arthur some important lessons about life and leadership, Merlin used a well-known tool of his trade, <u>metamorphosis</u>, to turn himself into a bird.

27. **mors** (Latin: death)
<u>remorse:</u> (re—again + mors) deep feeling of guilt
(mortal, immortality, mortified, mortuary, mortgage, postmortem)

As a result of the national <u>remorse</u> over refusal to enact anti-lynching legislation earlier, the Senate finally issued a public apology to the victims and their descendents.

28. **nasci, nas** (Latin: to be born)
<u>renascence:</u> (renasci, renascent—to be born again; re—again + nasci—to be born) being reborn; showing new life and strength; reviving
(cognate, native, nature, nativity, innate, nation, natal, pregnant)

A **renascence** of old Broadway musicals had a surprising effect: young people began singing the lyrics their parents and grandparents had once known and loved, strengthening the bond between the generations.

29. **nomen** (Latin: name)
<u>nominal:</u> (nomenalis—pertaining to a name) in name only; not in fact
(misnomer, nom de plume, nomenclature, nominate, denomination, ignominy)

The <u>nominal</u> respect paid to the newly established dictator by neighboring countries belied the fear and distrust they actually felt.

30. **nunciare, nuntio, nounc** (Latin: to tell)
<u>renounce:</u> (re—back + nunciare—to tell) to give up; to cast off; to deny; to forsake

You can ask me to give up all my bad habits or force me to go to bed at a decent hour; you can cut my hair and take away my computer, but do not ask me to <u>renounce</u> my instant internet access camera phone.

<u>denounce:</u> (de—from or away from + nunciare) to declare solemnly; to threaten; to inform against

While the hostile country prepared to report their intention to create a nuclear military device, the U.S. and its allies <u>denounced</u> it as a threat to the free world.

(pronounce, enunciate, announce, pronunciation, annunciation)

31. **numerus** (Latin: to number)
<u>innumerable:</u> (in—not + numer—to number + able—adjective-forming suffix) too many to be counted
(enumerate, numerous, numero uno, numerical, innumeracy)

She would not begin to list the <u>innumerable</u> mistakes the boy had made in his turbulent teenage years for fear he might slip back into his old ways.

32. **onerare, onus** (Latin: load, burden)
<u>exonerate:</u> (ex—away from + oner—burden + ate—verb-forming suffix) to unload; to disburden; to relieve from blame; to absolve or clear
(onerous, onus)

The two security guards who had been identified as suspects at the scene of the crime were <u>exonerated</u> when the witness admitted to authorities he had been lying to protect his friend.

33. ortho (Greek: straight)

<u>unorthodox:</u> (un—not + ortho + dox—opinion) going against accepted beliefs
(orthodontist, orthography, orthology, orthopedic, orthoptic, orthotropic)

**<u>Unorthodox</u> behaviors that usually result in conflict and then isolation
can often be better understood in the light of more knowledge of cultural
differences and tolerance for others.**

34. paidos, ped (Greek: child)

<u>pedant:</u> (ped + ant—a person or thing that performs) one who overrates trivial
points of learning; a narrow-minded teacher
(pedantic, pedagogue, pedagogical, pedagogy, pediatrics, pediatrician)

**The <u>pedant</u> who uses extreme measures to insure precision in grammar and
syntax will often discourage students from taking risks in writing creatively.**

35. paschein, path, pathy (Greek: to suffer, to feel)

<u>antipathy:</u> (anti—against + pathy—feeling) feeling of strong dislike

**The unusually severe <u>antipathy</u> between the two families had transpired for so
many generations that no one could remember how or why the feuding began.**

<u>apathy:</u> (a—without + pathy) lack of interest, concern, or desire to act

**Of all the reasons for an eroding of the natural resources of water, air, and land,
the one most shameful but preventable factor is humankind's <u>apathy</u>, which
causes him to look the other way and deny there is a problem.**

<u>telepathy:</u> (tele—far + pathy) the apparent communication of one mind to another
directly, without the use of speaking, writing, or using gestures

**The identical twins, who had participated in one research study after another,
gained widespread recognition from the <u>telepathy</u> that enabled them to
communicate with each other by using only their eyes.**

(pathetic, pathos, pathology, psychopath, empathy, sympathy, osteopath)

36. pater (Latin: father)

<u>patriarch:</u> (pater + arch—rule) the father and head of a family, tribe, colony,
religion, business or other group

**When the warm and benevolent <u>patriarch</u> who started the company and ran it
efficiently for forty years died, his cold and ruthless son took over, and within**

six months their financial rating had plummeted.

patron: (pater) protector, benefactor, advocate, supporter

The well-known patron of the visual arts, Margaret Redmon, hosted the annual Museum of Fine Arts fundraiser and contributed 1.5 million dollars of her own wealth to the Impressionist wing.

(patronize, patriot, compatriot, expatriate, patrician, paternal)

37. **pax, pac:** (Latin: peace)
    pacify: (pac + facere—to make) to appease, to calm, to make peaceful or calm
    (peace, appease, Pacific, pacifism)

The flight attendant, moving down the center aisle as efficiently as possible with her narrow cart, pacified the hungry, irritable passengers with snacks and beverages.

38. **pellere, pul, puls** (Latin: to drive, to urge)
    compulsory: (com—with, together + puls + ory—relating to) involving or using force; imposed as a requirement

Mark, unfamiliar with the compulsory ninety-day visa waiver established by the office of Homeland Security, was deported from the country after overstaying his visit by eighteen months.

dispel: (dis—apart, away + pel) to drive away; to cause to vanish; to disperse or scatter

Even though nontoxic fumes filled the air surrounding the train derailment, the sheriff's department tried without success to dispel the dangerous rumor spreading throughout the countryside.

repel: (re—back + pel) to drive off by causing distaste, dislike, or aversion; to repulse; to resist

The idea of eating bugs may repel most people, but the government's latest suggestion for saving the nation's crops from plant-devouring insects is now favorably reported to be a substantial source of protein for humans.

(appellate, compel, compulsion, expel, expulsion, impel, impulse, propel, propulsion, repulse, repellant, pelt, pulse)

39. pes, ped (Latin: foot)
impediment: (im—not + ped + ment—noun-forming suffix: literally to hold the feet) hindrance or obstacle; something that stops the progress of
(impede, expedite, expedition, expedient, pedal, pedometer, pedicure, centipede, pedigree, biped)

Roberta's greatest <u>impediment</u> to success ceased to be a problem when, after more positive reflecting, she turned her unhealthy obsession with chocolate into a chain of thriving chocolate shops nationwide.

40. placare, plac (Latin: to please, to quiet, to soothe)
placate: (plac + ate—cause) to satisfy, stop from being angry or upset

Although no bottle, pacifier, or toy would <u>placate</u> the screaming baby, a ride in the car at two in the morning produced a precious few hours of sleep for everyone.

placid: (plac + id—belonging to) calm, peaceful, undisturbed

It was on a noisy New York subway in the middle of rush hour when he finally discovered the most <u>placid</u> place in the world: inside his head, a little memory of a cabin on the lake where once he had caught the biggest fish of his life.

(placable, implacable, placebo)

41. plicare, plic (Latin: to fold)
inexplicable: (in—not + ex—out + plic—fold + able—capable of; literally not capable of being unfolded and laid out) not able to be explained
(complicate, implicate)

<u>Inexplicable</u> by definition, the intuitive feeling he had about seeing his daughter alive again was as real to him as if he had already received the news of her whereabouts.

42. potens (Latin: powerful)
omnipotent: (omnis—all + potens) almighty; all-powerful; possessing unlimited power
(potent, potential, impotent, potentate)

Possessing a seemingly <u>omnipotent</u> ability, the young tennis star outplayed every top athlete on the circuit, eventually winning the championship prize.

43. scire, sci (Latin: to know)
omniscient: (omni—all + scientia—knowledge) having knowledge of all things; having infinite knowledge
(science, conscience, prescience)

The scientist, having a mistaken and dangerous confidence in his own omniscient ability, presented to the world his plan to clone human embryos.

44. seguire, sequi (Latin: to follow)
obsequious: (obsequy—to comply with: ob—completely + sequi—to follow) excessively willing to serve or obey; servile

Everyone in the office shrank back in disgust and disillusionment at the obsequious behavior of the law firm's junior partner who would do anything to obtain special recognition.

segue: (seguire—to follow) to make a transition directly from one section or theme to another

A tour of Ireland after finishing graduate school produced the perfect segue between her life as a student and the life she would soon begin as an assistant to the U.S. ambassador to the Republic of Ireland.

(consequence, consecutive, sequel, subsequent, sequence, sequential, prequel)

45. similes, simil, sem (Latin: to make like, resemble)
assimilate: (ad, as—toward + simil) to take in and make part of oneself; absorb, incorporate
(assembly, ensemble, resemble, similarity, semblance, verisimilitude, simile, facsimile, simulation, simultaneous)

When Liz and her family moved to Australia, they assimilated as much of the culture as possible, with the exception of eating grub worms and roasted kangaroo.

46. solvere, solv (Latin: loosen from, free from)
absolve: (ab—turn away + solv) to set someone free from obligations or responsibilities

After a bleak three-month duration of being grounded, I made a serious list of fifty chores that would help my mother, the only one who could absolve me from my sentence.

solvency: (solv + ency—quality, action) able to be solved, cleared up, or made plain

The solvency of the school district's literacy problem became clear when the administration, having made a connection between learning and class size, required schools to form classes of no more than twenty students.

(absolute, resolution, solution, dissolution, soluble)

47. **somnus** (Latin: sleep)
insomnia (in—not + somnus) inability to sleep
(somniferous, somnolent, somnambulism, somnambulate, somnificent)

The bumpy flight, compounded by numerous cups of strong coffee, led to insomnia, a most unfortunate position for a man who would be driving across the country when his plane landed.

48. **spectare, spect** (Latin: to see)
retrospect: (retro—backwards + spect) a thoughtful review of past events
(spectacle, respect, disrespect, inspect, spectator, specter, spectral)

The plan to merge the two companies, in retrospect, could not possibly achieve the projected goals because the truth about their unstable financial conditions had not been revealed.

49. **spir** (Latin: to breathe)
conspire: (con—with, together + spir) to work or act together; plan or plot together: literally to breathe life into something together
(inspire, aspire, aspiration, respiration, spirit, perspire)

The two boys, only eight years old but clever and energetic, conspired to build a rocket to Mars and waited patiently for the day that scientists would give the two young entrepreneurs their opportunity.

50. **stringere, string, strict** (Latin: to draw tight, bind together)
constrict: (con—with, together + strict) to make smaller, narrower

If a good idea could be constricted by narrow-minded people with no vision for the future, Jake and his fear of failure could do it.

stringent: (string + ent—person or thing that performs an action) rigidly maintained

Despite the stringent requirements for buying a house, Jenny convinced the

bank to take a chance on her good credit and lend her the money.

(strict, restrict, stricture)

51. **struere, stru, struct** (Latin: to build)
<u>construe:</u> (con—with, together + stru) to explain the meaning of; interpret: literally to put together facts to build meaning
(construct, misconstrue, obstruction, destruction, instruct, instrument, structure)

By doing appropriate research and observing the artifacts in the field, the scientists were able to <u>construe</u> the mysteries surrounding the culture of the tribe that once inhabited the island.

52. **tacere, tacit** (Latin: to be silent)
<u>reticent:</u> (Latin reticens—from re, again + tacere, to be silent) habitually silent or uncommunicative; indisposed to talk; reserved
(tacit, taciturn)

The missionaries rescued the <u>reticent</u> twelve-year-old boy from a glue house in the slums of Moscow, and only after weeks of learning to trust them did he begin to relate the unspeakable misery of his past.

53. **temnein, tom** (Greek: to cut)
<u>dichotomy:</u> (di, dicha—two, twice + tom) a splitting into two parts; separation, division

Until the <u>dichotomy</u> between the two cultures is reconciled, the country will never act as one unified nation.

<u>epitome:</u> (epi—upon + tom) that which summarizes or represents the whole

Mr. Wynn promised the city that his hotel, the tallest and largest in both rooms and staff, would be the <u>epitome</u> of hotels in that city of entertainment.

(atom, anatomy, tome, epitome, entomology, appendectomy, tonsillectomy)

54. **tempus, temporarius** (Latin: time, pertaining to time)
<u>contemporary:</u> (con—with or together + temporaries) living or happening in the same period of time; one who lives at the same time as another
(temporal, temporary, tempo, tempest, extemporaneous)

Christopher Marlowe, a <u>contemporary</u> of the mysterious man named Shakespeare, of whom the world has scant knowledge, is purported by some to

be the real author of the plays.

55. **tenere, tenax, tenacis, ten** (Latin: to hold)
<u>tenacious:</u> (tenacis + ous—having) having a firm hold or grip; holding fast or firmly; cohesive; persistent; stubborn
(retentive, retain, tenacity, contain, maintain, maintenance, detain, tenable)

Only the firefighters' <u>tenacious</u> grip on the little boy saved him from the undertow of the murky flood waters that rapidly covered the town.

56. **theos** (Greek: god)
<u>monotheism:</u> (mono—one + theos) the doctrine or belief in the existence of one god

Although the Christian religion is philosophically based in <u>monotheism</u>, it took its roots in an environment in which the neighboring Greeks, among others, were still worshipping many gods.

<u>polytheism:</u> (poly—many + theos) belief in more than one god
(theocracy, theology, atheism, pantheism, polytheist, Pantheon, apotheosis, enthusiasm)

If you have ever read the stories of Greek mythology, you have studied the <u>polytheism</u> of a people whose concepts and explanations of life began with the stories of their gods and goddesses.

57. **tithenai, thet, thes** (Greek: to put or place)
<u>antithesis:</u> (anti—against + thesis) opposition or contrast of thoughts; the exact opposites

The <u>antithesis</u> of good and evil, portrayed in literature by many well-known characters, often shapes the tension of opposites in the conflict of a story.

<u>hypothesis:</u> (hypo—under + thet) an assumption made in order to draw out and test its logical consequence

The group of social scientists from around the world met at a mutually agreed upon location and time, undisclosed to the media, in order to draw up their first <u>hypothesis</u> in the most up-to-date analysis of terrorism.

<u>hypothetical:</u> (hypo—under + thet + ical—of the nature + al—adjective-forming suffix) of or depending on situation; conditional; assumed; supposed

Rather than looking at an actual historical example of the results of war, they examined the <u>hypothetical</u> model and made comparisons with new elements not considered before.

(thesaurus, thesis, synthesis, parentheses, parenthetical, prosthesis, anathema, epithet, apothecary)

58. **tangere, ting** (Latin: to touch)
<u>contingent:</u> (con—with or together + ting + ent—adjective-forming suffix) conditional; likely to happen; possible
(tangent, tangential, tangible, intangible)

My future apparently depends on my GPA in high school and the score on my college entrance exam, which is <u>contingent</u> on my decision to defer my insatiable desire to play on the computer and to study instead.

59. **testis, test** (Latin: witness)
<u>attest:</u> (at—to + test) to bear witness to
(test, testify, testimony, testimonial, testament)

Martin and George, the two students who were helping the soccer coach draw the lines on the field that afternoon, were asked to <u>attest</u> to the fact that an alien space craft actually did touch down in the field right before their eyes.

60. **torquere, torte** (Latin: to twist)
<u>retort:</u> (re—back + torte) a quick, sharp, witty reply, especially one that turns the words of the previous speaker back upon himself

The defense attorney quickly <u>retorted</u> that, if indeed the witness had been visiting his mother that day, it must have been impossible for him to have attended her funeral the year before.

<u>tortuous:</u> (tortuosus, from torquere—twist) twisted; full of turns, curves, or windings; crooked

Vines, trees, and undergrowth matted in a seemingly impenetrable mesh blocked the engineers' <u>tortuous</u> path that twisted its way through the jungle and down to the river's edge where the bridge was to be constructed.

(torch, contortion, torture, distort, extortion, torment, torque, tortoise, tortellini, tortilla)

61. **trahere, tract** (Latin: to draw)

abstract: (L. abstractus: ab, from + trahere, to draw) verb: to draw from; adjective: not easy to understand; not concrete; not able to be understood or perceived through the senses
(detract, retract, subtract, contract, extract, protractor)

Because the various computer languages may appear <u>abstract</u> and difficult to comprehend, the programmer must find the language that is easiest to use yet most suitable to the project on which he is working.

62. **tribuere, trib** (Latin: to assign, to give)
<u>attribute:</u> (L. attribuere: ad, to + tribuere, to assign or give) verb: to explain by giving a cause; noun: a characteristic of a person or thing
(contribute, distribute, tribute, tributary, retribution, tribe, tribune, tribunal)

Beth Storey, the star of track and field events for women at the university, <u>attributes</u> her amazing athletic success to exercise and nutrition, not steroids.

63. **ultra, ult** (Latin: ultimatus—to come to an end)
<u>ultimatum:</u> (Latin ultimatum) any final proposal or statement of conditions
(ultimate, penultimate, ulterior, ultra, utmost)

When the mold multiplying on the leftover lasagna under Roger's bed began to spread to the carpet, his mother issued an <u>ultimatum</u>: no food in his room or find another place to live.

64. **undulates, unda, und** (Latin: wave)
<u>redundant:</u> (L. redundare: re, again + unda, wave) overabundant; repetitive; excessive; wordy; more than enough
(abound, abundance, inundated, surround, undulate, undulation)

When Sylvia repeated the story about the miserable date she had with my cousin, I wondered if she was being <u>redundant</u> or trying to give me a message.

65. **unus, uni** (Latin: one)
<u>unify:</u> (L. uni + facere, to make) to make or form into one

Although the object of the European Union, which at the outset seemed like a workable and effective solution to several problems, was to <u>unify</u> and strengthen the European countries economically, the dissention among nations turned it into a fiasco.

<u>unilateral:</u> (L. uni + latus, lateris, side) of, occurring on, or affecting one side only; involving one party only; one-sided

The Democrats' <u>unilateral</u> stand on health care provisions for people in the U.S. resulted in its demise without the necessary support of the Republicans.

(united, unison, unity, unicycle, unisex)

66. **vacare, vac, void** (Latin: to be empty)
<u>vacuum:</u> (L. vacuums, vacua—empty) a completely empty space
(vacation, vacancy, vacuous, avoid, void, evacuee, evacuate, devoid, null and void)

He stared at the large decorative glass bubble that occupied the center of the room and thought of the <u>vacuum</u> that depicted his own empty and barren life, one in which a man could see his future as only a hopeless void.

67. **valare, vale, val** (Latin: to be strong, to have power)
<u>validity:</u> (L. validitas from valare, strong) strength or force from being supported by fact

The <u>validity</u> of the archeologist's report on discovering the oldest human was based on careful scientific research as well as the experience and reputation of the scientist.

<u>valor:</u> (L. valare) courage, bravery

The New York City firefighters and policemen who risked their lives to save others from the smoke-filled Twin Towers in the 9/11 crisis displayed the kind of <u>valor</u> that Americans will always remember.

(value, valuable, validate, valid, valentine, valiant, valence)

68. **varius, vari** (Latin: bent)
<u>prevaricate:</u> (L. prae, pre—before + varicus, bent) to lie; to evade the truth
(various, variety, vary, variegated, variant, variation, variance)

The once-promising young attorney could either <u>prevaricate</u> and support the criminal element he now defended, or he could tell the truth and risk his own execution.

69. **vertere, versare** (Latin: to turn)
<u>avert:</u> (a, ab—from, away + vertere) to turn from or away; to ward off or prevent

After hearing stories of hungry bears entering tents and attacking park visitors,

June and her friends <u>averted</u> disaster and stayed in a motel.

<u>divert:</u> (divertere, from dis, di—apart + vert) to turn a person or thing aside from a course; to deflect

The fact that Allen had to study for finals, no small matter that could be taken lightly, was sufficient enough for the moment to <u>divert</u> his attention from the recent death of his dog.

<u>introvert:</u> (intro—within, in + vert) one who turns inward or directs one's mind or interest upon oneself

The day Eric strolled into school in a clown suit with a battery-powered red flashing nose was the day everyone agreed he would never be called an <u>introvert</u> again.

<u>extrovert:</u> (extra—outside + vert) outgoing, expressive person; one who turns outward

As an <u>extrovert</u> who loved getting attention, Julie would stumble, feign an injury, and soak up the concerned gallantry of the one she had her eye on.

<u>versatile:</u> (versatilis—that which turns around, from versare) that may be turned or moved around; turning with ease from one thing to another; competent in many things

The international pump company was looking for a <u>versatile</u> new employee, one with no family obligations who could work both in sales and in the field.

70. **verus, ver** (Latin: true)
<u>verify:</u> (L. verus, true + facere, to make) to confirm, to prove the truth of
(averred, very, verification, veracious, veritable, veracity, verity)

Airplane Security is most interested in passengers who can <u>verify</u> who they are, where they live, and why they're on the flight.

71. **vestire, vestis, vest** (Latin: to dress)
<u>travesty:</u> (L. trans, over + vest, dress) to translate, treat, or imitate so as to render ridiculous, or ludicrous
(vest, vestments, vestry, invest, investiture, divest, reinvest)

The <u>travesty</u> of his behavior on the field trip to the theatre reached a crescendo when Jonah climbed onto the stage and joined the confused actors, surprised by

the unexpected intrusion.

72. **vivere, viv** (Latin: to live)

<u>convivial:</u> (convivalis—a feast, from com, con—together + vivere) jovial; social; festive; having good times with friends

The photographer, who captured the <u>convivial</u> atmosphere of the party, resplendent in its magnificent decorations, its festive music, and its happy faces, preserved many precious memories for the bride and groom.

<u>vitality:</u> (vita—life + ity—state of) power to live or go on living

Lost in the mountains for three days on a family camping trip, Matt endured low temperatures at night with unusual <u>vitality</u> and survived with only a canteen of water and the belief that he would be rescued.

<u>vivacious:</u> (vivi + ous—full of) spirited, energetic, full of life

The <u>vivacious</u> two-year-old had already climbed out of her crib, gone downstairs, and cracked a dozen eggs on the living room carpet by the time her sleepy mother arrived on the scene.

<u>vivify:</u> (vivi + by—make) to give life to

Rachel gazed at the painting and smiled, knowing the artist had indeed captured the spirit of the quiet coastal town of Italy that he tried to <u>vivify</u>, for she had been there and seen it for herself.

(revive, revival, revitalize, survive, viable, victuals, curriculum vitae/vita/vitae, vital, vitamin, aqua vitae, viva!, von vivant, vivid, vivisection)

73. **vocare, voc** (Latin: to call)

<u>avocation:</u> (avocatio—calling off; a—away + voc + tion—noun-forming suffix) something one does in addition to his vocation or regular work; hobby

Although gardening was an <u>avocation</u> that provided endless hours of pleasure, her books on the subject provided an income that afforded her the luxury of the hobby.

<u>convocation:</u> (con—with, together + voc + tion—noun-forming suffix) group of persons called together for a purpose

As the waiter brought us our dinner on the patio, a strange and humorous entertainment began: a <u>convocation</u> of grackles who began prancing to and fro, puffing up their feathers and doubling their size, and arguing in their bird-like language about who was going to court their feathered lady nearby.

(provocation, evoke, vociferous, invocation, vocation, revoke, irrevocable, advocate, equivocate)

74. **volens, vol, velle** (Latin: to wish, to will)
<u>malevolent:</u> (male—ill, badly + volens) having an evil disposition toward another; wishing evil to others; bringing calamity

The <u>malevolent</u> tornado, with its evil eye and merciless swirling dance, left a path of destruction with its deadly touch.

<u>volition:</u> (voil, volo + tion) the act of willing; exercise of will; determination by the will

The computer, as if by its own <u>volition</u>, stopped responding to my commands and began to erase the lines of code as fast as I typed them.

75. **vorare** (Latin: to swallow whole)
<u>devour:</u> (devorare, from de—intensive + vorare) to eat greedily

Ethan, who never learned the art of close, intensive study, <u>devoured</u> every book he could at incredible speed to satisfy his appetite for a wide range of knowledge.

<u>voracious:</u> (voracis, from vorare) greedy in eating; ravenous; very eager; insatiable

The students who volunteered for the beach's all-day clean-up campaign brought their <u>voracious</u> appetites to the cookout that night, a well-deserved reward for such physically enervating work.

(voracity, carnivorous, herbivore)

LATIN IN OUR EVERYDAY SPEECH
• • • • •

Latin may be considered a "dead" language, that is, not spoken by any particular group of people today, but its presence in the speech we use every day in all walks of life is indicative of just how alive Latin really is. And it isn't just law and medicine or the church or classical scholars who use it. It's ordinary folk like us who grab just the right word when we need it, which happens to be Latin sometimes. It's all of us who have ever read the myriad of abbreviations of terms that govern our lives—a.m., p.m., AD, BC, R.I.P., i.e.. Writers and public speakers today know that borrowing Latin words, phrases, and sayings from famous Roman and Greek poets, playwrights, philosophers, statesmen, and leaders helps them communicate meaning in a way that may lend more power to their own thoughts and ideas.

The words, phrases, and sayings listed in this chapter will give your writing more power, too. Read through the lists and put a star by the ones whose meanings strike you as something you could use to support your own ideas or philosophy of life. A pronunciation guide follows this section should you want to add this Latin influence to your speech as well.

Latin Words and Phrases

Ad astra per aspera: to the stars through difficulties

Ad infinitum: to infinity, with no limit

Ad lib, ad libitum: extemporaneously (literally, at pleasure)

Ad nauseum: to the point of nausea, something that seems to go on forever

Alter ego: an inseparable friend (literally, another I)

Alma mater: the school from which you graduated (literally, nourishing mother)

Ante bellum: before the war (U.S. Civil War)

A priori: from what is already known (in deductive reasoning, assumptions that derive from prior knowledge)

Aqua vitae: whiskey (literally, water of life; see *Twelfth Night*)

Arcanum arcanorum: secret of secrets

Bona fide: in good faith

Cacoethes loquendi: compulsive talking

Cacoethes scribendi: an incurable itch to write

Concordia discors: harmony in discord (Horace in *Epistles*)

Consensus omnium: agreement of all

Cornu copiae: horn of plenty (Zeus endowed the horn of a goat with the capability of producing whatever the owner of the horn desired.)

Curriculum vitae: a resume (literally, the course of one's life)

De facto: in reality, rather than legality (literally, from the fact)

Deus ex machina: an unlikely and providential intervention; the person or thing that seems to appear out of nowhere to save the day in fiction or drama (literally, god out of a machine)

Ex post facto: retroactive action, usually not legal; knowing all the answers after you know how something has turned out (literally, from what is done afterward)

Flagrante delicto: "red-handed" (caught with the evidence)

Habeas corpus: protection against arbitrary imprisonment (Literally, you may have the body.)

In loco parentis: a guardian (literally, in place of the parent)

Ipso facto: absolutely (literally, by that very fact)

Lacrima Christi: the tear of Christ (In Hawthorne's "Rappaccini's Daughter" it is a symbolic sweet red Italian wine called Lachryma Christi.)

Magnum opus: one's crowning achievement (literally, a great work)

Mea culpa: my fault (I am to blame—literally, through or by my fault.)

Modus operandi: scheme or plan for doing a job (literally, manner of working)

Ne plus ultra: perfection (literally, not more beyond)

Nihil nimis: nothing in excess (also *ne quid nimis*; quoted by Terence, Horace, Lucan, and Voltaire)

Prima facie: on or at first appearance (Prima facie evidence seems enough to convict.)

Quid pro quo: something given in return for something (literally, something for something)

Satis verborum: less talk, more action (literally, enough of words)

Sine qua non: absolutely necessary; an indispensable condition (literally, without which not)

Summum bonum: the highest good

Tabula rasa: a clean slate; often denotes a mind devoid of preconceptions

Tempus edax rerum: time, the devourer of all things (from Ovid's *Metamorphoses*)

Terra firma: solid land as opposed to being out at sea or in a plane

Vice versa: changed and turned, turned about

Volens et potens: willing and able

Famous Latin Sayings

(Some of the following sayings are anonymous and some are documented.)

Acta est fabula: It's all over. (Literally, the drama has been acted out. Life, too?)

Age quod agis: Pay attention to what you're doing. (Literally, do what you are doing.)

Albo lapillo notare diem: Mark the day with a white stone (white: symbol of happiness to the Romans).

Amor vincit omnia et nos cedaneus amori: Love conquers all, and let us yield to it.

Atque inter silvas Academi quaerere verum: And seek for truth in the groves of Academe.

Audi partem alteram: Hear the other side.

Carpe diem, quam minimum credula postero: Sieze the day, trusting little in tomorrow.

Caveat emptor: Let the buyer beware.

Cave quid dicis, quando, et cui: Beware what you say, when, and to whom.

Cognito ergo sum: I think, therefore I am.

Cucullus non facit monachum—**Medieval proverb:** The cowl does not make a monk.

Cui bono? Who stands to gain?

De calcaria in carbonarium: Out of the frying pan, into the fire.

De nihilo nihil—**Persius:** Nothing comes from nothing.

Favete linguis: Hold your tongue.

Finis coronat opus—**Ovid:** The end crowns the work.

Forsan et haec olim meminisse iuvabit: Perhaps some time it will be pleasant to remember even these things.

Fronti nulla fides: Never judge a book by its cover. (Literally, no reliance can be placed on appearance.)

Glaudeamus igitur,
Iuvenes dum sumus—**students' song, c. 1267**
Let us live then and be glad
While young life is before us.

Homo homini lupus: Man is a wolf to man. Scottish poet Robert Burns's interpretation is "man's inhumanity to man" (123).

Insanus omnis furere credit ceteros: Every madman thinks everybody else is mad.

Mater atrium necessitas: Necessity is the mother of invention.

Memento mori: Remember that you must die. (Literally, remember to die. It refers to the fact that we are all human and will eventually die.)

Nil desperandum: Never say die.

Non est tanti: No big deal (Literally, it is not of such great importance.).

Non scholae sed vitae discimus: We learn not for school, but for life.

Non semper ea sunt quae videntur: Things are not always what they appear to be.

Non sequitur: It does not follow. (It indicates something that does not seem logical.)

Parvis e glandibus quercus: Tall oaks from little acorns grow.

Pax vobiscum: Peace be with you.

Piscem nature doces: You're teaching a fish to swim.

Possunt quia posse videntur: They can because they think they can.

Qui desiderat pacem, praeparet bellum: Let him who desires peace prepare for war.

Qui me amat, amat et canem meam: Love me, love my dog.

Quos deus vult perdere prius dementat: Those whom God wishes to destroy, he first makes mad.

Res ipsa loquitur: The facts speak for themselves. (Literally, the thing itself speaks.)

R.I.P. (***Requiescat in pace***): May he or she rest in peace.

Salus populi suprema lex: The people's safety is the highest law.

Semel emissum volat irrevocabile verbum:
Once a word has been allowed to escape, it cannot be recalled.

Sic ego nec sine te nec tecum vivere possum: So I can't live either without you or with you.

Tanta stultitia mortalium est: What fools these mortals be. (Borrowed by Shakespeare in *Midsummer Night's Dream.*)

Tempora muntantur, nos et mutamur in illis: Times change, and we change with them, too.

Tempus fugit: Time flies.

Tempus omnia revelat: Time reveals all things.

Te nosce: Know thyself.

Usus promptos facit: Practice makes perfect.

Vade in pace: Go in peace.

Vincit omnia veritas: Truth conquers all things.

Vive, vale: Live, be well.

Latin Abbreviations

AD: *Anno Domini*—in the year of (our) Lord

a.m.: *ante meridiem*—before noon

c., circ., circa, circum: about, used with dates

e.g.: *exempli gratia*—for example (literally, for the sake of)

et al: *et alii* or *et alia*—and other people or things (*et alibi*—and elsewhere)

etc.: *etcetera*—and the rest, and so forth

ibid.: *ibidem*—in the same place (used in footnotes, if the reference is the same as the previous one)

i.e.: *id est*—that is

no.: *numero*—by number

op. cit.: *opere citato*—in the work cited (used in footnotes instead of repeating the title of a book you have already mentioned)

p.m.: *post meridiem*—after noon

pro and **con:** *pro et contra*—for and against

sic: thus (used inside brackets following a word or phrase when a writer wants to indicate an apparent misspelling or doubtful word or phrase in a source being quoted)

vs., v.: versus—against

Latin Pronunciation

The pronunciation of Latin roots and words is not difficult once you know a few basic rules. Most of the consonant and vowel sounds in Latin are similar to our sounds in English. The key is knowing a few basic rules.

Vowels:

Pronunciation	English word	Latin word
Ah	mom	the **a** in <u>a priori</u>
Ay	take	the **e** in <u>fecit</u>
Aw	call	the **a** in <u>astra</u>
E	get	the **e** in <u>et</u>
Eh	set	the **e** in <u>petere</u>
Ee	meet	the **i** in <u>vita</u>
Ih	pig	the **i** in <u>tibi</u>
Oh	know	the **o** in <u>pro</u>
Oo	soon	the **u** in <u>publica</u>
Uu	put	the **u** in <u>umbra</u>

Diphthongs:

Diphthong	Pronunciation
Ae	long *I* as in hike
Au	*ow* as in now
Oe	*oy* as in boy
Ui	*we*
Ei	*ay* as in eight

Consonants:

Consonant	Pronunciation
C and ch	*k* as in cash
T	*t* as in tie, never like *sh*
G	*g* as in go
V	*w* as in was
I	*y* as in you
X	*z* as in xenophobia
S	*s* as in say
Gu, qu	*gw*, *qw* as in queen

Accents:

1. Place the accent on the next-to-last syllable if that syllable is long.

2. Place the accent on the third-to-last syllable if the next-to-last syllable is short.

3. Place the accent on the first syllable if the word has only two syllables.

Not to go back is somewhat to advance,
And men must walk, at least, before they dance.
Alexander Pope
Imitations of Horace, 1733

CHAPTER 16

Five-Minute Grammar

The study of grammar can be laborious and ineffective if students are asked to complete stacks of worksheets for weeks at a time with long, dry intermittent stretches of no attention to grammar at all. What I'm describing, of course, is usually the exception rather than the rule, but there is a better way to learn grammar that involves knowing why you're learning it in the first place. There's nothing wrong with practice, but your time spent practicing must have an end that produces more than the practice itself. Grammar study should improve your writing.

Five-Minute Grammar is a program in which you can learn about grammar and syntax, or the way words and phrases are arranged in sentences, through parsing and writing sentences in only five minutes a day. The truth is, it can take a little longer if you need more time, but the principle behind this practice is "little by little does the trick," beginning with simple sentences and moving gradually toward compound-complex sentences with various kinds of phrases.

We live in a world where people understand connections through visual sources. Parsing sentences on paper is a visual way that helps you to see how words and phrases are connected in structure and meaning. It is important to remember, however, that examining each word in a sentence is a means, not the end, for studying the structure of our language. Included in this chapter is a list of grammatical terms as well as an activity for improving your ability to write more complicated sentences. When you complete the initial activity, use the thirty-two models given to continue constructing sentences that will add complexity, fluency, and variety to your writing.

Students who use more complicated structures in writing have a greater chance of having more sophisticated writing. Kellogg Hunt, in 1962 at Florida State University, reported his research on the qualities that he found in the writing of fourth-, eighth-, and twelfth-grade students and educated adults. He found that writers constructed sentences with length and complexity that increased with the maturity of the writer. Hunt devised a way to determine this maturity through terminable units, or t-units, the smallest part of a sentence that can stand on its own without leaving any sentence fragments. His study showed that fourth graders averaged 8.60 words per t-unit, eighth graders 11.50 words, twelfth graders 14.40 words, and educated adults 20.20 words per t-unit. Hunt found that it was the length of the t-unit that indicated complexity, not the length of the sentence.

Whether a student uses phrases or clauses, building meaning through any method beyond simple sentences communicates ideas in a more complex way. Many students exhibit this behavior: They write the way they think—in simple sentences or in fragments. They don't want to take the time to revise, or they don't know how, and often do not do it. Therefore, their writing lacks clarity and sophistication.

What are your writing habits? Will writing become artificial if you pay attention to the number of phrases and clauses that you use? The answer may be yes—at first, but as you remember your options and begin to use them, writing with a variety of constructions will seem more natural. If you want to find out the number of t-units in your own writing, follow these instructions:

1. Count the number of words in your sentences.
2. Divide the number of t-units (complete sentences) into the number of words.
3. Remember that each independent clause in a compound sentence counts as a t-unit. A complex sentence would count as one t-unit. A compound-complex sentence would count as two, depending on the number of independent clauses in the sentence.
4. Compare the number of t-units you get after dividing with Kellogg Hunt's results. Where do you stand?

The exercises below will show you how you can build sentences that communicate information in a clear, interesting way while increasing the maturity of your writing.

Directions: Use any of the information given below that you might need to write your sentences. Use phrases and clauses to add information as well as complexity. Avoid wordiness, lack of clarity, and run-ons.

Choose from the following structures ways of adding information to the subject-predicate pattern for your advanced structures.
1. Prepositional phrases (adjective and adverb phrases)
2. Appositive phrases
3. Participial, gerund, and infinitive phrases
4. Noun clauses
5. Adjective clauses
6. Adverb clauses
7. Absolute phrases

Use this information to write your new syntactically mature sentences:

1. It was an extremely cold day and because of the weather people's pipes froze and they

had to call plumbing companies. The plumbers couldn't take all the calls in one day. People were angry. This problem affected their lives in an upsetting way.

2. It was her birthday. She wanted a party but her aunt and uncle from Australia that her mom hadn't seen in six years were coming to visit. Her parents wanted her to have a quiet dinner with the family instead.

3. Mark and his friends wanted concert tickets but couldn't get the cash. Parents wouldn't give it, the boys didn't have any savings, nor did they have part-time jobs. One of them decided that they should all sell something to get the money. Everyone except Ted got the tickets.

4. Sean forgot to do his homework. He thought his homework was to write an essay on *To Kill a Mockingbird*. He would get two grades for this assignment. He arrived at school. He worked on the essay all day. His class was the last one of the day. He tried to work on it during every class and at lunch. He finished it and turned it in. It was on the wrong book.

5. The field trip to the museum was on Friday. It included a film, a hands-on demonstration by the university's recent Nobel Prize winner in chemistry, and a tour of the museum. Students did not have to take notes. They were asked to write an essay and a letter to the Environmental Protection Agency. They learned about chemicals and the effects on our environment.

GRAMMAR TERMS
• • • • •

THE PARTS OF SPEECH

Noun: word that names a person, place, thing, or idea. Nouns have many uses: subject, object, appositive, predicate nominative, adverbial noun. Examples: boy, school, kite, love

Pronoun: word that takes the place of a noun or noun phrase. There are many different kinds of pronouns:

<u>Personal</u>: refer to persons speaking, persons being spoken to, and persons spoken about. Examples: I, you, he, we, they, me, your, her, our, their, them

<u>Reflexive</u>: personal pronouns that end in –self or –selves. Example: herself

<u>Relative</u>: pronouns (who, whom, whose, which, that) used to introduce adjective clauses. Example: The book *that* I borrowed...

<u>Interrogative</u>: pronouns (Who? Whose? Whom? Which? That?) used in questions

<u>Demonstrative</u>: pronouns (this, that, these, those) used to point out a specific person or thing

<u>Indefinite</u>: pronouns that do not refer to a definite person, place, or thing

all	anything	everyone	most
another	both	everything	much
any	each	few	neither
anybody	either	many	nobody
anyone	everybody	more	none
no one	other	some	someone
one	several	somebody	

Adjective: word that modifies a noun or pronoun. Example: *delicious* ice cream

Adverb: word that modifies a verb, an adjective, or another adverb. Example: ran *quickly*

Verb: word that expresses action or state of being, or helps to make a statement

Action verbs can be *transitive* (take an object) or *intransitive* (do not have an object).
Example: *wrote* a poem (transitive), *sailed* into the harbor (intransitive)
Linking verbs show a connection between two words in a sentence. The most common linking verbs are **be** verbs: **is, am, are, was, were**, and the forms **be, being, been**, which take a helping, or auxiliary verb. <u>Be</u> is often part of the infinitive form <u>to be</u>. The complements that follow a linking verb are predicate nominative and predicate adjective. Other common linking verbs that often precede a predicate adjective are

grow, remain, appear, become, seem

look, smell, taste, sound, feel

stay, turn

Comman helping verbs are *be* verbs and the verbs *do, does, did, have, has, had, may, might, must, can, could, shall, should, will, would.*

Verbals:

<u>Participle</u>: present or past participial form of a verb that is used as an adjective

Examples: a *broken* watch, a *frozen* pizza, a *swimming* pool

Pushing his way through the crowd, Jim managed to get to the front of the line.

<u>Gerund</u>: present participial form of a verb (ending in –ing) that is used as a noun

Examples: *Reading* is fun (subject).

I like *reading* (direct object).

My hobby is *reading* (predicate nominative).

I give *reading* much of the credit for my ability to write (indirect object).

I have a great interest in *reading* (object of preposition).

My assignment for tonight, *reading* a poem, will be enjoyable (appositive).

<u>Infinitive</u>: verb form preceded by the word *to* that can be used as a noun, adjective, or adverb. Examples: *To keep* your assignments in a planner is a good idea (noun).

An interesting book *to read* is *Avenger* (adjective).

The senator was not available *to talk* to us (adverb).

Preposition: word that relates nouns and pronouns to other words in the sentence, usually nouns, pronouns, verbs, adjectives, and adverbs. The preposition comes first in the phrase followed by its object. The preposition helps to show relationships in sentences, serving as a kind of glue that holds that part of the sentence together. Here is a list of common prepositions:

aboard	beneath	in	throughout
about	beside	inside	till
above	besides	into	to
across	between	like	toward
after	beyond	near	under
against	but	of	underneath
along	by	off	until
among	concerning	on	up
around	down	out	upon
at	during	over	with
before	except	past	within
behind	for	since	without
below	from	through	

Think of a stationary object like a tree and a moveable object in relation to that tree. What kind of relationship can that moveable object have to the tree? If it's a squirrel, it can run to the tree, up the tree, around the tree, near the tree, behind the tree, beside the tree, by the tree, down the tree, into the tree, past the tree, toward the tree. You get the picture. Those prepositions help to show where the squirrel is in proximity to the tree. Adding prepositional phrases to your sentences can increase not only the details but also the complexity of your writing.

Conjunction: word that joins other words or groups of words. Three kinds of conjunctions help the writer do this:

<u>Coordinating</u>: conjunctions that connect two or more items of the same kind or of equal weight. And, but, or, nor, for, yet, so

<u>Correlative</u>: conjunctions that also connect two or more like items but are found in pairs: both…and, not only…but also, either…or, neither…nor, whether…or

<u>Subordinating</u>: conjunctions that introduce adverb clauses:

after	before	unless
although	if	until
as	in order that	when
as if	since	whenever
as long as	so that	where
as soon as	than	wherever
because	though	while

Interjection: word that expresses emotion, often followed by an exclamation mark but sometimes by a comma if the interjection is mild. Examples: Help! Well, …

PARTS OF A SENTENCE
● ● ● ● ●

Simple subject: the main word or group of words in the complete subject that shows who or what is doing the acting or is being acted upon or that shows who or what exists
   Example: The *quarterback* ran down the field for a touchdown.
Simple predicate: the main word or group of words in the complete predicate which shows the action or state of being in the sentence
   Example: The quarterback *ran* down the field for a touchdown.
Complete subject: the simple subject and all its modifiers and appositives
   Example: *The quarterback* ran down the field for a touchdown.
Complete predicate: the simple predicate and all its modifiers and complements
   Example: The quarterback *ran down the field for a touchdown.*
Complements:
   <u>Predicate Nominative</u>: noun or pronoun in the predicate that follows a linking verb and renames the subject. Example: Shane is our student council *representative.*
   <u>Predicate Adjective</u>: adjective in the predicate that follows a linking verb and modifies the subject. Example: The athlete seemed *tired* after running four miles.
   <u>Objects</u>
      Direct Object: a noun or pronoun that follows a transitive verb and receives the action of that verb, answering *what* or *whom* after the verb. Example: James bought a *book* about camping in national parks.
      Indirect Object: a noun or pronoun that precedes a direct object and answers the question "to whom or what" or "for whom or what" the action is done. Example: The volunteer read the *children* a story.
      Retained Object: noun or pronoun object that is kept in its position following a passive voice verb. Example: If the active voice sentence, "The Student Council gave Marie an award" is made passive, "Marie was given an award by the Student Council," *award* retains its object position.
      Objective complement: noun, noun-equivalent, or adjective that completes the meaning of the object. Example: I found him *funny*. (adjective) They named the baby *Christopher* (noun).

Appositive: noun or pronoun that follows another noun and adds information to it to identify or explain it. Example: My sister *Sarah* is traveling to England (not set off by commas). Sarah, my *sister* from Ohio, is traveling to England (set off by commas).

KINDS OF SENTENCES

• • • • •

Simple: an independent clause. Example: *They played computer games after school.*

Compound: two or more independent clauses connected by a coordinating conjunction. Example: *They played computer games after school, and then they did their homework.*

Complex: a combination of one independent clause and one or more subordinate clauses. Example: *After they played computer games, they did their homework.*

Compound-complex: a combination of two or more independent clauses and one or more subordinate clauses. Example: *After they played computer games, they did their homework, but they went to bed too late.*

PHRASES

• • • • •

Prepositional Phrase: group of words beginning with a preposition and ending with a noun or pronoun called the *object of the preposition*. Prepositional phrases serve as adjectives and adverbs. Examples: I went *to the store* (adverb phrase modifying *went*). I picked up the book *on the table* (adjective phrase modifying *book*).

Appositive Phrase: appositive and its modifiers. Example: Dr. Wingate, *the latest Nobel Prize winner at our university*, is in the engineering department.

Participial Phrase: participial and its modifiers and complements, which serve as an adjective. Example: *Yawning widely*, the cat stretched herself out for a nap.

Gerund Phrase: gerund and its modifiers and complements, which serve as a noun. Example: Jim enjoys *running six miles around the track.*

Infinitive Phrase: infinitive with its modifiers and complements. Example: *To get enough sleep each night* is important to your mental and physical well-being.

Absolute Phrase: a construction of words that helps to develop ideas in the main clause which appears to be a complete sentence but is missing the linking verb or the helping (auxiliary) verb. An absolute phrase can appear anywhere in the sentence where it can add information. Example #1: He cast his line into the stream, *his mind far away in another place and time.* Example #2: He sat down to watch the play, *the seat next to him taken by a beautiful girl who appeared to be alone.* Key: Write a sentence with *was* or *were*, strike this helping or linking verb, and put the phrase into your sentence wherever it can best add information.

CLAUSES

• • • • •

Independent Clause: group of words having a subject and predicate and expressing a complete thought, also called a simple sentence. Example: *I finished my homework.*

Dependent Clauses

    Adjective Clause: subordinate clause that modifies a noun or pronoun in an independent clause. Example: The sport *that I enjoy most* is soccer. (The relative pronoun *that* connects the subordinate clause to the independent clause.)

    Adverb Clause: subordinate clause that modifies a verb, an adjective, or an adverb. Example: *Because it rained,* we canceled the picnic. (The adverb clause begins with a subordinating conjunction, which in this sentence is *because*.)

    Noun Clause: subordinate clause used as a noun (subject, predicate nominative, appositive, direct object, indirect object, object of a preposition). Example: I don't know *what I did with my planner* (noun clause used as a direct object).

USAGE

• • • • •

Subject-Verb Agreement: Subjects that are singular in number take verbs that are singular. Examples: *James likes* peaches. (*James* is singular; *likes* is singular.) The *students are* happy about the upcoming holidays. (*Students* is plural; *are* is plural.)

Pronoun Agreement: A pronoun agrees with its antecedent (the word to which a pronoun refers) in number and gender. Examples: *Jeff* gave *his* speech in class today. (*Jeff* is singular in number and masculine in gender; *his* is singular in number and masculine in gender.) The *people* on the new road paid *their* tolls. (*People* is plural; *their* is plural.)

PRACTICE SENTENCES

• • • • •

Model 1: Subject-Verb-Prepositional Phrase

1. My little sister came to the movie with me on Friday.
2. In class on Tuesday we will be writing about plot structures.
3. A monkey in a plaid suit appeared out of nowhere.
4. According to my calculations, we should leave by six a.m.
5. Five members of the class had traveled to Europe.
6. Several passengers on the train boarded with their bags in their hands.

Model 2: Subject-Verb-Prepositional Phrase (with appositive, contraction, adverbial noun)

1. Michael, an excellent student, didn't study last night for the test on colonization.
2. The students, all twenty-six of them, were waiting outside the door of my classroom after the bell.
3. During summers, my older sister works at the Children's Museum, the best hands-on museum in Texas.
4. The Smiths, our newest neighbors, subscribe to a weekly newspaper, the *Sycamore Times.*
5. The love of a sport, the best reason for competition, can grow in a wholesome atmosphere.
6. Hasn't that little boy, the one in the red shirt, been sitting under that tree all afternoon?
7. The bottle of vitamins on the shelf in the bathroom belongs to Aunt Betsy, my mother's sister from Pennsylvania.

Model 3: Subject-Predicate-Direct Object

1. Before the storm, the boy brought his sheep down the mountain.
2. James made a touchdown in the final minute of the game.
3. The juniors at Plainview High School are planning a field trip to the Railroad Museum, a view of cultured society in turn-of-the-century Galveston.
4. The puppy, a thirsty little mutt, drank water from the puddle in the street.
5. The four boys, all best friends, rode their bikes down the long dirt road.
6. Last night I saw a great movie, a swashbuckling adventure with pirates and treasure.
7. How many cases of chicken soup did the store manager order?
8. The old radio in my grandfather's study played all of my favorite songs, four by the Beatles.
9. My next-door neighbor, Mr. Colvin, donated money to our class project.

Model 4: Subject-Predicate-Direct Object (with a participle)

1. Swirling the beaker of liquid, Angie, the lab assistant, observed the solution slowly changing color.
2. Neil watched the waves gently rocking the boat in the evening tide.
3. Charging like an angry bull, the customer demanded his money back.
4. Living in Nebraska, we learned respect for blizzards.
5. Worried about an allergic reaction, the teacher took the swelling boy, stung by a bee, to the clinic.
6. Kept in a sunny corner of the patio, the catnip plants entertained the cats for weeks.
7. Patrick, unaware of the broken bottle on the sidewalk, cut his foot on the shard of glass rising up from the pavement.

8. Disappointed with the grade on her test, Betsy quietly slipped the paper into the back of her binder.

Model 5: Subject-Predicate-Direct Object (with compound subject and appositive)

1. Purple and gold, my two favorite colors, remind me of the LSU Tigers, the best college team in its league.
2. Walking proudly onto the stage, James and Mark, two of the investigators in the experiment, accepted first prize in the contest.
3. Devouring the hot beef stew with enthusiasm, the Boy Scouts and their leader, Mr. Atkins, ate in silence after a long day on the trail.
4. Only a broken watch and chain, its owner's most valuable possessions, filled the knot hole of the oak tree standing on the edge of the Radley lot.
5. Singing "Old McDonald" at the top of their lungs, Jake and Kelly, best friends, completed their initiation into the 4H Club.
6. Socrates and Plato, two Greek philosophers of influence on Western thought, promoted the tenet of truth as the universal good.

Model 6: Subject-Compound Predicate-Direct Object (with participles and appositive)

1. Educated Americans in the nineteenth century, a time of growing wealth, found more time for the arts and enjoyed the music of many composers, especially Beethoven.
2. Visiting his transplanted French family in New Orleans in the mid 1800s, Impressionist painter Edgar Degas lived in this cultural society and painted the daily life of his relatives.
3. Deeply marked by the tragedy of the Spanish Civil War, poet Pablo Neruda had a long history of social consciousness and wrote odes of love—love of nation in particular.
4. Henry David Thoreau, known for his experiment at Walden Pond, wrote *Walden*, the book recording those experiences, and later traveled on the Merrimack River in a canoe with his brother John.
5. George Gershwin and Irving Berlin, America's greatest composers, charmed audiences with their fascinating new tunes from Tin Pan Alley, the uptown Broadway district of music publishing firms, and established names for themselves in the hearts of people everywhere.
6. Mary and John, two French students, read the original *Cyrano de Bergerac* and, hoping for extra credit, performed scenes from the play for their class in French.
7. Arriving at the end of a long line for the roller coaster, the children and their parents walked to a nearby restaurant and ordered their meal, a tasteless hamburger with fries still frozen.

Model 7: Subject-Predicate-Indirect Object-Direct Object

1. Marvin the Monkey, swinging from the chandelier, broke Mother's antique vase and caused her great consternation.
2. Please hand me that blue book, the one sitting on the left side of my desk.
3. The whale, taking revenge on the Essex, rammed its head against the bow and gave the sailors the dreaded fright of their lives.
4. Carving Elizabeth's name on the old oak tree in the park, the boy pledged her his eternal love and then hurried home for his date with Sue.
5. The librarian collected her props around her and told the children gathered together for story time the tale of St. George and the dragon.
6. My three best friends from my old school in Atlanta threw me the greatest birthday party in the world.

Model 8: Subject-Predicate-Indirect Object-Direct Object (imperative sentence with you as the subject)

See sentence 2 in Model 7.

Model 9: Subject-Linking Verb-Predicate Nominative (with appositive)

1. Franklin D. Roosevelt, our thirty-second president, was a well-respected leader during WW II.
2. Lisa, an accomplished mime, has also been a stage actress for ten years.
3. Lucky Dime, the most stunning horse in that race, and Beautiful Dreamer, a slow beginner without a very good record, had once been the property of my grandmother's first cousin once removed.
4. William W. Wodenhouse, a patron of the Alley Theatre for twenty years, has been a board member of the MFA and a driving force in the construction of our new performing arts center.
5. The evening of January 6, better known as Twelfth Night, is also the Feast of the Epiphany, the celebration of the Three Kings.

Model 10: Subject-Linking Verb-Predicate Nominative (with participle)
(See Model 9, numbers 1-5)

Model 11: Subject Linking Verb-Predicate Adjective (with participle)

1. The Renaissance band performing on the stage tonight looks strange but sounds interesting.
2. The hot, steaming oatmeal topped with butter and brown sugar smelled good and tasted delicious on this frosty morning.
3. The velvety petals of Sandburg's rose, folded over and under in the mystery of nature,

soon turned brown, withering on the windowsill.

4. Jill was indifferent about the family's trip to Austin but appeared amenable about the decision, not wanting any conflict with her parents.
5. The crowd, responding to the dictator's speech, became hostile and stormed the building, growing violent with every minute.
6. The rough, uneven stones along the rocky shore felt sharp under my bare feet, cutting into the tough flesh of my heels.

Model 12: Subject-Linking Verb-Predicate Adjective (with compound PA and participles)

1. The lotion, smelling of oranges and lemons, felt cool and soothing on my parched skin.
2. The noise coming from the A/C system grew louder and louder and remained a low, dull static sound for the rest of the day.

Model 13: Subject-Predicate-Direct Object (gerund DO)

1. You should try starting your homework earlier.
2. Our cat hates being kept in her cage on road trips to the farm.
3. James began writing his essay on the train from New York.
4. Have you ever tried balancing schoolwork, a job, and athletics at the same time?
5. The student council vetoed spending the money on a monument for the courtyard.

Model 14: Gerund Subject

1. Appearing exhausted and worn did not increase her marketability.
2. Remaining broken during a week of captivity resulted in the loss of the wolf's leg.
3. Smelling old and rotten is the nature of fruit left in the refrigerator for several weeks.
4. Staying shut up in a dark room for even one day could cause insanity.
5. Flooding in the small Mississippi town was the result of a swollen river exceeding its banks.

Model 15: Subject-Linking Verb-Predicate Adjective (with gerund OP)

1. Frozen pizza and Kool-aid are adequate for having a party at the last minute.
2. The dance club at school quickly became interested in sponsoring the winter holiday dance.
3. Dropping out of obedience school was definitely not conducive to Rover's behaving himself in front of guests.
4. Our vacation seemed successful because of carefully planning a three-day field trip to a dude ranch in Texas.
5. The students on the trip grew weary after walking twenty miles from the London Eye to the Hard Rock Café.

Model 16: Gerund Appositives

1. My favorite sport, swimming, became my ticket to a college scholarship.
2. My only homework assignment, studying for the history test, took four hours.
3. My punishment for wrecking the car, raking three weeks of leaves in our half-acre yard, seemed unfair.
4. In times of trouble, my way of coping, watching television, offered anesthetic relief.
5. Behind the set of the drama class's first production, the two crew members stirred up trouble and made noises: whistling, stomping, and clapping.

Model 17: Compound Sentence

1. Inspired and awed by the number of supporters in the stands, the Katy Tigers pounded the Longview Lobos, and they captured the state championship title with a score of twenty-four to three.
2. Gracefully executing a turn, the skater fell on the ice and in a flash she saw her chance for the gold slipping away from her.
3. Jim saved his money after exhausting work, and he spent every hard-earned penny on games.
4. At first Elizabeth and Jeremy fought over the remote control, but they finally made popcorn and rented a movie.
5. The frozen pizza and lumpy bags of peas fell out of the freezer and hit the kitchen floor with a thud, but fortunately no one had heard me sneaking a midnight ice cream sundae.

Model 18: Compound Sentence (with compound subjects)

1. Excited about their first trip to Disney World, Alexis and her best friend Tia checked in with their drill team leader, and, after loading their bags, the girls claimed seats in the back of the bus.
2. Freezing in the icy winter drizzle, Raymond and Andrew pulled their hoods over their heads, and the two started running toward the school bus slowly creeping toward them.
3. Imitating the animals at the zoo, Marvin and Michael began munching on tree leaves, and later on the bus the teacher heard them squealing like hyenas.
4. Swimming to the side of the pool, the instructor and his students pulled themselves out of the water, but they soon jumped back in for the next lesson.
5. Racing in terror down the corridor, Mickey and Minnie looked for an escape from the cat, but the ferocious feline chased them relentlessly.

Model 19: Subject-Linking Verb-Predicate Nominative (with infinitive subject)

1. To clone a human being is a controversial issue.
2. To inform everyone about the next meeting is the purpose of calling people on the

list.
3. To insist on the teacher giving a due date for the project was a mistake.
4. To be a success means hard work, perseverance, and a strong desire for improvement.
5. To study or not to study is really the question.

Model 20: Subject-Predicate-Direct Object (infinitive DO)

1. Marcus and Alicia tried to call their parents several times after the dance.
2. Tired of losing their games, the basketball team decided to try a new strategy.
3. Tomorrow I plan to write a letter to the mayor about the poor quality of our playgrounds.
4. After eyeing the cat in the grass, the mockingbird began to swoop down upon her repeatedly, pecking at the base of the cat's tail.
5. Putting aside my pride and getting on my knees, I begged to go to the concert.

Model 21: Compound Sentence: S-V-DO (with infinitives)

1. I want to buy a new CD but I don't have enough money.
2. I am hoping to see Joan's written report on our fund-raising efforts before leaving for our vacation, but that doesn't give her much time.
3. Before taking the exam, several of us plan to form study groups; we have much to cover before Friday.
4. Do you want to come with me to the movie, or are you too tired?
5. Haven't you ever wanted to sleep just one more hour, but your little brother insisted on playing with you?

(The following sentences contain infinitives that take subjects.)
6. Getting into a good high school encourages me to study hard, but that isn't the only reason to do my best.
7. My brother forced me to go to the movie with him last night by threatening to tell Mom about the dent in the car and the broken window.
8. The police, surrounding the scene of the crime, warned intruders not to go beyond the yellow tape.
9. The booklet in the box instructed the owner of the new desk to connect the numerous parts together, but several important pieces of hardware were missing.
10. Mom helped me make the cake for Jen's birthday, but I went to my friend's house, forgetting to watch the cake after putting it in the oven.
11. In geometry Ms. Baun makes us learn theorems and postulates, and the list gets longer and longer every single day.

Model 22: Subject-Linking Verb-Predicate Nominative (with adjective infinitive phrase)

1. Early mornings are the best time to study for me.
2. It is a good idea to run several miles each day, but you need to be in good shape.
3. A good way to lose weight is to eat moderately.
4. The best movie to see this summer is *The Legend of Muddy River.*
5. The item at the top of the congressman's agenda was the bill to write for better medical care for children.

Model 23: Compound Subject-Predicate-Adverb Infinitive Phrase

1. After two sets of tennis, Liz and Beth were too tired to play any more, but they managed to bicycle to the beach and back.
2. Moving closer to the edge of the pier to get a better look, the investigator and his partner found the necessary clues to help them solve the case.
3. The lightning and lashing rain followed me home, pelting my face and soaking my clothes to force me to run faster.
4. Marissa and her friends got up early to watch their best friend Jill swim in the championship meet.
5. Alex, Margaret, and Joe met in the library to review for the test.

Model 24: Adjective Clause (that)

1. This is the book on public policy that I was telling you about for your debate.
2. Do you know the answer that I am going to give you?
3. Max was responsible for the idea that we used for our science project.
4. Is this the address that I need for my letter to the governor ?
5. The problem that we must address today is one of grave concern for all Americans.

Model 25: Adjective Clause (*which* with a preposition)

1. Marguerite asked the question for which the professor had no answer.
2. Jung's theory regarding the collective unconscious, on which the archetypal approach to literature is based, has become the subject of numerous books.
3. The question for which there is no one particular answer is the one that asks the meaning of life.
4. The article in the newspaper, to which I must dutifully reply, was poorly written with numerous grammatical errors and incorrect statements.
5. The argument on which I originally based my case has now been thoroughly destroyed.

Model 26: Adjective Clause (whose)

1. We met the vocalist whose CD was released this week.
2. The farmer whose crops failed in the midst of the drought received relief from the government.
3. The boy, whose only mistake was in loving the girl, became a recluse.
4. Maggie gave Sarah a small gift for her cousin, whose book recently won a Pulitzer.
5. The cat, whose tail had been caught in a door blown shut by the wind, was forever psychologically impaired by the event.

Model 27: Adjective Clause (who and which)

1. Griffins, which are mythological beasts, are common designs on coats of arms.
2. Laurie, who lives for swimming, has decided to spend all of her spare time on the swim team this year.
3. Students who challenged the decision to incarcerate innocent men gained recognition for their investigative journalism.
4. Students who questioned the data on which the theory was based won fame and recognition for their work.
5. I am the kind of person who cannot refuse chocolate, but I have no use for other sweets.

(The following sentences contain adjective clauses introduced by <u>when</u> and <u>where</u>.)

6. They showed us the stadium where the game would be played.
7. Summer is the season when I feel happiest.
8. Have you chosen a time when we can get together and study?
9. The theatre where we saw the play is being renovated and will not be ready for three months.
10. I remember so clearly the birthday when I received my first pair of skates.

Model 28: Adverb Clause

1. After I proofread my paper, I made the necessary corrections.
2. You may watch TV as long as you do your homework first.
3. Please sign this form as soon as you can.
4. Because it rained, the game was canceled.
5. I see a play whenever I am in London.
6. Because of the tumultuous nature of the crowd, manifesting itself in violent rioting, the police used tear gas whenever it was necessary.
7. I climbed fifty steps to the top of the plaza so that I could see Bernini's fountain, the beautiful sculpture adorning the Spanish Steps in Rome.
8. Although Frank enjoys riding his bike around his neighborhood, he avoids the

freeways in an effort to live longer.

9. Before Emina practices her violin, she spends time each day thinking of ways to help her beloved country of Bosnia.

10. Although Nathan usually has a strong opinion about everything, expressed in an assertive but humorous manner, his serious repertoire of good qualities includes his willingness to help others.

11. Being a vegetarian is more difficult than Jon imagined, but he continues to pursue the battle against the fur and meat industry in his own small way.

Model 29: Noun Clause (subject)

1. What Amelie likes to do best is dance.
2. Who gave me the note is of no concern to you.
3. Whoever climbs tall, treacherous mountains successfully usually becomes famous.
4. Whatever we can do to make this world a better place is our lifelong duty to humanity.
5. What we must do to convince the jury of your innocence is simply present the facts, which will speak for themselves.

Model 30: Noun Clause (introduced by *that*)

1. I knew that it was too late to repair the relationship, and I felt very sad.
2. That he would win the golf tournament over Tiger Woods came as a surprise.
3. He told the teacher that the dog ate his homework, and he was finally telling the truth.
4. Do you understand that I can't go with you to confess your crime to your parents?
5. That I made the highest grade on the algebra test made me the happiest person at school.

Model 31: Noun Clause (direct object)

1. After a moment he realized who the girl in the pink sweater was.
2. I said that I wanted to go to the movie, but I was really too exhausted from spending the day at the beach.
3. The judges did not question how we arrived at our answer, and they gave us the point.
4. Did you know who wrote the note, or were you just hoping?
5. Have you discovered whom the president selected to be the next ambassador to Ireland?

Model 32: Noun Clause (indirect object)

1. The manager of the store gave whoever came in without shoes and a shirt the boot,

and that was just a warning.
2. Grandfather told whoever would listen the fascinating story of his mail-order bride, my grandmother!

Model 33: Noun Clause (predicate nominative)

1. The winner of the drawing contest will be whoever shows the most creativity with pen and ink.
2. Harvey's excuse for not going to school was that he was ill from eating too many figs.
3. The question of most concern was where he was going at that time of night.

Model 34: Compound-Complex Sentences

1. School began late this year because we experienced a hurricane, but we will make up the days in June.
2. A strong wind blew through the trees, and, although it did no real damage, it rocked our tree house.
3. Our top athlete ran for three touchdowns while the roar of the crowd was deafening, yet he still had to turn in his research paper the next day.
4. As long as I can ride my bike on the weekends, I don't mind doing chores, but sometimes Dad wants me to help him in the shop all day on Saturday.
5. I am freezing in this movie theatre because I didn't bring a sweater, and I may need to leave.

Model 35: Absolute Phrases

1. Alfonso finally packed up his books, his friends patiently waiting.
2. Marissa connected the wires in her science project, her hands trembling with excitement.
3. The next contestant stepped up to the platform, the outcome resting on this final speech.
4. It was almost midnight when a subtle sadness settled over the party, the merriment coming to an end.
5. She covered her face at the sight of the tragedy, the stark reality of the fragility of life clear and present at that moment.

A Guide for Punctuation and Grammar Usage
● ● ● ● ●
Punctuation

Comma Rules

1. Use a comma to separate items in a series when not joined by a conjunction.

Example: Jack bought paper, a notebook, and three pens at the store.
2. Use a comma to separate short independent clauses in a series.
   Example: Mom made the salad, Dad grilled the fish, and I set the table.
3. Use a comma to separate two or more adjectives preceding a noun when *and* can be logically inserted between the adjectives.
   Example: The beautiful, functional, and practical piece of furniture was also very expensive.
4. Use a comma to separate two independent clauses connected with *and*.
   Example: The squirrel inched his way to the seed tray, and the birds moved out of his way.
5. Use a comma to set off nonessential clauses from the rest of the sentence.
   Example: The student, *who left his book in his locker and had to retrieve it,* was late to class.
6. Use a comma to set off introductory phrases and clauses.
   Example: Because it rained, we had to cancel the game.
7. Use a comma to set off introductory words such as *yes, no, well, ah, why,* etc.
   Example: Yes, I would like some ice cream.
8. Use a comma to set off appositives and appositive phrases. Sometimes a one-word appositive follows the noun it adds information to without a pause and requires no comma. Example: My sister Beth is coming to visit me. The appositive Beth is said quickly and needs no pause and no comma. ·
9. Use a comma to set off words of direct address.
   Example: Jane, please take the attendance slip to the office.
10. Use a comma to set off parenthetical expressions such as *in fact, in my opinion, moreover, nevertheless, however, consequently,* etc. *Not* is parenthetical when used in a contrasting phrase. Example: Hand me the red cup, not the blue one.
11. Use commas to separate items in dates and addresses.
    Example: I live at 43057 Walker Way, Houston, Texas, 77057.
12. Use a comma to separate items in letters:
    Salutation in a friendly letter.
    > Dear Jane,

    Closing of any letter:
    > Sincerely,
    > Jane
13. Use a comma after a title following a name, such as Jr., M.D., Sr.
    Example: Sarah Dooley, M.D., is our speaker today.

Semicolon Rules
1. Use a semicolon between independent clauses linked together with transitional expressions such as *for example, nevertheless, however, therefore,* etc.
   Example: I studied for the test; therefore, I feel confident I will pass.
2. Use a semicolon to separate independent clauses or other items in a series if the clauses and other items contain commas.

Example: Millie, Ryan, and Michelle worked on the graphics for the project; and Philip and Robert wrote the text.

Colon Rules

1. Use a colon after expressions such as *as follows* and *the following*.
   Example: The writing topics are *as follows:*
2. Use a colon after the salutation of a business letter. (British English uses a comma instead of a colon.)
   American example: Dear Ms. O'Connor:
   British example: Dear Ms. O'Connor,

Italics and Underlining Rules

1. Use italics or underlining for the following titles: books, plays, films, periodicals, works of art, long musical compositions, television programs, long narrative poems, ships, and planes. Example: Last night I finished reading *The Icon*.
2. Use italics or underlining for words, letters and figures referred to as such, and for foreign words. Example: The delicious cake was the chef's *piece de resistance*.

Quotation Marks Rules

1. Use quotation marks for the following short works: short stories, articles, short poems, essays, songs, episodes of television programs, chapters of a book.
   Example: One of my favorite poems is Frost's "The Road Not Taken."
2. Use quotation marks for quoted material from a published work.
   Example: In her speech, Smith states, "Women are 70% of the world's poor."
3. Use quotation marks for dialogue in a story, book, or nonfiction article or book.
   Example: "Don't be foolish," Atticus said.
4. When using quotation marks for quoted sentences and dialogue, place the period and comma inside the quotation marks.
5. Do not place any other punctuation inside the quotation marks unless it is part of the quotation. Example: "Do you have something in mind?" he asked.
6. Use single quotation marks to indicate a quotation within a quotation.
   Example: At the end of the story, the author writes, "The old man looked up and said one word, 'No'."

Apostrophe Rules

1. To form the possessive case of a singular noun, add an apostrophe and an *s*.
   Example: boy's book
2. To form the possessive case of a plural noun ending in *s*, add only an apostrophe.
   Example: students' books
3. When a singular noun ends in the *s* or *z* sound, you may form the possessive by adding an apostrophe and *s*. One syllable words add an apostrophe and *s*. If the word sounds awkward, you may add just the apostrophe.
   Example: the frieze's decorative appearance
   Gus's paper

Mr. Michaels' notes (*Mr. Michaels's* is awkward.)

4. Do not use an apostrophe with possessive personal pronouns.
   Example: hers, its, theirs
5. In compound words or words showing joint ownership, use an apostrophe with only the last word. Example: Hart & Caper's best selling books; Sharifa and Kylie's science project
6. Use an apostrophe for each name when two or more persons own something individually. Example: Cai's and Jacob's report cards
7. Use an apostrophe to show time or amount. Example: today's assignment; a dollar's worth of candy
8. Use an apostrophe to form plurals of letters, numbers, signs, and words. Example: A's, 6's, $'s, the's
9. Use an apostrophe in contractions where letters have been omitted. Example: The package *hasn't* arrived.

Hyphen Rules

1. Use a hyphen to divide a word at the end of a line.
2. Use a hyphen with compound numbers from twenty-one to ninety-nine.
3. Use a hyphen with fractions used as adjectives but not with nouns. Example: He drank one half of the milk. He drank a one-half cup of milk.
4. Use a hyphen with the prefixes *ex-*, *self-*, *all*, etc. Example: *self-appointed*
5. Use a hyphen with the suffix *elect*. Example: *president-elect*
6. Use a hyphen with all prefixes before a noun or adjective. Examples: *ex-president, self-made, mid-August, pre-World War II.*

Dash Rules

1. Use a dash to indicate a sudden break in thought or speech. Example: I—I can't go through with it.
2. Use a dash to indicate an unfinished sentence. Example: Don't put that glass on the—

Parentheses Rules

1. It is acceptable to use parentheses to enclose words that are added but nonessential information. Avoid doing so. You have added the information for a reason. If it isn't necessary, don't include it.
2. Use parentheses for citing sources in an essay or report. Follow these guidelines:
   - Enclose only the page number or source name inside the parentheses. Do not write the word *page* or any abbreviation of *page*. Example: (54)
   - Place the page number or source name in parentheses after the quoted material—outside the quotation marks. Example: "Well, it'd be sort of like shootin' a mockingbird, wouldn't it?" (Lee 276).
   - Put a period after the closed parentheses if the citation comes at the end of a sentence. Put no additional punctuation if the citation falls within

the sentence. Example: Clinton explains the importance of suffrage, that "bloodless war," (10) in her speech to the UN conference.

Usage

Subject-Verb Agreement

1. Verbs must agree with their subjects in number. Singular subjects take singular verbs.
   Example: He writes well. (singular subject *He* with singular verb *writes*)
   They write well. (plural subject *They* with plural verb *write*)
   Note: When prepositional phrases follow the subject, do not look at the number (singular or plural) of any word except the subject when determining the number of the verb. Example: One of the boys *is* the writer of the story. (Do not think *boys are.* Think *One…is.*)
2. The following indefinite pronouns are singular: *each, either, neither, one, everyone, everybody, no one, nobody, anyone, anybody, someone, somebody.*
3. Compound subjects take a plural verb. Example: James and Shane *are* going to movie.
4. Singular subjects joined by *or* or *nor* take a singular verb. Example: Either John or Patrick is the winner of the competition.
5. When a singular subject and a plural subject are joined by *or* , the verb agrees with the number of the subject nearer the verb. Example: Either John or his two sons are going to take me to the airport.
6. *Here* and *there* at the beginning of sentences are used as adverbs, not subjects. The subject usually follows the verb and must agree with the verb in number. Invert the subject and verb to test for correctness. Example: Here is your newspaper
   Your newspaper is here.
7. Words that state an amount are usually considered singular in number.
   Example: Five dollars *is* a reasonable sum.
8. Words that state number are usually considered plural in number.
   Example: Five cows *are* being auctioned today.
9. Titles of works of art, music, and literature are considered singular in number.
   Example: *Blue Dancers* is my favorite painting by Degas.

Pronoun Agreement

1. A pronoun must agree with its antecedent in number and gender (male, female, neuter). An antecedent (*ante*: before plus *ced*: to come) is the word to which a pronoun refers.
   Example: The students brought *their* books to class.
   The student raised *his* hand.
   Every one of the students has *her* book.
   All of the students did *their* homework.
2. Use a singular pronoun to refer to the singular indefinite pronouns.

Example: *Each* of the boys played *his* guitar.

No one on the dance team forgot *her* uniform.

One of the dogs escaped from *its* compound.

3. Two or more antecedents joined by *and* should be referred to by a plural pronoun.
Example: *Sara* and *Philip* joined the group because *they* had time to work on the project.

4. Over time, habits in language actually change accepted language use. It is more convenient today for people to avoid the *his* and *her* conflict when referring to the singular antecedent. Informal speech already accepts the following:

Everyone brought *their* homework to class today.

In writing, however, it is best to follow the stricter rules of pronoun agreement.

Everyone brought *his* or *her* homework to class today.

Correct Use of Verbs

Learn the difference between the following pairs of verbs by memorizing the spelling, principal parts, and meaning of each one:

1. lie/lay

To lie:

Principal parts: lie, lay, lain, lying

Meaning: to rest or recline

Example: I will lie down under this tree. I lay down under this tree yesterday. I have lain under this tree many times before. I am lying under this tree right now.

To lay:

Principal parts: lay, laid, laid, laying

Meaning: to put or place

Example: I will lay the book on the table. I laid the book on the table yesterday. I have laid the book on the table before. I am now laying the book on the table.

2. sit/set

To sit:

Principal parts: sit, sat, sat, sitting

Meaning: to rest oneself in an upright position

Example: I sit on this bench and wait for my ride. I sat on this bench yesterday. I have sat here many times before. I am sitting on this bench right now.

To set:

Principal parts: set, set, set, setting

Meaning: to put or place

Example: I set out the science equipment for Mrs. Arnold every day. I set the equipment out yesterday. I have set the equipment out many times before. I am setting out the equipment today.

3. **rise/raise**

To rise:

Principal parts: rise, rose, risen, rising

Meaning: to become elevated, to go or get up

Example: I rise early in the morning. I rose early yesterday. I have risen early many times before. I am rising early now.

To raise:

Principal parts: raise, raised, raised, raising

Meaning: to cause or make something to go up, to ascend, or to grow

Example: I raise my hand to speak. I raised my hand yesterday. I have raised my hand before. I am raising my hand to speak now.

4. **affect/effect**

To affect:

Principal parts: affect, affected, affected, affecting

Meaning: to have an influence on something

Example: I affect my grades with good study habits. I affected my grades when I didn't study. I have affected my grades in a positive way. I am affecting my grades in a negative way without enough sleep.

To effect:

Principal parts: effect, effected, effected, effecting

Meaning: to bring about a change

Example: People can effect the desired outcome of the election by voting. Their behavior effected the change in the political climate. Not voting has effected a negative outcome in many an election. I am effecting change now by learning more about the candidates.

Effect is used more often as a noun meaning *an outcome or result*.

Note: *Affect* and *effect* are most often confused when affect is used as the noun form *effect*. Remember, *affect* is often used as a verb and *effect* as a noun.

Spelling Troublesome Words

Spelling often becomes difficult with words that are homonyms and homographs. It can be helpful to students of English to understand what they're up against. Learn to recognize them by memorizing the spelling and the meaning of each, but first understand what these tools of language are.

- Homonym: one of two or more words that have the **same sound** but often different

spelling, meaning, and origin. Think of the Greek origin: *homos,* same; *onyma,*
onama, name. Example: stationary, stationery

- Homograph: one of two or more words that have the **same spelling** but differ in
  origin, meaning, and sometimes pronunciation. Think of the Greek origin: *homos,*
  same; *graphein,* to write. Example: *pine,* to languish; *pine,* a tree. (In *Twelfth Night,*
  Viola says, "She *pined* in thought and with a green and yellow melancholy sat like
  patience on a monument, smiling at grief"(2.5.124-5.)

- Homophone: one of two or more words that have the same sound but differ in
  spelling, origin, and meaning. Think of the Greek origin: *homos,* same; *phone,* voice
  or sound. **Another name for *homophone* is *homonym.***

Become aware of the differences in these words and the correct usage of each.

Alright: nonstandard form of *all right*

Accept: receive, take in
Except: besides, other than

Adapt: adjust to
Adopt: take in as belonging to you

Affect: influence
Effect: result (noun), to bring about (verb)

A lot: many
Alot: incorrect spelling of *a lot*

Anyway: transitional word meaning *at any rate* or *nevertheless*
Anyways: colloquial use of *anyway*

Beside: by the side of
Besides: in addition to

Brake: a device for slowing or stopping motion
Break: to crack or split open

Capital: official seat of government; assets
Capitol: building in which a state legislature or the U.S. Congress assembles

Chord: combination of three or more concordant tones sounded simultaneously
Cord: string or rope
Cordially: sincerely

Chose: (past tense of *choose*)
Choose: (present tense) to select

Complement: something that completes, makes up a whole, or brings to perfection
Compliment: an expression of praise or admiration

Counsel: consultation, advice, guidance
Council: assembly of persons called together for discussion or deliberation

Desert: dry, barren, sandy region
Dessert: a portion of a sweet food usually served after a meal

Hear: to perceive by the ear; to listen
Here: at or of this place or time

Immigrate: to enter and settle in a country not one's own
Emigrate: to leave one's country to settle in another

It's: It is.
Its: possessive personal pronoun

Lead: present tense of verb *to lead*: to show the way; a soft, bluish-white metallic element
Led: past tense of verb *to lead*

Loose: not fastened or restrained
Lose: present tense of verb *to lose*: to be unable to find; to be deprived of

Principal: highest in importance
Principle: basic truth, law, or assumption

Quiet: silent
Quite: to a great extent; really; very
Quit: stop

Sight: ability to see; something that is seen
Cite: to quote as an authority or example
Site: place or setting

Stationary: not moving
Stationery: writing paper and envelopes

Than: subordinate conjunction used to introduce a dependent clause; word used in comparisons
Then: at that time in the past

Their: third person plural possessive pronoun of *they*
There: at or in that place
They're: contraction of *they are*

Threw: past tense of *throw*: to propel through the air
Through: in one side and out the opposite; among or between

To: in a direction toward
Too: also
Two: number 2

Vain: not yielding the desired outcome; excessively proud
Vane: a device on a rooftop that indicates the direction of the wind
Vein: a vessel that transports blood; a lengthy strip of ore or color—as in a streak

Ware: articles of the same general kind, e.g., silverware, glassware
Wear: to have or put on, such as clothes
Where: at or in what place, situation, or position
Were: first, second, and third person plural past tense of verb *to be*

Your: that or those belonging to you
You're: contraction of *you are*

Verb Use:
Active and Passive Voice

Active voice: The verb expresses an action performed ***by the subject***.
Example: The boy kicked the football.

Passive voice: The verb expresses action performed ***on the subject***.
Example: The football was kicked by the boy.

(The **object** becomes the **subject** in passive voice. The subject in active voice becomes the object of the preposition in passive voice.)

Passive voice emphasizes the person or thing receiving the action rather than on the one performing it. Look at the examples in both active and passive voice that follow.

Active	Passive
They began their journey.	The journey was begun by them.
They saw the accident.	The accident was seen by them.
He rode the horse.	The horse was ridden by him.
She knew the secret.	The secret was known by her.
He stole the base.	The base was stolen by him.
He blew the horn.	The horn was blown by him.
They chose a hotel.	The hotel was chosen by them.
They broke bread.	Bread was broken by them.
They drove the car.	The car was driven by them.
They froze the cookies.	The cookies were frozen by them.

Forming Passive Voice

To form the passive voice of a verb, follow this formula:

Use a form of **be** plus the past participle of any verb.
(Forms of the verb **be**: is, am, are, was, were, be, being, been)
Example: is + given = is given (The award is given to a deserving student.)

Let us read and let us dance—
two amusements that will never do any harm to the world.
Voltaire (1694-1778)

Chapter 17

Traditions That Enrich Our Language

An Introduction to **YOU**: A Two-Page Spread
● ● ● ● ●

This colorful introduction that my students share with me and each other is a ritual that lasts the whole year. Everyone looks forward to each month. Here's how it works. At the beginning of every school year, I ask students to prepare a colorful, artistic two-page spread about themselves, covering specific required information and anything else they would like to tell the world about themselves. I also ask that at least one recent photo be included. Baby pictures are also welcomed. Then each month, in celebration of everyone's birthday, I place the two-page spreads for that month on a large bulletin board in my room. For one whole month, we read about and celebrate those lives. Here's an outline of the instructions and information you will need in order to make your own.

1. Start with two blank sheets of paper, white copier paper or construction. You may connect them in any way, side to side or end to end. If desired, you may use a colorful backing, but it is not required.

2. Plan an overall design or theme for your spread. What colors will you use? Will your illustrations be photos, magazine pictures, computer graphics, line drawings, cartoons, a combination of these media?

3. Be sure to include a recent photo of yourself, perhaps on a holiday or doing what you like to do best.

4. Include the following information in whatever format you plan:
    a. Full name
    b. Information about your family (names or anything else)

    c. Birth date (month, day, year)

    d. Where you were born (city, state, country)

    e. Hobbies, interests, favorites, and goals

    f. Your favorite quotation (Give credit to the person you are quoting.)

5. Be sure the writing is neat and large enough for everyone to read.

6. When you bring your two-page spread to class, be prepared to show it to your classmates and say a few words about it.

VALENTINES IN LITERATURE
• • • • •

Valentines Day is a day we often observe to celebrate love. It is also a day in English class when we can bring together characters we have loved in literature at various times in our lives. Many years ago I began asking students to think about the books they had read and the Valentine messages they might have one character send to another, characters in either the same book or two different ones. With paper and markers and scissors, they created beautiful cards with literary allusions, and it's a project we have continued with great pleasure.

Through the years Jesse, in *Bridge to Terabithia*, has expressed his love for his sister May Belle as he makes her queen of his imaginary kingdom, and Wilbur, in *Charlotte's Web*, has professed his gratitude to his benefactor Charlotte, the spider who saves his life. Often a student will quote a passage from a book, choosing instead to let the author speak for him. Robert Cormier's message from Mike to his grandmother in "The Moustache" is one of love. In plain and simple words of forgiveness, Mike sees the redemptive power of love at work in the now peaceful, dying eyes of his grandmother Meg..

To the student's amazement, he often finds the author's poignant Valentine messages dispersed throughout the book, and it is just a matter of finding the one that captures the heart. Through this activity, I'm sure my students have continued to learn about theme and characterization and style even without the dissecting and labeling of parts of the literary piece. While most of the students choose to make predictions about characters involved in the same plot, some do not. Nipa's bittersweet Valentine message mourned a love that would never be for two characters that she loved. To Nipa, Shakespeare's Portia and Cervantes' Don Quixote belonged together. Her writing expresses the misfortune: "In the course of a lifetime, nothing is so tragic as the passing of two hearts that never met."

THE QUEST LETTER
• • • • •

Every year in May, when the eighth graders are looking ahead toward new and more challenging days in high school, I ask them to stop and reflect on their year. What were the highlights? The low points? What were the subjects, people, musicians, entertainers, sports heroes, and world events that made an impact on them? I then ask them to write these things down in a letter addressed to themselves, with the knowledge that I will mail these letters to them when they become seniors about to graduate, another turning point just as leaving middle school had been. But that's not all. The last part of this letter to themselves is a prediction that I ask students to make about high school. What were their lives like as seniors? What did they accomplish in high school? Where will they go to college? Did they have any unusual experiences, a car, a job, a romance—just beginning or long term? Of course, these are only predictions, but getting that letter four years later and comparing the predictions with reality can be quite interesting, and sometimes humorous and enlightening. Each year before my former students receive their letters as high school seniors, they are invited to attend a celebration before they all head off for college. It is unusual that high school graduates would look forward to attending a middle school reunion, but here again is a testament to the necessity of rituals in our lives. A topic of discussion at the dinner is always, when are the quest letters going to be mailed?

So now it's your turn. Below you will find some guidelines for putting your own quest letter together, so named for the four-year journey that intervenes between writing and receiving this letter. In addition to writing a letter to yourself, feel free to write to your friends. Put those letters in *their* envelopes, though, not yours. Your friends will receive your letters with their own in four years. Follow these steps:

1. Bring a self-addressed, stamped, large brown envelope. Letters and photographs will need the space.

2. Write your letter to yourself and include a detailed description of your life as an eighth grader. Then write a prediction of what you think your life was like as a senior. Look back at some of your journal entries for ideas to include about yourself. When you're finished, put your letter in your envelope behind the appropriate alphabetical divider in the box marked Quest Letters.

3. Write letters to your friends and put them in their envelopes. Don't show them the letters you wrote. Let them be surprised when they get their letters four years later. Use discretion when writing to other people. Fill your letters with fond memories and kind thoughts. This is not the time to be vindictive or to retaliate for something that happened in sixth grade. Make your letters positive and don't burn any bridges.

4. My policy is that I do not read students' letters. I respect their privacy and trust their judgment. I do not, however, seal the letters until I mail them in May four years later. I also put my own letter to students in their envelopes as well as photographs I may have collected over the year. If in the next four years students want to add a letter to their friends' envelopes, they simply pay me a visit and do so. I have the letters organized in four boxes labeled with graduation years.

A Reading List
● ● ● ● ●

Many years ago a survey was conducted asking universities to indicate their own recommendations to prepare high school seniors who would be entering college. My favorite response to this survey was, read everything; just put books of all kinds on a scale and read as many pounds as possible. What should these freshmen have read? Obviously every educated reader has his or her favorite list of must-reads. But the question will always remain. What should be included in the reading repertoire of any teenager preparing for college?

The books included in this list have been recommended by various individuals, groups, scholars, and friends as being essential to the literate mind. Keep in *your* mind, however, that books on any list merely reflect the opinion of individuals whose taste may not necessarily concur with yours. This is simply a place to begin. Add your own favorite titles, books read and books to be read. These are listed alphabetically by author.

Abbey, Edward
> *Fire on the Mountain*
> *The Monkey Wrench Gang*

Agee, James
> *A Death in the Family*

Alcott, Louisa May
> *Little Men*
> *Little Women*

Algren, Nelson
> *The Man with the Golden Arm*
> *A Walk on the Wild Side*

Allende, Isabel
> *The House of the Spirits*
> *Eva Luna*
> *Of Love and Shadows*

Alvarez, Julia
> *How the Garcia Girls Lost Their Accents*

Anaya, Rudolfo
> *Bless Me, Ultima*

Angelou, Maya
> *I Know Why the Caged Bird Sings*

Aristotle
> *Poetics*
> *Rhetoric*

Augustine, Saint
> *Confessions*

Austen, Jane
>*Emma*
>*Mansfield Park*
>*Northanger Abbey*
>*Persuasion*
>*Pride and Prejudice*
>*Sense and Sensibility*

Baines, Keith
>*Malory's Le Morte d'Arthur, a prose rendition by K.B.*

Baldwin, James
>*Go Tell It on the Mountain*

Blackmore, R.D.
>*Lorna Doone*

Bradbury, Ray
>*The Illustrated Man*
>*The Martian Chronicles*

Bronte, Anne
>*The Tenant of Wildfell Hall*

Bronte, Charlotte
>*Jane Eyre*

Bronte, Emily
>*Wuthering Heights*

Brown, Claude
>*Manchild in the Promised Land*

Buck, Pearl S.
>*Dragon Seed*
>*The Good Earth*

Burke, Edmund
>*A Philosophical Enquiry into the Origin of Our Ideas of the Sublime and the Beautiful*
>*Reflections on the Revolution in France*

Campbell, Joseph
>*The Hero with a Thousand Faces*
>*Myths to Live By*
>*The Power of Myth*
>*Transformations of Myth through Time*

Capote, Truman
>*In Cold Blood*
>*Music for Chameleons*

Cather, Willa
Death Comes for the Archbishop
My Antonia
A Lost Lady
One of Ours
O Pioneers
The Professor's House
The Song of the Lark
Uncle Valentine and Other Stories

Carroll, Lewis
Alice's Adventures in Wonderland and Through the Looking Glass

Cervantes
Don Quixote

Chaucer, Geoffrey
The Canterbury Tales

Cheever, John
The Stories of John Cheever

Chopin, Kate
The Awakening and Other Stories

Cisneros, Sandra
The House on Mango Street

Cohlho, Paulo
The Alchemist
The Pilgrimage

Collins, Wilkie
The Moonstone

Conrad, Joseph
The Heart of Darkness and *The Secret Sharer*
Lord Jim

Conroy, Pat
The Great Santini
The Water Is Wide

Cooper, James Fenimore
The Deerslayer
The Last of the Mohicans

Cormier, Robert
The Bumblebee Flies Anyway
The Chocolate War
Eight Plus One
I Am the Cheese
Tunes for Bears to Dance to

Courtenay, Bryce
The Power of One

Crane, Stephen
     The Red Bade of Courage and Other Stories
Defoe, Daniel
     Moll Flanders
     Robinson Crusoe
Dennis, Patrick
     Auntie Mame
Diamant, Anita
     The Red Tent
Dickens, Charles
     David Copperfield
     Great Expectations
     A Christmas Carol
     Nickolas Nickleby
     Oliver Twist
     The Pickwick Papers
     A Tale of Two Cities
Dillard, Annie
     An American Childhood
     The Living
     Pilgrim at Tinker Creek
     The Writing Life
Dostoyevsky, Fyodor
     The Idiot
     Notes from the Underground
     Crime and Punishment
     The Brothers Karamzov
Doyle, Sir Arthur Conan
     The Adventures of Sherlock Holmes
     The Memoirs of Sherlock Holmes
     The Return of Sherlock Holmes
     The Case-Book of Sherlock Holmes
     The Hound of the Baskervilles
Dreiser, Theodore
     Best Short Stories
     Sister Carrie
Dumas, Alexandre
     Camille
     The Count of Monte Cristo
     The Man in the Iron Mask
     The Three Musketeers
Du Maurier, Daphne
     Rebecca

Jamaica Inn

Edinger, Edward
    Ego and Archetype

Eliot, George
    Middlemarch
    The Mill on the Floss
    Silas Marner

Ellison, Ralph
    Invisible Man

Emerson, Ralph Waldo
    Selected Essays
    Essential Writings of Ralph Waldo Emerson

Estes, Clarissa Pinkola
    Women Who Run with the Wolves

Farrell, James
    Studs Lonigan

Faulkner, William
    Absalom, Absalom!
    As I Lay Dying
    Go Down, Moses
    Intruder in the Dust
    Light in August
    The Sound and the Fury

Fielding, Henry
    Tom Jones
    Joseph Andrews

Fitzgerald, F. Scott
    Babylon Revisited and Other Stories
    The Great Gatsby
    The Stories of F. Scott Fitzgerald

Flagg, Fannie
    Fried Green Tomatoes at the Whistle Stop Café

Forester, C.S.
    The Horatio Hornblower novels:
        The Happy Return
        A Ship of the Line
        Flying Colours
        Lord Hornblower

Forster, E.M.
    The Celestial Omnibus and Other Stories
    Howards End
    A Passage to India
    A Room with a View

Forsyth, Frederick
    The Afghan
    Avenger
    The Day of the Jackal
    Icon
    The Veteran
Frank, Ann
    The Diary of Ann Frank
Frankl, Victor
    Man's Search for Meaning
Golding, William
    Lord of the Flies
Graves, Robert
    Greek Myths
    I, Claudius
Greene, Graham
    The Man Within
    Stamboul Train (Film Version: Orient Express)
    Brighton Rock
    The Power and the Glory
    The Heart of the Matter
    The End of the Affair
Grimm, Jacob and Wilhelm
    Grimm's Fairy Tales
Hamilton, Edith
    Mythology
Hammett, Dashiell
    The Maltese Falcon
Hardy, Thomas
    Far from the Madding Crowd
    Jude the Obscure
    The Mayor of Casterbridge
    Return of the Native
    Tess of the d'Urbervilles
Harte, Bret
    The Luck of Roaring Camp and Other Sketches
Hawthorne, Nathaniel
    The Celestial Railroad and Other Stories
    The House of the Seven Gables
    The Marble Faun
    Mosses from an Old Manse
    The Scarlet Letter
    Twice-Told Tales

Heller, Joseph
    Catch-22
Hemingway, Ernest
    A Farewell to Arms
    For Whom the Bell Tolls
    The Short Stories
Henry, O.
    Cabbages and Kings
    Collected Stories
Hesse, Hermann
    Siddhartha
    Steppenwolf
Hollis, James
    Creating a Life
    The Eden Project
    Finding Meaning in the Second Half of Life
    Why Good People Do Bad Things
Houston, Jeanne Wakatsuki and James D. Houston
    Farewell to Manzanar
Hughes, Langston
    The Ways of White Folks, Stories by Langston Hughes
Hugo, Victor
    Les Miserables
Hurston, Zora Neale
    Their Eyes Were Watching God
    Dust Tracks on a Road
    I Love Myself When I Am Laughing and Then Again When I Am Looking Mean
        and Impressive
Isherwood, Christopher
    The Berlin Stories
Jackson, Shirley
    The Lottery and Other Stories
    We Have Always Lived in the Castle
James, Henry
    Daisy Miller and Other Stories
    The Portrait of a Lady
    The Turn of the Screw and Other Short Fiction
Jewett, Sarah Orne
    Deephaven
    The Country of the Pointed Firs
Johnson, James Weldon
    Autobiography of an Ex-Coloured Man
    God's Trombones

Joyce, James
 Finnegans Wake
 Ulysses
 A Portrait of the Artist as a Young Man
Kafka, Franz
 The Metamorphosis
 In the Penal Colony
 The Trial
 The Castle
 Amerika
Kerouac, Jack
 On the Road
 The Dharma Bums
 The Subterraneans
 Doctor Sax
 Lonesome Traveler
 Visions of Cody
Kidd, Sue Monk
 The Secret Life of Bees
 The Mermaid's Chair
King, Stephen
 Carrie
 The Shining
 The Stand
 The Dead Zone
 Firestarter
 Cujo
 It
 Christine
 The Dark Half
 Night Shift
Kingsolver, Barbara
 The Bean Trees
 The Poisonwood Bible
Kipling, Rudyard
 Barrack-Room Ballads
 Captains Courageous
 Just So Stories
 Kim
 The Light That Failed
 The Man Who Would Be King and Other Stories
 Puck of Pook's Hill
 Rewards and Fairies

Knowles, John
> *A Separate Peace*

Kubler-Ross, Elizabeth and David Kessler
> *Life Lessons*

Lardner, Ring
> *Best Short Stories*
> *Haircut and Other Stories*
> *You Know Me, Al*

Lawrence, D.H.
> *Sons and Lovers*

Lee, Gus
> *China Boy*

Lee, Harper
> *To Kill a Mockingbird*

Le Guin, Ursula
> *A Wizard of Earthsea*
> *The Tombs of Atuan*
> *The Farthest Shore*

Lerouz, Gaston
> *The Phantom of the Opera*

Lewis, Sinclair
> *Main Street*
> *Babbitt*
> *Arrowsmith*
> *Elmer Gantry*
> *Dodsworth*

London, Jack
> *The Call of the Wild*
> *To Build a Fire and Other Stories*
> *White Fang*

Macken, Walter
> *Rain on the Wind*
> *Seek the Fair Land*
> *The Silent People*
> *Scorching the Wind*

Mailer, Norman
> *The Naked and the Dead*

Malamud, Bernard
> *The Natural*
> *The Assistant*
> *The Fixer*
> *The Magic Barrel*

Mansfield, Katherine
  The Garden Party, and Other Stories
Marquez, Gabriel Garcia
  One Hundred Years of Solitude
  Love in the Time of Cholera
  Leaf Storm and Other Stories
  No One Writes to the Colonel and Other Stories
  Collected Stories
Martel, Yann
  Life of Pi
Maugham, W. Somerset
  The Moon and Sixpence
  The Razor's Edge
McCullers, Carson
  The Heart Is a Lonely Hunter
  The Member of the Wedding
McMillan, Terry
  Disappearing Acts
  Waiting to Exhale
McMurtry, Larry
  Lonesome Dove
  The Last Picture Show
  Streets of Laredo
  Terms of Endearment
  Buffalo Girls
  Sin Killer
McPherson, James
  Hue and Cry
  Elbow Room
Melville, Herman
  Moby Dick
  Billy Budd and Other Stories
Mitchell, Margaret
  Gone with the Wind
Michener, James
  Tales of the South Pacific
  Hawaii
  Centennial
  Chesapeake
Momaday, Scott
  House Made of Dawn
  The Way to Rainy Mountain

Morrison, Toni
> *Beloved*
> *The Bluest Eye*

Murdoch, Iris
> *Under the Net*
> *The Flight from the Enchanter*
> *A Severed Head*
> *The Nice and the Good*
> *The Black Prince*
> *Henry and Cato*

Nordhoff, Charles and James Norman Hall
> *Mutiny on the Bounty*
> *Men against the Sea*
> *Pitcairn's Island*

O'Connor, Flannery
> *The Complete Stories*

O'Connor, Frank
> *Collected Stories*
> *Guests of the Nation*
> *Crab and Apple Jelly*
> *The Midnight Court*
> *Kings, Lords, and Commons*

O'Faolain, Sean
> *Collected Stories of Sean O'Faolain*
> *A Life of Daniel O'Connell*
> *Midsummer Night Madness and Other Stories*
> *A Nest of Simple Folk*

O'Grady, Standish James
> *The Bog of Stars*
> *The Flight of the Eagle*

Orwell, George
> *Animal Farm*
> *1984*

Pasternak, Boris
> *Dr. Zhivago*

Plath, Sylvia
> *The Bell Jar*

Plato
> *The Portable Plato, ed. Scott Buchanan*

Poe, Edgar Allan
> *The Tell Tale Heart and Other Writings*

Porter, Katherine Anne
>> *Ship of Fools*
>> *The Collected Stories of Katherine Anne Porter*
>> *Pale Horse, Pale Rider*
>> *Flowering Judas*

Pullman, Philip
>> *The Ruby in the Smoke*

Rand, Ayn
>> *Anthem*
>> *Atlas Shrugged*
>> *The Fountainhead*

Rawlings, Marjorie Kinnan
>> *Cross Creek*
>> *The Yearling*

Rostand, Edmund
>> *Cyrano de Bergerac*

Rhys, Jean
>> *Wide Sargasso Sea*

Saki
>> *Beasts and Super-Beasts*

Salinger, J.D.
>> *The Catcher in the Rye*

Saroyan, William
>> *The Human Comedy*

Scott, Sir Walter
>> *The Heart of Midlothian*
>> *Ivanhoe*
>> *Kenilworth*
>> *Old Mortality*
>> *Rob Roy*
>> *The Waverley Novels*

Seybold, Alice
>> *The Lovely Bones*

Shelley, Mary
>> *Frankenstein*

Shreve, Anita
>> *Fortune's Rocks*
>> *Light on Snow*
>> *The Pilot's Wife*
>> *Sea Glass*
>> *A Wedding in December*

Singer, Isaac Bashevis
>> *The Family Moskat*

The Magician of Lublin
A Crown of Feathers
The Image and Other Stories
Collected Stories
Stein, Gertrude
    The Making of Americans
Steinbeck, John
    Cannery Row
    East of Eden
    The Grapes of Wrath
    Of Mice and Men
    Sweet Thursday
    Tortilla Flat
    Travels with Charley
    The Winter of Our Discontent
Stoker, Bram
    Dracula
Stowe, Harriet Beecher
    Uncle Tom's Cabin
Swift, Jonathan
    Gulliver's Travels
Thackeray, William Makepeace
    Vanity Fair
Thoreau, Henry David
    Walden
    A Week on the Concord and Merrimack Rivers
    The Maine Woods
    "Civil Disobedience"
Thurber, James
    My Life and Hard Times
Tolkien, J.R.R.
    The Hobbit
    The Lord of the Rings
Tolstoy, Leo
    Anna Karenina
    War and Peace
Trollope, Anthony
    Barchester Tower
Twain, Mark
    The Adventures of Huckleberry Finn
    The Adventures of Tom Sawyer
    A Connecticut Yankee at King Arthur's Court
    The Prince and the Pauper

Verne, Jules
  Journey to the Center of the Earth
  Twenty Thousand Leagues Under the Sea
  The Mysterious Island
  Around the World in Eighty Days
Voltaire
  Candide
Von Arnim, Elizabeth
  The Enchanted April
Vonnegut, Kurt
  Slaughterhouse-Five
  Cat's Cradle
Walker, Alice
  The Color Purple
Well, H.G.
  The Invisible Man
  The Time Machine
  War of the Worlds
Welty, Eudora
  The Collected Stories
  A Curtain of Green
  Delta Wedding
  Losing Battles
  One Writer's Beginnings
Werner, E.T.C.
  Myths and Legends of China
White, Bailey
  Mama Makes Up Her Mind
  Quite a Year for Plums
White, T.H.
  The Once and Future King
  The Book of Merlyn
Wiesel, Elie
  Night
  The Town beyond the Wall
  A Beggar in Jerusalem
  Souls on Fire
  The Testament
  The Forgotten
Wister, Owen
  The Virginian
Wodehouse, P.G.
  Blandings Castle and Elsewhere

How Right you Are, Jeeves
Leave It to Psmith
Life with Jeeves
The Wodehouse Clergy
Woolf, Virginia
Mrs. Dalloway
To the Lighthouse
Orlando
A Room of One's Own
Wright, Richard
Black Boy
Native Son

Works Cited

Adventures in Babysitting. Screenplay by David Simkins. Dir. Chris Columbus. Perf. Elisabeth Shue and Keith Coogan. Dir. Chris Columbus. Touchstone, 1987.

Alvarez, Julia. *How the Garcia Girls Lost Their Accents.* New York: PLUME, 1992.

Angelou, Maya. *The Complete Collected Poems.* New York: Random House, 1994.

---. *I Know Why the Caged Bird Sings.* NY: Bantam, 1997.

Annas, Julia. *An Introduction to Plato's Republic.* Oxford: Clarendon, 1981.

Aristotle. *Poetics.* Trans. Malcolm Heath. London: Penguin, 1996.

Aristotle. *Poetics and Rhetoric, Aristotle.* Ed. Eugene Garver. New York: Barnes, 1995.

Bartlett, John. *Bartlett's Familiar Quotations.* Boston: Little, 1980.

Barton, John. *RSC in Playing Shakespeare.* London: Methuen, 1984.

Baym, Nina. Introduction. *The Scarlet Letter.* New York: Penguin, 1986.

Benet, Stephen Vincent. "The Devil and Daniel Webster." *The Devil and Daniel Webster.* New York: Penguin, 1999.

---. "A Tooth for Paul Revere." *Twenty Grand Short Stories.* New York: Bantam, 1968.

Berry, Cicely. *The Actor and the Text.* New York: Applause, 1992.

Best Plays Theater Yearbook, 2005-2006. 86th ed. New York: Limelight, 2006.

Biedermann, Hans. *The Dictionary of Symbolism, Cultural Icons, and the Meanings Behind Them.* New York: Penguin, 1994.

Bierce, Ambrose. "The Coup de Grace." *Classic American Short Stories.* New York: Oxford UP, 1989.

Blayney, Peter W.M. *The First Folio of Shakespeare.* Washington, D.C.: Folger, 1991.

Bloom, Harold. *Shakespeare, the Invention of the Human.* New York: Riverhead, 1998.

Book of Common Prayer. New York: Church Pension, 1945.

Bowker Annual of Library and Book Trade Information. 31 July 2007: 516. TRR hmm Houston Public Library eServices.

Bradbury, Ray. *The Illustrated Man.* New York: Bantam, 1951.

---. *The Martian Chronicles.* New York: Bantam, 1979.

Brooks, Gwendolyn. *African American Poetry.* Ed. Michael S. Harper and Anthony Walton. New York: Random, 2000.

Brush, Katherine. "Fumble." *Twenty Grand Short Stories.* New York: Bantam, 1963.

Buchanan, Scott, ed. *The Portable Plato.* New York: Penguin, 1977.

Buck, Pearl. "The Enemy." *Harpers Magazine.* Nov. 1942. 2 Jan. 2008 <http://*www. harpers.org/archive/1942/11/0020381*>.

Burke, Edmond. *A Philosophical Enquiry into the Origin of Our Ideas of the Sublime and the Beautiful.* Oxford: Oxford UP, 1998.

Burns, Robert. *Poems and Songs of Robert Burns.* Ed. James Barke. Glasgow: Collins, 1971.

Burrows, David J., Frederick R. Lapides, and John T. Shawcross, eds. *Myths and Motifs in Literature.* New York: Free, 1973.

Burt, Daniel S. *The Literary 100: A Ranking of the Most Influential Novelists, Playwrights, and Poets of All Time.* New York: Checkmark, 2001.

Byron, George Gordon, Lord Byron. *Childe Harold's Pilgrimage and Other Romantic Poems.* New York: Odyssey, 1936.

Campbell, Joseph. *The Hero with a Thousand Faces.* Princeton: Princeton UP, 1968.

---. *Myths to Live By.* New York: Penguin, 1972.

---. *The Power of Myth.* New York: Doubleday, 1988.

---. *Transformations of Myth Through Time.* New York: Harper, 1999.

Capote, Truman. "Children on Their Birthdays." *Selected Writings of Truman Capote.* New York: Random, 1948.

Carpenter, Thomas H. and Robert J. Gula. *Mythology, Greek and Roman.* Wellesley Hills: Independent School, 1977.

Cavendish, Richard, ed. *Legends of the World.* New York: Barnes, 1994.

---. *Mythology, an Illustrated Encyclopedia.* New York: Barnes, 1992.

Cerf, Bennett and Van H. Cartmell, eds. *24 Favorite One Act Plays.* New York: Broadway, 1958.

Chain Reference Bible. Comp. and ed. Frank Charles Thompson. Indianapolis: Kirbride, 1964.

Chaucer, Geoffrey. *Canterbury Tales, An Interlinear Translation.* Trans. Vincent F. Hopper. NY: Barron's, 1970.

Cheney, Theodore A. Rees. *Getting the Words Right: How to Revise, Edit, and Rewrite.* Cincinnati: Writers Digest, 1983.

Children on Their Birthdays. Screenplay by Douglas Sloan. Dir. Mark Medoff. Based on Truman Capote's short story "Children on Their Birthdays." Artisan, 2002.

Chute, Marchette. *Shakespeare of London.* New York: Dutton, 1949.

Cirlot, J. E. *A Dictionary of Symbols.* New York: Barnes, 1971.

Clinton, Hillary Rodham. "Women's Rights Are Human Rights," The United Nations Fourth World Conference on Women, China: Beijing, 1995. *American Rhetoric, Top 100 Speeches.* 2 Jan. 2008 <http://www.un.americanrhetoric.com/speeches/hilla ryclintonbeijingspeech.htm>.

Coelho, Paulo. *The Alchemist.* New York: Harper, 1993.

Columbia Encyclopedia 5th Edition. Ed. Barbara Chernow and George A. Vallasi. New York: Columbia UP, 1993.

Cooper, J.C. *An Illustrated Encyclopedia of Traditional Symbols.* London: Thames, 1978.

Cormier, Robert. "The Moustache." *Eight Plus One.* New York: Bantam/Starfire, 1985.

---. *Tunes for Bears to Dance to.* New York: Bantam, 1992.

Crain, W.C. "Kohlberg's Stages of Moral Development." *Theories of Development.* New York: Prentice, 1985.

Cullen, Countee. "Incident." *African American Poetry.* Ed. Michael S. Harper and Anthony Walton. New York: Random, 2000.

---. "Saturday's Child." *African American Poetry.* Ed. Michael S. Harper and Anthony Walton. New York: Random, 2000.

---. "Scottsboro, Too, Is Worth the Song." *African American Poetry.* Ed. Michael S. Harper and Anthony Walton. New York: Random, 2000.

Dahlke, Rudiger. *Mandalas of the World.* New York: Sterling, 1992.

Dancing: New Worlds, New Forms. Created by Rhoda Grauer. Thirteen/WNET and RM Arts, 1993
Dickinson, Emily. *The Complete Poems of Emily Dickinson.* Boston: Back Bay, 1976.

Dillard, Annie. *An American Childhood.* New York: Harper, 1987.

---. *Pilgrim at Tinker Creek.* New York: Harper, 1974.

---. *The Writing Life.* New York: HarperPerennial, 1990.

Donne, John. "Devotions upon Emergent Occasions, XVII Meditation." 1624. *The Complete Poetry & Selected Prose of John Donne.* Ed. Charles M. Coffin. New York: Modern Library, 1994. 441.

Driver, Tom F. *Liberating Rites*. Boulder: Westview, 1998.

Dunbar, Paul. "We Wear the Mask." *African American Poetry*. Ed. Michael S. Harper and Anthony Walton. New York: Random, 2000.

---. "The White House." *African American Poetry*. Ed. Michael S. Harper. and Anthony Walton. New York: Random, 2000.

Durant, Will. *The Story of Philosophy*. New York: Simon, 1961.

Edgar, Christopher and Ron Padgett, eds. *Classics in the Classroom*. New York: Teachers and Writers Collaborative, 1999.

Edinger, Edward F. *Ego and Archetype*. Boston: Shambhala, 1972.

Ehrlich, Eugene. *Amo, Amas, Amat and More*. New York: Harper, 1985.

Ellis, Havelock. *The Dance of Life*. New York: Modern Library, 1951.

Emerson, Ralph Waldo. "Gifts." *The Essential Writings of Ralph Waldo Emerson*. Ed. Brooks Atkinson. New York: Modern Library, 2000.

---. "Self-Reliance." *Ralph Waldo Emerson, Selected Essays, Lectures, and Poems*. Ed. Robert D. Richardson, Jr. New York: Bantam, 2007.

The Emperor's Club. Screenplay by Neil Tolkin. Dir. Michael Hoffman. Perf. Kevin Kline. Based on the short story "The Palace Thief" by Ethan Canin. Universal, 2002.

Encyclopedia of Literature. Springfield: Merriam-Webster, 1995.

Estes, Clarissa Pinkola. *Women Who Run with the Wolves*. New York: Ballantine, 1992.

Ever After. Screenplay by Susannah Grant, Andy Tennant, and Rick Parks. Dir. Andy Tennant. Perf. Drew Barrymore, Dougray Scott, and Anjelica Huston. Twentieth Century, 1998.

The Fantasticks. Screenplay by Tom Jones and Harvey Schmidt. Dir. Michael Ritchie. Based on the play by Tom Jones and Harvey Schmidt. MGM, 1995.

Far and Away. Screenplay by Bob Dolman. Dir. Ron Howard. Perf. Tom Cruise and Nicole Kidman. Universal, 1992.

Fields, Bertram. *Players, The Mysterious Identity of William Shakespeare.* New York: ReganBooks/HarperCollins, 2005.

Finding Forrester. Screenplay by Mike Rich. Dir. Gus Van Sant. Perf. Sean Connery. Columbia, 2001.

Flaubert, Gustave. *Madame Bovary.* Trans. Francis Steegmuller. NY: Modern, 1992.

Foner. Eric and John A. Garraty, eds. *The Reader's Companion to American History.* Boston: Houghton, 1991.

Forsyth, Frederick. "The Veteran." *The Veteran.* New York: St. Martin's, 2001.

---. "Whispering Wind." *The Veteran.* New York: St. Martin's, 2001.

Frankl, Viktor E. *Man's Search for Meaning.* New York: Simon, 1984.

Frost, Robert. *The Poetry of Robert Frost.* New York: Holt, 1969.

---. *Robert Frost, A Tribute to the Source.* Ed. Dewitt Jones and David Bradley. New York: Holt, 1979.

Gallo, Donald R., ed. *Connections, Short Stories by Outstanding Writers for Young Adults.* New York: Dell, 1989.

---. *Sixteen Short Stories by Outstanding Writers for Young Adults.* New York: Dell, 1984.

Gershwin, Ira. *The Complete Lyrics of Ira Gershwin.* Ed. Robert Kimball. New York: Alfred A. Knopf, 1993.

Gibaldi, Joseph. *MLA Handbook for Writers of Research Papers.* 6th ed. New York: MLA, 2003.

Greenblatt, Stephen, Walter Cohen, Jean E. Howard, and Katharine Eisaman Maus, eds. *The Norton Shakespeare.* New York: Norton, 1997.

Guerin, Wilfred L., Earle Labor, Lee Morgan, Jeanne C. Reesman, and John R. Willingham. *A Handbook of Critical Approaches to Literature.* New York: Oxford UP, 1992.

Halprin, Anna. *Dance as a Healing Art.* Medicino: Life Rhythm, 2000.

Hamilton, Edith. *Mythology*. Boston: Bay Back, 1942.

Hansberry, Lorraine. *A Raisin in the Sun*. New York: Vintage, 1994.

Harper, Michael S. and Anthony Walton, eds. *African American Poetry*. New York: Random, 2000.

Harrison, G. B., ed. *Shakespeare, Major Plays and the Sonnets*. New York: Harcourt, 1948.

Hawthorne, Nathaniel. "Dr. Heidegger's Experiment." *The Celestial Railroad*. New York: Signet, 1963.

---. *The House of the Seven Gables*. New York: Bantam, 1981.

---. "The Maypole of Merry Mount." *The Celestial Railroad*. New York: Signet 1963.

---. "The Minister's Black Veil." *The Celestial Railroad*. New York: Signet, 1963.

---. *Mosses from an Old Manse*. New York: Modern Library, 2003.

---. "Rappaccini's Daughter." *The Celestial Railroad*. New York: Signet, 1963.

---. *The Scarlet Letter*. New York: Penguin, 1986.

---. *Twice-Told Tales*. New York: Modern Library, 2001.

---. "Young Goodman Brown." *The Celestial Railroad*. New York: Signet, 1963.

Heath, Malcolm. Introduction. *Poetics* by Aristotle. London: Penguin, 1996.

Henry, Patrick. "Patrick Henry, Liberty or Death!" 23 Mar. 1775. Richmond, Virginia. *The History Place, Great Speeches Collection*. 2 Jan. 2008 <http://*www.historyplace.com/speeches/henry.htm*>.

Herder, Freiburg. *The Herder Dictionary of Symbols*. Wilmette: Chiron, 1978.

Hinton, S. E. *The Outsiders*. New York: Puffin, 2003.

Hobsbaum, Philip. *Essentials of Literary Criticism*. London: Thames, 1983.

Hoeller, Stephan A. *Jung and the Lost Gospels*. Wheaton: Quest, 1994.

Hoffman, Edward, ed. *The Wisdom of Carl Jung.* New York: Citadel, 2003.

Holiday, Billie. "Strange Fruit." *Strange Fruit: 1937-1939.* Jazzterdays Records, 2000.

Hollis, James. *Creating a Life.* Toronto: Inner City, 2001.

---. *Why Good People Do Bad Things.* New York: Gotham, 2007.

Holy Bible, the Washburn College Bible. Oxford ed. New York: Oxford UP, 1979.

Honan, Park. *Shakespeare, A Life.* London: Oxford UP, 1999.

Houston Chronicle. <http://www.houstonchron.com>.

Houston, Jeanne Wakatsuki and James D. Houston. *Farewell to Manzanar.* New York: Bantam, 1973.

Howard-Hill, T. H. *Twelfth Night, by William Shakespeare.* The Blackfriars Shakespeare. Dubuque: Brown, 1969.

Hubert, Karen M. *Teaching and Writing Popular Fiction in the American Classroom.* New York: Teachers and Writers Collaborative, 1983.

Hughes, Langston. "Cross." *African American Poetry.* Ed. Michael S. Harper. and Anthony Walton. New York: Random, 2000.

---. "Mother to Son." *African American Poetry.* Ed. Michael S. Harper and Anthony Walton. New York: Random, 2000.

---. "Theme for English B." *African American Poetry.* Ed. Michael S. Harper and Anthony Walton. New York: Random, 2000.

Hunt, Kellogg. *Grammatical Structures Written at Three Grade Levels.* Champaign: NCTE, 1965.

Hyde, Maggie and Michael McGuinness. *Introducing Jung.* Cambridge, UK: Icon, 1999.

I Know Why the Caged Bird Sings. Teleplay by Leonora Thuna and Maya Angelou. Dir. Fielder Cook. Perf. Diahann Carroll, Ruby Dee, Esther Rolle. Based on the novel by Maya Angelou. Artisan, 1978.

The Importance of Being Earnest. Screenplay by Oliver Parker. Dir. Oliver Parker. Perf. Reese Witherspoon, Colin Firth, Rupert Everett, and Frances O'Connor. Based on the play by Oscar Wilde. Miramax, 2002.

Irwin, Terence. *Plato's Ethics.* New York: Oxford UP, 1995.

Jenkins, Harold. "Creative Devices Make *Twelfth Night* a Great Comedy." *Readings on the Comedies.* Ed. Clarice Swisher. San Diego: Greenhaven, 1997.

Jones, Suzanne W., ed. *Growing up in the South.* New York: Penguin, 1991.

Jones, Tom. "Trying to Remember." *The Fantasticks.* New York: Applause, 1964.

Jones, Tom and Harvey Schmidt. *The Fantasticks.* New York: Applause, 1964.

The Journey of Natty Gann. Screenplay by Jeanne Rosenberg. Dir. Jeremy Kagan. Perf. Meredith Salenger, John Cusack, and Ray Wise. Walt Disney, 1985.

Jung, C. G. *The Basic Writings of C. G. Jung.* Trans. R.F.C. Hull. Ed. Violet S. de Laszlo. Bollingen Series. Princeton: Princeton UP, 1990.

---. *Four Archetypes.* Princeton: Princeton UP, 1969.

---. *Memories, Dreams, Reflections.* Trans. Richard and Clara Winston. Ed. Aniela Jaffe. New York: Vintage, 1989.

Kidd, Sue Monk. *The Secret Life of Bees.* New York: Penguin, 2003.

King, Martin Luther, Jr. "I Have a Dream." Speech. 28 Aug. 1963. Washington, D.C. *The U.S. Constitution Online.* 2 Jan. 2008 <http://*www.usconstitution.net/dream. html*>.

King, Stephen. *On Writing.* New York: Pocket, 2000.

Kirby, Dan. "Images of Childhood." Speech Given to the Greater Houston Area Writing Project Conference. Feb. 1986.

Knowles, John. *A Separate Peace.* New York: Bantam, 1988.

Kohlberg, Lawrence. *The Philosophy of Moral Development: Moral Stages and the Idea of Justice.* New York: HarperCollins, 1981.

Krull, Kathleen. *12 Keys to Writing Books That Sell.* Cincinnati: Writers Digest, 1989.

Labyrinth. Story by Dennis Lee and Jim Henson. Screenplay by Terry Jones. Dir. Jim Henson. Perf. David Bowie and Jennifer Connelly. Lucasfilm, Columbia Tristar, 1999.

Laing, Jennifer. *Art & Society in Roman Britain.* Phoenix Mill, UK: Sutton, 1997.

Lee, Gus. *China Boy.* New York: PLUME, 1994.

Lee, Harper. *To Kill a Mockingbird.* New York: Warner, 1960.

Lincoln, Abraham. Second Inaugural Address. 4 Mar. 1865. Washington, D.C. *The History Place.* 2 Jan. 2008 <http://*www.historyplace.com/lincoln/inaug-2.htm*>.

Linklater, Kristin. *Freeing Shakespeare's Voice.* New York: Theatre Communications, 1992.

Littleton, Scott C., ed. *Mythology, The Illustrated Anthology of World Myth and Storytelling.* San Diego, CA: Thunder Bay, 2002.

LoMonico, Michael. *The Shakespeare Book of Lists.* Franklin Lakes: New Page, 2001.

London, Jack. "The Heathen." *South Sea Tales.* Kila: Kessinger, 2004.

Longfellow, Henry Wadsworth. Letter to Nathaniel Hawthorne. MSS68. 8 Feb. Nathaniel Hawthorne Collection. Phillips Library, Salem, MA.

---. "Nature." *Keramos, and Other Poems.* Ann Arbor: SPO, 2006.

--- "The Sound of the Sea." *The Complete Poetical Works of Henry Wadsworth Longfellow.* New York: Lightyear, 1993.

---. "The Tide Rises, the Tide Falls." *Twenty Poems from Henry Wadsworth Longfellow.* Illus. Ernest W. Longfellow. Ann Arbor: SPO, 2006.

Lowell, Robert. *Near the Ocean.* New York: Farrar, 1967.

Macrone, Michael. *Brush Up Your Classics.* New York: Gramercy, 1991.

---. *Brush Up Your Mythology.* New York: Gramercy, 1992.

Mad About Mambo. Written and dir. John Forte. Perf. William Ash, Keri Russell, and Brian Cox. Universal, 2000.

Manning, Frankie. *Learn to Dance, Savoy-Style Lindy Hop.* Perf. Frankie Manning and Erin Stevens. Living Traditions, 1998.

Marquez, Gabriel Garcia. *Leaf Storm and Other Stories.* New York: Harper, 1972.

Maslow, Abraham H. *Motivation and Personality.* New York: HarperCollins, 1987.

"The Master of Conspiracy." Interview with Frederick Forsyth. *Sun-Herald.* 19 Sept. 2004 2 Jan. 2008 <*http://www.smh.com.au/articles/2004/09/19/1095532173658.html*>.

McCaughrean, Geraldine and Victor G. Ambrus, Illus. *The Canterbury Tales by Geoffrey Caucer (Retold).* Oxford: Oxford UP, 1984.

McCrum, Roger and Robert MacNeil. "Muse of Fire." *The Story of English.* MacNeil-Lehrer Productions/BBC, 1986.

McKay, Claude. "If We Must Die." *African American Poetry*. Ed. Michael S. Harper and Anthony Walton. New York: Random, 2000.

---. "The White House,. *African American Poetry.* Ed. Michael S. Harper and Anthony Walton. New York: Random, 2000.

Mellow, James R. *Nathaniel Hawthorne in His Times.* Baltimore: Johns Hopkins UP, 1980.

Meredith, Robert C. and John D. Fitzgerald. *Structuring Your Novel.* New York: Harper, 1993.

The Milagro Beanfield War. Screenplay by David Ward and John Nichols. Dir. Robert Redford. Based on the novel by John Nichols. Universal, 1988.

Moore, Bob and Moore, Maxine. *Dictionary of Latin and Greek Origins.* New York: NTC, 1997.

Murray, Donald. *Learning by Teaching.* Portsmouth: Boynton, 1982.

Nelson, Cary, ed. *Anthology of Modern American Poetry.* New York: Oxford UP, 2000.

Neruda, Pablo. *The Selected Odes of Pablo Neruda.* Berkeley: University of California Press, 1990.

Nicholas Nickleby. Written for the screen and dir. Douglas McGrath. Perf. Jamie Bell and Anne Hathaway. Based on the novel by Charles Dickens. MGM, 2002.

Nixon, Joan Lowery. Address to National Scholastic Winners at Barnes and Noble Writing Workshop. Houston, Texas. 8 June 2002.

Novakovich, Josip. *Writing Fiction Step by Step*. Cincinnati: Story, 1998.

Obama, Barack. "Out of Many, One." 2004 Democratic National Convention Keynote Address. 27 July 2004. Fleet Center, Boston, MA. *American Rhetoric Online Speech Bank*. 2 Jan. 2008 <http://www.americanrhetoric.com/speeches/convention2004/ barackobama2004dnc.htm>.

O'Connor, Frank. "Guests of the Nation." *Collected Stories*. New York: Vintage, 1982.

Oliver, Mary. *Dream Work*. New York: Atlantic, 1986.

---. *A Poetry Handbook*. New York: Harcourt, 1994.

---. *Thirst*. Boston: Beacon, 2006.

Open Range. Screenplay by Craig Storper. Dir. Kevin Costner. Perf. Robert Duvall, Kevin Costner, and Annette Benning. Touchstone, 2004.

Papp, Joseph and Elizabeth Kirkland. *Shakespeare Alive!* New York: Bantam, 1988.

Paterson, Katherine. *Bridge to Terabithia*. NY: HarperTrophy, 2005.

Pearson, Carol S. *The Hero Within: Six Archetypes We Live By*. New York: HarperCollins, 1989.

Person, Leland S. "Nathaniel Hawthorne: A Chronology." *The Scarlet Letter and Other Writings*. 731-2. NY: Norton, 2005.

Plato. "Apology." *The Last Days of Socrates*. Trans. Hugh Tredennick. New York: Penguin, 1969.

Plato. *The Dialogues of Plato*. Trans. Benjamin Jowell. London: Oxford UP, 1971.

Plato. "Phaedo." *The Last Days of Socrates*. Trans. Hugh Tredennick. New York: Penguin, 1969.

Plato. "The Republic II." Trans. Benjamin Jowett. *The Portable Plato*. Ed. Scott Buchanan. New York: Penguin, 1977. 327-28.

Plato. "The Republic VII." Trans. Benjamin Jowett. *The Portable Plato*. Ed. Scott

Buchanan. New York: Penguin, 1977. 546-49.

Porter, Katherine Anne. "The Grave." *The Collected Stories of Katherine Anne Porter.* San Diego: Harcourt, 1972.

Princess Bride. Screenplay by William Goldman from his book. Dir. Rob Reiner. Perf. Robin Wright and Cary Elwes. MGM, 1987.

A Raisin in the Sun. Screenplay by Lorraine Hansberry from her play. Dir. Daniel Petrie. Perf. Sidney Poitier, Claudia McNeil, and Ruby Dee. RCA/Columbia, 1961.

Reagan, Ronald. "Tear Down This Wall, Remarks at the Brandenburg Gate." 12 June 1987. West Berlin, Germany. *The Ronald Reagan Foundation Speeches.* 2 Jan. 2008 <http://*www.reaganfoundation.org/reagan/speeches/wall.asp*>.

Regarding Henry. Screenplay by Jeffrey Abrams. Dir. Mike Nichols. Perf. Harrison Ford and Annette Benning. Paramount, 1991.

Reynolds, David S. *Beneath the American Renaissance.* Cambridge: Harvard UP, 1988.

Roberts, J.M. *History of the World.* New York: Oxford UP, 1993.

Roberts, Paul. *Understanding Grammar.* New York: Harper, 1954.

Robertson, Stuart and Frederic G. Cassidy. *The Development of Modern English.* Englewood Cliffs: Princeton UP, 1969.

Robinson, Dave and Judy Groves. *Introducing Plato.* Cambridge, UK: Icon, 2000.

Rodenburg, Patsy. *The Actor Speaks: Voice and the Performer.* New York: St. Martin's, 2000.

Roosevelt, Franklin D. "The 'Four Freedoms' Speech." Annual Message to Congress. 6 Jan. 1941. Washington, D.C. *Franklin D. Roosevelt Presidential Library and Museum.* 2 Jan. 2008 <http://*www.fdrlibrary.marist.edu/4free.html*>.

Rosenblatt, Louise M. *Literature as Exploration.* New York: Noble, 1978.

Rowse, A. L. *Shakespeare the Man.* New York: St. Martin's, 1988.

Runaway Jury. Screenplay by Brian Koppelman, David Levien, Rick Cleveland, and Matthew Chapman. Dir. Gary Fleder. Perf. John Cusack, Gene Hackman, Dustin Hoffman, and Rachel Weisz. Twentieth Century Fox, 2003.

Sacks, Kenneth S. *Understanding Emerson.* Princeton: Princeton UP, 2003.

Sahakian, William S. and Mabel Lewis Sahakian. *Ideas of the Great Philosophers.* NY: Barnes, 1966.

Sandburg, Carl. *Honey and Salt.* New York: Harcourt, 1963.

Savage, Anne. *The Anglo-Saxon Chronicles*, collected and translated into English. New York: Barnes, 2000.

The Scarlet Letter. Adapted for television by Allan Knee and Alvin Sapinsley. Dir. Rick Hauser. Perf. Meg Foster, John Heard, and Kevin Conway. WBGH/Boston Education Foundation, 1979.

Schiff, Hilda, ed. *Holocaust Poetry.* New York: St. Martin's, 1995.

Scholastic Art & Writing Awards. 2 Jan. 2008 <_http://www.scholastic.com/ artandwritingawards/index_pages6.htm_>.

School Ties. Screenplay by Dick Wolf and Darryl Ponicson. Dir. Robert Mandel. Perf. Brendan Fraser, Matt Damon, Ben Affleck, and Chris O'Donnell. Paramount, 1992.

Sebranek, Patrick, Verne Meyer, and Dave Kemper. *Writers Inc.* Wilmington: Write Source, 1996.

Seger, Linda. *Creating Unforgettable Characters.* New York: Holt, 1990.

Sense and Sensibility. Screenplay by Emma Thompson. Adapted from the novel by Jane Austen. Dir. Ang Lee. Perf. Emma Thompson, Alan Rickman, Kate Winslet, and Hugh Grant Columbia Pictures, 1995.

Serendipity. Screenplay by Marc Klein. Dir. Peter Chelsom. Perf. John Cusack and Kate Beckinsale. Miramax, 2001.

Shadow Magic. Dir. Ann Hu. Perf. Jared Harris and Yu Xia. Sony Pictures Classic, 2001.

Shakespeare, William. "Hamlet." *The Norton Shakespeare.* Based on the Oxford Edition. Ed. Stephen Greenblatt. New York: Norton, 1997.

---. "King John." *The Norton Shakespeare.* Based on the Oxford Edition. Ed. Stephen Greenblatt. New York: Norton, 1997.

---. "The Merchant of Venice." *The Norton Shakespeare.* Based on the Oxford Edition. Ed. Stephen Greenblatt. New York: Norton, 1997.

---. "Othello." *The Norton Shakespeare.* Based on the Oxford Edition. Ed. Stephen Greenblatt. New York: Norton, 1997.

---."The Rape of Lucrece." *The Norton Shakespeare.* Based on the Oxford Edition. Ed. Stephen Greenblatt. New York: Norton, 1997.

---. "Richard II." *The Norton Shakespeare.* Based on the Oxford Edition. Ed. Stephen Greenblatt. New York: Norton, 1997.

---. "*Romeo and Juliet.*" NY: Oxford UP, 2000.

---. *Twelfth Night.* The New Folger Library Shakespeare. New York: Washington Square, 1993.

---. "Venus and Adonis." *The Norton Shakespeare.* Based on the Oxford Edition. Ed. Stephen Greenblatt. New York: Norton, 1997.

Shaw, George Bernard. *Plays by George Bernard Shaw: Man and Superman; Arms and the Man; Mrs. Warren's Profession; Candida.* Foreword by Eric Bentley. New York: Signet, 1960.

Spenser, Edmund. *The Works of Edmund Spenser: A Variorum Edition.* Ed. E. A. Greenlaw, F. M. Padelford, et al. 10 vols. Baltimore: Johns Hopkins UP, 1931-49.

Steinbeck, John. "Flight." *Masters of the Modern Short Story.* New York: Harcourt, 1955.

Storr, Anthony and Anthony Stevens, *Freud & Jung: A Duel Introduction.* New York: Barnes, 1998.

Strathern, Paul. *Plato in 90 Minutes.* Chicago: Dee, 1996.

Strunk, William, Jr. and E.B. White. *The Elements of Style.* New York: Macmillan, 1979.

Takaki, Richard. *A Different Mirror.* Boston: Back Bay, 1994.

Thoreau, Henry David. *Walden.* New York: Signet, 1980.

Thurber, James. "The Secret Life of Walter Mitty." *The Thurber Carnival.* New York: HarperPerennial, 1999.

To Kill a Mockingbird. Screenplay by Horton Foote. Based on Harper Lee's novel. Dir. Robert Mulligan. Perf. Gregory Peck. Universal, 1998.

Tobias, Ronald B. *Twenty Master Plots.* Cincinnati: Writers Digest, 1993.

Twain, Mark. "William Dean Howells." *The Complete Essays of Mark Twain.* Ed. Charles Neider. Cambridge: Da Capo, 2000.

Twelfth Night. Screenplay by Trevor Nunn. Based on William Shakespeare's play. Dir. Trevor Nunn. Fine Line Features, Renaissance Films, 1996.

Van Doren, Mark. *Nathaniel Hawthorne: A Critical Biography.* New York: Viking, 1949.

Van Druten, John. *I Am a Camera: A Play in Three Acts.* New York: Random, 1952.

Van Tassel, Wesley. *Clues to Acting Shakespeare.* New York: Allworth, 2000.

Voorhies, Felix. *Acadian Reminiscences.* New Orleans: Rivals, 1907.

Warga, Richard G. *Personal Awareness: A Psychology of Adjustment.* Dallas: Houghton, 1974.

Wells, Stanley. *The Cambridge Companion to Shakespeare Studies.* Cambridge: Cambridge UP, 1986.

Westbury, Virginia. *Labyrinths: Ancient Paths of Wisdom and Peace.* New York: Da Capo, 2001.

White, Bailey. *Mama Makes Up Her Mind.* New York: Vintage, 1993.

White, E. B. *Charlotte's Web.* New York: HarperTrophy, 2004.

Wiesel, Elie. *Night.* New York: Bantam, 1982.

Willis, Meredith Sue. *Personal Fiction Writing.* New York: Teachers and Writers Collaborative, 2000.

Wineapple, Brenda. *Hawthorne, A Life.* New York: Random, 2004.

Wodehouse, P.G. *The Most of P.G. Wodehouse.* New York: Simon, 1916.

Woodman, Marion and Elinor Dickson. *Dancing in the Flames.* Boston: Shambhala, 1997.

Wright, Richard. "The Man Who Was Almost a Man." *Eight Men: Short Stories.* New York: HarperPerennial, 1996.

Yeats, William Butler. *The Collected Poems of W.B. Yeats.* Ed. Richard J. Finneran. New York: Scribner, 1989.

Zulu. Screenplay by John Prebble and Cy Endfield. Dir. Cy Endfield. Perf. Stanley Baker, Jack Hawkins, Ulla Jacobsson, and Michael Caine. MGM, 1964.

A

A/B script 46, 47, 48

ABBA 15

abbreviations 72, 315, 321

Absolute phrase 295

actions 18, 22, 24, 34, 44, 47, 53, 55, 72, 82, 87, 106, 112, 138, 142, 155, 156, 157, 159, 182, 185, 195, 197, 214, 215, 224, 258

active voice 73, 329, 350

actor 137, 233, 252, 254, 255, 288, 289, 290, 371, 382

Adam 150, 151

adapt/adopt 222, 348

adjective 180, 202, 295, 298, 301, 302, 309, 310, 311, 325, 326, 327, 329, 330, 331, 334, 335, 337, 338, 339, 344

adjective clause 325, 326, 331, 338, 339

adultery 166, 186

adverb 295, 325, 327, 328, 330, 331, 338, 339

adverb clause 331, 339

Aegeus 222

affect/effect 14, 17, 23, 28, 36, 37, 52, 65, 66, 73, 85, 86, 87, 88, 103, 144, 153, 166, 173, 183, 202, 203, 214, 228, 253, 302, 347, 348

African American 98, 99, 105, 189, 190, 215, 373, 374, 376, 377, 380

African American Poetry 105, 215, 371, 373, 374, 376, 377, 380

Alabama 16, 205

The Alchemist 7, 213, 214, 215, 238, 357, 373

allegory 7, 19, 76, 87, 114, 142, 144, 145, 146, 157, 158, 159, 162

allegory of the cave 19, 114, 144, 145, 146

alliteration 87

allusion 78, 82, 87, 165, 173, 218

a lot/alot 17, 49, 59, 72, 106, 225, 283, 287, 348

altar 126, 132, 158, 236

Alvarez, Julia 54, 355, 370

ambiguity 20, 165, 181, 201, 202, 203, 205, 206, 209, 215, 219

American Renaissance 6, 12, 91, 93, 100, 101, 167, 234, 382

amplification 76, 233, 256

analogy 85, 87, 184

anaphora 76, 79, 87

anecdote 87

angel 166, 167, 168, 172, 185, 186

Angelou, Maya 20, 54, 105, 188, 191, 355, 370, 377

anima 136

animals 35, 49, 71, 101, 119, 137, 142, 150, 186, 233, 336

animus 137

antagonist 22, 87

antidote 151, 201, 202

antithesis 7, 51, 72, 75, 76, 79, 83, 84, 86, 87, 103, 120, 142, 144, 146, 149, 153, 159, 162, 165, 166, 170, 171, 172, 174, 175, 181, 182, 184, 185, 192, 195, 196, 205, 210, 255, 258, 309

apostrophe 343, 344

appeals 76, 77, 78, 80

appositive 295, 325, 326, 327, 329, 330, 331, 332, 333, 334, 342

archetypal warrior 202

archetype 6, 32, 85, 87, 116, 118, 119, 120, 133, 136, 142, 144, 145, 147, 149, 153, 162, 196, 198, 219, 222, 230, 296, 359, 374

Ariadne 69, 222

Aristotle 12, 19, 22, 26, 27, 28, 29, 31, 33, 76, 111, 232, 255, 355, 370, 376

art 7, 13, 15, 18, 20, 49, 75, 76, 81, 86, 87, 91, 93, 115, 126, 131, 132, 150, 163, 182, 183, 186, 187, 188, 190, 221, 289, 292, 294, 298, 315, 343, 345, 375, 379, 383

Arte of Rhetorique 233, 256

assertion 75, 143, 179, 201

Assonance 87

Atropos 186

Attis 130, 132

audience 15, 45, 50, 53, 55, 56, 75, 76, 78, 82, 88, 124, 125, 128, 143, 144, 145, 189, 191, 228, 230, 233, 240, 253, 257, 278, 279, 301

autobiography 87, 190, 206, 207, 361

Avenger 23, 327, 360

axis mundi 132, 133, 171, 183

B

Bacon, Francis 232

balance 12, 52, 53, 56, 64, 68, 83, 84, 89, 103, 135, 137, 138, 139, 142, 146, 149, 150, 151, 154, 159, 162, 166, 170, 171, 184, 221, 223, 252, 255

Baltimore Consort 140, 293

Barton, John 288, 291, 370

Baym, Nina 128, 370

BBC 231, 290, 380

bean 41, 92, 192, 230, 240, 242, 243, 362

bearbaiting 230, 231

Benet, Stephen Vincent 54, 370

Berry, Cicely 252, 254, 255, 288, 371

bestiality 7, 20, 208, 217, 219, 220

betrayal 7, 20, 45, 78, 80, 120, 151, 166, 173, 181, 189, 192, 200, 201, 202, 203, 207, 210, 211, 212, 214, 215, 222

be verbs 6, 66, 72, 73, 180, 327

Bible 78, 79, 116, 134, 228, 232, 238, 290, 362, 372, 377

Biedermann, Hans 85, 371

Bierce, Ambrose 371

black 7, 16, 41, 56, 79, 84, 96, 122, 137, 143, 147, 148, 151, 153, 154, 155, 158, 162, 163, 167, 169, 172, 173, 176, 177, 182, 184, 187, 188, 189, 190, 191, 192, 194, 205, 209, 222, 245, 287, 365, 369, 376

blank verse 144, 252, 255

Blayney, Peter 371

blazing 158, 159

blood 106, 130, 137, 159, 173, 178, 222, 231, 350, 356

Bloom, Harold 228, 229, 230, 288, 371

Blue 13, 158, 345

Blue Dancers 13, 345

body paragraphs 64

Bontemps, Arna 191

Book of Common Prayer 232, 236, 371

boundaries 32, 33, 75, 134, 188, 196, 224

Bradbury, Ray 54, 356, 371

Brahmins 91

breathing 251, 255

Broadside Band 250

brook 17, 170, 171, 178, 288

Brooks, Gwendolyn 188, 192, 371

Brook Farm 92, 129

brown 7, 58, 59, 84, 86, 108, 122, 157, 158, 159, 162, 204, 241, 242, 270, 289, 334, 335, 354, 356, 376, 377

Buchanan, Scott 113, 365, 371, 381, 382

Buck, Pearl S. 205, 206, 356, 371

"The Buffens" 140

Burbage, James 233

Burke, Edmond 27, 356, 371

Burns, Robert 220, 319, 371

business letter 343

butterfly 101, 148, 152, 162

Byron, George Gordon Lord 22, 95, 372

C

Caesar, Julius 235, 237, 294

caesura 252, 253, 254, 255

Campbell, Joseph 119, 120, 356, 372

canon 188, 229

Canterbury Tales 357, 372, 380

capital/capitol 237, 270, 348

Capote, Truman 43, 356, 372

The Celestial Railroad 360, 376

Celtic 118, 133, 295

center 57, 58, 60, 83, 124, 126, 128, 130, 131, 132, 133, 139, 140, 141, 148, 150, 151, 152, 171, 193, 195, 212, 221, 223, 229, 230, 251, 271, 278, 304, 312, 334, 368, 381

chameleon 152

character 5, 16, 22, 23, 24, 25, 27, 28, 32, 33, 34, 35, 36, 37, 38, 43, 45, 46, 47, 48, 49, 53, 56, 76, 77, 81, 83, 87, 88, 89, 136, 138, 139, 140, 153, 154, 156, 157, 161, 162, 165, 166, 168, 170, 180, 182, 184, 185, 189, 195, 198, 206, 210, 215, 231, 239, 253, 257, 258, 259, 353

Chaucer, Geoffrey 49, 357, 372

childhood 32, 33, 34, 49, 69, 70, 83, 102, 128, 184, 188, 194, 358, 373, 378

Children on Their Birthdays 43, 372

Chillingworth 64, 166, 167, 171, 174, 175, 176, 177, 178, 179, 180, 183, 184, 185

China 45, 54, 69, 118, 238, 363, 368, 373, 379

choppy 73

chord/cord/cordially 69, 150, 250, 348

chose/choose 12, 23, 25, 28, 33, 34, 35, 36, 40, 44, 45, 47, 48, 50, 51, 55, 56, 61, 72, 73, 81, 82, 100, 105, 106, 115, 117, 121, 131, 132, 140, 153, 157, 158, 159, 162, 163, 165, 180, 187, 192, 195, 199, 201, 204, 205, 206, 207, 208, 209, 210, 211, 213, 216, 224, 225, 227, 239, 240, 256, 258, 271, 287, 292, 325, 348, 349, 351, 353

Christmas 97, 132, 229, 240, 244, 358

Chronicles, Holinshed's 233

Chronology 6, 8, 92, 93, 167, 236, 381

Cinderella 150

circle 8, 11, 12, 33, 84, 85, 125, 126, 129, 137, 140, 141, 142, 152, 171, 172, 221, 240, 250, 251, 258, 259, 260, 277, 296

Circle Dance 8, 250, 258, 259, 260

circuit 222, 223, 305

circular pattern 49, 221

Cirlot, J.E. 372

civil disobedience 166, 202, 367

Civil Rights Act 194

Civil War 91, 99, 100, 191, 209, 316, 333

clarity 66, 67, 182, 202, 301, 325

climax 22, 87, 88, 89

Clinton, Hillary Rodham 77, 79, 373

Clotho 186

cloud 104, 152, 158, 183, 297

clown 197, 234, 256, 313

Coelho, Paulo 7, 20, 213, 214, 373

cohesive 12, 309

cohesiveness 65, 180

collective unconscious 87, 116, 117, 131, 139, 296, 338

colon 74, 255, 343

colors 70, 71, 130, 137, 142, 187, 333, 352

comedy 54, 143, 227, 229, 235, 236, 238, 258, 366, 378

comma 73, 143, 255, 329, 341, 342, 343

comma splice 73

commentary 64, 65, 67, 173, 180, 288

communicate 13, 18, 21, 37, 41, 53, 55, 66, 73, 80, 82, 85, 90, 102, 105, 106, 122, 165, 170, 303, 316, 325

communication 81, 303

compare 74, 82, 123, 174, 197, 210, 216, 325

complacency 203

complement 12, 76, 329, 349

complete plot 26

complex sentence 295, 325

compliance 201, 202, 203, 215, 299

compound sentence 73, 143, 325, 336, 337

conclusion 55, 63, 65, 68, 74, 76, 77, 143, 173, 182, 197

conflict 5, 7, 22, 23, 36, 37, 38, 41, 45, 48, 49, 51, 52, 54, 56, 83, 87, 137, 142, 146, 150, 165, 166, 172, 174, 182, 183, 184, 185, 201, 204, 218, 233, 303, 309, 335, 346

conjunction 73, 328, 341
  coordination 73, 328, 330
  correlative 328
  subordinating 328, 331, 349

conscience 138, 160, 173, 199, 200, 306

consonant 87, 322, 323

content 18, 66, 74, 88, 111, 250, 253, 255

contraction 332, 350

contractions 72, 344

contrast 74, 82, 88, 113, 185, 309

Cooper, J. C. 131, 373

Cormier, Robert 212, 213, 353, 357, 373

"The Coup de Grace" 209, 215

Creating a Life 213, 361, 377

credibility 76, 77, 83

Cullen, Countee 188, 190, 191, 192, 373

cultural diversity 224

culture 12, 13, 32, 45, 50, 72, 85, 91, 93, 115, 118, 119, 123, 130, 132, 139, 155, 162, 189, 190, 196, 201, 216, 217, 221, 224, 225, 227, 231, 232, 254, 258, 294, 295, 298, 306, 308

Curious George 225

Cybele 84, 130

Cyrano de Bergerac 143, 333, 366

D

Daedelus 222

Dahlke, Rudiger 373

dance iii, 1, 6, 7, 8, 11, 12, 13, 15, 22, 57, 59, 60, 61, 63, 75, 83, 91, 103, 116, 122, 123, 125, 126, 130, 140, 142, 144, 145, 146, 148, 164, 172, 188, 193, 194, 200, 212, 213, 215, 222, 227, 234, 241, 244, 248, 250, 256, 258, 259, 260, 263, 270, 272, 274, 275, 276, 277, 278, 279, 281, 282, 284, 286, 294, 315, 324, 335, 337, 340, 345, 352, 357, 373, 374, 375, 380

The Dance of Life 13, 294, 374

dancing 5, 11, 12, 13, 15, 75, 76, 84, 123, 124, 125, 128, 130, 142, 145, 146, 148, 149, 164, 172, 186, 193, 194, 222, 231, 240, 258, 259, 275, 284, 294, 373, 386

Dancing in the Flames 75, 164, 386

dark 30, 71, 72, 75, 86, 107, 108, 129, 142, 146, 149, 152, 155, 158, 159, 162, 163, 166, 177, 231, 235, 249, 291, 335, 362

darkness 75, 85, 104, 112, 133, 136, 137, 144, 145, 148, 151, 152, 154, 155, 158, 163, 171, 172, 183, 184, 196, 230, 259, 357

dark house 231

dash 344

dawn 130, 152, 364

death 6, 40, 44, 69, 77, 78, 83, 85, 86, 98, 110, 111, 112, 118, 119, 120, 127, 128, 129, 133, 135, 136, 137, 142, 143, 144, 146, 147, 148, 149, 150, 151, 152, 153, 155, 157, 158, 161, 162, 167, 171, 172, 173, 177, 194, 198, 200, 209, 212, 222, 230, 238, 246, 247, 249, 250, 259, 263, 301, 313, 355, 357, 376

Degas, Edgar 13, 96, 333, 345

Demeter 118, 135

denotation 87

denouement 22, 87, 89

dependent clause 349

description 25, 29, 30, 36, 51, 64, 68, 82, 88, 114, 132, 146, 174, 197, 224, 239, 354

destiny 152, 155, 171, 172, 183, 186, 187, 200

detail 161, 174

details 22, 25, 26, 28, 37, 41, 43, 45, 47, 56, 68, 143, 165, 173, 187, 278, 290, 295, 328

de Vere, Edward 232

dialect 32, 52, 88, 191

dialectic 6, 75, 76

dialogue 5, 32, 41, 46, 47, 48, 52, 53, 55, 67, 146, 180, 343

Dickinson, Emily 96, 373

Dickson, Elinor 75, 164, 386

Diction 5, 50, 64, 66, 68, 72, 75, 78, 80, 81, 86, 88, 206, 233

Dictionary of Symbols 372, 376

didactic 88

Dillard, Annie 15, 20, 100, 101, 102, 358, 373

Dimmesdale, Arthur 166, 167, 168, 171, 172, 174, 175, 176, 177, 178, 179, 181, 183, 184, 185
direct address 342
direct object 327, 329, 331, 332, 333, 334, 335, 337, 340
discourse 6, 18, 19, 66, 75, 76
diversity 8, 66, 224
Donne, John 211, 373
"Dr. Heidegger's Experiment" 7, 122, 147, 162
dragon 8, 71, 83, 119, 132, 230, 241, 244, 245, 246, 247, 248, 334, 356
dramatic irony 38, 41, 84, 88, 145, 146, 165
dream 45, 77, 79, 91, 97, 105, 125, 140, 144, 158, 159, 161, 169, 209, 214, 235, 237, 270, 274, 320, 378, 381
Driver, Tom 374
Dunbar, Paul 188, 191, 192, 374

E

Edinger, Edward 139, 221, 359, 374
edit 51, 143, 276, 372
ego 19, 75, 116, 120, 122, 138, 139, 142, 165, 202, 203, 205, 211, 215, 316, 320, 359, 374
Ego and Archetype 359, 374
Elements of Style 31, 384
eleven 132, 155, 173, 212, 222, 223, 294
elide 252
Eliot, T.S. 105
elision 252
Elizabethan 8, 81, 227, 228, 229, 230, 231, 232, 233, 236, 239, 240, 250, 258, 288, 289, 290, 291
Elizabeth I 232, 233, 237, 239, 244
ellipsis 67
Ellis, Havelock 13, 294, 374
Emerson, Ralph Waldo 12, 19, 20, 92, 93, 100, 109, 111, 115, 117, 129, 220, 359, 374, 383
emotional impact 27
Endicott, John 83, 84, 124, 126, 127, 142, 168
"The Enemy" 205, 215
England 41, 42, 91, 92, 94, 97, 105, 123, 125, 126, 128, 129, 130, 176, 178, 189, 200, 208, 217, 227, 233, 236, 237, 238, 239, 244, 250, 289, 291, 292, 294, 295, 329
English Renaissance 8, 12, 13, 227, 289
English sonnet 235
Enjambment 252, 253, 255
esprit de corps 20, 189, 200, 202, 203, 210, 214, 215
essay 7, 15, 17, 18, 63, 65, 67, 68, 69, 73, 76, 90, 109, 115, 143, 147, 162, 173, 179, 180, 288, 326, 335, 344
  analytical 20, 74, 179
  personal 20, 68, 69
essay topics 179, 180
ethos 76, 77, 78, 80

Evangeline 98, 101, 102
Eve 150, 151
evil 29, 39, 43, 91, 120, 127, 128, 137, 139, 151, 155, 158, 162, 167, 177, 186, 198, 208, 230, 234, 240, 244, 250, 273, 309, 315
exposition 26, 88
extroverted 139
eye 45, 68, 116, 149, 152, 203, 211, 221, 313, 315, 335, 365

F

fable 88
The Faerie Queene 54, 236, 237, 244, 245
fairy tale 24, 150, 151, 153, 224, 360
faith 29, 84, 131, 157, 158, 160, 161, 168, 169, 176, 248, 316
fall 12, 13, 25, 50, 85, 107, 139, 142, 177, 218, 229, 230, 247, 261, 270
falling action 22, 88
The Fantasticks 42, 53, 114, 123, 143, 144, 147, 374, 378
Farewell to Manzanar 206, 215, 361, 377
Fates 186
fear 19, 27, 33, 38, 39, 40, 50, 118, 120, 136, 153, 154, 155, 156, 167, 179, 201, 206, 214, 217, 246, 297, 302, 307
Feeling 70, 286
feet 11, 15, 22, 69, 71, 80, 92, 110, 122, 125, 134, 141, 178, 248, 250, 252, 253, 256, 275, 277, 285, 305, 335
feminine 132, 136, 150, 152, 172, 253, 254
fertility 11, 130, 183
Feste 230, 259
fiction 5, 12, 15, 16, 17, 18, 19, 20, 22, 24, 26, 30, 31, 34, 50, 53, 54, 91, 92, 116, 167, 195, 198, 213, 214, 217, 224, 317, 361, 377, 381, 385
figurative language 20, 68, 72, 76, 82, 86, 102, 105, 106, 107, 116, 122, 142, 165, 173, 174, 181, 192, 195, 218
film 5, 7, 34, 41, 43, 44, 45, 145, 146, 194, 195, 227, 230, 231, 326, 360
filmmaking 162
Finch, Atticus 16, 49, 194, 199, 205
fire 85, 104, 114, 137, 139, 158, 159, 164, 171, 178, 238, 245, 246, 247, 276, 290, 319, 355, 363, 368, 380
The First Folio 227, 291, 371
Fitzgerald, John 31, 380
Five-Minute Grammar 324
flame 159, 169
flashback 49
Flaubert, Gustave 123, 213, 375
"Flight" 54
fluency 65, 67, 73, 80, 180, 182, 324

foil 88

Folger Library 227, 231, 384

food 13, 94, 225, 240, 250, 258, 272, 284, 311, 349

foot 86, 128, 250, 252, 253, 254, 256, 305, 332

Foote, Horton 194, 195, 385

foreshadowing 88, 150, 196

forest 84, 86, 119, 124, 125, 126, 150, 152, 157, 158, 167, 171, 172, 177, 178, 179, 192, 234, 256

form 11, 12, 17, 24, 54, 63, 66, 67, 74, 75, 87, 88, 99, 106, 116, 122, 125, 134, 139, 142, 166, 172, 203, 204, 205, 206, 207, 208, 209, 210, 212, 225, 251, 252, 298, 299, 301, 307, 311, 327, 337, 339, 343, 344, 347, 348, 351

Forsyth, Frederick 16, 20, 23, 63, 119, 120, 121, 122, 210, 212, 215, 360, 375, 380

"For Whom the Bell Tolls" 361

four 43, 69, 70, 71, 74, 78, 79, 84, 107, 119, 121, 122, 123, 128, 129, 133, 136, 137, 139, 143, 147, 148, 152, 158, 162, 187, 190, 191, 198, 199, 205, 210, 211, 221, 223, 228, 229, 235, 250, 251, 265, 280, 288, 294, 329, 332, 336, 354, 378, 382

fourth wall 53, 84

Frankl, Viktor 207, 208, 360, 375

Freud, Sigmund 6, 12, 19, 99, 116, 122, 123, 138, 139, 142, 155, 205, 215, 220, 384

Freud and Jung 12, 123, 138

friendship 7, 33, 50, 62, 119, 129, 186, 189, 196, 197, 198, 202, 204, 217, 219, 258, 259, 263

Frost, Robert 105, 258, 343, 375

Fuller, Margaret 92

G

garden 90, 101, 106, 150, 151, 152, 169, 171, 182, 233, 292, 364

gardener 150

gender 16, 34, 45, 184, 188, 196, 205, 209, 239, 299, 331, 345

generalization 64, 65, 87, 93

Geneva Convention 204

Genevan Bible 232

genre 31, 52, 53, 88, 116, 122, 229, 299

Gershwin, George 333

Gershwin, Ira 12, 375

gerund 295, 325, 327, 330, 335, 336

gift 30, 71, 102, 115, 151, 213, 339

The Globe Theatre 237

gloom 142, 152, 154, 158, 168, 173

god 85, 118, 132, 135, 136, 309, 317

goddess 75, 84, 119, 130, 135, 271

gods 118, 130, 135, 295, 309

gold 21, 98, 137, 152, 169, 172, 183, 186, 224, 248, 301, 333, 336

Gothic 134, 221

grammar 8, 13, 89, 232, 233, 295, 299, 303, 324, 326, 341, 382

"The Grave" 49

Great Britain 97, 295

Great Depression 205

Greek 8, 12, 20, 22, 27, 76, 85, 86, 88, 102, 111, 113, 118, 130, 133, 134, 135, 186, 222, 294, 295, 296, 297, 298, 299, 300, 301, 303, 308, 309, 316, 333, 347, 348, 360, 372, 380

Greek roots 20, 294

Greeks 76, 221, 309

green 74, 106, 107, 108, 125, 134, 136, 137, 177, 248, 270, 272, 348, 359, 368

Greenblatt, Stephen 227, 292, 375, 383, 384

"Guests of the Nation" 203, 215

gules 173

H

Hades 118, 135

Hadrian's Wall 294

hair 45, 58, 59, 70, 127, 137, 172, 177, 245, 264, 265, 266, 270, 277, 302

Hall, Peter 229

Halprin, Anna 188, 375

hamartia 27, 213

Hamlet 109, 138, 158, 235, 237, 383

hand 42, 70, 84, 90, 105, 106, 112, 124, 125, 127, 135, 137, 145, 172, 176, 177, 178, 179, 183, 185, 212, 244, 245, 248, 249, 250, 266, 271, 274, 282, 283, 285, 286, 287, 334, 342, 345, 347

Hansberry, Lorraine 16, 20, 189, 209, 376, 382

Harlem 188, 189, 190, 191, 193, 194

Harlem Renaissance 188, 189, 190, 191, 193, 194

Harmony 193

harmony 150, 152, 193, 201, 213, 217, 220, 221, 222, 299, 316

Harper, Michael S. 105, 215, 371, 373, 374, 376, 377, 380

Hawthorne, A Life 385

Hawthorne, Nathaniel 6, 7, 16, 20, 21, 39, 54, 64, 83, 84, 85, 86, 91, 92, 93, 97, 98, 100, 101, 102, 103, 117, 122, 123, 124, 128, 129, 130, 131, 134, 135, 139, 142, 143, 144, 146, 147, 148, 149, 151, 153, 154, 155, 156, 157, 158, 159, 161, 162, 163, 164, 165, 166, 167, 168, 170, 171, 172, 173, 174, 175, 176, 177, 181, 182, 183, 184, 185, 186, 200, 227, 317, 360, 376, 379, 380, 381, 385

Hawthorne, Sophia Peabody 92, 129, 130, 299

"He's Mine!" 57

heart 16, 26, 30, 69, 70, 84, 85, 92, 102, 109, 110, 120, 125, 126, 128, 131, 136, 152, 154, 155, 169, 175, 176, 177, 178, 179, 182, 183, 184, 192, 193, 214, 218, 231, 232, 245, 250, 353, 357, 360, 364, 366

Heath, Malcomb 27, 370, 376

"The Heathen" 204, 215

heaven 116, 137, 157, 158, 160, 179, 223, 246, 253

Heminges and Condell 234

hemlock 111, 112

Henry, Patrick 77, 78, 80, 376

Heritage of Humanity 189, 200, 202

hero 25, 32, 88, 118, 119, 120, 121, 122, 144, 145, 158, 194, 246, 356, 372, 381

hero's journey 119, 120, 121, 122

heroic couplet 88

Hierarchy of Needs 7, 198

Hill, Georgine Susan White 13

History 21, 191, 235, 239, 264, 289, 375, 376, 379, 382

"Hoboken Brawl" 250

Holiday, Billie 192, 377

Hollis, James 156, 213, 361, 377

Holocaust 105, 207, 212, 215, 383

Holocaust Poetry 105, 215, 383

home schematic 33, 46

homograph 348

homonym 347, 348

homophone 348

Houston, Jeanne Watatsuki and James D. 206, 361, 377

Houston, Texas 260, 342, 381

Houston Arboretum 107

Houston Chronicle 17, 377

How the Garcia Girls Lost Their Accents 54, 355, 370

Hubert, Karen 31, 377

Hubris 72, 88

"Hugging the Wind" 69

Hughes, Langston 20, 188, 190, 192, 209, 361, 377

humanitarian law 204

Hunt, Kellogg 18, 324, 325, 377

Hyde, Maggie 131, 377

hyperbole 72, 88

hyphen 344

hypothesis 76, 309

I

I Am a Camera 16, 385

I Know Why the Caged Bird Sings 41, 54, 191, 355, 370, 377

iamb 252

iambic pentameter 106, 228, 251, 252, 253

Id 138

illusion 159, 161, 163

imagery 11, 64, 68, 69, 142, 144, 166, 170, 181, 205, 206, 218

Images of Childhood 32, 34, 378

imago Dei 221

imago mundi 132, 133

immortality 118, 135, 137, 142, 148, 301

incident 34, 35, 40, 49, 68, 128, 147, 192, 194, 195, 206, 284, 373

independent clause 325, 330, 331

indirect object 329, 331, 334, 340

individuation 11, 139, 202, 203

Industrial Revolution 91

Infinitive 295, 325, 327, 330, 336, 337, 338

Inhumanity 201, 220, 319

interjection 329

internet 26, 201, 221, 302

Introducing Jung 377

introduction 9, 18, 35, 63, 64, 65, 68, 74, 76, 131, 140, 143, 144, 150, 164, 173, 227, 230, 288, 289, 292, 352, 370, 376, 384

introverted 139

Ireland 98, 203, 237, 306, 340

irony
  dramatic, verbal, irony of situation 38, 41, 79, 83, 84, 88, 142, 145, 146, 165, 181, 192, 197, 205, 206, 219, 229, 298

Italian sonnet 106, 234

italics 74, 143, 343

items in a series 74, 341, 342

J

Jacobean 8, 236, 289

jargon 257

"Joe King" 69

Johnson, James Weldon 190, 361

Jones, Tom and Harvey Schmidt 53, 143, 144, 145, 359, 374, 378

journal 5, 7, 13, 19, 20, 21, 23, 24, 27, 28, 30, 32, 33, 34, 35, 40, 41, 43, 44, 45, 48, 92, 93, 101, 111, 113, 114, 121, 140, 147, 148, 149, 153, 156, 157, 158, 159, 161, 162, 163, 164, 165, 173, 179, 187, 192, 194, 195, 204, 205, 206, 207, 208, 209, 210, 211, 212, 213, 215, 216, 217, 219, 220, 232, 240, 270, 280, 285, 354

journey 3, 13, 16, 17, 21, 25, 32, 36, 42, 84, 86, 118, 119, 120, 121, 122, 131, 144, 145, 146, 151, 152, 157, 158, 160, 171, 212, 213, 222, 223, 245, 254, 351, 354, 368, 378

Jung 11, 12, 19, 32, 39, 87, 109, 116, 117, 119, 123, 131, 136, 137, 138, 139, 145, 153, 154, 155, 156, 157, 161, 162, 189, 202, 203, 207, 215, 220, 221, 338, 376, 377, 378, 384

Junior Great Books 75

K

Kidd, Sue Monk 16, 30, 362, 378
Kimball, Robert 375
King, Jr., Martin Luther 77, 79, 80, 378
King, Stephen 31, 362, 378
Kirby, Dan 32, 378
kiss 78, 150, 151, 173, 263
Knowles, John 20, 188, 189, 208, 217, 363, 378
Kohlberg, Lawrence 20, 189, 195, 199, 205, 220, 373, 378
Krull, Kathleen 31, 379

L

labyrinth 42, 69, 170, 221, 222, 223, 379
Lachesis 186
Laing, Jennifer 379
lamb's wool 241
Latin 86, 186, 232, 275, 277, 282, 284, 294, 295
  pronunciation 321, 322
  roots 20, 244, 294, 296, 297, 298, 299, 300, 301, 302, 303, 304, 305, 306, 307, 308, 309, 310, 311, 312, 313, 314, 315, 380
  sayings 20, 72, 220, 315, 316, 318
Leaf Storm and Other Stories 364, 380
Learning by Teaching 380
Lee, Harper 16, 20, 49, 101, 105, 188, 194, 196, 197, 198, 205, 215, 363, 371, 372, 373, 374, 376, 377, 379, 380, 382, 385
legacy 200, 201, 202
legend 72, 102, 118, 196, 338
Les Romanesques 143
lie/lay 346
life 12, 13, 15, 16, 17, 18, 19, 20, 21, 23, 25, 28, 30, 31, 32, 33, 34, 36, 37, 38, 39, 40, 42, 43, 44, 54, 67, 68, 69, 71, 72, 76, 81, 84, 85, 86, 87, 90, 91, 92, 93, 100, 102, 103, 104, 105, 106, 107, 109, 110, 111, 112, 113, 115, 117, 118, 119, 120, 121, 122, 123, 124, 125, 126, 127, 128, 129, 130, 131, 132, 133, 135, 136, 137, 138, 139, 142, 143, 144, 145, 146, 147, 148, 149, 150, 151, 152, 153, 154, 155, 156, 157, 158, 159, 160, 161, 162, 163, 165, 166, 167, 168, 170, 171, 172, 173, 174, 177, 178, 182, 183, 184, 185, 186, 187, 189, 190, 191, 193, 194, 195, 196, 198, 199, 201, 204, 206, 207, 208, 212, 213, 214, 221, 222, 223, 224, 225, 227, 228, 229, 230, 231, 232, 233, 234, 239, 240, 247, 248, 259, 265, 286, 288, 289, 292, 294, 295, 296, 297, 298, 299, 301, 305, 306, 307, 309, 312, 314, 315, 316, 317, 318, 319, 333, 338, 341, 353, 354, 358, 361, 362, 363, 364, 365, 367, 369, 373, 374, 375, 377, 378, 384, 385

life/death/life 118, 136, 142, 143, 144, 146, 147, 148, 149, 150, 151, 153, 162, 222, 230
light 28, 58, 59, 63, 71, 72, 86, 102, 104, 109, 112, 114, 124, 126, 132, 133, 134, 136, 137, 142, 144, 145, 146, 148, 149, 152, 155, 158, 159, 162, 163, 166, 170, 172, 183, 184, 186, 196, 197, 221, 230, 243, 244, 272, 276, 303, 359, 362, 366
lightning 152, 338
Lincoln, Abraham 78, 79, 91, 99, 100, 379
Lindy Hop 193, 380
line 33, 55, 83, 88, 89, 90, 97, 103, 128, 163, 200, 226, 233, 242, 243, 251, 252, 253, 254, 255, 256, 257, 276, 287, 291, 327, 330, 333, 344, 352, 359, 385
Linklater, Kristin 252, 254, 289, 379
literal 85, 88, 114, 158, 159, 160, 165, 168, 182
literary terms 81, 87, 111, 251
Literature as Exploration 229, 290, 382
Locke, Alain 189
logic 76, 92, 232, 270
logical appeals 77
logos 76, 77, 78, 80
London 15, 94, 95, 129, 138, 200, 211, 233, 234, 236, 237, 238, 239, 288, 290, 292, 294, 335, 339, 370, 372, 373, 376, 377, 381
London, Jack 204, 363, 379
Longfellow, Henry Wadsworth 91, 93, 98, 99, 100, 101, 102, 106, 128, 129, 234, 379
long lines 252, 253
losses and gains 33
love 3, 11, 15, 16, 17, 24, 25, 29, 35, 39, 45, 50, 56, 58, 59, 70, 84, 85, 102, 106, 120, 122, 125, 129, 130, 136, 142, 143, 144, 145, 146, 147, 148, 151, 152, 166, 167, 168, 171, 172, 173, 174, 178, 182, 183, 185, 189, 208, 214, 222, 224, 229, 230, 231, 232, 234, 235, 236, 244, 249, 253, 256, 258, 259, 265, 266, 272, 277, 282, 284, 288, 296, 297, 318, 320, 326, 332, 333, 334, 353, 355, 361, 364
love motif 85, 136
Lowell, Robert 105, 379
lyric 88, 106

M

Macbeth 98, 228, 235, 238
magazines 33, 75, 224, 261, 264
magic 11, 22, 45, 119, 132, 259, 301, 363, 383
main idea 65, 67, 84, 90
Mama Makes up Her Mind 69
Mama Mia 15
Man's Search for Meaning 207, 215, 360, 375
Mandala 221, 222
Mandalas of the World 373

Manning, Frankie 193, 380

Marlowe, Christopher 232, 233, 236, 290, 291, 308

Marquez, Gabriel Garcia 54, 364, 380

Mask 137, 144, 145, 146, 151, 155, 192, 245, 358, 374

Maslow, Abraham 20, 189, 195, 198, 202, 205, 220, 380

Maypole 11, 13, 54, 83, 84, 86, 91, 103, 122, 123, 124, 125, 126, 127, 128, 130, 131, 134, 135, 140, 141, 142, 143, 144, 162, 168, 200, 227, 376

"The Maypole of Merry Mount" 54, 83, 84, 86, 91, 103, 122, 123, 124, 130, 134, 135, 140, 141, 143, 144, 162, 168, 200, 227, 376

maze 82, 221

McGuinness, Michael 131, 377

McKay, Claude 20, 188, 190, 192, 380

Melville, Herman 92, 98, 364

memoir 68

Mercier, Jeanne Felicie 13

Meredith, Robert 31, 380

metaphor 11, 13, 15, 51, 72, 76, 80, 82, 88, 102, 103, 104, 106, 142, 144, 145, 146, 149, 165, 173, 174, 218, 224, 229, 233, 256, 259

meteor 171, 177, 183, 184

meter 88, 106, 107, 227, 251, 252, 257

metonymy 88

metric 252, 253, 254

Millay, Edna St. Vincent 105

"The Minister's Black Veil" 84, 122, 153, 155, 162

Minos 221, 222

Minotaur 221, 222

mirror 60, 83, 85, 104, 148, 149, 152, 171, 188, 201, 264, 280, 384

model for essay writing 63

moirae 186

mood 30, 56, 68, 78, 82, 88, 122, 142, 196

moon 85, 144, 145, 146, 148, 171, 221, 231, 364

moral ambiguity 20, 165, 181, 202, 205, 206, 209, 215, 219

moral exemplar 167, 168

moral relativism 165, 181, 205

mosaics 294

Mosses from an Old Manse 360, 376

mother 3, 13, 16, 42, 43, 56, 70, 127, 128, 130, 132, 135, 145, 146, 167, 169, 171, 172, 173, 176, 177, 178, 183, 192, 203, 233, 245, 248, 283, 300, 306, 310, 311, 314, 316, 319, 332, 334, 377

motif 26, 85, 118, 121, 122, 135, 136, 142, 143, 145, 150, 151, 296

motive 22, 25, 47, 167, 198

Murray, Donald 32, 68, 380

Musson, Celestine 13

Musson, Germain 13

mystery 29, 56, 81, 101, 123, 125, 128, 130, 148, 171, 176, 224, 244, 258, 259, 276, 278, 280, 285, 286, 334

myth 50, 89, 119, 131, 133, 139, 196, 197, 198, 222, 356, 372, 379

mythology 11, 67, 86, 117, 118, 119, 131, 132, 133, 134, 135, 137, 150, 152, 157, 171, 173, 186, 309, 360, 372, 376, 379

N

narration 53, 55, 89

narrative poem 54, 89, 101, 234

National Public Radio 69

nature 15, 23, 68, 72, 77, 81, 92, 100, 101, 102, 104, 105, 106, 107, 117, 118, 119, 131, 132, 148, 156, 166, 175, 176, 180, 182, 184, 201, 203, 210, 218, 228, 229, 231, 301, 309, 320, 334, 335, 339, 379

needle 16, 106, 167, 171, 186, 187

needlework 176, 183, 186

Neruda, Pablo 105, 200, 333, 380

Newspaper 66, 74, 97, 258, 259, 260, 267, 270, 274, 280, 281, 282, 283, 284, 285, 332, 338

New England 41, 91, 92, 126, 128, 130, 178, 189, 200, 208, 217, 239

New Orleans 13, 333, 385

Night 13, 54, 81, 97, 102, 152, 206, 215, 227, 228, 229, 230, 231, 235, 237, 240, 241, 243, 244, 245, 251, 254, 255, 256, 257, 258, 259, 288, 289, 291, 292, 316, 320, 334, 348, 362, 365, 368, 377, 378, 384, 385

nineteenth century 92, 93, 100, 101, 109, 149, 165, 167, 333

Nixon, Joan Lowery 31, 34, 381

Nobel Prize 96, 200, 326, 330

nonessential clause 342

notebook 20, 163, 268, 276, 280, 341

noun 295, 297, 299, 305, 311, 314, 325, 326, 327, 329, 330, 331, 332, 340, 342, 343, 344, 347, 348

noun clause 331, 340

Novakovich, Josip 31, 381

numbers 73, 79, 137, 143, 146, 159, 165, 168, 181, 205, 211, 223, 334, 344

Nunn, Trevor 231, 385

O

O'Connor, Frank 20, 203, 365, 381

Obama, Barack 78, 79, 381

obedience 335

objective complement 329

Oliver, Mary 20, 105, 106, 381

Onions, C.T. 290
onomatopoeia 89
opposites 72, 79, 83, 87, 137, 139, 146, 165, 166,
    172, 182, 223, 255, 309
organization 13, 66, 67, 68, 80, 106, 143, 272
Othello 112, 228, 235, 384
Our Town 144
Ovid 143, 232, 318, 319
Oxymoron 72, 82, 89, 142, 165, 173

P

pace 22, 48, 73, 146, 320
paradigm shift 27, 28, 29, 31, 44, 72
paradise 104, 131, 133, 135, 136, 139, 142, 150,
    151, 152, 153, 162, 171, 182, 223
paradox 197, 202, 213
parallel 67, 73, 79, 104, 117, 119, 133, 139, 194
parallelism 76, 79, 89
paranoia 154, 156
paraphrase 67
Parcae 186
parentheses 28, 55, 67, 310, 344
parenthetical reference 64, 66, 182
Participial Phrase 330
participle 327, 332, 334, 351
passive voice 73, 180, 329, 350, 351
path 13, 70, 107, 108, 113, 144, 152, 158, 177, 189,
    222, 223, 303, 310, 315
pathos 76, 77, 78, 80, 189, 303
patriarchal 168, 183, 184, 186
Payne, Iden 144
Peabody, Sophia 129, 130
pearl 166, 167, 171, 172, 176, 177, 178, 179, 181,
    183, 184, 185, 187, 204, 205, 206, 356, 371
"The Peascods" 140
Peck, Gregory 194, 385
pentameter 106, 228, 251, 252, 253
period 67, 91, 93, 136, 140, 188, 191, 193, 221, 227,
    230, 239, 251, 255, 258, 266, 293, 294, 296,
    298, 308, 343, 344
persecution 156
Persephone 118, 135
person 23, 25, 27, 28, 31, 32, 33, 34, 35, 36, 37, 38,
    49, 66, 68, 72, 75, 77, 87, 89, 90, 103, 112,
    113, 119, 120, 121, 130, 131, 134, 136, 139,
    154, 160, 163, 179, 180, 185, 186, 195, 198,
    203, 204, 208, 209, 212, 214, 217, 221, 231,
    239, 270, 294, 297, 300, 303, 307, 311, 313,
    317, 326, 327, 339, 340, 350, 353
persona 31, 137, 145, 151, 154
personification 82, 89, 103, 142, 165, 173, 174, 218
perspective 17, 33, 34, 53, 166, 203, 215
persuasive 75, 78
philos 27

philosophy 12, 19, 20, 21, 72, 81, 86, 92, 100, 104,
    105, 109, 111, 115, 116, 122, 136, 137, 142,
    190, 197, 220, 229, 236, 286, 289, 290, 295,
    316, 374, 378
phrase 20, 71, 73, 79, 84, 88, 103, 232, 252, 321,
    326, 328, 330, 331, 332, 337, 338, 342
phrases 12, 67, 73, 87, 89, 103, 143, 230, 233, 252,
    255, 256, 295, 316, 324, 325, 328, 330, 341,
    342, 345
phrasing 251, 252, 254
Pierce, Franklin 128, 129
pilgrim 15, 16, 100, 101, 223, 296, 358, 373
The Pilgrimage 214, 357
Pilgrim at Tinker Creek 15, 100, 101, 358, 373
pine 107, 108, 126, 130, 348
pink 16, 157, 158, 340
plagiarism 25, 26
Plato 12, 19, 75, 77, 109, 111, 112, 113, 114, 135,
    143, 144, 145, 146, 157, 220, 333, 365, 370,
    371, 378, 381, 382, 384
Plautius 294
playwright 191, 194, 210, 232, 235, 251
play production 55
plot 15, 16, 22, 23, 24, 25, 26, 27, 28, 32, 33, 34, 35,
    36, 37, 38, 39, 40, 45, 46, 47, 48, 49, 50, 51,
    52, 53, 54, 55, 56, 81, 83, 87, 105, 119, 122,
    123, 131, 144, 146, 150, 162, 165, 166, 175,
    181, 183, 184, 189, 196, 204, 210, 217, 229,
    237, 238, 258, 259, 307, 331, 353
Poe, Edgar Allan 92, 93, 98, 365
Poetics 355, 370, 376
poetry 17, 19, 82, 88, 90, 92, 101, 102, 103, 104,
    105, 107, 188, 190, 191, 201, 215, 224, 253,
    371, 373, 374, 375, 376, 377, 380, 381, 383
point of view 89, 234
Portable Plato 113, 365, 371, 381, 382
Porter, Katherine Anne 49, 366, 382
Poseidon 221, 222
possessions 32, 86
possessive 343, 349, 350
power 15, 25, 37, 43, 44, 75, 82, 85, 86, 87, 91, 110,
    113, 119, 120, 135, 137, 148, 151, 155, 168,
    171, 172, 177, 184, 186, 188, 202, 230, 234,
    244, 259, 286, 294, 305, 312, 314, 316, 353,
    356, 357, 360, 372
practical exemplar 168
practice sentences 331
predicate 73, 325, 326, 327, 329, 331, 332, 333, 334,
    335, 336, 337, 338, 340
predicate adjective 327, 329, 334, 335
predicate nominative 326, 327, 329, 331, 334, 336,
    337, 340
preposition 73, 327, 328, 330, 331, 338, 350
prepositional phrase 330, 331, 332

principled conscience 199

private 109, 134, 165, 166, 167, 174, 175, 176, 182, 185, 208, 228, 234, 240

private vs. public 165, 167, 174

producing a play 55

pronoun 180, 326, 327, 329, 330, 331, 345, 346, 349, 350

  demonstrative 326

  indefinite 345

  interrogative 326

  personal 104, 326, 343

  reflexive 326

  relative 326, 331

pronoun agreement 331, 345, 346

pronunciation 81, 256, 302, 316, 321, 322, 323, 348

proofread 72, 143, 276, 339

prose 82, 106, 142, 144, 188, 228, 251, 253, 257, 290, 356, 373

protagonist 22, 23, 34, 87, 89

proverbs 111

Prynne, Hester 16, 103, 128, 166, 167, 168, 172, 175, 180, 182, 183, 184, 186

psyche 119, 154, 202

Psychology 20, 21, 75, 116, 122, 131, 138, 142, 156, 199, 220, 221, 296, 385

public 60, 69, 75, 96, 129, 165, 166, 167, 174, 176, 182, 183, 185, 190, 222, 228, 255, 294, 299, 301, 316, 338, 371

punctuation 67, 73, 180, 251, 252, 253, 254, 255, 341, 343, 344

Puritans 73, 84, 91, 123, 124, 126, 127, 128, 130, 131, 142, 165, 167, 168, 174, 175, 176, 183, 185, 186, 200, 227, 228, 231, 233, 234

purple 108, 137, 151, 333, 368

Q

quadrant 223

quaternity 221

quest letter 13, 353, 354

quilt 13, 186, 187

quotations 66, 67, 74, 180, 205, 210, 211, 228, 370

quotation marks 67, 74, 143, 343, 344

R

rainbow 104, 130, 137, 210

A Raisin in the Sun 16, 189, 209, 215, 376, 382

Rape of Lucrece 234, 384

"Rappaccini's Daughter" 122, 149, 150, 151, 162, 168, 317, 376

reading list 12, 224, 355

Reagan, Ronald 78, 79, 382

rebirth 85, 118, 121, 130, 133, 135, 136, 142, 143, 146, 147, 148, 151, 152, 158, 171, 172, 185, 230, 236, 259

recipe 173, 225

recognition 18, 25, 27, 28, 31, 32, 164, 191, 296, 303, 306, 339

red 71, 106, 108, 121, 158, 170, 173, 183, 245, 246, 247, 248, 250, 265, 313, 317, 332, 342, 358

redemption 83, 119, 128, 146, 152, 166, 168, 170, 181, 296

Red Cross Knight 245, 246, 248, 250

reform 92, 165, 167, 168, 210, 299

rejection 123, 128, 154, 176

repression 154, 155

The Republic 112, 113, 114, 157, 381, 382

Repunzel 150

resolution 26, 35, 56, 83, 88, 89, 259, 307

response group 51

retained object 329

revenge 25, 38, 84, 166, 167, 178, 224, 230, 258, 284, 334

reversal 27, 29, 31

revision 51

Reynolds, David 128, 167, 382

rhetoric 19, 75, 76, 80, 232, 255, 256, 355, 370, 373, 381

rhetorical device 77, 78, 79, 80, 233, 255, 256

rhyme 89, 106, 107, 192, 235, 251, 252, 253

rhymed couplet 235, 252

Richard II 104, 235, 237, 384

righteousness 200, 202, 215, 258

Rillieux, Marie Antoinette 13

Rillieux, Marie Celeste 13

Rillieux, Vincent 13

The Ring of Gyges 19, 113

rise/raise 347

rising action 22, 89

rites of passage 189, 217

ritual 13, 37, 222, 230, 352

road 69, 70, 146, 158, 183, 213, 222, 331, 332, 335, 343, 361, 362

Rodenburg, Patsy 252, 254, 255, 290, 382

Romance 235

Romans 130, 294, 295, 318

Romanticism 89

Romeo and Juliet 144, 145, 150, 228, 235, 236, 253, 384

Roosevelt, Franklin Delano 78, 79, 80, 334, 382

Rose 171

Rosenblatt, Louise 32, 81, 229, 290, 382

Rostand, Edmund 143, 366

Royal Shakespeare Company 288, 291

rules of civility 202, 209, 215

"Rumpelstiltskin" 150

run-on 73

S

sable 173

Sacred Marriage 120

Sacrifice 24, 37, 112, 118, 120, 121, 130, 136, 137, 145, 146, 150, 151, 152, 153, 155, 158, 159, 162, 168, 173, 192, 221, 222, 231, 298

"St. George and the Dragon" 230, 244

Salem 102, 128, 129, 157, 158, 192, 213, 291, 379

salutation 342, 343

Sandburg, Carl 105, 383

sandwiching 73

savior 150, 151, 153, 219, 244, 248, 250

Savoy 193, 380

scansion 252, 254

The Scarlet Letter 13, 16, 18, 21, 86, 98, 103, 128, 129, 164, 165, 166, 168, 170, 173, 174, 175, 179, 181, 182, 183, 184, 185, 186, 187, 360, 370, 376, 381, 383

Schiff, Hilda 105, 215, 383

Scholastic Art & Writing Awards 13, 17, 20, 49, 383

Scotland, PA 228

Scottsboro Trial 194

Script 47, 48, 53, 54, 55, 56, 240, 257

Seasons 69, 85, 118, 133, 135, 142, 144, 146, 147, 151, 196, 198, 222

Secret 16, 30, 32, 54, 68, 79, 135, 154, 155, 156, 166, 168, 170, 172, 174, 175, 177, 178, 197, 249, 258, 280, 285, 316, 351, 357, 362, 378, 384

The Secret Life of Bees 16, 30, 362, 378

Self 19, 32, 39, 61, 70, 72, 92, 109, 110, 120, 136, 139, 147, 151, 152, 155, 171, 172, 177, 185, 189, 198, 199, 202, 216, 217, 221, 230, 231, 269, 297, 298, 326, 344, 354, 374

self-actualization 198, 202

"Self-Reliance" 19, 92, 109, 374

semicolon 74, 255, 342

sentence structure 18, 73, 296

A Separate Peace 188, 189, 208, 215, 217, 219, 363, 378

setting 25, 26, 35, 37, 43, 52, 56, 68, 69, 83, 88, 89, 92, 124, 131, 133, 144, 145, 150, 162, 165, 189, 196, 203, 204, 205, 206, 207, 208, 209, 211, 212, 217, 236, 239, 258, 346, 349

seven 13, 65, 69, 70, 79, 98, 101, 128, 129, 137, 166, 172, 178, 186, 222, 223, 232, 255, 280, 360, 376

shadow 45, 71, 110, 125, 136, 151, 153, 154, 155, 156, 157, 159, 162, 163, 169, 170, 172, 174, 196, 202, 203, 207, 208, 215, 383

Shadow Magic 45, 383

shadow theory 155, 156, 157, 162, 203, 207, 215

Shakespeare 15, 20, 24, 54, 81, 104, 109, 112, 130, 138, 143, 144, 150, 158, 200, 224, 227, 228, 229, 230, 231, 232, 233, 234, 235, 236, 237, 238, 239, 240, 250, 251, 252, 253, 254, 255, 256, 257, 258, 259, 288, 289, 290, 291, 292, 293, 308, 320, 353, 370, 371, 372, 375, 376, 377, 379, 381, 382, 383, 384, 385

shared line 252, 253

Shaw, George Bernard 99, 201, 384

She's the Man 228

short fiction 17, 19, 20, 22, 26, 50, 54, 195, 361

short line 252, 253

short story 20, 23, 24, 29, 34, 43, 49, 50, 51, 54, 55, 74, 89, 92, 100, 124, 134, 203, 204, 205, 209, 210, 227, 372, 374, 384

Show, don't tell 51

silver 21, 105, 152, 245

simile 82, 89, 165, 173, 174, 218, 306

sin 154, 155, 156, 157, 159, 160, 161, 170, 174, 175, 176, 185, 223, 364

sit/set 346

skeleton 147, 148

sky 69, 70, 71, 107, 108, 158, 172, 177, 183

Sleeping Beauty 150

smoke 159, 246, 247, 312, 366

snake 104, 158

snapshot 32, 82

social contract 199

Socrates 76, 77, 109, 110, 111, 112, 135, 333, 381

Socratic method 75, 111

sonnet
  Petrarchan 107, 234
  Shakespearean 235

Sophists 75, 113

Soul 15, 110, 112, 130, 133, 137, 148, 152, 174, 193, 213, 214

South 43, 96, 129, 188, 189, 191, 204, 297, 364, 378, 379

Southampton 96, 234

spelling 67, 72, 128, 143, 346, 347, 348

Spenser, Edmund 54, 236, 237, 244, 245, 384

sphere 152, 171, 172, 173, 183

spider 108, 152, 353

spirit 32, 52, 110, 131, 145, 155, 163, 168, 171, 182, 183, 184, 193, 200, 202, 229, 259, 281, 307, 314

spondaic foot 252

spring 11, 82, 92, 100, 130, 131, 135, 136, 137, 144, 169, 190, 191, 230, 246, 297

square 172, 187, 221, 226, 292, 384

staccato 73

Standish, Miles 227

stanza 90

stars 102, 108, 123, 145, 158, 213, 316, 365

static 218, 335
Steinbeck, John 54, 367, 384
Stevens, Anthony 155, 384
stock devices 234, 256
story elements 25, 34, 44, 83, 119, 197
"Strange Fruit" 192, 377
stress 26, 70, 221, 253, 255
student models 20, 181
style 18, 24, 29, 30, 31, 52, 69, 86, 88, 113, 116, 123, 134, 142, 151, 189, 256, 274, 296, 353, 380, 384
sub-points 64
subject 31, 65, 68, 72, 73, 90, 104, 131, 141, 283, 314, 325, 326, 327, 329, 331, 332, 333, 334, 335, 336, 337, 338, 340, 345, 350
subject-verb agreement 331, 345
subtext 47, 48, 54
summary 36, 37, 65
sun 16, 23, 69, 82, 85, 118, 133, 137, 144, 145, 146, 152, 172, 189, 209, 214, 215, 222, 264, 376, 380, 382
sunshine 49, 85, 148, 152, 172
superego 19, 84, 116, 138, 140, 142, 155, 165, 205, 215, 258
support 3, 12, 16, 18, 51, 63, 65, 67, 76, 77, 84, 104, 105, 117, 123, 127, 142, 143, 146, 149, 153, 157, 158, 159, 162, 166, 171, 179, 180, 181, 182, 183, 189, 196, 201, 202, 205, 208, 211, 220, 254, 312, 316
swan song 112
syllable 252, 253, 254, 256, 323, 343
symbol 11, 13, 85, 86, 90, 117, 131, 132, 134, 137, 148, 149, 150, 154, 163, 171, 172, 174, 183, 185, 244, 254, 296, 318
symbolic 83, 85, 117, 118, 119, 120, 121, 130, 131, 132, 133, 150, 157, 159, 160, 162, 163, 182, 210, 222, 223, 259, 263, 317
Symbolic Illusions 162
symbolism 11, 39, 51, 85, 86, 117, 122, 123, 131, 132, 137, 142, 145, 147, 149, 150, 154, 156, 159, 162, 163, 164, 166, 170, 172, 181, 182, 183, 184, 187, 189, 197, 198, 205, 210, 222, 223, 263, 371
synchronicity 297
synecdoche 80, 90
synergistic 86, 201
synthesis 75, 310

T

t-unit 325
The Taming of the Shrew 227, 228, 235, 236
tasting party 13, 225
teens 34, 54
temptation 43, 132, 151, 157, 160, 161, 167, 189

tension 22, 23, 37, 38, 39, 40, 41, 43, 44, 45, 50, 51, 52, 54, 79, 81, 83, 87, 146, 165, 166, 172, 174, 175, 182, 193, 210, 214, 255, 259, 261, 309
tension of opposites 79, 83, 146, 165, 166, 172, 182, 309
Ten Things I Hate about You 228
terminable unit 324
textual support 18, 179, 180, 181, 182, 205, 211
theme 13, 24, 55, 56, 64, 84, 88, 90, 103, 117, 122, 123, 139, 142, 144, 146, 147, 149, 151, 155, 159, 162, 165, 166, 171, 189, 192, 197, 198, 205, 206, 259, 275, 306, 352, 353, 377
Theseus 69, 222
thesis 18, 64, 65, 67, 74, 75, 76, 77, 90, 161, 162, 173, 180, 181, 182, 309, 310
The unexamined life 112
Thoreau, Henry David 12, 20, 92, 94, 99, 100, 101, 102, 111, 333, 367, 384
thread 11, 16, 67, 69, 71, 125, 170, 171, 181, 183, 185, 186, 187, 222
Three 56, 68, 75, 91, 121, 171, 189, 240, 244, 265, 328, 334, 358, 377, 385
Three Fates 186
Three Times Three 56
Thurber, James 54, 367, 384
Thurman, Wallace 191
Time-Life 231
Tin Pan Alley 12, 333
To Kill a Mockingbird 16, 49, 188, 194, 195, 196, 198, 199, 205, 210, 215, 326, 363, 379, 385
Tobias, Ronald 24, 385
tolerance 20, 200, 201, 202, 203, 206, 215, 234, 303
tolerance for ambiguity 202
tone 30, 56, 68, 71, 78, 82, 90, 122, 125, 127, 142, 196, 257, 262, 280
"A Tooth for Paul Revere" 54, 370
topic 17, 19, 64, 65, 72, 74, 93, 141, 143, 165, 180, 239, 240, 255, 276, 278, 354
topic sentence 74
Touchstones 224
traditions 86, 123, 166, 216, 251, 294, 352, 380
tragedy 83, 136, 194, 198, 199, 235, 300, 333, 341
Transcendentalism 91, 92
transformation 24, 75, 177, 185, 224
transition 65, 306
tree 84, 85, 100, 104, 107, 108, 118, 123, 130, 131, 132, 133, 137, 139, 142, 145, 146, 150, 158, 163, 196, 198, 230, 240, 247, 328, 332, 333, 334, 336, 341, 346, 348
triangle 171
trimeter 252
trochaic foot 252, 253
troublesome words 72, 347

truth 29, 48, 65, 72, 74, 76, 79, 84, 85, 92, 97, 109, 110, 113, 131, 143, 146, 148, 151, 152, 155, 167, 170, 171, 172, 176, 177, 184, 196, 208, 213, 218, 228, 232, 249, 255, 307, 312, 313, 318, 321, 324, 333, 340, 349

Tunes for Bears to Dance To 212, 215

Twain, Mark 66, 96, 367, 385

Twelfth Cake 242

Twelfth Night 229, 230, 240, 241, 243, 244, 245, 334

Twelfth Night 13, 54, 81, 227, 228, 229, 230, 231, 235, 237, 251, 254, 255, 256, 257, 258, 259, 288, 289, 291, 292, 316, 348, 377, 378, 384, 385

Twenty Grand 54, 370, 371

Twice-Told Tales 91, 97, 129, 360, 376

two 12, 16, 17, 18, 21, 23, 26, 29, 33, 34, 35, 36, 37, 38, 39, 42, 43, 44, 45, 46, 47, 48, 53, 54, 56, 64, 70, 71, 72, 73, 74, 75, 76, 82, 84, 85, 87, 88, 89, 92, 97, 100, 103, 106, 107, 108, 111, 113, 114, 119, 120, 124, 127, 129, 133, 135, 136, 139, 143, 144, 145, 146, 149, 150, 155, 157, 159, 163, 165, 167, 170, 173, 174, 183, 190, 191, 194, 195, 196, 199, 203, 205, 208, 211, 215, 217, 218, 222, 223, 229, 232, 234, 235, 236, 240, 243, 250, 252, 254, 255, 256, 257, 258, 260, 261, 264, 265, 267, 269, 270, 271, 278, 291, 294, 302, 303, 305, 307, 308, 310, 314, 323, 324, 325, 326, 327, 328, 330, 333, 336, 338, 342, 344, 346, 347, 348, 350, 352, 353, 358

two-page spread 352, 353

U

Una 244, 245, 246, 247, 248, 249, 250

unconscious 87, 116, 117, 131, 136, 138, 139, 154, 155, 172, 202, 221, 296, 338

underlining 74, 143, 343

union of opposites 139

V

Valentines 312, 353, 357

Van Druten, Jon 16, 385

Van Tassel, Wesley 228, 251, 254, 292, 385

veil 84, 122, 153, 154, 155, 156, 162, 376

Venus and Adonis 234, 384

verb 73, 74, 302, 311, 327, 329, 330, 331, 332, 334, 335, 336, 337, 345, 347, 348, 349, 350, 351

verbal 83, 88, 138, 165

verb tense 349, 350

verse 107, 144, 191, 227, 228, 230, 231, 251, 252, 253, 254, 255, 257, 288, 290, 291, 292

verse speaking 228, 230, 231, 251, 252, 254, 288, 290, 291, 292

"A Very Old Man with Enormous Wings" 54

"The Veteran" 210, 215, 360, 375

voice 17, 31, 45, 52, 68, 70, 73, 178, 180, 254, 255, 263, 266, 271, 279, 280, 288, 289, 290, 329, 348, 350, 351, 379, 382

vowel 87, 254, 322

W

Walden 92, 99, 100, 333, 367, 384

wall 30, 53, 84, 105, 110, 152, 158, 222, 236, 294, 368, 382

Walton, Anthony 105, 215, 371, 373, 374, 376, 377, 380

wassail 230, 240, 241

water 18, 41, 56, 85, 95, 101, 103, 104, 108, 133, 145, 147, 148, 149, 151, 158, 159, 162, 171, 172, 174, 192, 230, 237, 241, 258, 265, 267, 279, 297, 303, 314, 316, 332, 336, 357

web 152, 353, 385

Wells, Stanley 292, 293, 385

Westbury, Virginia 385

Whispering Wind 16, 119, 120, 122, 212, 215, 375

white 13, 16, 31, 69, 79, 88, 107, 108, 119, 158, 167, 169, 184, 187, 189, 191, 192, 193, 194, 196, 204, 205, 222, 243, 244, 249, 318, 349, 352, 361, 363, 368, 374, 380, 384, 385

White, Bailey 69, 368, 385

whiteness 152, 170, 171

Whitman, Walt 92, 94, 99

Wiesel, Elie 206, 207, 368, 385

Wilde, Oscar 99, 122, 378

Wilder, Thornton 144

William the Conqueror 295

Wilson, Thomas 233, 256

Wind 16, 22, 30, 66, 69, 71, 103, 107, 119, 120, 121, 122, 155, 158, 212, 214, 215, 339, 341, 350, 363, 364, 375

wine 133, 152, 155, 170, 250, 317

Wineapple, Brenda 128, 129, 130, 166, 385

wisdom 68, 69, 70, 109, 112, 113, 133, 145, 152, 157, 171, 199, 213, 214, 229, 234, 377, 385

wisdom tradition 213

Wodehouse, P.G. 55, 368, 385

Woodman, Marion 75, 164, 386

word bank 50, 51, 66

word choice 52, 82, 116, 182, 197

World War II 188, 189, 211, 344

wounded vision 213

Wriothesley, Henry 234

writing 3, 12, 13, 15, 17, 18, 19, 20, 21, 22, 24, 25,
        26, 29, 30, 31, 32, 33, 34, 41, 46, 49, 50, 51,
        52, 53, 55, 56, 63, 64, 66, 67, 68, 69, 72, 75,
        76, 78, 81, 82, 89, 91, 101, 105, 109, 111, 115,
        116, 123, 129, 130, 133, 142, 143, 144, 147,
        161, 162, 165, 167, 169, 173, 179, 180, 181,
        182, 188, 189, 190, 194, 195, 201, 217, 220,
        221, 224, 225, 231, 232, 233, 251, 256, 268,
        269, 270, 274, 276, 286, 292, 295, 303, 316,
        324, 325, 328, 331, 335, 343, 346, 349, 353,
        354, 358, 373, 377, 378, 379, 381, 383, 385
writing guide 66, 162, 179
Writing Workshop 33, 381
  Part 1 24, 34
  Part 2 34

Y

Yeats, William Butler 11, 105, 386
York 13, 18, 41, 43, 96, 97, 128, 189, 190, 193, 222,
        288, 289, 290, 291, 292, 293, 294, 305, 312,
        335, 370, 371, 372, 373, 374, 375, 376, 377,
        378, 379, 380, 381, 382, 383, 384, 385, 386
"Young Goodman Brown" 84, 86, 122, 157, 158,
        159, 162, 376

Z

Zeus 130, 135, 139, 317